Infants and Young Children with Special Needs

Infants and Young Children with Special Needs

A Developmental and Ecological Approach

SECOND EDITION

by

S. Kenneth Thurman, Ph.D.
Professor of Special Education
Temple University
Philadelphia

and

Anne H. Widerstrom, Ph.D.
Professor of Special Education
San Francisco State University
San Francisco

Baltimore · London · Toronto · Sydney

Paul H. Brookes Publishing Co.
P.O. Box 10624
Baltimore, Maryland 21285-0624

Typeset by The Composing Room, Inc., Grand Rapids, Michigan.
Manufactured in the United States of America by
The Maple Press Company, York, Pennsylvania.

The frontispiece photograph was provided by Susan Sandall, Department of
Individual and Family Studies, University of Delaware. Photographs in Chapters
1, 2, 3, 9, and 11 were taken by Anne Widerstrom at St. John's Special School,
Woodford, England. All other photographs were taken by Anne Widerstrom at
Kay Rowe Nursery, Borough of Newham, London, England.

Library of Congress Cataloging-in-Publication Data
Thurman, S. Kenneth.
    Infants and young children with special needs : a developmental
and ecological approach / by S. Kenneth Thurman and Anne H.
Widerstrom. — 2nd ed.
        p.   cm.
    Rev. ed. of: Young children with special needs / S. Kenneth
Thurman, Anne H. Widerstrom.
    Includes bibliographical references.
    ISBN 1-55766-031-X
    1. Handicapped children—Education (Preschool)—United States. 2.
Handicapped children—United States—Development.   3. Mainstreaming in
education—United States.   I. Widerstrom, Anne H.   II. Thurman, S.
Kenneth. Young children with special needs.   III. Title.
LC4019.2.T48   1990
371.9—dc20   89-39649
                                                               CIP

Contents

Foreword

WHILE A FEDERAL COMMITMENT to early intervention was formalized in 1986 with the passage of PL 99-457, the advocacy for comprehensive services for handicapped infants, young children, and their families had preceded the law by more than a decade. The first edition of this book, published in 1985, was one of the sources of such advocacy, presenting the rationale as well as strategies for early intervention efforts. With this second edition, the authors have updated the theoretical content in terms of empirical findings and revised the material with particular reference to the provisions of PL 99-457.

This text constitutes an important resource for all professionals involved in work with at-risk and handicapped young children and their families in that it encompasses the major themes that are current in early intervention. The stage for these themes is set in the first chapter in the identification of six key challenges facing the field of early intervention. In the context of addressing these challenges, the following themes reflect the relevance and comprehensiveness of this volume.

The first theme that emerges is a recognition of the complexity of early intervention and its uniqueness as a domain for helping professionals. A clear case is made for a differentiated approach that takes into account the unique populations, settings, and services indicated in early intervention. A complementary theme is the emphasis placed on the importance of a multidisciplinary approach to endeavors involving infants and young children with special needs. While the specific manner in which a multidisciplinary approach is implemented will vary as a function of policy as well as practice, the commitment to such an approach is widely endorsed. A third theme that builds on the need for a multidisciplinary approach and the complex nature of early intervention is the emphasis on individualization in work with families. This is a theme that the authors have effectively merged with the provisions of PL 99-457 regarding the Individualized Family Service Plan (IFSP).

Complementing the above three themes, which are methodological in nature, are three content-oriented themes pertaining to development, the family, and the environmental context. Drawing on theoretical contributions, the authors consider the development of the child as transactional in nature in which outcomes are determined by mutual exchanges between child and family over time. A further elaboration of the dynamic nature of development is the recognition of the goodness of fit of the child and family with the environmental demands. The centrality of the family in the development of the child and the ecological contexts of child and family are the fifth and sixth themes that permeate the text and provide a basis for assessment as well as intervention activities.

The belief in the benefits of early intervention is now being recognized as a formal commitment to at-risk and handicapped infants and their families. This text embodies that belief and provides a systematic approach to the implementation of theoretically sound and feasible interventions.

Rune J. Simeonsson
University of North Carolina at Chapel Hill

Preface

SINCE THE FIRST EDITION of this book was published in 1985, the field of early childhood special education has come to be recognized nationally as a discipline in its own right, with its own university training and research programs, an active national professional organization, several professional journals of quality, and a significant voice in the formulation of policy at national, regional, and local levels. Early intervention for families with infants and young children with special needs is on the way to becoming universally available in the United States, thanks to the passage of PL 99-457 in 1986 and the growing commitment of professionals in many disciplines to serve these families.

As services expand, the need for comprehensive preparation of educators, therapists, psychologists, and health professionals to work with children under the age of 5 and their families also expands. This fact is reflected in the increasing number of university-level programs throughout the country that are faced with the task of preparing teachers, speech/language pathologists, occupational and physical therapists, school psychologists, social workers, and program administrators to implement the mandate of PL 99-457. We are already faced with the prospect of personnel shortages in early intervention, and projections for the 1990s are more serious yet. Those of us engaged in university teaching have a very big and important job ahead, if we are to emerge at the end of the century with a universal service delivery system of high quality. The primary factor that determines quality in an early intervention program is the effectiveness of the professionals who work in it, and effectiveness, obviously, is directly related to quality of training.

It is to the problem of providing effective personnel preparation that the second edition of this book, like the first, is addressed. While the number of textbooks in early childhood special education has increased since the first edition was published, and it is no longer the case that appropriate books are unavailable, we believe there continues to be a need for the unique approach that our book offers. This approach places strong emphasis on typical and atypical child development, combined with an ecological view of intervention.

The second edition is organized around the same two basic premises that characterized the first edition: 1) that early intervention professionals require firm grounding in the typical sequences of development that children experience from birth, and 2) that effective intervention must take an ecological perspective (i.e., the context of the infant's or young child's environment must be taken into account). In this edition, we have placed more emphasis on these two premises by devoting the first section to a developmental perspective and the second to an ecological perspective.

Generally speaking, the passage of PL 99-457 has provided the impetus for the updating of the original book. It sets the context for discussion of developmental research and theory, assessment and intervention, and addressing family needs. It is also reflected in the addition to the title that acknowledges the new emphasis on early intervention programs for infants from birth.

Part I begins with a review of certain issues pertinent to the early intervention field, including the concepts of being at risk and the least restrictive environment. The majority of the section is then devoted to an updated review of typical and atypical cognitive, language, physical, and social development.

Part II begins with a greatly expanded section on assessment, with a chapter on screening and traditional assessment procedures and a new chapter on ecological assessment including information on developing an Individualized Family Service Plan (IFSP). The second half of Part II is devoted to program planning and implementation from an ecological approach. It includes an expanded and updated chapter on family needs that reflects the content of PL 99-457.

Chapter 1 sets the context for the rest of the book by explaining the developmental and ecological perspectives on which it is based, and showing how the two perspectives are interrelated. Chapter 2 reviews the most common factors associated with infancy and early childhood that place the child at risk for handicaps. The final chapter of the first subsection discusses the least restrictive environment in the context of PL 99-457.

Beginning with Chapter 4, Cognitive Development, and continuing through Chapter 5, The Development of Language, Chapter 6, Social and Emotional Development, and Chapter 7, Physical Development, the primary research and theory related to typical and atypical development are reviewed for each developmental area. These chapters are comprehensive in scope and provide a review of relevant recent research in special education, psychology, occupational and physical therapy and medicine.

Chapter 8 presents an overview of screening and assessment issues and techniques, and includes information on how professionals from related disciplines conduct assessments, and how assessment procedures can be modified for children with special problems that make assessment difficult. In Chapter 9 the rationale for conducting ecological assessments is discussed, and the process involved in an effective ecological assessment is described. The second subsection begins with Chapter 10, Individualized Program Planning, which has been updated to take account of the requirements set out in PL 99-457. Chapter 11 continues the subject of individualized planning with information on how to implement IEPs and IFSPs. Chapter 12 provides an updated and comprehensive discussion of families, again within the context of PL 99-457, as well as a full review of recent research. The final chapter presents some recent program models that have received national attention for the effectiveness in serving families of infants and young children with special needs.

Like the first edition, we hope that this second edition proves to be a useful resource for students of early intervention, teachers, psychologists, counselors, therapists, health professionals, and others interested in services to infants, young children, and their families. The reference section, which we considered to be a strength of the first edition, has been expanded to include some 200 additional references. The objectives at the beginning of each chapter have been retained as a means for providing the reader a context in which to place chapter content. We hope that the addition of new figures, tables, and photographs will enhance the book's readability.

Finally arrives the pleasant task of acknowledging those whose help was so important in making this second edition possible. First, we wish to acknowledge the lasting influence of Dr. Terry D. Meddock as one of the early conceptualizers of the book, whose enthusiasm at the beginning of the first edition gave us the momentum we needed to launch the project. We know he is happy to see how far we have actually come, having published a second edition. We thank him for his support.

Second, we would like to acknowledge the work of Dr. Allen Sandler, who wrote the very sound chapter on parents for the first edition. We continue to be grateful for that contribution. Next, we would like to thank the anonymous reviewer who gave us invaluable information and advice for developing the second edition by providing us a thorough, comprehensive, and sympathetic review.

In producing this edition, several people at Paul H. Brookes Publishing Co. deserve special recognition. First, we were fortunate to have Vice President Melissa Behm as our editor, and we are grateful for her excellent editing skills and fine attention to detail. She put an unusual amount of time, energy, and caring into this edition, and we believe it is reflected in the quality of the book. Roslyn Udris, production manager, was able to bring the book out on schedule and in an attractive, readable format. We are grateful to both of them and the rest of the competent Brookes staff.

Finally, each of us has special thanks for family members, friends, colleagues, and students who have been especially helpful to us during the preparation of this second edition. I (SKT) as always had the complete love and support of my wife, Marcia, and my son, Shane. Both of them know how lucky I am. Thank you both. Thank you also to my aunt, Charlotte Schneyer, whose scholarship is second to none and who has always provided a model and support for my academic endeavors. I appreciate all she's done for me. And I (AHW) completed my work on the book during sabbatical leave at the University of London Institute of Education, and wish to thank colleagues, students, and staff who assisted me. Special thanks go to Julie Newman and Rachel Cohen, teacher and head at Kay Rowe Nursery School in Stratford; Peter Johnson, deputy head at St. John's Special School in Woodford; and Will Fletcher, teacher at Watling View School in St. Albans, all of whom helped to obtain photographs used in the book. And very special thanks to Professor Klaus Wedell, Department of Educational Psychology and Special Needs at the Institute, who provided the flexible lecture schedule necessary for writing the book, and arranged the many stimulating visits to British schools and child development centers that are reflected in the book. Finally, much thanks from both of us to Betty Robichaw for getting through the references.

Infants and Young Children with Special Needs

1

A DEVELOPMENTAL PERSPECTIVE

1A

Perspectives
and Issues

1

Infants and Young Children with Special Needs

1. What are some of the challenges of early intervention besides those mentioned in this chapter?
2. In what ways are a developmental and an ecological perspective compatible with each other?
3. What do you see as the personal rewards you may gain as an early interventionist?

THIS BOOK IS ABOUT children from birth to age 6. It is about children whose developmental patterns lie outside the range considered "normal." It is about children whose environments and social settings place them at risk. It is about children who have special needs.

Special needs are those that require care or intervention beyond that normally required to ensure the best possible developmental outcome in young children. All young children require stimulating, nurturing environments. All young children require love and trust. Children with special needs in addition require specialized treatment and interventions. Low birth weight infants, for example, may be required to spend the first weeks of life in an intensive care nursery. A 3½-year-old who is not talking may require language therapy. A 5-year-old whose behavior is oppositional may require a behavior management program in order to be ready for public school. As you read this book you will become familiar with the various types of problems and special needs that young children may have. You will also learn about ways in which these special needs can be addressed to minimize or remediate their effects.

THE CHALLENGES OF EARLY INTERVENTION

The future of early intervention is sure to be affected by the passage of PL 99-457, the Education of the Handicapped Act Amendments, passed in late 1986. This law has set the stage for the development of new and expanded services for handicapped and at-risk infants and preschool children. Bricker (1988) suggested that this law has legit-imized early childhood special education. At the same time the passage of the law has created challenges to the field of early inter-vention. While some of these challenges ex-isted prior to the passage of PL 99-457, the law provides new impetus to confront these challenges. As Odom and Warren (1988) have advised, a proactive view of the future is necessary if the challenges put forth here are to be met.

Before discussing these challenges in de-tail, it is necessary to delineate the provi-sions of PL 99-457. The provisions of the law directly affect services for children from birth to age 5 who have handicaps or who are at risk for developing handicaps. Specifi-cally, the law extends all of the provisions of PL 94-142 (the Education for All Handi-capped Children Act of 1975) to children 3 to 5 years old. All states are required to pro-vide these services by the 1990–1991 school year or they will lose federal monies set aside for preschool programs for children with handicaps. A second set of provisions in PL 99-457 is directed at children from birth to age 2. These provisions provide for the establishment and maintenance of ap-propriate early intervention services in every state. The legislation defines the eligi-ble population as all children from birth to age 2 who are developmentally delayed, who have conditions that typically result in delay, or who are at risk for significant de-velopmental delay. The legislation requires that each state define the criteria for devel-opmental delay and for risk. Thus, the pop-ulations eligible for services will vary from state to state. In addition to providing a defi-nition for the term "developmentally de-layed," the law requires the following mini-mum components of a statewide system:

- availability of a multidisciplinary evalua-tion for every infant and toddler with a handicap
- availability of an individualized family service plan (IFSP) for each infant and toddler
- maintenance of a comprehensive child find system
- maintenance of a public awareness pro-gram focusing on early identification
- maintenance of a central directory of ser-vices, resources, and experts available in the state
- maintenance of a comprehensive system of personnel development and appropri-ate standards for qualified personnel
- maintenance of a single line of responsi-bility (lead agency) for general admin-istration, supervision, and monitoring of programs and activities, including re-sponsibility for carrying out the entry into formal interagency agreements
- maintenance of a policy pertaining to contracting with service providers
- maintenance of a procedure for timely reimbursement from agencies responsi-ble for payment
- maintenance of procedural safeguards for parents and guardians
- maintenance of a data collection system

Each governor also has the responsibility of establishing an interagency coordinating council composed of consumers and repre-sentatives from relevant state agencies and provider organizations. The purpose of the council is to provide advice to the governor on the development, implementation, and maintenance of the statewide system.

The provisions of PL 99-457 are alluded to throughout the text, and the reader is urged to become familiar with them. In ad-dition, the provisions of PL 99-457 help to put into perspective the challenges to the field discussed below.

The challenges of early intervention for young children with special needs include the following:

1. Provision of programs without stigmatizing through labels
2. Inclusion of family members in programs without destroying family integrity
3. Continued financial support of programs in times of declining resources
4. Development of personnel from a variety of disciplines who understand children with and without special needs
5. Development of interagency and interdisciplinary models of service
6. Provision of early intervention services in the least restrictive environment (LRE)

Each of these challenges is examined below.

Early intervention must counteract the effects of special needs without creating self-fulfilling prophecies regarding the developmental outcomes and potentials of these children. Thus, the first challenge is to identify and provide programs for young children with special needs without labeling the children. In order to do this, early interventionists must be aware that children with special needs fall outside of the accepted parameters of normalcy, but they must also resist placing inhibiting labels on these children. Thurman and Lewis (1979) have pointed out how the early labeling of children may contribute to the development of prejudice toward them. Thurman and Lewis contend that early intervention programs should stress the confrontation of difference in a positive way and, by so doing, reduce the possibilities of developing negative prejudices. In fact, early intervention programs, if properly designed, should reduce the probability of a child being labeled. Take, for example, the case of an oppositional 5-year-old whose pattern of behavior could, if left untreated, result in his being labeled as behavior disordered or emotionally disturbed in first grade. Proper intervention designed to make the child less oppositional could prevent such labeling. In cases in which labeling is unavoidable, early intervention can be useful in reducing the severity of the label. For example, a child born without arms is destined to be labeled. Early intervention, however, can minimize the child's disability and, therefore, his label, at, say, age 6.

A second challenge for early intervention programs is family involvement. It is accepted practice to involve families in intervention programs for young children with special needs. Some programs, in fact, are actually structured so that parents are responsible for any intervention that a child receives (see Chapter 3). Too often, however, interventionists have failed to recognize that families that include young children with special needs are families with special needs. While it is not unreasonable to expect families to put forth additional effort on behalf of their special-needs children, it must be remembered that each family is different and includes individual members whose ability to respond effectively varies greatly. Turnbull and Turnbull (1982) have suggested that professionals tend to respond to parents with a standardized set of expectations. They go on to identify the problems associated with such an approach. The early interventionist would do well to remember that individual family members are as different from each other as are individual special-needs children. The principle that special-needs children should be responded to as individuals is especially applicable to responding to their families. To this end, PL 99-457 provides for the mandatory development of individualized family service plans (IFSPs). The development of IFSPs requires professionals working in the field of early intervention to become more skillful at using techniques designed to assess the needs of families and to develop programs that provide for these needs. Chapter 12 addresses the needs and involvement of families with special-needs children.

A third challenge facing the early interventionist is the problem of maintaining programs financially, a problem some predict will continue into the foreseeable future (Odom & Warren, 1988). This challenge is salient in times of declining federal and state support. Early interventionists must provide cost-efficient programs and use each resource to its maximum. Effective use of volunteers, for example, may reduce overall program cost. Staff-made materials often cost less than mass-produced ones and at the same time can be more responsive to the individual needs of the children. The financial stability of a program is critical if high-quality services are to be maintained. The morale and effectiveness of direct intervention staff decline when they are constantly concerned with whether there will be money to run the program. The challenge of providing financial solvency lies primarily with program administrators, who should be prepared to tap a variety of different funding sources. One mistake often made by program administrators is to rely too heavily on a single source of funds. Generally, a program ought not to rely on one source for more than 25%–30% of its operating funds. While this is not always possible, the challenge of financial solvency can be more readily met if programs are developed with

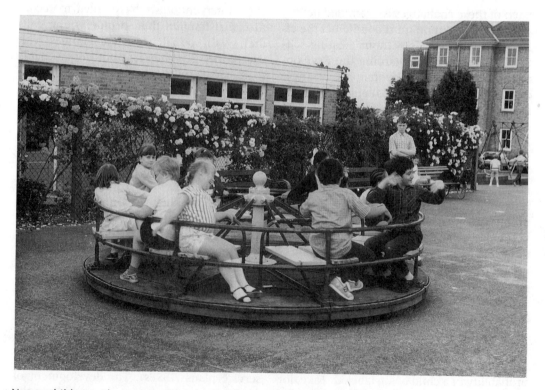

Young children with special needs present unique challenges to professionals to provide effective early intervention.

multiple funding bases. As you read the program descriptions in Chapter 13, you may want to recall this point and think about how well each program seems to be meeting the challenge of financial solvency through the use of cost-effective methods and multiple funding bases.

The fourth challenge to be discussed deals with the development of personnel to provide early intervention to young children with special needs. These people must come from a wide variety of disciplines, including special education, psychology, early childhood education, nutrition, audiology, speech, and language pathology, occupational therapy, physical therapy, nursing, social work, and pediatrics. These professionals must be provided with expertise on the needs of both children with and children without special needs. While it is up to colleges, universities, and professional schools to offer preservice programs to train early interventionists, individual early intervention programs must take the responsibility for providing meaningful ongoing staff development programs. These programs should inform staff of the latest theories and techniques as they apply to young children with special needs. The bases of both preservice and inservice training should be familiarity with the theories of normal development and their relationship to intervention with young children with special needs. Our commitment to this belief is manifest in this book, which has as one of its major foci normal developmental patterns in children from birth to age 6.

Moreover, the growing consensus among professionals in the field of early childhood special education is that competencies for personnel working primarily with infants must be differentiated from those for personnel working with 3- to 5-year-old children (Bailey, Palsha, & Huntington, 1988; Bricker & Slentz, 1989). Thus, it is important that personnel preparation programs, whether preservice or inservice, be targeted specifically for each group.

Each professional involved in early intervention must take up the challenge of his or her own professional development. Interventionists must think of themselves as self-directed learners and must stay abreast of the field by reading professional literature and by attending conferences. At the same time, they must use their own programs as a source of knowledge and professional development. They can learn not only from peers but also from the children and families for whom they provide services. Careful recordkeeping and data collection can provide important information about the effectiveness of various techniques and procedures. Systematic observation can provide valuable insight into children's development as well as into their patterns of interaction with their environments. Many of these themes are further elaborated in later chapters of this book.

The fifth challenge confronting the early interventionist is the development of interdisciplinary and interagency program models. The necessity for IFSPs and individualized education programs (IEPs) called for by PL 99-457 underscores the challenge of developing interdisciplinary service models. These models must include professionals from a variety of disciplines who are involved not only in the assessment and evaluation of infants and young children with handicaps, but also in a team approach to the ongoing provision of service to these children and their families. It is important to recognize that maintaining an interdisciplinary approach requires a commitment to teamwork by all involved. It also requires the recognition that no single discipline has all the answers. With constant communication among team members, an atmosphere of mutual respect can evolve that leads to improved service delivery to children and families, and to a work environment that promotes professional growth and development.

A related challenge is that of establishing effective interagency cooperation. This challenge grows from the recognition that families with young children with handicaps often have multiple needs that cannot be adequately addressed by the resources of a single agency or service provider. Perhaps the most important interagency challenge is that of bringing about a smooth transition for the child and his or her family from the early intervention service system to that of the public schools. These transitions are often stressful for families (Fowler, 1982) and require sensitivity on the part of both the early intervention agency and the public school system. In order to effect smooth, nonstressful transitions and maintain interagency cooperation, early interventionists must put in place workable case management systems. Case management provides the backbone for effective interagency service models.

Yet another challenge facing the field of early intervention is that of providing services in the least restrictive environment (LRE). LRE refers to that environment that is as close to that of one's nonhandicapped peers as possible. The application of the concept of LRE grew in large part from the passage of PL 94-142, which requires that special educational services be rendered in the least restrictive environment.

Although research has demonstrated that early intervention services that integrate children with handicaps and children without handicaps can be successful (Odom & McEvoy, 1988), the challenge that remains is determining how to establish environments that best meet the needs of individual children. As Peterson (1987) has suggested, the determination of what is least restrictive must be made for each child individually.

This challenges early intervention professionals to develop an array of services that can meet the needs of different kinds of young children with special needs and their families. Infants and preschool children without special needs are served through day care centers, day care homes, nursery schools, Head Start programs, preschool programs, babysitters, and nannies. Which of these services is least restrictive is a matter of conjecture. In addition, how these services can be offered in an integrated fashion to both infants and young children with handicaps and infants and young children without handicaps remains to be determined.

Implementation of early intervention services using the concept of LRE will require further staff training. Such training must focus not only on establishing positive attitudes toward young children with special needs and their families, but also on providing personnel with the skills to address these special needs.

The future of early intervention programs for children with special needs depends on how well we are able to respond to these six challenges. We hope that through reading this book you will become better able to meet the challenges of early intervention. The knowledge that you gain should be a point of departure and not an end in your own professional development. To that end, each chapter, including this one, begins with a series of thought questions designed to encourage you to think about the issues raised.

A DEVELOPMENTAL ECOLOGICAL PERSPECTIVE

As you read this book, you will find that it approaches young children with special needs from two separate yet interrelated perspectives. On the one hand, the first part of the book is developmental in approach. Our goal is to provide the reader with a knowledge of typical patterns of cognitive, language, social/emotional, and motor development. In addition, specific problems that may occur in children from birth to age 6 are addressed. Our focus on development stems from our belief that two of the major functions of early intervention are to facilitate development and, as will be discussed in the next chapter, reduce risk to young children. Effective early intervention, then, should improve the quality of development beyond the point that would be expected were intervention not provided. To improve the development of children with special needs, we must understand normal development, including the problems that may occur in normal developmental patterns.

An equally important perspective that characterizes this book is an ecological one. An ecological perspective recognizes that a child is not a free-floating developing human being, but assumes rather that every child is part of an ecological system. An ecological approach is concerned with the child as a developing organism in interaction with the environment. *Ecology* is defined as the study of an organism's interaction with its environment. In an ecological approach, attention must be given to the goodness-of-fit between the child and the environment. To elucidate goodness-of-fit, Thurman (1977) developed the concept of ecological congruence (the degree to which an individual and his or her environment are mutually tolerant). This tolerance is in part a function of the developmental status of the individual child.

An ecological approach complements a developmental one because it provides the context within which developmental intervention occurs. Development can only be improved within some context. The ecological system provides the context. Thus, while it should seek to improve the developmental status of a child, early intervention should also recognize that the child's development has meaning only within its ecological context. Chapters 9 and 10 discuss the ecological congruence model in detail and describe how to design early interventions that develop a higher level of tolerance or congruence within the ecological system. In short, a child's development cannot be assessed without examining the ecological system within which that child functions. It is only in a well-balanced ecology that development is facilitated and maintained.

SUMMARY

This chapter has focused on the challenges that face professionals who are providing early intervention services. Many of these challenges are inherent in PL 99-457 that became law in 1986 and that set the stage for increased services to infants and young children with special needs and their families. These challenges include: providing services without labeling, including families in meaningful ways, assuring financial support for programs, developing a wide array of personnel to provide services, developing interagency and interdisciplinary models of service, and providing services in the least restrictive environment. In addition, the chapter discusses the relationship between ecological and developmental approaches. These two approaches are complimentary to each other and can be used together to develop effective early intervention programs. Essentially, development is meaningful only within the context of the ecological setting of each individual. In summary, the challenges of providing early intervention are great. A commitment to meeting those challenges can result in meaningful personal rewards. It is hoped that those rewards will be yours.

2

Determinants of Risk in Infants and Young Children

---

1. What factors can put an infant or young child at risk?
2. Does being at risk necessarily imply a negative outcome?
3. What are the implications of incidence and prevalence for the study of young children who are at risk?
4. Why is it important for interventionists to understand the concept of risk?

THE PURPOSE OF THIS chapter is to identify the determinants of risk and disability in young children. The concepts discussed are derived from psychology, sociology, and medicine. This chapter addresses factors that help determine the degree of risk experienced by children in infancy and early childhood. It also provides perspective on the pervasiveness of developmental problems in young children through a discussion of incidence and prevalence.

THE CONCEPT OF BEING AT RISK

In one sense, we are all at risk. Every time we get into an automobile, cross a street, or participate in sports, we risk personal injury and even death. Most of the risks we take as well-adjusted adults are voluntary risks: no one forces us to play football or jog across a busy street. As a matter of fact, most of us have a point beyond which we will not take risks. For example, you may be perfectly willing to drive your car down the highway at 55 miles per hour but unwilling to drive at 100 miles per hour, since the latter speed would not only increase your likelihood of receiving a stiff fine but would also put you at much greater risk of injuring or killing yourself. Essentially, we are all at risk to a certain extent but at the same time we have a certain amount of control over the degree of risk to which we are exposed.

The same thing could not have been said about us during prenatal and early postnatal periods. Being at risk begins with the moment of conception. Early developmental intervention is crucial because of the developmental risk that exists both prenatally and during the first several years of life. The roots of much of our early developmental programming for young children are found in the desire to reduce exposure to risk for these children. Thus, we have established special programs for those young children whom we consider to be especially at risk. By reducing the risk to which a child is exposed, we increase the probability that the child will develop to the fullest extent possible. Typically, the greater the degree of perceived risk, the more intensive the intervention.

FACTORS CONTRIBUTING TO RISK

Solnit and Provence (1979) have suggested that the degree of potential risk is determined in part by the vulnerability of the child. They suggest that "vulnerability refers particularly to the weaknesses, deficits, or defects of the child, whereas risk refers to the interaction of the environment and the child" (p. 800). This section examines a number of factors related to the vulnerability and risk of infants and young children. These factors include: socioeconomic status, prematurity and low birth weight, hereditary and genetic conditions, prenatal factors, and events occurring during birth and delivery.

Understanding risk factors takes on added importance in light of PL 99-457. The provisions of the law apply to at-risk populations, with each state free to define its own at-risk population. Undoubtedly each state will use different criteria for defining those infants who are at risk. However, it is likely that several of the factors discussed below are likely to be used in defining these populations.

Socioeconomic Status

Socioeconomic status (SES) is associated with vulnerability and risk more often than any other identifiable variable. Lower SES mothers are more likely than higher SES mothers to give birth to premature infants (Butler & Alberman, 1969; Guthrie et al., 1977) and SES remains the single best predictor of later IQ scores (McCall, Hogarty, & Hurlburt, 1972): infants and young children born and reared in lower SES environments have a greater risk of exhibiting lower IQ scores in subsequent years than do their higher SES peers.

Generally, children born into lower SES environments tend to be more vulnerable throughout infancy and the preschool years than those born into higher SES environments. This is true if we base our conclusions solely on statistical evidence, for the statistics show that such factors as nutrition, mother-child interaction patterns, and language experience are less likely to promote optimal development in lower SES families than in middle- and upper-class families (Golden & Birns, 1976). Nevertheless, it would be false to assume that middle- and upper-income families are by definition better at caring for their children than are lower-income families, or that lower SES parents may automatically be categorized as producing at-risk children. Obviously, many disabled children are identified from all SES groups. Vulnerability and risk must be considered on an individual basis.

Prematurity and Low Birth Weight

Prematurity and low birth weight contribute to the risk of infants by increasing their vulnerability in different ways. *Prematurity* refers to a relatively short gestational period, usually less than 37 weeks. Infants born prematurely usually have low birth weights; however, their weights at birth are often appropriate for their gestational ages.

The classification of *low birth weight* (LBW) applies to any infant weighing under 2,500 grams at birth. *Very low birth weight* (VLBW) is the term applied to infants weighing under 1,500 grams and *very, very low birth weight* (VVLBW) or *extremely low birth weight* (ELBW) designates babies weighing under 1,000 grams. The lower the birth weight of the infant, the greater the degree of risk for later medical and developmental problems. The National Center for Health Statistics reports that in 1986, 6.8% of all infants born were of low birth weight, and 11% of all births were premature. If an infant is *small for gestational age* (SGA), that is, weighs less than normal for its gestational age, then the degree of risk is even greater than would be expected if the infant were of appropriate gestational age. By examining Table 2.1, the reader can see that an infant born at 31 weeks gestation on average would weigh about 1,500 grams. Thus, an infant who weighed only 1,250 grams who was born at 31 weeks gestation would be both premature and small for gestational age. This baby would be at higher risk for problems than would a baby whose weight was appropriate for its gestational age. Hunt (1976) has suggested that any baby, whether premature or full term, be considered SGA if it is 3 standard deviations below the average birth weight for its gestational age.

Before the mid-1960s it was common practice to consider low birth weight and premature infants as a single group (cf. Gruenwald, 1965). More recently, Robinson and Robinson (1976) and Fox (1978) have suggested that the validity of research with low birth weight babies has been compromised by the inclusion of both premature and SGA babies in the same experi-

Table 2.1. Average fetal weight and size by gestational age

Week (*postconception*)	Weight (g)[a]	Length (cm)
8	1	4.0
9	2	4.0
10	4	6.5
11	7	6.5
12	14	9.0
13	25	9.0
14	45	12.5
15	70	12.5
16	100	16.0
17	140	16.0
18	190	20.5
19	240	20.5
20	300	25.0
21	360	25.0
22	430	27.5
23	501	27.5
24	600	30.0
25	700	30.0
26	800	32.5
27	900	32.5
28	1,001	35.0
29	1,175	35.0
30	1,350	37.5
31	1,501	37.5
32	1,675	40.0
33	1,825	40.0
34	2,001	42.5
35	2,160	42.5
36	2,340	45.0
37	2,501	45.0
38	2,775	47.5
39	3,001	47.5
40	3,250	50.0
41	3,501	50.0
42	4,001	52.5
43	4,501	52.5

[a]454 grams = 1 pound.

From Rossetti, L.M. (1986). *High risk infants: Identification, assessment and intervention.* Boston: College-Hill Press. Reprinted by permission.

mental samples. Fox (1978) reports that SGA babies, as compared to premature babies, "are associated with . . . higher rates of seizure and mental retardation in the absence of cerebral palsy, but lower rates of spastic diplegia [a type of cerebral palsy] and deafness" (p. 2). In discussing risk factors in development, Kopp (1983) has urged researchers to "define samples so that interpretation of findings is not hampered by lack of clarity about sample characteristics" (p. 1165). Such factors would include birth weight, degree of prematurity, and type and extent of complications during hospitalization.

Examination of the literature since the early 1970s reveals an improving prognosis for low birth weight infants, especially those weighing less than 1,500 grams. Mortality rates among this population have improved. Sell (1986) reports that survival rates in neonatal intensive care units (NICUs) improved for infants with birth weights between 500 and 750 grams from 20.9% in 1978 to 36.1% in 1983. Similarly, the survival rates for infants with birth weights between 751 and 1,000 grams rose from 50.4% in 1978 to 66.1% in 1983. Raju (1986) indicates that VVLBW babies accounted for 57% of the neonatal mortality rate in the period from 1982 to 1984 as compared with 80% 10 years earlier. The long-term outcomes of these infants also seems to be improving. While Drillen (1964) showed a negative correlation between birth weight and developmental status at age 4, other studies in the 1970s (e.g., Fitzhardinge & Ramsey, 1973; Rawlings, Reynolds, Stewart, & Strange, 1971) show much more favorable outcomes. Kitchen and his colleagues (Kitchen, Ford, Rickards, Lissenden, & Ryan, 1987) present data on the developmental status of 5-year-olds whose birth weights were less than 1,000 grams. Their data indicate that 60% of these children were

not impaired in any way, and that another 20% had only minor neurobehavioral difficulties. Although some of these children without impairments may show learning problems when they reach school age (Hunt, Tooley, & Harvin, 1982), the data presented by Kitchen and colleagues does suggest that the prognosis for these babies is improving. The improvement in survival rates of these babies and their generally improved prognosis can be attributed to improved medical treatment and better methods of early intervention. While evidence does suggest that the course of VLBW infants is improving, this population is still at greater risk than infants with normal birth weights. Brooten (1983) has concluded that only about 40% of these infants are free from morbidity during their first year of life, while the figure for all infants is 70%.

Prematurity and low birth weight are clearly factors that contribute to the risk status of an infant. Treatment of these infants in NICUs has lead to their increased survival, as indicated above. However, because of their vulnerability these infants often suffer additional complications as a result of their treatment. These complications include bronchopulmonary dysplasia (BPD), a type of damage to the lungs resulting from prolonged maintenance on respirators; retinopathy of prematurity (ROP), a visual impairment resulting from increased oxygen and blood flow to the retina; and necrotizing enterocolitis (NEC), a dying off of the intestine often associated with feeding or infection. Other complications are often present at birth when an infant is born prematurely. Many of premature infants suffer from respiratory distress syndrome (RDS), also known as Hyaline membrane disease, a condition in which the infant lacks surfactant, a protein that wets the lining of the lungs and decreases surface tension to facilitate inhaling. Another common condition in premature infants is jaundice, which results from hyper-bilirubinemia, or abnormally large amounts of bilirubin, a red bile pigment, circulating in the blood that can lead to central nervous system damage. Premature babies also have difficulty maintaining body temperature and the under-development of their immune systems often makes them particularly susceptible to infection. Any of these complications can significantly increase the risk to the infant.

Hereditary and Genetic Conditions

Between 15% and 25% of developmental disorders in young children are related to genetic factors, that is, abnormalities in the makeup of either genes or chromosomes.

The *gene* is the functional unit of heredity, the means by which characteristics of parents are transmitted to their children. Each gene occupies a specific place on a *chromosome*. Chromosomes are arranged in pairs and are present in every cell of the body. There are 23 pairs of chromosomes in the normal human being. Of these 23 pairs, 22 pairs are *autosomal*. The other pair, which determines an individual's sex, is referred to as the *sex chromosomes*. The sex chromosomes are labeled XX for females and XY for males. Genetic material, coded on the chromosomes, is contained in molecules of DNA (deoxyribonucleic acid). When additional chromosomal material is present or when a certain amount is lacking, the infant is at risk of developmental disorder or delay.

Genetic disorders are referred to as either autosomal or X-linked, and either dominant or recessive. Dominant disorders are more likely to be inherited than recessive disorders. A child whose parent carries a gene for a dominant disorder is more likely to manifest the abnormal condition because the dominant gene takes precedence over the other parent's recessive gene. For example,

tuberous sclerosis is a genetic disorder related to a dominant gene. If one parent carries this dominant gene, the child faces a 50% risk of inheriting tuberous sclerosis. If both parents carry the gene the risk increases to 100%. Hurler syndrome, though, is an autosomal recessive disorder. Autosomal recessive disorders are the most common of the genetic disorders, although they carry a lower risk factor than do dominant ones. When only one parent carries the abnormal gene, the other parent's normal dominant gene takes precedence. Of course, if both parents carry this recessive gene, the risk increases greatly. Duchenne's muscular dystrophy is an example of a sex-linked chromosomal disorder. It occurs on the X chromosome and is thus more common in boys than girls, since boys have only one X chromosome. In girls, the harmful action of genes on one X chromosome is usually suppressed by dominant genes on the other X chromosome.

Many genetic disorders manifest themselves in metabolic dysfunction. That is, due to genetic error, the infant is born with a lack of a certain enzyme. Infants with galactosemia, for example, lack the enzyme necessary to convert galactose, a milk sugar, into glucose. Many metabolic disorders can now be controlled by dietary means or through enzyme replacement therapy.

While some genetic disorders are inherited through either dominant or recessive genes, others are due to chromosome abnormalities. These abnormalities, resulting from additions or deletions of chromosomal material, are referred to as *cytogenetic conditions*. Unlike dominant and recessive conditions, cytogenetic conditions are not typically passed from generation to generation. That is, they are not inheritable. Several of the better known cytogenetic conditions that place infants and young children at risk for developmental delays are Down syndrome (trisomy 21), trisomy 18, and cri du chat syndrome.

Recent advances in medical techniques have made it possible to identify many genetic disorders prenatally. Through such procedures as amniocentesis, chorionic villi sampling (CVS), sonar scanning, and fetoscopy, parents can be informed of potential problems before birth. *Amniocentesis* involves removing a sample of amniotic fluid from the womb and analyzing it for a variety of possible birth defects. Tay-Sachs disease, for example, can be identified through this method. *Chorionic villi sampling* involves removing a small piece of the placenta very early in pregnancy and testing it for genetic and other defects. *Sonar scanning* or *ultrasound,* is used to identify possible problems in the developing fetus. *Fetoscopy* consists of viewing the fetus in utero by means of an endoscope. Another diagnostic technique is the analysis of the levels of alpha-fetoprotein (AFP) in maternal blood samples taken during the second trimester of pregnancy. Increased levels of AFP may indicate a neural tube defect (spina bifida) (Hayden & Beck, 1982).

Parents whose infants are at risk for developmental disorders may receive genetic counseling, which includes diagnosis, an appraisal of risk factors, discussions relating to etiology of various conditions, and information concerning alternatives. First trimester abortions are often performed on women whose infants would have been born with serious chromosomal abnormalities. In other cases, counseling may result in the pregnancy proceeding with appropriate therapy, either during pregnancy or immediately following birth.

The foregoing section provides only an overview of the relationship between being at risk and the genetic endowment of individuals. Many other conditions related to genetic factors may be associated with signifi-

cant risk of developmental delay. The interested reader should consult Carter (1975) or Jones (1988) for a more comprehensive coverage of these and other genetically related conditions.

Prenatal Factors

While it provides maximum protection for the rather vulnerable organism within it, the uterus does not provide an absolutely safe environment. Every fetus is at some degree of risk during the prenatal period. A number of events that can occur during pregnancy place the developing fetus at risk. Infants born following a pregnancy that includes such factors are usually more vulnerable than infants delivered following normal pregnancies.

Two sets of factors can place the fetus at risk prenatally. First are those related to the physical and health status of the mother and the general quality of the uterus. These factors include age, level of nutrition, and specific health problems, such as hypertension and diabetes. The second group of factors are those that interfere more directly with the developmental progress of the fetus regardless of the conditions of the general intrauterine environment. These factors include radiation, prenatal anoxia, drug use, and viral and bacterial infections.

Maternal Age Maternal age directly affects the degree of risk associated with pregnancy. Increased maternal (over 35 years) and paternal age significantly raise the risk of giving birth to an infant with Down syndrome or an infant who manifests other types of chromosomal abnormalities (Abroms & Bennett, 1980). The incidence of Down syndrome births in the general population is about 1 in 600 (Hirshhorn, 1973). For women under 30, the figure is 1 in 1,500, as compared with 1 in 65 for women over 45 (Smith & Wilson, 1973). Lilienfeld and Pasamanick

(1956) report an increased risk of giving birth to a child with mental retardation for mothers under 20 and over 35.

Maternal Nutrition The major studies of maternal nutrition have been performed on animals because of the ethical considerations surrounding the manipulation of diets during human pregnancy. Winick and Rosso (1973), for example, have shown retarded fetal and placental growth and a reduction in the number of brain cells in rats whose mothers' protein intake was restricted during pregnancy.

An in-depth study of pregnancies during the siege of Leningrad (Anatov, 1947) indicated that the poor nutrition of the mothers resulted in only slightly reduced birth weights but significant increases in spontaneous abortion and premature births. A later follow-up of babies born during the food blockade of Holland in 1944 showed few identifiable developmental defects (Stein, Susser, & Marolla, 1972).

Winick (1970) has pointed out that a major factor in fetal malnutrition is incomplete development of the placenta. Thus, inadequate nutrition in the fetus may be related to the structure and function of the placenta itself or, as discussed above, to the general nutritional status of the mother during pregnancy.

Specific Maternal Health Problems Hypertension, or high blood pressure, during pregnancy places both the mother and infant at risk. Robinson and Robinson (1976) suggest that 20% of all pregnancy-related maternal deaths can be accounted for by disorders related to high blood pressure in the third trimester of pregnancy. Hellman and Pritchard (1971) estimated that as many as 25,000 fetal deaths occur annually because of maternal hypertension.

Diabetes increases the likelihood that mothers will become hypertensive during pregnancy, and can also put the fetus at risk by affecting the development of the placenta. Mothers with diabetes often develop vascular problems that manifest themselves in inadequate nutritional exchange via the placenta. Diabetic mothers are also more likely to have larger babies, which may result in birth complications. Babies of diabetic mothers are often hypoglycemic. Although techniques for managing diabetes have improved over time and have reduced the risk to both mother and fetus during pregnancy, diabetic women experience greater risks during pregnancy than do nondiabetic women.

The interaction between mother and fetus is a complex one and includes many factors related to risk in pregnancy. The specific effects of these factors are, at best, difficult to measure. In general, age, health, and nutritional status of the mother before and during pregnancy can contribute to the overall development of the child. Other factors are more specifically linked to risk in prenatal development and to later behavioral deficits.

Radiation Radiation can contribute to risk during prenatal development. Its hazard is related to its ability to alter genetic structures and cause mutations, or changes in the genes. Radiation is most dangerous during early pregnancy. Unfortunately many women do not even realize they are pregnant when these effects can be greatest.

Microcephaly is a common manifestation of prenatal radiation. Although Wilson (1974) has suggested that less than 1% of all developmental defects can be linked to radiation, it is imperative that women who believe they might be pregnant inform their physicians prior to submitting to any kind of X ray. Ultrasound appears not to have the negative effects of X rays on the fetus. It is being used more and more commonly to assess the prenatal condition of the uterus, placenta, and fetus during pregnancy.

Prenatal Anoxia Prenatal anoxia, or the deprivation of oxygen to the fetus, can damage the central nervous system. The condition may develop in several ways. First, a pregnant woman's oxygen supply may be cut off through accident or suffocation. If prolonged, this can result in the fetus experiencing anoxia. Women with deficient hearts are prone to produce anoxic conditions in fetuses during pregnancy. One possible result of anoxia is anacephaly, or the total absence of a differentiated brain. A second factor that can result in prenatal anoxia is the closing off of the umbilical cord. This can occur through accident or through premature separation of the placenta from the uterine wall. In rare instances, the fetus may actually become entangled in the umbilical cord and anoxia can result. Prenatal anoxia greatly increases the risk to the fetus during pregnancy.

Maternal Drug Use   Ingestion of drugs, including prescription, over-the-counter, and illicit drugs, can place the developing fetus at risk. Wilson (1973) has reported that over 600 drugs have been related to later birth defects in animals, although only about 20 have been linked to similar effects in the human beings. He estimates that only 2%–3% of the defects present in the human population can be related to drugs taken during pregnancy. In addition to drugs, it is quite likely that increased exposure to environmental pollutants is increasing the risk to many fetuses. Cassarett and Doull (1975), for example, have reported the effects of mercury pollution on mothers and their offspring. The combined risk of drugs and pollutants and of various drugs taken simultaneously has been virtually unexamined, in spite of reports indicating that 92% of all women surveyed used drugs during pregnancy (Apgar, 1965) and that on the average, women recall the use of four different medications during pregnancy (Barnes, 1968). More recently, Stewart, Cluff, and Philp (1977) reported that mothers consumed a mean of 11 different drugs during pregnancy. Hill, Craig,

Chaney, Tennyson, and McCulley (1977) surveyed 241 upper-middle-class, pregnant women who reported taking a mean of 9.6 different drugs, of which an average 6.4 were prescribed by physicians.

Thalidomide is a drug frequently cited for creating significant risk during prenatal development. Mellin and Katzenstein (1962) linked the use of this relatively mild tranquilizer to a number of babies born in Europe with physical anomalies. About 20% of the children whose mothers took the drug during critical periods of pregnancy were affected (Robinson & Robinson, 1976). While their mental development did not seem to be affected in most cases, these children experienced increased risk of severe developmental problems because of the prenatal influence of the drug. Additional research by McFie and Robertson (1973) suggests that there may be a supression of IQ in some of these children.

Alcoholic mothers put their infants at risk. Their infants often develop what has come to be recognized as fetal alcohol syndrome (Furey, 1982; Jones, Smith, Ulleland, & Stressguth, 1973; Umbreit & Ostrow, 1980). Manifestations of the syndrome are retarded physical and mental development, microcephaly, short eye slits, and possible limb and cardiac anomalies. About 40% of the children born to chronically alcoholic mothers display fetal alcohol syndrome (Green, 1974; Jones & Smith, 1974). Green (1974) points out, however, that many alcoholic mothers are also subject to environmental factors (e.g., low SES, poor nutrition, anxiety), which may also place the fetus at risk.

Recent research suggests that even moderate drinking may be related to central nervous system dysfunction and retardation of growth. Babies born to moderate drinkers show the effects of maternal drinking but do not have all of the features associated with fetal alcohol syndrome (Abel, Randall, & Riley, 1983).

Other drugs have also been shown to increase the risk to the fetus during prenatal development. Mothers addicted to heroin often pass on the addiction to their offspring and their infants must undergo the trauma of withdrawal (Hans, Marcus, Jeremy, & Auerbach, 1984). The growing popularity of cocaine has taken its toll on newborns. Chasnoff, Burns, Schnoll, and Burns (1985) present data that suggest that cocaine use during pregnancy leads to placental vasiconstriction and subsequently to reduced fetal blood supply. Data from the same study indicate a higher incidence of spontaneous abortion among cocaine users. Chasnoff and colleagues also found that infants of mothers who abused cocaine during pregnancy experienced higher incidences of abnormal sleep patterns, tremors, and poor feeding relative to other infants. Some evidence suggests that these babies are also of lower birth weights, have decreased head circumference, and are shorter in length than other infants (Bingol, Fuchs, Diaz, Stone, & Gromisch, 1987; Oro & Dixon, 1987).

Nicotine has been linked to lower birth weights in infants. Vorhees and Mollnow (1987) report that "birth weight deficits found in children are dose dependent and average about 200 g. Perhaps most significantly, the risk of having a low birth weight child (less than 2,500 g.) is doubled among women who smoke" (p. 947). Other research suggests that the offspring of smoking mothers may have deficits in auditory processing (Picone, Allen, Olsen, & Ferris, 1982).

There is then, ample evidence that maternal exposure to drugs and other types of chemical agents increases the risk to the fetus during pregnancy. Professionals concerned with reducing the risk of developmental difficulties among young children should provide information about the hazards of drug use during pregnancy to women likely to become pregnant. In general pregnant women should use any kind of drug prudently, if at all, and only with the advice of a physician.

Maternal Infection Many bacterial and viral infections contracted during pregnancy can place the fetus at significant risk of later developmental problems. Rubella, or German measles, is one of the best known conditions affecting prenatal development (Gregg, 1941). Typically, childhood rubella is very mild and results in few, if any, complications. In a pregnant woman, however, rubella can have devastating effects on the developing fetus. This is especially true if the disease occurs during the first trimester of pregnancy. Children exposed prenatally to rubella are often profoundly mentally and physically disabled (Cooper & Krugman, 1966). Women contemplating pregnancy must determine whether or not they need to be vaccinated against rubella prior to conceiving. A simple blood test can determine whether vaccination is necessary.

Blood tests can also help screen for the presence of spirochete bacteria that cause syphilis. In spite of improved detection techniques, the incidence of syphilis is rising. Syphilis is not only potentially fatal to the person contracting it, but can also have grave effects on a developing fetus. A woman who has syphilis can pass on the infection to her fetus, possibly resulting in visual handicaps, damage to the central nervous system and even death, depending upon the progress of the disease. Antibiotics can be used to cure syphilis in the mother and the risk to the fetus can be dramatically reduced prior to approximately the 18th week of gestation.

At least two other more chronic viruses have been linked to increased risk to the fetus if contracted by the mother during pregnancy. *Cytomegalic inclusion disease* may result in a wide variety of developmental disorders. *Herpes virus hominus* leaves mild manifestations in adults, but can greatly increase the risk to the fetus by introducing a higher incidence of brain lining infections. The mortality rate for infants infected with herpes is 50%.

Acquired immunodeficiency syndrome (AIDS), which is caused by the human immunodeficiency virus (HIV), can be passed on to the fetus by an infected mother. It is difficult to diagnose the presence of HIV at birth because the mother passes her antibodies to the infant across the placenta. In most cases, the disease will become symptomatic within the first 24 months of life (American Academy of Pediatrics Task Force on Pediatric AIDS, 1988). Symptoms include failure to thrive, chronic diarrhea, pneumonia, meningitis, and bone and joint infection. These infections are often recurrent. Developmental disabilities and neurological dysfunction are also common in AIDS children. "Reported overall mortality in children with AIDS is 65%, with the majority of deaths occurring during the first 24 months of life" (American Academy of Pediatrics Task Force on Pediatric AIDS, 1988, p. 942). The care and treatment of infants and young children with AIDS should include provisions for the safety of both the child with the disease and others in the environment. The American Academy of Pediatrics (1988) has issued guidelines for care providers who are working with HIV-positive children. If these guidelines are followed, there is virtually no risk of the disease being transmitted to others in the environment.

Pregnant women should, of course, take precautions against contracting any infections during pregnancy since the degree of risk created by other microbic agents is not well understood.

Perinatal Risk Factors

Not all factors that increase the risk of later developmental difficulties occur during preg-

nancy. A number of factors occurring during birth, infancy, and early childhood may contribute to developmental problems. The perinatal period lasts from the 28th week of gestation to the 7th day after delivery.

Birth Complications and Prematurity

Birth complications often result in anoxia, or lack of oxygen. In a breech birth, for example, the infant is born buttocks first rather than head first. While it is often possible for the obstetrician to turn the baby with instruments, use of instruments contributes to the risk of direct damage to the baby's head. The risk of anoxia occurs in breech birth because the umbilical cord can rather easily become wrapped around the infant's neck.

Precipitous labor, or labor lasting less than 2 hours, often sets the stage for anoxia. In this situation, anoxia results from premature separation of the placenta from the uterine wall. Prolonged labor may also lead to anoxia through an incomplete separation of the placenta.

Drugs used during labor may also affect the infant. Heavy anesthesia used during delivery may affect the baby, since anesthetic crosses the placental barrier quickly. Exposure to anesthetic may reduce the infant's ability to breathe independently and cause a general depression of the central nervous system (Brackbill, 1979). After an in-depth analysis of the use of drugs during birth, Brackbill concluded that "drugs given to mothers during labor and delivery have subsequent effects on infant behavior and no study has demonstrated functional enhancement following obstetrical medication" (p. 109). In addition, these effects may persist into the first year of life. Drugs administered during labor and delivery should thus be used judiciously.

Prematurity also greatly increases the chances of anoxia. Premature infants tend to lack the physiological maturity in their respiratory systems needed to breathe independently. Thus, when the umbilical cord is severed the child may become anoxic and need assistance in breathing.

While a number of birth complications can lead to anoxia, it is not well established just how much anoxia an infant can withstand before irreparable nervous system damage occurs. Generally, even brief episodes of anoxia should be avoided at birth to decrease the risk of later developmental problems.

Infant Status at Birth Because labor and delivery increase the risk to the infant, the infant's status must be assessed immediately after birth. The status of the infant is an index of vulnerability and is, thus, important in identifying infants who are significantly at risk just after birth. The most widely used measure of determining an infant's status at birth is the Apgar scale (Apgar, 1953), discussed in Chapter 8. While low Apgar scores seem to predict neonatal death rates in groups of infants (Apgar, Holaday, James, Berrien, & Weisbrot, 1958; Apgar & James, 1962), they may or may not predict behavioral outcomes or death in a given infant (Self & Horowitz, 1979).

DEFINING RISK

No single test can accurately predict the degree of risk to which an infant is exposed. Recognition of this fact led Parmelee, Sigman, Kopp, and Haber (1975) to develop the concept of cumulative risk. Their method of identifying infants at risk uses multiple assessments at different ages and measures a wide range of variables. The cumulative risk score system devised by Parmelee and colleagues is comprised of certain items related to each period, as follows:

Neonatal risk score items
1. Obstetric complications
2. Postnatal events
3. Newborn neurological examination

4. Visual attention
5. Sleep polygraph

Three and four month risk score items
6. Pediatric events and examination
7. Gesell test
8. Visual attention
9. Sleep polygraph

Eight and nine month risk score items
10. Pediatric events and examination
11. Gesell test
12. Cognitive test
13. Hand precision/sensory-motor schemes
14. Exploratory behavior

Parmelee, Sigman, Kopp, and Haber (1976) provide a more complete description of these items, to which the interested reader is referred.

Simply defined, risk is a prediction of the manifestation of later developmental disability. Parmelee and colleagues (1975) asserted that the greater the number of predictor variables, the more accurately risk status can be assigned to an individual infant. This argument is only one half of the story, however, for Parmelee's system is designed to measure only the biological status of the infant, that is, the infant's vulnerability. However, Parmelee and colleagues (1975) did recognize that "one important recurring observation is that outcome measures are strongly influenced by the socioeconomic circumstances of the children's environments, and this influence is often stronger than that of earlier biological events" (p. 114).

As we stated earlier, being at risk is a function of the child's biological status in interaction with the environment. Thus, as Anastasi (1958) suggested three decades ago and as Bixler (1980) reiterated more recently, both nature and nurture contribute to a child's development. Our mission is to determine how these two influences interact to place children at risk.

Successful interactions with caring and competent adults increase the child's chances for optimal development.

Sameroff and Chandler (1975) took this interactional view one step further, suggesting that neither environmental nor biological factors are static. They suggest a transactional model, in which the biological nature of the child influences the caregiving environment, which, in turn, influences the child. Prematurity, for example, does not imply that an infant will ultimately be at risk or manifest a developmental problem. However, a baby's prematurity may set the stage for transactions with the caregiving environment that may result in developmental delay.

Kearsley (1979) has presented the concept of *iatrogenic retardation*, a syndrome of learned incompetence. His concept provides an excellent illustration of the way an in-

fant's transactions can be governed by a biological event such as prematurity. He presents evidence to suggest that a modification of the transactional pattern between the infant and the caregiving environment can significantly alter the course of the child's development. His argument demonstrates the way labeling a child as vulnerable can create a self-fulfilling prophecy by establishing an overprotective and understimulating set of transactions. In such cases, it may be the label "prematurity," rather than the biological event of prematurity, that contributes most to the child's risk status. Kearsley's argument is sobering when one considers the negative effect of labels that have been recognized by sociologists (e.g., Bogdan, 1980; Dexter, 1964; Farber, 1968; Mercer, 1973). Labels have significant effects on the life chances (Farber, 1968) and status (Mercer, 1973) of school age children and adults. Apparently, labels potentially may have similar effects on infants, beginning even at birth.

In summary, we have pointed out a number of factors that can contribute to the risk status of the infant. These factors are both biological and environmental in nature and interact to define the degree of risk assigned to any infant or young child. Accepting the premise of Sameroff and Chandler (1975) allows us to see this interaction as a dynamic one, and to suggest that a modification of the child's transactions with the environment may significantly alter his or her eventual developmental status. As we discuss in later chapters, early developmental intervention is often the key to effective modifications in the young child's transactions with the environment, and, consequently, in the child's degree of risk and eventual developmental status.

INCIDENCE AND PREVALENCE OF DEVELOPMENTAL PROBLEMS

Now that we have examined some of the factors related to increased risk in young children, it is necessary to explore the pervasiveness of the developmental problems exhibited by preschool children. To accomplish this, we consider the incidence and prevalence of various developmental problems in infants and preschool children.

Both incidence and prevalence relate to the actual occurrence of a particular developmental problem. While the two terms are related and have often been used interchangeably, they are not synonymous. *Incidence* refers to the frequency with which a particular condition occurs within a population. For example, the expected incidence

of Down syndrome is approximately 1 in 600 births. The actual incidence, however, would be defined by how many Down syndrome children were actually born during a particular period of time, so that the actual incidence of the condition may have been 87 out of 35,000 births in a given year. Changes in incidence figure may reflect what society is doing about preventing a particular condition. For example, the world-wide incidence of smallpox has been zero over the last several years, reflecting the success of mass immunization programs.

Prevalence refers to the actual number of individuals identified as having a particular condition at a given time. Thus, while the incidence of Down syndrome has decreased as a result of genetic counseling and amniocentesis, the prevalence has increased as a result of the increased ability to prolong the life of people with Down syndrome. Prevalence figures reveal how much of a particular problem there is to deal with; incidence figures can provide the basis for predicting the need for future services.

Although several prevalence studies have been completed to determine the number of children with a particular disability, no studies yet provide data on specific disabling conditions in children under 6. The figures that are presented are based on estimates extrapolated from census data. For example, the National Advisory Committee on the Handicapped (1976) estimated that there were 1,187,000 disabled children 6 years old or younger during the 1975–1976 school year. Of these, they estimated that approximately 737,000 were unserved.

Two main reasons account for the lack of definitive prevalence data on disabled children under the age of 6. First, such studies are difficult to conduct, especially at a national level, and are, therefore, costly. Second, and perhaps more important, is the difficulty in adequately defining a population of preschool children with handicaps. As was seen in the first section of this chapter, a number of factors contribute to an infant or young child being at risk. However, being at risk does not per se make a child disabled. Since many disabilities manifest themselves, at least in part, through deficits in academic performance, it is only when children reach school age that they are clearly identified as disabled. Thus, accurate prevalence figures for school age populations are easier to develop than for preschool ones. PL 99-457 requires states to engage in active child find. This effort may lead to more availability and accuracy of prevalence figures for children under 6 years of age with disabilities.

In some instances, however, even preschool children can be identified, classified, and accounted for as disabled. These instances arise when the disabling condition has obvious physical and/or behavioral manifestations, as with birth defects or many genetically determined syndromes such as those discussed above. Preschool children with multiple disabilities tend to be more easily accounted for than those with single disabilities. For example, in an early prevalence study of visually impaired children, Graham (1967) determined that 86% of the children under 6 had one or more additional disabilities.

As with prevalence figures, incidence figures depend on one's ability to identify the actual condition of concern. Again, more severe and more obvious conditions are identifiable at birth. Thus, a number of incidence figures are available for the more obvious congenital anomalies and birth injuries. Table 2.2 presents incidence figures for 1984 and 1985 for a number of major birth anomalies. These figures are probably underreported because of inaccurate recording or the failure to recognize certain anomalies at birth. Obviously, an anomaly must be recognized before it can be recorded. Further un-

Table 2.2. Incidence of selected birth anomalies, 1984–1985

Congenital anomaly	1984	1985
Anencephalus	2.6	2.7
Hydrocephalus	5.6	5.6
Down syndrome	.8	.7
Spina bifida	5.0	4.5
Cleft palate	5.6	6.0
Cleft lip	8.9	8.9
Tracheo-esophageal fistula	1.2	2.9
Clubfoot	24.8	26.0
Reduction deformity of upper limb	1.5	1.7
Reduction deformity of lower limb	.8	1.1
Trisomy 18	.9	1.3

Note: Data are based on 10,000 live births.

derscoring this point is a survey of 44 state Departments of Education that found that only seven states have definitions of preschool children with handicaps (Lessen & Rose, 1980). Lessen and Rose concluded from their results that

> identifying the pre-school handicapped population may seem difficult for a number of reasons including variability in normal development, questionable identification and diagnostic instruments, and variability in quality and quantity of environmental experiences. Because of these difficulties, the identification and definition and accounting for this population is at best tenuous. (1980, p. 469)

The provisions of PL 99-457 require states to develop definitions that can be applied to infants and preschool children with handicaps. Thus, over the next several years useable definitions for identifying the population should become available.

SUMMARY

This chapter discusses various factors that can put infants and young children at increased risk for developmental delay. These factors include prematurity and low birth weight, as well as genetic traits. There are also factors like maternal nutrition, drug use, smoking, and maternal infection that can increase risk during the prenatal period. Risk is a dynamic concept and may be affected by subsequent environmental or biological events. Thus, the assessment of risk status is cumulative and must be reassessed on an on-going basis. Finally, this chapter considers the incidence and prevalence of develop-mental problems in infants and young children. Incidence and prevalence figures are important indicators of society's effectiveness in dealing with a particular problem. In addition, these figures are necessary to plan for and develop early intervention services. The importance of these figures is recognized in PL 99-457 that calls for establishing definitions of at-risk and disabled infants and young children, as well as for conducting child counts indicating their prevalence.

Early Intervention in the Least Restrictive Environment

1. What has been the role of litigation in bringing about the integration of children with handicaps into programs for children without handicaps?
2. Why is imitation thought to be an important means for learning for children in integrated settings?
3. What major arguments have been put forth for and against educating preschool children in the least restrictive environment?

SINCE THE PASSAGE OF PL 99-457 there has been a renewed effort to ensure that early intervention programs for children with handicaps are carried out in integrated settings. This results from the stipulation in the law, deriving from PL 94-142, that all children must be educated in the least restrictive environment (LRE). Research has shown that many children below age 5 with handicapping conditions can profit in terms of cognitive, social, and communication development from interactions with peers without handicaps (Bartel & Guskin, 1980). Until the 1980s, however, integrated programs were rare, primarily because preschool programs were not generally available for children without handicaps. Now, with the advent of

PL 99-457 and the greater availability of child care and other preschool programs for children without handicaps, the least restrictive environment is more accessible to young children with handicaps.

The concept of integration has often been misinterpreted by parents and professionals. This chapter attempts to clarify the concept as it is applied to children from birth to age 5. We begin a review of the legal precedents that established the concept, then briefly examine the historical context in which it developed. Some arguments for and against integration are then presented. Finally, we review Head Start integration policy, which by law has provided integrated education for children with handicaps since 1975.

29

LITIGATION AND LEGISLATION

According to Bricker (1978), the prevailing social philosophy in the United States has been gradually changing to include more and more children with handicaps in public education programs. Whereas formerly only a select group was eligible, today all children between ages 3 and 21 with handicaps must be provided services. This change had particularly strong impact in two areas: the education of preschool children with handicaps and the education of children in kindergarten through 12th grade with severe handicaps. As the public schools adjusted to accommodate these two groups into special, usually self-contained, programs, the same social philosophy has prompted a movement of children with moderate handicaps from segregated to integrated programs.

The social philosophy to which Bricker refers is reflected in a series of court and legislative decisions passed down during the last 20 years that relied on the Fourteenth Amendment of the U.S. Constitution. The *equal protection clause* of that amendment has been used repeatedly to justify the extension of educational services to children with handicaps. That clause states that any opportunity provided by a state must be made available to all citizens on an equal basis.

Court decisions relating to the least restrictive environment may be divided into two groups, those mandating the right to treatment for institutionalized children (deinstitutionalization) and those mandating the right to education in the least restrictive environment (integration) for noninstitutionalized children. Combined, these decisions constitute a strong movement toward normalization of life for all citizens with handicaps (Wolfensberger, 1975). They are briefly reviewed below.

Right to Appropriate Education

Cases dealing with the right to an appropriate education involved two issues. First, the contention was made that many children with handicaps were being denied a free public education because they were denied access to the public schools. These were primarily children who were labeled moderately to severely mentally retarded, and who were either living in institutions or remaining at home without schooling. Second, there were large numbers of children placed inappropriately in special classes for the mentally retarded. These children, while served by the public school system, were not being provided an appropriate education. Many of these children were from minority backgrounds. For example, in a study of 505 southern school districts in 1974, the Children's Defense Fund found that over 80% of the children in classes for the mentally retarded were black (Children's Defense Fund, 1974).

The major litigation dealing with these two issues took place between 1968 and 1973 and is summarized below.

1968 *Arreola et al. v. Board of Education* involved seven Mexican-American children in Santa Ana, California, who had been placed in special classes for the mentally retarded. Their placement had been based on IQ scores obtained from tests administered in English. The children were retested in Spanish and scored within the normal range on an individually administered intelligence test.

1970 *Diana v. Board of Education* involved nine Mexican-American children who had been tested by means of a group IQ test and found to be mentally retarded. When retested individually in English and/or Spanish, seven of the children scored well above 70, the eighth scored 70, and the ninth 67, for an average gain of 15 points each. The court ruled that a group IQ test score could not be used for the purpose of labeling a child mentally retarded.

1970 *Stewart v. Philip* was a classification suit involving seven children from low SES black families in Boston who had been classified as mentally retarded. Re-testing found them to be functioning within the average intellectual range. The court based its decision on the following points: the children had been placed outside the regular classroom because they were considered behavior problems; they had been classified on the basis of a single test; standardized tests discriminate against children who are not of white middle-class backgrounds; and standardized tests fail to discriminate among various learning disorders, only one of which is mental retardation.

1971 *Hobson v. Hansen* was a suit filed by a group of black parents in Washington, D.C., against the tracking system, in which children were tested at an early age and sorted into ability groups. The court found that the low track consisted predominantly of low SES black children and that the low track program was of poor quality. The court further found that the aptitude test used for sorting was biased in favor of white middle-class children, and its use for tracking purposes violated the Fourteenth Amendment.

1972 *Mills v. Board of Education* was a class action suit brought against the Washington, D.C. Board of Education on behalf of nine children with handicaps who had not been allowed to enroll in the public schools. The court ruled that the children must be provided educational services by the public school system, that lack of funds could not be used as an excuse for not educating children with handicaps, and that due process procedures must be instituted to protect children from arbitrary administrative decisions.

1972 *Larry P. v. Riles*, a landmark case in San Francisco, involved six black elementary school children who had been tested and improperly placed in classes for the mentally retarded. Stating that the children were "victims of a testing procedure which fails to recognize unfamiliarity with white middle-class culture," the judge ruled that a second criterion in addition to the IQ test was necessary in order to classify a child mentally retarded. He instructed the educational system to find an IQ test that was not culturally biased against minority children. Seven years later when such a test had still not been developed, he ruled that IQ tests could not be used at all in the classification of minority children.

1972 *Pennsylvania Association for Retarded Children v. Commonwealth of Pennsylvania,* another landmark case in the right to education litigation, challenged the constitutionality of the state law that excluded mentally retarded children from public schools. Basing its decision on both the Fifth and Fourteenth Amendments, the court mandated free public programs for all retarded children in Pennsylvania between the ages of 6 and 21. These programs were stipulated to be appropriate to the needs of the child and to be carried out in the least restrictive environment. Due process protections were included.

1973 *Lebanks v. Spears*, a case brought in Louisiana on behalf of children in special education classes, resulted in an opinion that the regular classroom with support services is preferable to special class placement. The decision called for a written individual educational plan for each child with a handicap.

Right to Treatment

Although the five years from 1968 to 1973 were years of significant progress in the delineation of educational rights of some children with handicaps, it was not until 1972 that an important case was brought on behalf of those children with severe handicaps who were spending their lives in institutions without adequate treatment. In *Wyatt v. Stickney* (1972) the court stated that citizens in a state institution have the right to appropriate treatment, education, and habilitation, and that these services must be in the form of an individual program fitted to their needs. This landmark case was affirmed by the United States Supreme Court, making it a decision of national importance. Two similar cases, *Welsch v. Likens* in Minnesota (1974) and *New York Association for Retarded Citizens v. Carey* (1975) affirmed the right to treatment based on the Eighth Amendment protection against cruel and unusual punishment.

The result of nearly a decade of court decisions broadening access to free, appropriate education was a series of state and federal laws culminating in PL 94-142, the Education for All Handicapped Children Act of 1975. This law established the following mandates, which derive from the court decisions of the previous 8 years.

1. All children between the ages of 3 and 21 with handicaps must be provided free, appropriate educational programs. Only those states already serving 3- to 5-year-olds without handicaps in public

schools need serve preschool children with handicaps.

2. These programs must be based on an individualized education program (IEP) developed for each child and revised at least annually.

3. The IEP must be developed by means of assessment procedures that take account of the child's cultural background, primary language, and previous experience.

4. The education program chosen must be the least restrictive alternative. This means that the child must be placed in as normal a setting as he or she can prosper in, preferably together with children without handicaps. This will vary according to the individual capabilities of each child.

5. Parents must be involved in the planning of their child's educational program. They are accorded carefully defined due process procedures for appealing educational decisions that they find inappropriate, and they must be consulted whenever program changes are made.

In 1986, the rights accorded to 5- to 18-year-olds in PL 94-142 were extended to 3- and 4-year-olds in the form of amendments to the 1975 act known as PL 99-457. (See Chapter 1 for a complete review of this law.) Essentially, PL 99-457 requires that 3- and 4-year-olds with handicaps be provided early intervention services in the least restrictive environment. Whether or not a state provides preschool programs for preschool children without handicaps is no longer a criterion for serving those with handicaps.

PL 99-457 made very clear its intent in regard to the education of preschool children with handicaps. It clearly intends that children with mild to moderate handicaps be integrated, or placed in programs with their peers without handicaps for most or all of their program. The expectation for more severely impaired children is that they be integrated with nonhandicapped children for certain portions of their program. The remainder of this chapter explores the appropriateness and feasability of integrating young children with handicaps with children without handicaps.

HISTORICAL PERSPECTIVE

The history of educational programs for young children with handicaps is a short one. Traditionally, children with handicaps have been kept at home or placed in institutions soon after birth. Since they were not considered educable, the expenditure of funds for their education was generally considered wasteful (Hutt & Gibby, 1976). It was seen to be in the best interests of all to keep children with handicaps at home, both to prevent them from harming nonhandicapped peers and to protect them from too demanding an environment.

Until the early twentieth century, the public schools had a limited role in the education of children with handicaps. The major function of the public schools was deemed to be the socialization and education of nonhandicapped children. Gradually that view changed, and mentally retarded children were accepted into the public school system in segregated classes. By 1910, 99 U.S. cities had classes for children with mental retardation within the public school system (Hutt & Gibby, 1976). The 1920s, 1930s, and 1940s saw an expansion of such programs for school age retarded children. During the 1950s and 1960s, there was a gradual movement to provide public educational programs to school age children

with physical handicaps, visual and hearing impairments, and learning disabilities. However, although the public school system finally accepted responsibility for these children after the age of 6, it has been only recently that a similar commitment to preschool children has been made, and this is the result of strong encouragement from lawmakers in the form of PL 99-457. Currently, most public education programs for preschool children with handicaps are federally funded, and until 1987, few were integrated.

Until the passage of PL 99-457, educational programs for children under 5 were typically not based in public schools but rather fell into one of three general categories: 1) private nursery schools for children from middle- and upper-class families, 2) early intervention programs for children from lower-class families who were considered to be disadvantaged, and 3) programs sponsored by community and private agencies for the benefit of young children with handicaps. The latter category included some short-term, hospital-based programs.

While it is beyond the scope of this chapter to discuss programs based on social and economic class, it is important to note that during the 1960s much national attention was focused on efforts to help lower-class children "catch up" with the middle-class majority. The provision of public programs for these children (e.g., Head Start, Follow Through) provided some legitimacy for the public education of preschool children with handicaps. Indeed, Head Start's requirement that 10% of enrolled children be labeled handicapped not only sanctioned services to preschool children with handicaps, but required that such services be provided in the least restrictive environment.

In summary, integrated programs have been more difficult to achieve for preschool children than for school age children. Although the same attitudes that account for the mainstreaming movement in public schools prevail, the machinery—that is, classes of normally achieving children—are less readily available at the preschool level. This has meant that mainstreamed programs for young children are much less common and will probably continue to be so until public schools become more involved in the education of all children below age 5.

Arguments for Integration

Ethical Arguments Surely the goal of serving all children within the public sector is a noble one with which few argue. But should children with handicaps and children without handicaps be educated together? Unless integration is beneficial to both groups of children, it cannot be wholeheartedly supported. Much has been written on this topic, with a few references standing out. Dunn (1968) was among the first to question the education of children with mild retardation in segregated classes. In an article that has since become a classic in the field of special education, Dunn presented educational and social arguments suggesting that special classes generally provided inadequate programs for children with handicaps. Expectancy studies during the late 1960s and early 1970s (Avery, 1971; Beez, 1968; Scott, 1969) indicated that teacher expectations are lower for labeled children than for those without handicap labels. Lowered expectations lessen the chances of children with handicaps achieving average levels in their academic and social performance.

Evidence confirms that children with handicaps do not necessarily receive an appropriate education within the special class setting. Ethical considerations, too, have provided much of the rationale for integration of children of all ages. The traditional segregation of children with handicaps is as much a result of negative social attitudes toward these children as it is motivated by a desire to improve conditions for them. Bartel and Guskin (1980) argue that society creates children with handicaps by selecting certain attributes (e.g., normal intelligence) and calling them desirable while labeling others (e.g., mental retardation) undesirable. They further maintain that whether a child is labeled handicapped depends on the child's social class, parents, income, educational level, and race. Those children from socially less desirable backgrounds tend to be labeled handicapped more often (Mercer, 1973) and, therefore, segregated from the mainstream. Thus, society has tended to deal with difference or deviance by segregating it so that it can be ignored.

Placing a child with a handicap in an environment comprised exclusively of other children with handicaps may result in an inadequate environment for that child. Since an impoverished environment may have caused the handicap in the first place, a segregated environment can only maintain that impoverishment and perpetuate the handicap (Bartel & Guskin, 1980). Such an environment does not provide typical role models for the child and thus hinders the child's learning of typical behavior. Bartel and Guskin claim that, indeed,

> segregation of handicapped children in special programs is one aspect of a larger social phenomenon: the formal management of deviance by our society. It includes prisons for the behaviorally different, mental institutions for the emotionally different, residential institutions and special classes for the intellectually different, hospitals for the physically different, and ghettos for the ethnically and racially different. (p. 64)

Integration is more compatible with the recent emphasis in this country on a multicultural approach to education that values differences between individuals. Multicultural education and integration share the same goal: to achieve acceptance by the public school system of children who for cultural, intellectual, or behavioral reasons deviate from the norm significantly enough to be noticed. However, public schools are only a reflection of the larger society they serve. We must ask whether expectations for social reform can be realistically posited in them. It can be argued that the attitudes of all citizens, not only those of children, must be changed if people who are different are to be allowed to lead average lives. This seems a fearsome and unrealistic responsibility to place on public schools.

Developmental Arguments

Peer Interaction   In the review of developmental or psychological arguments for integration, the work of Harlow and his colleagues with rhesus monkeys is a good starting place. For nearly 20 years, Harlow and his colleagues studied the social relationships of monkeys in order to gain a better understanding of primates in general. Their conclusions regarding the role of peer relationships in social development have implications for mainstreaming. Suomi and Harlow (1975), for example, believe the importance of peer friendships has traditionally been underestimated by researchers in social development. They present evidence that competent and adaptive social activity in the adult monkey is predicated on the development and maintenance of peer friendships immediately following infancy and throughout the developmental years. They found peers to be the most salient influence in a monkey's everyday life after infancy; this influence is primarily in the form of play, through which social roles are established and maintained. Suomi and Harlow maintain that peer interactions have an important developmental purpose not

only for rhesus monkeys but for other primates, including humans. They believe that as humans, we share with other primates a genetically acquired potential for social activity that is shaped by peer interactions.

The role of play in children's cognitive and moral development (Piaget, 1932, 1954; Sproule, 1988; Wilkinson, 1980) and social and affective development (Bruner, Jolly, & Sylva, 1976; Hartup, 1983; Rubin & Pepler, 1980; Sproule, 1988) has been well documented (see Chapter 6). It is through play that children try out new roles, experiment with their environment, and test their limits in physical and mental activity. Play also provides a safe forum in which a child may experiment with aggression and sexual arousal as a means of learning how to handle these feelings without fear of adult disapproval. Mueller and Cohen (1986) point out that peer relations allow toddlers to develop some autonomy from their parents, and, subsequently, to master the skills of peer play that will later form the basis of friendships. In play activity with peers, children encounter an egalitarian environment with fewer constraints than in adult-child relationships. This environment facilitates social, cognitive, moral, language, and motor learning. Indeed, inadequate peer relations are prognostic indicators of social and emotional trouble in young children, for loners more often end up as delinquents, or develop adjustment difficulties in adulthood.

Evidence suggests that differentiated social relationships develop early in infancy. Musatti (1986) reported that infants as young as 3 months differed in the amount of approach behavior they directed toward other infants. By 18 months, differences are clear (Jacobson, Tianen, Willie, & Aytch, 1986); some infants have developed a more responsive, reciprocal style of interacting with peers. Other research (Stambak & Verba, 1986) indicates that reciprocity is an important aspect of toddler friendship, and that imitation plays a role in establishing peer interactions during the first and second years of life (Mueller & Cohen, 1986). Thus, peer interaction, or lack of it, is an important feature in a child's early life.

Peer interactions in the form of play are important to preschool children. They may be even more important to children with handicaps who have experienced deprived environments, as Bartel and Guskin (1980) have suggested. Before we address the question of whether integrating preschool children increases their peer interaction, let us examine for a moment some aspects of peer relationships.

STAGES OF PEER INTERACTION According to Mueller and Lucas (1975) and Stambak and Verba (1986), young children between the ages of 12 and 18 months are predictable in their development of peer interactions. The first stage is an outgrowth of sensorimotor behavior. It consists of two children acting on an object in an identical fashion. Because 1-year-olds are used to acting on objects, the object, which is naturally admired by both children, becomes the focus of contact. This stage is dyadic, and three-person interactions are not observed until age 2. This stage is sometimes known as parallel play, terminology that actually ignores the peer interaction involved. The beginnings of imitative behavior are seen here, since the two children behave in similar fashion with the object.

By the second stage, children are actively seeking and receiving what Mueller and Lucas (1975) term "contingencies," that is, actions contiguous in time and space. These are comparable to Piaget's secondary circular reactions. That is, child A initiates an action, such as laughing, and child B's response to that action causes child A to repeat the action. A circular reaction that involves a good deal of imitation is set up. The

children's behaviors gradually become reciprocal. For example, child A honks a horn, child B then honks the horn, child A then honks it again. As the imitation and the reciprocal activity increase, both children notice each other and actively seek more interaction.

By stage three, the interchanges have become complementary in nature. The participants do different but intercoordinated things. The activity is reciprocal in the sense that child B now does the opposite of what child A does or responds with his or her own action. Therefore, by definition, stage three is no longer imitative. The activities at stage three require a sensitivity between the children to each other's movements. For example, two children playing a game of catch, rolling a ball back and forth between them, requires one to throw and the other to catch, and each must be sensitive to the movements of the other. Thus, a developmental sequence is identified that begins with sensorimotor intelligence and develops through imitation to reciprocal interactions, all during the first 18 months of life.

TYPES OF PEER INTERACTION Hartup (1983) has reported three ways in which peers influence each other. The first and earliest to develop is *peer modeling*. We have noted previously that imitation plays an important part in the socialization of young children. Peer modeling, Hartup reports, is influential in the development of problem-solving behavior, sex-role activity, and social interaction. It is evidently enhanced if the child sees the peer model receive a reward (Bandura & Menlove, 1968) and if the child and the model are of the same sex. Hartup notes that children enjoy being imitated and are more apt to be friendly toward the imitator, a factor to be considered in mainstreaming children with handicaps.

A second kind of peer influence is *peer reinforcement*. Peer reinforcement is related to the efficacy of peer modeling. Hartup

Peer interactions are an important source of learning. Children with special needs can benefit from interactions with nonhandicapped peers.

found that children who had experienced positive interactions with their peers were better able to imitate models than those who had not. He cites many examples from research showing how effective peer reinforcement can be for shaping behaviors.

Finally, Hartup suggests *peer tutoring* as a means of providing opportunity for social interaction between preschool children. Both children benefit from the peer tutoring experience. The tutor gains in self-esteem flowing from the increased status the role of tutor provides and has an opportunity to experience a nurturing role, which helps to increase his or her sensitivity to others. The tutored child benefits from the individual attention that is provided and has an opportunity for increased cognitive growth.

Hartup maintains that all of these forms of peer interaction are helpful in the socialization process. He cautions, however, that peer interactions must be carefully planned if they are to help children with handicaps get along with children without handicaps. This brings us back to the question, does integrating preschool children increase their social interaction with their nonhandicapped peers? Research evidence does not provide a clear answer. Some interesting work has been done, however. Gottlieb and Leyser (1981) reported that in a free play situation, preschool children select playmates with similar cognitive levels.

Guralnick and his colleagues have done a great deal of work in this area. They report that simply introducing children without handicaps into a play setting does not guarantee that they will play together with children with handicaps. In an early study, Devoney, Guralnick, and Rubin (1974) found that children with handicaps could be encouraged to play both among themselves and with children without handicaps if the teacher structured the environment to promote interactions. When this was done, it was observed that the children with handicaps played in a more organized way and with more sophistication and fantasy than had been noted before their contacts with children without handicaps. In a later study, Guralnick (1976) found that peer modeling and peer reinforcement by children without handicaps significantly increased the cooperative play of children with handicaps.

Two factors have been identified by Guralnick (1980) and others (Peck, Apolloni, Cooke, & Raver, 1978) that have an important effect on how much preschool children interact when they are integrated. The first factor is training. It appears that preschool children with developmental disabilities imitate nonhandicapped children if they are trained to do so and reinforced for it. Peck, Apolloni, Cooke, and Raver (1978) found, moreover, that this training generalized to other situations. In their experiment, they trained retarded children to imitate nonhandicapped children and found that the behaviors learned from peer models were displayed in other situations. They noted that the generalization was more successful when the children were closest in developmental level. This is the second factor to emerge from the research. Children seem to choose playmates who are at similar developmental levels. This suggests that older children with handicaps should be integrated with younger children without handicaps so that they might approximate the same developmental level and share similar interests and ability levels. As a matter of fact, interest in mixed-

age peers is not restricted to mainstreaming. Research on nonhandicapped preschool children in mixed-age classes indicates that such environments produce more mature play and may contribute to greater socialization (Epstein, 1986; Hartup, 1983; Rubin, 1980).

LANGUAGE ACQUISITION   Another area in which peers may be important for preschool children with handicaps is language acquisition. Here again, the evidence is not clear-cut. Bates, Bretherton, Beeghly-Smith, and McNew (1982) reported that children who spend more time with peers than with adults are at a disadvantage in learning language. Bates and her colleagues (1982) show that twins who talk only to each other tend to be retarded in language development; that first-borns have better language than younger siblings because they talk more to adults than to peers; and that institutionalized children have poor language if adult speech is not available to them. The same children show no effects from peer talk or the lack of it. Thus, the level of language development has been found to be highest in children who associate primarily with adults.

It would seem from this that peers do not have a great influence on the language acquisition of children with handicaps. Evidence suggests, however, that other children are an important source of communication for a child, and that children are sensitive to the communicative needs of each other. In an important study, Shatz and Gelman (1973) found 4-year-olds to speak differently to adults, to peers, and to 2-year-olds. All the 4-year-olds in that study adjusted their speech for the 2-year-olds, making it shorter, simpler, and more directive.

Since language acquisition appears to depend on availability of simple, clear, grammatically correct, and redundant language (known as ''motherese'' by language acquisition researchers), the fact that young children can apparently provide this sort of language to their peers is important. Guralnick (1978b) reported that children without handicaps adjust their speech when addressing children with handicaps to match their listener's cognitive and linguistic levels. He concludes that peers without handicaps can provide a linguistic environment for children with handicaps that is sufficiently complex to stimulate language development and still remain at the appropriate developmental level for the listener.

Garvey (1986) reported several advantages of play for the development of language. Children are accustomed to commenting on what is going on in their play, often providing a running commentary of events. This process appears to be associated in some way with the child's language and cognitive development, but more specifically, it allows the partner in play to interpret and follow the action and thus to participate more fully in the play. Another advantage of play is that child-child interactions demand greater responsibility on the part of the child than do adult-child interactions, requiring children to work at regulating and maintaining their conversations with peers in a way not required in exchanges with adults.

In a study designed to explore children's dyadic relationships, Shugar and Bokus (1986) concluded that children under 3 use peer interactions to practice their roles as agents of actions in which they explore spatial and temporal relationships. Language is used to draw other children into their action fields.

In summary, there appear to be many benefits available to children with handicaps in an integrated preschool classroom, as long as the environment is properly structured and children are provided some training and reinforcement in order to take advantage of the peer models without handicaps. None of the research reported above found any ill effects

for the children with handicaps in their studies. But the question remains whether the effects on the children without handicaps are positive. Although little work has been done on this subject, what evidence there is suggests that the effects on children without handicaps are beneficial. Early studies by Bricker and Bricker (1971), Guralnick (1978), and Peck, Apollini, Cooke, and Raver (1978) suggest that children without handicaps benefit from integrated programs to at least the same degree and sometimes to a greater degree than would have been expected if they had attended nonintegrated preschools. These studies found no negative effects on the children without handicaps in these programs. More recently, Odom, De-Klyen, and Jenkins (1984) have presented evidence that "normally" developing preschool children experience similar levels of achievement whether they are placed with peers who are handicapped or with peers who are nonhandicapped. Guralnick (1978b) compared the positive effects on children without handicaps to similar effects found for tutors in peer tutoring situations, namely, that the child who is tutoring receives different but just as significant benefits from the experience as does the tutored child.

Arguments Against Integration

Teacher Attitudes The principal arguments against the mainstreaming of children with handicaps come from data based on elementary school and high school age children. We stated earlier that some of these data reveal the inadequacy of segregated programs for elementary school age children with handicaps. Such children, however, also encounter problems in the regular classroom, and these appear to be primarily related to teacher attitude. Palmer (1979, 1980), for example, studied instructional prescriptions that teachers prepared for normally achieving, learning disabled, and mentally retarded children, and found that teachers prescribed more remedial lessons for labeled children than for normally achieving children, even if all were performing at grade level. They evidently expected the labeled children to perform less ably. In another study, MacMillan, Meyers, and Yoshida (1978) found that regular classroom teachers perceived integrated students formerly in classes for the mentally retarded to be significantly weaker than regular classroom students in both academic achievement and social acceptance, even though there was little measured difference between the two groups of students. In a study of teacher attitudes toward mainstreaming, Moore and Fine (1978) reported that regular classroom teachers were less accepting of integration than other teachers, and that they were less positive about children with mental retardation being integrated than children with learning disabilities. These attitudes are partially confirmed in interviews conducted with regular and special education teachers in England and Wales (Huggett, 1986).

These studies suggest that teacher attitudes may adversely affect the classroom environment for the integrated child. Although there is no direct evidence of this at the preschool level, it must be inferred that a negative attitude on the part of preschool teachers toward children with handicaps in their classrooms would have similar adverse effects.

Teacher Attention A fear of parents of children with handicaps is that a mainstream classroom will not provide the individual attention that children have traditionally enjoyed in segregated settings (Sarason & Doris, 1979). It is true that teacher-child ratios for segregated classrooms are generally established by law and are usually quite favorable, whereas regular classroom settings tend to be less strictly regulated. Nevertheless, integrated preschool programs generally have a higher teacher-child ratio than regular programs because the need for more individual attention is recognized.

Finally, an argument raised against integration by parents of children without handicaps is that their children will suffer a reduction in attention and instructional time because the children with handicaps will absorb more than their share. There does not appear to be any basis for this fear, as an examination of some successful programs at the preschool level demonstrates. Indeed, the authors' personal experience indicates that the individualized programming that children with handicaps need, and must be provided, often spills over into the instructional environment of the children without handicaps. Regular classroom teachers who previously thought in terms of group activities and group achievement have learned through their work with children with handicaps to plan for individual needs more successfully.

With the main arguments for and against mainstreaming in mind, let us examine the way in which children with handicaps have been integrated into Head Start programs.

Head Start

As noted above, Head Start programs have been required by Congress for many years to reserve 10% of their enrollment space for children identified as handicapped. Head Start classes tend to be small, in keeping with their performance standards, which require procedures for individualized planning and evaluation of each child's growth. As a result of this emphasis on meeting the special needs of each child, such classes have been conducive to integration. Because the children come from low-income families, the majority have special needs, and so there is a tradition in Head Start of identifying specific skill areas that need extra remedial effort. This tradition extends readily to children with handicaps. As a result, integration has become a major activity for Head Start. More than any other preschool institution, Head Start has promoted the integration of children with handicaps.

Because of the grass-roots nature of the Head Start experience, it is difficult to generalize about Head Start programs. Local autonomy has been the rule, with the result that regions may approach integration differently. Nevertheless, some general observations can be made.

In a series of manuals (Department of Health, Education, and Welfare, 1978) for Head Start teachers, the role of the classroom teacher was delineated as follows:

1. Developing and putting into effect an educational program that meets the special needs of a child with a handicap
2. Helping parents implement the learning program at home as a carryover from the classroom
3. Taking advantage of special services available to aid in program diagnosis, program planning, and implementation (e.g., handicap coordinator, social services coordinator, educational consultant)

One of Head Start's primary strengths has been the supplemental resources provided to local programs to meet the performance standards. These resources may include consultants in medical, dental, mental health, or nutritional needs; social workers; and evaluation teams provided by public schools under PL 94-142 and PL 99-457 Child Find mandates. Most of these services are available on a part-time basis, but some may be full time.

In addition, Resource Access Projects (RAP) were established in each region of the country in 1972 for the specific purpose of helping local Head Start programs in each region to serve children with handicaps more effectively. RAPs continue to offer valuable training and technical assistance to Head Start centers on a local, state, and regional basis. In cooperation with public health departments and resource centers in each region, RAPs provide information, equipment, and services through public health departments, community mental health centers, speech and hearing clinics, universities and colleges, developmental disabilities programs, and private agencies.

SUMMARY

This chapter reviews legal mandates for the least restrictive environment in early childhood special education in the context of past litigation and recent legislation. It also provides a summary of arguments for and against integration, followed by a review of progress made toward LRE in the early childhood sector, with special attention to Head Start. Finally, research on the efficacy of LRE is presented.

IB

Typical and Atypical Development

4

Cognitive Development

1. What is the role of the central nervous system in the development of cognition?
2. Can a single theoretical position explain cognitive development?
3. How are the basic cognitive processes of attention, perception, and memory affected by problems in cognitive development such as mental retardation?
4. Can learning disabilities be identified in 3- to 5-year-old children?

COGNITIVE DEVELOPMENT IS A complex topic, one that has received much attention from psychologists and neurologists since the nineteenth century. More recently, researchers who bridge both disciplines—known as neuropsychologists—have begun to examine cognitive development. Neuropsychologists believe the roots of cognition—and, in fact, all human behavior—are found in the central nervous system. The first part of this chapter examines the physiological processes associated with cognitive development. The latter part of the chapter focuses on several crucial cognitive processes.

In defining cognition from a psychological viewpoint, it is useful to use Piaget's (1954) term, "knowing." Indeed, the development of cognitive abilities is perhaps best described in the Piagetian manner as the child's construction of "knowledge." By this

phrase, Piaget meant that each of us develops our own unique understanding of the world based on our individual genetic and environmental backgrounds. This explains why no two people understand the world in exactly the same way.

Although cognitive development is unique for every individual, it occurs in an orderly and sequential manner. We can predict the general steps children will take in developing their understanding of the world. This topic has received extensive attention from developmental psychologists and is examined in this chapter.

From an evolutionary standpoint, human beings are well suited for a high level of cognitive activity. The human nervous system is genetically endowed for complex intellectual activity, and human beings have been successful in adapting to a variety of environments. Human neurological structures have proved able to adapt well to the environment.

Underlying the development of cognition are the basic neurological structures of the young child. These structures are the hardware through which cognition emerges. They are programmed through interaction with the environment. Put another way, the environment provides the software of cognition. Cognitive abilities develop in young children because of the interplay between neurological structures and cultural/environmental influences. While this interplay makes development for each child unique, similarities exist across children. For example, the cognitive abilities described by Piaget (1954)—classification, seriation, and conservation—develop in all young children in the same sequence; that is, children are able to arrange objects in order of size before they are able to conserve. Sensorimotor abilities, such as reaching for objects, smiling at them, or searching for them when they are hidden, also emerge in a uniform sequence in normally developing infants (Widerstrom, 1979, 1982a). However, the rate of acquisition varies depending on the characteristics of the child. Children with mental retardation, for example, follow the same sequence in their development of conservation, but their rate of development is slower (Gallagher & Reid, 1981). In general, then, differences in development affect the rate of acquisition, rather than the sequence, of specific cognitive abilities.

FACTORS AFFECTING COGNITIVE DEVELOPMENT

Cross-cultural studies have also revealed similarities and differences in cognitive development as having certain common elements. Like genetic predeterminants, these cultural elements account for the development of the structure and sequence of cognitive function. For example, all cultures expose children to objects, usually to count, match, or stack them. One-to-one mathematical correspondence is a cognitive concept learned by nearly all children everywhere because their cultures provide the necessary exposure to objects. Specific cultural differences are related to differences in the content of cognition rather than to its sequence and structure. Inuit children, for example, generally know more about snow than do Hawaiian children.

This argument can be carried one step further and applied to human environments in general. All environments inhabited by human beings have certain common elements that define the general course of development. At the same time, every environment has unique features that help to account for the individual variations in cognitive function. Development at any point is a function of both environmental and biological factors. Normal development depends on a set of standard biological and environmental conditions. How a person functions cognitively depends on various factors, past and present, that are based on both biology and experience.

Figure 4.1 provides a matrix for categorizing various factors that affect cognitive development. The cells on the left side of the matrix contain examples of biological factors; those on the right identify some environmental factors. These factors are then divided into those that may have affected the child's cognitive development in the past and those that may be affecting it in the present. These factors affect development both individually and through their interaction with each other. This means that a negative factor in the past may be counteracted by one or more positive factors in the present. For example, statistics tell us

	Biological	Environmental
Past	Failure to breathe at birth Genetic background Low birth weight Malnutrition during infancy	Father absent during first 3 years of life Involvement in day care Maternal attention to inappropriate behavior Confinement to a playpen Good prenatal care during mother's pregnancy
Present	Obesity Hunger Increased adrenalin Tiredness Need to defecate Absence of feeling thirsty	Positive reinforcement for attending to day care teacher A bright cheerful room Weekly visits to public library A puzzle to put together Mother and father in the same room

Figure 4.1. A matrix for classifying factors accounting for cognitive development.

that a child born into poverty is at risk for mental retardation. However, not all children born into poverty develop mental retardation. Factors such as positive parental attention, adequate nutrition, and appropriate intellectual stimulation can help to counteract the effects of a low SES background.

It should be clear that we shall never be able to isolate all of the factors that could be represented within Figure 4.1's matrix. The figure simply helps to illustrate that cognitive development depends on a variety of both biological and environmental factors.

COGNITION AND THE CENTRAL NERVOUS SYSTEM

No examination of cognitive development can proceed far without a discussion of the central nervous system (CNS). While a detailed review of the structure and function of the CNS is beyond the scope of this chapter, some basic understanding of the nervous system is necessary to understand cognition.

The nature of the human nervous system is determined by the genetic uniqueness of the human being. Without this underlying structure, human cognition would develop in a very different manner. The CNS consists of the spinal cord and the brain. In the following discussion, we look at the spinal cord as the body's main nerve pathway and describe the brain's structure and function. Before embarking on this discussion, however, it is useful to describe briefly the smallest functional unit of the central nervous system, the neuron.

The Neuron

The brain contains approximately 100 billion neurons, or nerve cells, which make possible the complex information processing carried out by the brain. The neurons are surrounded by billions of *glial cells*, which provide nutrients to the neurons and assist blood vessels in removing neural waste products (Grady, 1984). Blood vessels carry oxygen to the neurons in the brain and spinal cord.

Motor and sensory neurons comprise only about .02% of all neurons in the CNS (Johnson, 1980). The other 99.98% of neurons are required for the intricate network of information communication and storage that is the primary function of the central nervous system.

At birth, the brain contains most of the neurons that a person will have for life. The brain continues to develop through the first two years of life, however, during which time the number of neurons increases and the networks of cells grow more intricate and complex. Indeed, the brain increases in size and weight throughout a person's lifetime (Grady, 1984).

When neurons die, they are not replaced. This fact is not particularly significant, except in the case of brain injury, because of the enormous number of neurons contained in a healthy nervous system. Injured neurons have some ability to heal themselves, particularly if the injury occurs during the first two years of life (Johnson, 1980). The importance of healthy neural networks to the memory process will be discussed later in the chapter.

Neurons are very small, measuring 0.1 millimeter or less in diameter (Johnson, 1980). However, they may reach a meter (approximately 39.37 inches) in length, and their sizes and shapes are diverse. Each neuron consists of a central *cell body* (containing a nucleus), an *axon,* and many *dendrites.* The axon and dendrites work together to transmit information through the neuron, but each has a different function.

The cell body of the neuron branches into many tiny dendrites that reach in all directions toward surrounding cells. The dendrites receive information, in the form of electrochemical impulses, from these neighboring neurons through the axons of the neighboring neurons. The axon is a long branch extending from each cell body and terminating in several small *end feet,* or *terminals* (see Figure 4.2). The axon carries information from the cell body to the terminals where it is passed along to the dendrites

of neighboring neurons. In sum, axons send information, or impulses, to other neurons, and dendrites receive information.

The junction between the dendrites of one neuron and the axon of another is called the *synapse.* The synapse is critical to the efficient processing of information, since messages traveling through the brain and spinal cord must be able to flow smoothly from one neuron to the next.

Axons are coated with *myelin,* an insulating substance made of glial cells. As the nervous system develops in the first year following birth, the neural axons become encased in myelin, in a process known as *myelinization.* This is an important process in the developing nervous system because the insulation provided to the neurons by the myelin makes the transmission of information from one neuron to others in the network much faster and more efficient (see Figure 4.3).

As the CNS matures during the prenatal period and first two postnatal years, the nerve cells grow in size and develop increasingly complex interconnections by means of *dendritic branching* (see Figure 4.4). The dendrites of each neuron increase in number and make more numerous connections with neighboring neurons. As these interconnections increase, cognitive development proceeds.

When a nerve cell generates an electrical impulse, the impulse travels down the axon to the synapse. The impulse is passed across the synapse by one of several chemicals known as *neurotransmitters.* These neurotransmitters, which include serotonin, norepinephrine, dopamine, and acetylcholine, are released into the *synaptic cleft* upon stimulation by the electrical impulse. At the same time, other substances, called *neural inhibitors,* prevent impulses from backing up through the system. The complementary function of transmitters and inhibitors keeps

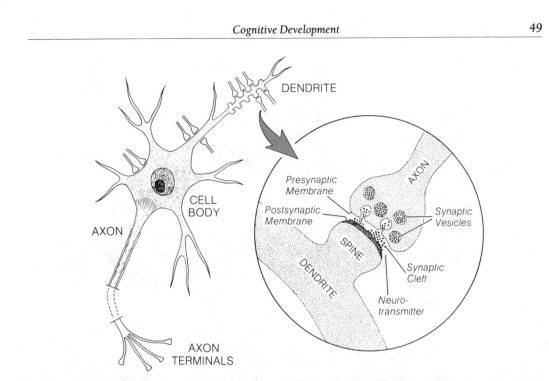

Figure 4.2. Neuron with cell body, axon, and dendrite. (From Batshaw, M.L., & Perret, Y.M. [1986]. *Children with handicaps: A medical primer* [p. 153]. Baltimore: Paul H. Brookes Publishing Co. Reprinted by permission.)

impulses moving through the CNS in a systematic and orderly manner.

The Spinal Cord

The spinal cord is a major component of the central nervous system and provides the main nerve pathway from various areas of the body to the brain. The function of the spinal cord in cognitive development is to relay nerve impulses to and from the brain. Major nerves of the body feed into the spinal cord, which in turn passes motor and sensory messages to the brain. Similarly, information from the brain passes down the spinal cord and into various regions of the body. The latter impulses account for many human behavioral responses. For example, walking depends on neural impulses traveling from the brain to the muscles of the legs and feet. A child born with spina bifida, or incomplete formation of the spinal cord, often cannot walk independently, even though the joints and muscles of the legs are perfectly normal, because neural impulses are unable to travel across the injured area of the spinal cord. Thus, in a sense, the spinal cord provides the link between an individual's cognitive programming and motor responses.

The Brain

The brain of a normal adult weighs approximately 1,400 grams, or about 3 pounds (Brierley, 1987), although human brains can vary considerably in size and weight. Scientists, however, have found no correlations between brain weight and intellectual ability, except where brain weight is well

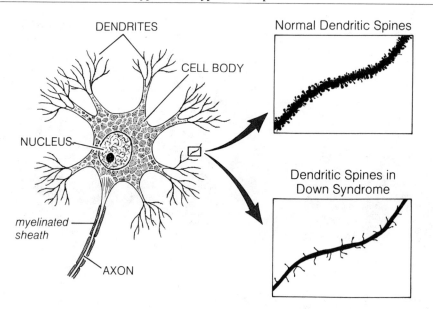

DENDRITES

CELL BODY

Normal Dendritic Spines

NUCLEUS

Dendritic Spines in
Down Syndrome

*myelinated
sheath*

AXON

Figure 4.3. The neuron and its components. The enlargements show the minute dendritic spines that increase the number of synapses, or junctures, between nerve cells. Note the diminished size and number of dendritic spines in a child with Down syndrome. (From Batshaw, M.L., & Perret, Y.M. [1986]. *Children with handicaps: A medical primer* [p. 152]. Baltimore: Paul H. Brookes Publishing Co. Reprinted by permission.)

below normal, that is, under 1,000 grams (Brierley, 1987).

The brain is soft and jellylike. It is protected from injury because it is completely immersed in a bath of cerebrospinal fluid, which circulates throughout the brain and spinal cord. The fact that the brain floats in liquid reduces its net weight to about 80 grams, making it much easier for the skeletal system to support (Carlson, 1986).

The major divisions of the brain are the forebrain, midbrain, and hindbrain. These are further subdivided into five regions. These five regions and the principal structures found in each region are presented in Table 4.1.

The Forebrain

The forebrain contains the *cerebral cortex,* the *thalamus* and the *hypothalamus.* The cerebral cortex is further divided into right and left hemispheres, each assigned specific functions. The two hemispheres are joined by the *corpus callosum,* a massive set of nerve fibers that makes communication possible between the two hemispheres. Since the brain is very complex and a full discussion of its structure and function is beyond the scope of this chapter, the following text concentrates on the forebrain, briefly describing the midbrain and hindbrain.

The Cerebral Cortex It is in the cerebral cortex, located in the forebrain, that activities such as thinking, moving, planning, reasoning, and speaking originate. When we talk about the brain and cognition, therefore, we really mean the cerebral cortex. It is here that perception and memory, two of the basic cognitive functions, reside.

The cortex grows very rapidly in infancy, especially during the first six months after

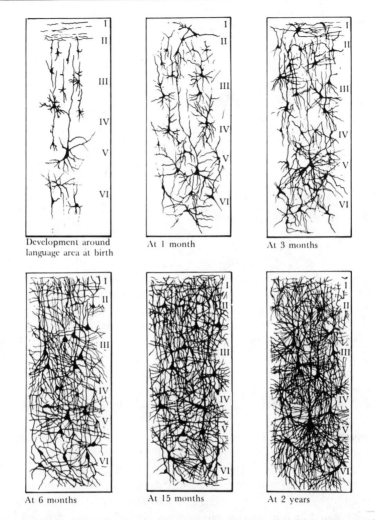

Figure 4.4. Dendritic branching. Sections from the cerebral cortex of children between the ages of birth and 2 years. (From Lindsay, P.H. & Norman, D.A. [1979]. *Human information processing* [2nd ed., p. 450]. New York: Academic Press. Reprinted by permission.)

birth. Growth is almost complete by age 2, with the brain reaching 80% of its adult size (Willis & Widerstrom, 1986).

The cerebral cortex is called the brain's "gray matter" because it is made up primarily of nerve cell bodies that are mostly grayish brown in color. Beneath the cortex run millions of axons that connect the neu-

rons with those located elsewhere in the brain. The large concentration of myelin insulating these axons gives this tissue a white appearance, hence the term "white matter" (Carlson, 1986).

THE SURFACE OF THE CEREBRAL CORTEX The surface area of the cerebral cortex is very large, averaging about 2,000 square cen-

Table 4.1. Anatomical subdivisions of the brain

Major divison	Subdivision	Principal structures
Forebrain	Telencephalon	Cerebral cortex Basal ganglia Limbic system
	Diencephalon	Thalamus Hypothalamus
Midbrain	Mesencephalon	Tectum Tegmentum
Hindbrain	Metencephalon	Cerebellum Pons
	Myelencephalon	Medulla oblongata

From Carlson, N.R. (1986). *Physiology of behavior* (3rd ed.). Boston: Allyn & Bacon. Reprinted by permission.

timeters (Brierley, 1987). The *motor strip* is located in the frontal lobe. It is here that voluntary movement of the body originates. Movement affecting each part of the body is located in a different part of the motor strip. To illustrate this fact, we can stimulate the neurons of the motor strip with a weak electrical shock, thus causing movement of a particular body part. If the current is then moved to a different part of the motor strip, a different body part will move (Carlson, 1986).

The other three lobes in each hemisphere are specialized for sensory perception (Figure 4.5). The *occipital lobe* contains the primary visual cortex, and the *temporal lobe* contains the primary auditory cortex. The sensory cortex is located in the *parietal lobe,* where tactile information and information related to pain and body temperature are received.

THE HEMISPHERES OF THE CEREBRAL CORTEX Much research has been conducted during the past century to discover the functions of the various parts of the brain. While scientists have been successful in isolating many functions, particularly those of the forebrain, midbrain, and hindbrain, a great deal about the brain and how it works remains a mystery (Squire, 1987). This is es-

pecially true of the differences between left and right hemispheres of the cerebral cortex.

The relationship between the brain's functions and its structures remains of great interest to researchers (Willis & Widerstrom, 1986). Disagreement remains over whether certain structures of the brain are responsible for certain functions. Some researchers (e.g., Springer & Deutsch, 1985) believe that the brain works in this way and others (Batuev, 1987; Hynd & Willis, 1987) argue that such a description is too simplistic to accurately convey the complexity of neurological function.

Some interesting research has illuminated the specialization of the two hemispheres. This research comes from two sources: laboratory experiments on animals (primarily rats) and clinical observations of humans who have suffered brain damage. The present discussion is based on the reporting of Cohen and Martin (1975); Gazzaniga and Blakemore (1975); Levy (1974); Levy, Trevarthen, and Sperry (1972); Lindsay and Norman (1979); and Sperry (1974). Results indicate that the brain consists of two fully equipped central processing systems joined by a very efficient communication system (the corpus callosum). While each hemisphere receives only part of the sensory in-

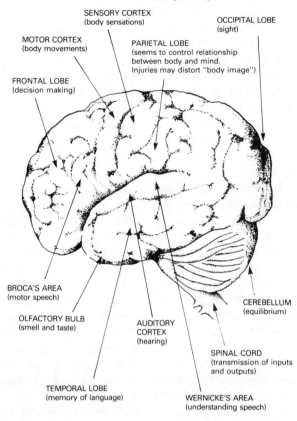

LEFT HEMISPHERE (outside)

SENSORY CORTEX
(body sensations)

OCCIPITAL LOBE
(sight)

MOTOR CORTEX
(body movements)

PARIETAL LOBE
(seems to control relationship
between body and mind.
Injuries may distort "body image")

FRONTAL LOBE
(decision making)

BROCA'S AREA
(motor speech)

CEREBELLUM
(equilibrium)

OLFACTORY BULB
(smell and taste)

AUDITORY
CORTEX
(hearing)

SPINAL CORD
(transmission of inputs
and outputs)

TEMPORAL LOBE
(memory of language)

WERNICKE'S AREA
(understanding speech)

Figure 4.5. The outside of the left hemisphere of the human brain. (From Brierley, J. K. [1987]. *Give me a child until he is seven: Brain studies and early childhood education*. New York: Falmer Press. Reprinted by permission.)

formation arriving from the various sensory receptors, the communicating fibers of the corpus callosum seem to be used to transfer the missing parts of the message to each cortex so that each half of the brain has a complete representation of the environment. For example, the left side of the brain receives its input from the right hand, right ear, and right half of the visual field; the right brain receives its information from the left side of the body. Thus, the two hemispheres create duplicate memories in a learning task, even when the sensory messages are restricted to only one hemisphere. Interestingly, however, when the two hemispheres are disconnected by severing the corpus callosum, each is capable of functioning independently. Each half can acquire and store the information needed to perform a learning task, even though each hemisphere receives only part of the environmental information. Congenital brain damage affecting the corpus callosum does not produce serious impairment of perceptual or intellectual abilities. Language abilities, however, will be affected, as seen below.

The left hemisphere is believed to be responsible for language, and is more skilled at analytical processing: it appears to process input in a sequential manner. The right hemisphere, however, is more adept at simultaneous processing of information, which makes it well suited to deal with visual-spatial tasks. The right hemisphere is said to be more holistic, or synthetic, in contrast to the analytic character of the left hemisphere (Cohen & Martin, 1975). For example, serious disturbances in orientation and awareness have been noted in patients with right hemisphere damage. These patients perform poorly on tasks involving form, distance, depth perception, and other space relationships, such as map reading, visual puzzles, and part-whole relationships (Springer & Deutsch, 1985). Musical ability also seems to be located in the right hemisphere, since patients who suffer left hemisphere damage lose their ability to speak but not to sing.

Another difference between the hemispheres is the way they are organized. Right hemisphere processes are distributed over larger regions of brain tissue than left hemisphere processes. This may be associated with the differences in function (i.e., analytic versus synthetic) noted above. For example, we would expect the left brain to be better at mathematical concepts requiring analysis and the right brain to be more efficient at processing concepts requiring a holistic approach.

Are there differences in brain asymmetry between right-handed and left-handed people? According to Springer and Deutsch (1985), 95% of right-handers and 70% of left-handers have left hemisphere control of speech and language. Of the remaining left-handers, half have right hemisphere control and half have bilateral control of speech and language. It is not known why this is so, or why most people are right-handed.

The possible link between handedness and the body's immune system is an interesting new development in the study of laterality. Springer and Deutsch (1985) reported that studies involving nearly 3,000 individuals identified as either strongly right-handed or strongly left-handed, significantly higher rates of allergies, migraines, thyroid disorders, learning disorders, and stuttering occurred among the left-handed subjects. Although these findings are not easily verifiable with very young children since laterality is not usually established until about age 7, they are of interest to early interventionists, who may wish to be alert to such problems as children enter primary school and begin to demonstrate their handedness.

The preceding discussion illustrates that the brain is an amazingly complex and flexible organ. The two halves share many functions and either half can take over should an emergency arise. The flexibility is greater in a young child than in an adult, as might be expected. After age 12, the brain loses much of this flexibility (Lindsay & Norman, 1979). The earlier in a child's life brain injury occurs, the better the chance for the intact hemisphere to take over the functions of the injured one. The more language has been developed, the more difficult is this process (Gazzaniga & LeDoux, 1978).

The Thalamus and Hypothalamus The *thalamus* and *hypothalamus* are located beneath the cerebral cortex, deep within the brain. The thalamus is responsible for sending to the cerebral cortex most of the sensory information received by the *peripheral nervous system* (i.e., the system of nerves located throughout the body and outside the brain and spinal cord). The thalamus also maintains the body in a conscious state.

The hypothalamus lies at the base of the brain and controls the *autonomic nervous system*. This nervous system overlaps both the central and peripheral nervous systems, since it shares some structures and functions with each. It is responsible for such unconscious functions as physiological regulation (e.g., hunger, waste elimination), the endocrine system, the pituitary gland (which governs body growth), and motivation (Willis & Widerstrom, 1986). The hypothalamus is also the source of the four behaviors known as the basics of survival, namely, fighting, feeding, fleeing, and mating (see Figure 4.6).

The Midbrain and Hindbrain The midbrain and hindbrain are located in the lower, or *caudal*, region of the brain, and are important in carrying out such activities as regulation of certain bodily functions (e.g., sleeping, arousal, maintenance of muscle tone, respiration), visual and auditory processing, and kinesthetic abilities.

The midbrain is responsible for conveying visual and auditory information to the thalamus and cerebral cortex. In the hindbrain, the most caudal of the brain's regions, are located the *cerebellum, pons,* and *medulla.* The cerebellum is responsible for coordinated gross and fine motor activities. The medulla regulates the cardiovascular system (heart rate, blood pressure) and respiration. The pons acts as a bridge between the cere-

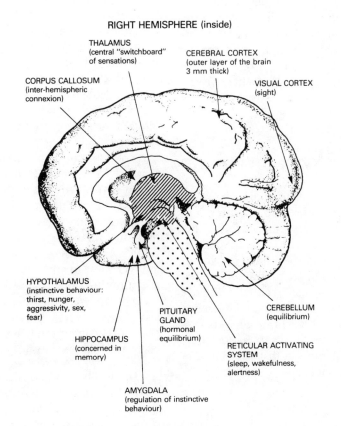

Figure 4.6. The inside of the right hemisphere of the human brain. (From Brierley, J. K. [1987]. *Give me a child until he is seven: Brain studies and early childhood education.* New York: Falmer Press. Reprinted by permission.) (Dotted area = bulb or lower brain stem. Hatched area = "old" brain or upper brain stem.)

brum and cerebellum, conveying information in both directions (Willis & Widerstrom, 1986). While these are critical functions for the well-being of the organism, they are only indirectly related to cognitive development.

Summary

The central nervous system plays a vital role in cognitive function. As mentioned earlier, using a computer as an analog, the structure of the nervous system can be described as providing the hardware for cognitive processing. Like a computer, the nervous system provides the general limits of the cognitive program and accepts its programming only in certain forms. Thus, the central nervous system provides the framework for the development of cognition. We return to this analogy of the computer again when we discuss the information-processing model of cognition.

BASIC COGNITIVE PROCESSES

We now turn to an examination of some basic cognitive processes, namely, attention, perception, and memory. Not only are these processes the most basic forms of cognitive activity, from which all others grow, but problems in cognition are most often related to deficits in these areas. Essentially, the development of cognitive structures depends on how efficiently the central nervous system functions (Benoit, 1959). Inefficiency, of course, results from both biological and environmental factors.

Attention

Attention may be defined as the process by which one focuses awareness. What is not directly attended to will not be perceived or remembered. According to Ross (1976), learning cannot take place unless the learner focuses attention on the relevant dimensions of the learning task. This requires *selective attention*, involving scanning the stimulus field, locating the relevant stimuli, and then attending to those stimuli over a period of time.

The concept of selective attention was developed by Zeaman and House (1963, 1979) in their research with mentally retarded children. In analyzing the children's ability to perform a visual discrimination task, Zeaman and House (1963) noted that there were two distinct phases to the children's learning. In the first phase, the attention phase, the children randomly attended to various aspects of the task. In the second phase, the learning phase, they were able to focus on the key features of the task. Zeaman and House (1963) suggested that it was this ability to attend selectively to certain critical information that facilitated learning the task.

In observations of retarded and nonretarded learners, Zeaman and House (1979) concluded that both groups of children went through the attention and learning phases they described. However, the mentally retarded children appeared to spend a longer time in the attention phase and were able to attend to fewer dimensions of a stimulus simultaneously.

Patton, Payne, and Bierne-Smith (1986) have drawn several implications from the work of Zeaman and his colleagues for teaching children with mental retardation:

1. The teacher should present stimuli that vary on only a few distinct dimensions. For example, a child might be presented with blue squares and circles, but not with different size and different color shapes.

2. The teacher should direct the child's attention to the relevant stimuli. For example, the teacher might say, "Look at the shape of this piece and this piece. How are they different?"
3. The teacher should remove extraneous stimuli that may distract the child from attending to the task.
4. The child should be rewarded for attending to the task. For example, the teacher might give the child a tangible reward, such as a toy or a token, or verbally praise the child.

This basic step, the ability to focus attention on the relevant, is one we take for granted in adults. It is actually an important prerequisite for successful cognitive development in young children with handicaps.

The poor ability to attend that often characterizes the child with learning disabilities has become of interest in recent years to neuropsychologists who study learning disorders. Children with *attention deficits*—once labeled brain damaged, dyslexic, or hyperactive—exhibit a variety of behaviors, including impulsivity, distractibility, and overactivity. Many differences of opinion currently exist among psychologists, psychiatrists, and educators concerning children with these problems. While those who take a medical perspective see the problem as primarily neurological, behavioral psychologists discount this explanation, concentrating instead on the child's total pattern of behaviors.

The child with attention deficits is discussed more fully later in this chapter. Here we simply wish to emphasize the importance of attention to the learning process. Without the ability to attend to information, the higher cognitive processes of perception and memory cannot take place and learning cannot occur.

Perception

The second basic cognitive process is perception. Perception refers to the interpretation of the sensory information provided to the brain by the sense organs for vision, hearing, smelling, touching, tasting, and movement. Sensory information refers to the data received by the central nervous system. A person with sensory impairments may be visually or auditorially impaired. Total impairment results in blindness or deafness. The deficit occurs in the sensory organ itself, or in the nerve connecting it to the brain.

Perception, by contrast, takes place in the brain. It is the process by which the sensory information is interpreted. Because sensory information is interpreted differently by different individuals, each person develops his or her own unique understanding of the world.

An important aspect of the perceptual process is the relating of new sensory information to past experiences. This is accomplished by recalling relevant past experiences from memory and comparing them to new information. In this way, we develop our perceptions of the world based on both new information we observe and information we have observed previously in other situations.

Perceptual Development in Infants In the developing infant, perception is highly dependent on the emerging sensory systems. In contrast to motor development, human sensory development is so rapid that all sensory systems are capable of functioning before birth (Gottlieb, 1983).

For example, as early as 7 to 8 weeks after conception, the fetus responds to stimulation of the oral-nasal region of the face. The tactile system is, thus, the earliest sensory system to develop, followed by taste, proprioception, smell, hearing, and vision. It is not clear just how functional the auditory and visual systems are at birth since they are the last to develop (Willis & Widerstrom, 1986).

Much of the information about sensory and perceptual development following birth comes from studies of preterm and full-term infants. Recent advances in technology have made it possible to study sensory responses more reliably. For example, researchers have used habituation, cortical evoked responses, the monitoring of heart rate, and the high amplitude suck to measure various responses of the infant to sensory stimulation (Willis & Widerstrom, 1986). For a more complete discussion of these procedures, the reader is referred to Cohen (1981) or Rose (1981) on habituation; Banks and Salapatek (1983) or Parmelee and Sigman (1983) on cortical evoked responses; Porges (1983) on heart rate; and Siqueland (1981) on high amplitude suck.

Studies of preterm infants have demonstrated that infants can attend to visual stimuli by the ninth month following gestation, and can probably attend to auditory information by the sixth to eighth month (Willis & Widerstrom, 1986). They can differentiate visual patterns very early (Haith, 1980) and can demonstrate visual recognition memory by 6 months of age (Rose, 1981). They are able to orient their heads toward sound at birth, and can distinguish one sound from another during the first year (Aslin, Pisoni, & Jusczyk, 1983).

Modes of Perception   Each sensory system (vision, hearing, smell, taste, touch) is associated with a mode of perception. The most commonly studied mode of perception, especially in infants, is the visual mode (Willis and Widerstrom, 1986). Because of the extensive body of work on the visual mode, it has been used to develop most models of perception.

Different perceptual abilities develop within each perceptual mode. Perception of depth, size, shape, color, brightness, and movement develop in the visual mode; perception of pitch, loudness, and language develop in the auditory mode.

Models of Perception   The brain is extremely complex and its functioning not well understood. In attempting to understand how the brain processes and stores information so efficiently, cognitive psychologists have developed several theoretical models.

Neisser (1976) contrasted two models of perception. One grows from a traditional view of perception based on an information-processing model; the other represents a more active view of perception based on what Neisser calls anticipatory schema. The information-processing model is described as being rather static; the active model, or perceptual cycle, is said to be more dynamic in character.

The Information-Processing Model   Neisser (1976) asserts that, in the information processing model,

> the image is not looked at but processed. Certain specific mechanisms in the visual system, called detectors, are assumed to initiate neural messages in response to certain equally specific features of the image. Information about these features is then passed on to higher stages of the brain. At the higher stages it is collated and combined with previously stored information in a series of processes that eventually results in perceptual experience. (p. 16)

This process is known as *feature analysis* and is shown in Figure 4.7. Essentially, the perceptual process defined in the information processing model is a static one. No change occurs in the perceptual process; environmental stimuli are simply sensed and perceived.

Anticipatory Schema Model   Neisser (1976) proposes a dynamic model of perception based upon anticipatory schema. He asserts that:

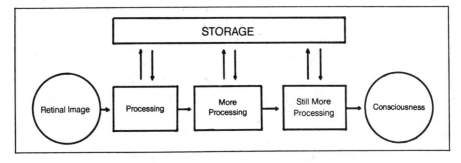

Figure 4.7. The information-processing model of perception. (From Neisser, U. [1976]. *Cognition and reality: Principles and implications of cognitive psychology.* San Francisco: W.H. Freeman. Reprinted by permission.)

at each moment the perceiver is constructing anticipations of certain kinds of information that enable him to accept it as it becomes available. Often he must actively explore the optic array to make it available, by moving his eyes or his head or his body. These explorations are directed by the anticipatory schemata, which are plans for perceptual action as well as readinesses for particular kinds of optical structure. The outcomes of the explorations—the information picked up—modifies the original schema. Thus modified, it directs further exploration and becomes ready for more information. (pp. 20–21)

This process (shown in Figure 4.8) is called a *perceptual cycle,* and is the mechanism that ensures continuity of perception over time (Neisser, 1976).

Consider the following example of a perceptual cycle. A young child sitting by himself in his playing area has called out for his mother. The perceptual cycle begins as he looks toward the door in anticipation of her appearance. At the same time, he listens for her footsteps. His anticipatory schemata direct his visual and auditory explorations. Now mother approaches the room and her appearance in the doorway confirms the child's expectation. The information he expected—his mother's person and voice within his perceptual field—requires no modification of his anticipatory schemata since her presence has confirmed them. But

suppose that not mother but father enters through another doorway of the room in response to the call. The child's perceptual cycle must now include a modification to take into account the unexpected, unanticipated visual and auditory information that his father's appearance provides. He has anticipated mother, but his perceptual abilities tell him it is father who has entered; therefore, he must modify his anticipatory schemata to expect father's voice and father's touch. In this way the cycle is continual, causing the child constantly to anticipate, explore, and assess information, and to modify anticipations.

Both of these models are based on the assignment of meaning to the world. Both provide the basis for interpretation of environmental events and so fit our earlier definitions of both cognition and perception.

Memory

Attention and perception are the most basic cognitive processes; all information gained from the environment stems from initial perceptual processing. For perception to occur, information must be stored in the nervous system. This is true whatever model of perception is adopted. Memory is the third and most complex of the basic cognitive

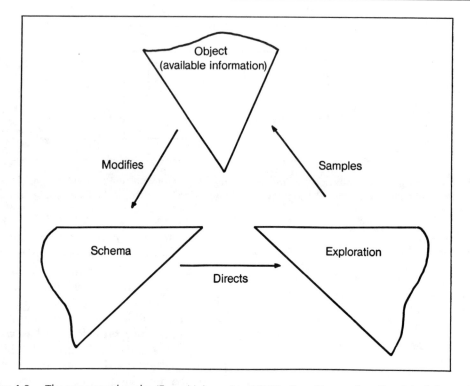

Figure 4.8. The perceptual cycle. (From Neisser, U. [1976]. *Cognition and reality: Principles and implications of cognitive psychology.* San Francisco: W.H. Freeman. Reprinted by permission.)

functions. It is the process by which information about the world is stored in the central nervous system. Attention, perception, and memory are interwoven processes, each depending on the others for effective information processing. Together they form the basis for all other cognitive processes.

To grasp this point, think about young children experiencing something new. Unless they can attend to the event, they cannot perceive or remember it. Unless they can remember a previous similar experience, they cannot accurately perceive or understand the new event because they have nothing to which to relate it. If they cannot understand what is happening in this new situation, they will not be likely to attend to it. To children with developmental delays, this learning process may be even more dif-

ficult because they are likely to have deficits in attention, perception, or memory.

Robinson and Robinson (1976) have suggested that memory can be divided into three stages. The first stage is *encoding*, which includes acquiring information from the sensory system and attaching some meaning to it. We recognize this as the process of perception. The second stage is *storage*, which includes the retention of the information within the brain. We might call this process learning. The third stage is *retrieval*, which includes drawing the information back from storage, or remembering.

Memory and the Developing Nervous System At least two processes that take place in the developing organism may account for the neurological function of memory. These two processes, nerve cell death and the development of synaptic connections through competition, allow for structural changes in the neurons at the synapses. Let us briefly examine each process.

Neural Death Research on visual development in rhesus monkeys has revealed that the monkey fetus has 2.85 million retinal axons, while the adult monkey has only 1.2 million (Squire, 1987). Most of this loss occurs between the 90th and 120th days of a 165-day gestation period. This phenomenon, known as neural, or cell, death, helps to explain the development of memory. As the monkey's visual system develops, its neurons become more specialized for certain functions. Fewer neurons are, thus, needed to make the necessary connections required for efficient vision. The unused neurons, with their axons and dendrites, die, eliminating millions of synapses from the system (Squire, 1987).

Competition Research with young frogs, cats, and monkeys has shown that structural changes occur in the visual system if one eye is damaged early in life. If the damage results in one eye receiving less visual input than the other, the active eye develops more synaptic connections in the brain. This results in a trimming of terminals from the deprived eye and the sprouting of terminals from the experienced eye.

This process demonstrates that networks of neurons can be altered at the synaptic level, resulting in changes in their structure. It is this kind of structural change that is necessary for long-term memory storage to occur (Squire, 1987).

The sight deprivation studies suggest that new experiences affect the central nervous system by directly strengthening or weakening the connections between neurons. This is useful in understanding the neurological basis for memory, for if memory involves structural changes that increase connectivity, then forgetting must depend on similar changes that decrease connectivity. In fact, scientists now believe that the use of memory is a dynamic process, with the information stored being constantly reorganized as new information is added. This reorganizing process causes structural change in the neural systems (Squire, 1987).

Remembering and Forgetting Neuropsychologists disagree over whether we ever forget something we have learned. One school of thought holds that nothing is ever lost from storage and that forgetting represents only the loss of access to memory. Such a position would be taken by Piaget and Freud, for example. Another school of thought believes that memory is not completely preserved, and that forgetting is a true loss of information from storage (Squire, 1987).

The neural death and competition processes described above appear to support the latter position. If synaptic connections are necessary for memory, and if those connections can be destroyed, it is logical that the information stored might also be destroyed.

Evidence also exists, however, that neural pathways partially atrophied from disuse will reactivate themselves when stimulated again (Squire, 1987). In addition, since one single memory represents many hundreds of synaptic changes, it is unlikely that any memory will be totally forgotten. Even in the case of injury, some of the synaptic changes would remain unharmed. It is probably true, however, that a loss of connectivity would diminish speed, efficiency, or completeness of recall.

Localization of Memory Much brain research has been devoted to determining where in the brain information is stored. Historically, there was disagreement over whether information was localized in one center or spread throughout the brain. The argument began in 1904, when Richard Se-mon, a German biologist, introduced the term *engram* to represent stored memory (Squire, 1987). Those who believed memory was localized spent much time searching for the location of the engram.

We know today that both points of view are correct, depending on the type of information stored. Representation, for example, is highly localized. Perhaps the best known example of a representation process, language, is organized in specific regions of the left hemisphere. Much evidence of this localization comes from patients who have become aphasic after suffering injury to the left side of the brain (Springer & Deutsch, 1985).

Current brain research indicates that other types of memory are widely distributed, with different parts of the brain storing different aspects of a whole piece of information. For example, not all information pertaining to motor activity is stored in the motor cortex (Squire, 1987). It appears that no separate memory centers, in which entire memories are stored, exist in the brain: there is no single engram in the brain for memory storage. Rather, different components of information are processed and stored by small, functionally specific assemblies of neurons. In this way, many areas of the brain are involved in the remembering of an entire event, each contributing in a different way to storage of the whole (Squire, 1987).

As evidence of just how highly specialized the brain is in carrying out its functions, consider that the areas of the brain devoted to information storage and retrieval are very small, containing fewer than a thousand neurons (Squire, 1987).

Short-Term Memory Psychologists and neuropsychologists distinguish between short-term and long-term memory. Some authors have also distinguished immediate from short-term memory. This latter distinc-

tion is not particularly useful, however, for the purposes of this discussion.

It was once thought that short-term memory constituted a working memory, a workspace in which to maintain information while it was being processed. The working memory was believed to be auditory-verbal, and allowed the learner to memorize information by means of verbal rehearsal (Squire, 1987).

It is now thought that the brain contains many working memories, or temporary storage capacities, within its information processing subsystems, one for each processing module (Klapp, Marshburn, & Lester, 1983; Monsell, 1984). These other working memories are not auditory-verbal since they do not process language. Each subsystem is believed to process its information in the modality (auditory, visual, tactile, kinesthetic, etc.) best suited to its purposes.

Short-term memory is further discussed in the Atkinson-Shiffrin model presented below.

Long-Term Memory Scientists have determined that long-term memory is localized in the medial temporal region of the brain and in certain other brain structures. If these areas are damaged, long-term memory is impaired, although short-term memory remains intact.

The formation of long-term memory depends on changes in synapse connectivity. These changes depend on several successive biological changes: metabolic change, synthesis of molecules, and the resulting structural change (Squire, 1987). Some of this synaptic connectivity occurs in the medial temporal region and some of it occurs in other parts of the brain.

While we still do not understand the links between short-term and long-term memory, studies of patients with amnesia have revealed that short-term memory is independent of the neural system damaged in amnesia. Long-term memory is affected by this damage, leading scientists to conclude that the two types of memory require different neurochemical processes. This finding does not contradict the idea that short-term memory can be converted to long-term memory if the proper conditions prevail, as, in fact, happens.

Inhibitors of protein synthesis in the brain have been found to block the formation of long-term memory (Davis & Squire, 1984). Therefore, it is assumed that the former is required for the formation of the latter. The protein must be synthesized and moved to the neural synapse in order for short-term memory to be converted to long-term memory.

A Model of Memory One of the most widely accepted models for explaining memory is that put forth by Atkinson and Shiffrin (1968), shown schematically in Figure 4.9. Because it is based on the input and output of information, it is called an information-processing model. The model begins with sensory memory, which has a large capacity but lasts only a very short period of time, typically about a quarter of a second. Through sensory memory, initial encoding occurs and the perceptual event enters the memory system. Whether a sensory memory enters the short-term memory store depends on attention. Information can be expected to remain in the short-term store for about 30 seconds. If the material is maintained beyond the normal limit, movement to the long-term store is facilitated. This facilitation is most commonly brought about through a rehearsal mechanism. *Rehearsal* is a strategy by which information in the short-term is repeated over and over, or is practiced in some organized manner. The deeper the level of analysis, the more likely information is to remain in the long-term store. Rote learning or memorizing, for example, represent fairly shallow levels of analysis. Information learned in such ways is not retained very long.

Young children do not rehearse information spontaneously and, consequently, must be provided with repeated experiences with the same environmental events in order for long-term memory (learning) to occur. Young children with developmental delays are even less likely to learn rehearsal skills independently and, of course, will do so at a later age. Most nondelayed children will acquire the use of rehearsal strategies between ages 7 and 9. While there is some evidence that older retarded persons can improve their rehearsal skills (Belmont & Butterfield, 1971; Brown, Campione, Bray, and Wilcox, 1973; Butterfield, Wambold, & Belmont, 1973), teachers of young children with developmental delays should help these children learn the prerequisite skills to effective rehearsal and should create learning environments in which rehearsal becomes an integral part of the teaching-learning process.

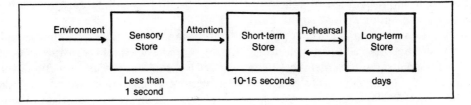

Figure 4.9. Schematic representation of the Atkinson-Shiffrin model. (Adapted from Bourne, L.E., Jr., Dominowski, R.L., & Loftus, E.F. [1979]. *Cognitive processes.* Englewood Cliffs, NJ: Prentice-Hall. Reprinted by permission.)

For example, young children working puzzles may, by trial and error, fit all the pieces together. The next day, however, they may not remember what pieces go where and may have to resort again to trial and error. With enough sessions of puzzle working (rehearsals), children remember where the pieces go and do not have to try each piece before finding the proper one. Repeated experiences with the same event thus aid learning.

Since learning is a direct outgrowth of memory, any deficiency in memory processes (i.e., encoding, storage, or retrieval) can result in overall cognitive deficits. It is difficult, however, to pinpoint where deficits occur. For example, take children who cannot point to the color red when asked to do so. Their inability to perform this task, given the necessary motivation, would suggest that they have not learned the color red. This lack of learning may be a result of any of several factors: 1) the child's inability to encode the necessary information, 2) the inability to attend to the necessary cues, 3) the inability to transfer the encoded information from short-term to long-term store, and 4) the inability to retrieve the information from the long-term store.

Research into the physiological mechanisms of memory has revealed some interesting facts about the storage and retrieval of information in long-term and short-term memory. Studies of victims of retrograde amnesia, a common form of amnesia brought about by a severe jolt to the brain, such as a fall or a blow to the head, reveal that the victims forget events prior to the accident. They tend completely to forget more recent events, but to remember events from long ago. Memory seems to be erased from the time of the accident, extending backwards for a duration that corresponds to the severity of the wound. Interestingly

enough, only memory for events appears to be affected. Other kinds of stored information, notably language comprehension and use, are not affected. These patients almost always recover their memories, and it is the old memories that return first.

This pattern confirms that different processes are responsible for storage and retrieval. It is the retrieval process, not the storage process, that is disrupted by brain trauma. Apparently, information in long-term store is resistant to destruction through brain damage. The neural process for retrieving the information is more vulnerable, however.

Other research has provided evidence that disruption of short-term memory interferes with storage of information in long-term memory. There is a direct relationship between short- and long-term store. Information apparently enters short-term store first and is then, if certain conditions take place, consolidated in long-term store. One of these necessary conditions may be the synthesis of protein in the neurons and at the synaptic junctions. These new proteins may then permanently alter the responsibilities of the neuron. Thus, short- and long-term memory may represent different phases of activity that occur at the neuron (Lindsay & Norman, 1979). There is a time period during which only temporary (short-term) memory exists. The period of time until the permanent trace (long-term) is established is called the *consolidation period*. The precise nature of the consolidation process is not known.

In summary, memory, perception, and attention are basic cognitive processes that interact to provide the basis for the development of later cognitive structures. Indeed, any cognitive structure is stored in memory and is thus dependent on the efficient function of memory to be useful. Deficits in attention, perception, or memory are likely to result in deficits in other areas of cognitive functioning.

THE DEVELOPMENT OF COGNITION

Buckminister Fuller relates the story of a father who, upon observing a picture drawn by his young son, inquired why the child had included both the moon and the sun in his picture since both are not in the sky at the same time. Fuller's query, which followed the anecdote, was, "But indeed aren't the sun and the moon in the sky at the same time?" Although meant to show both the innocence and wisdom of childhood, Fuller's story also points up an example of the qualitative difference in children's and adults' cognition. The young child in Fuller's story was unable to see anything unusual about the moon and the sun both being in the scene he had drawn. The father, however, had a different reality, or knowledge of the world.

Several authors have devised theoretical models to account for the development of cognition. One, the information-processing model, was alluded to in the discussion of perception and memory. Other models are examined below.

Hebb's Model of Cognition

A theory of neurophysiological development postulated by Hebb (1949) is particularly helpful in elucidating the relationship between neurological structures and cognitive development. Hebb's theory, first developed in the late 1940s, remains relevant today. It is useful, too, in demonstrating how environmental stimuli provide the basis for the software of cognitive development. Hebb suggests that through sensory input beginning at birth, repeated firing of adjacent neurons causes them to form units, or *cell assemblies*. By firing we refer to the transmittal of a neural impulse through the neuron, from the synapse along to dendrites and cell nucleus and then across another synapse to the next neuron (see Figure 4.3).

As more and more stimulation of the CNS continues, these cell assemblies are integrated into larger units, which Hebb refers to as *phase sequences*. Phase sequences grow out of repeated experiences employing cell assemblies, and provide the basis of perceptual integration. Finally, perceptual associations and concepts emerge as the repeated use of phase sequences leads to the formation of *phase cycles*. Phase cycles contain the cognitive structures associated with higher order cognitive functions, such as concept formation and reasoning.

It is important to point out that Hebb believed not only that early stimulation is necessary for the development of cell assemblies, phase sequences, and phase cycles, but that it is necessary to continue their stimulation to maintain their maximum function. Thus, Hebb's theory supports the need to provide young children with environments that stimulate cognitive growth. Such environments are even more vital to the development of children whose nervous systems may not be intact as a result of insults, or whose nervous systems do not operate as efficiently as possible. Hebb's theory thus provides a rationale for early intervention with young children.

This notion has been underscored by early research demonstrating that deprived environments can not only affect later perceptual processes, but may indeed alter anatomical structures in young organisms. Held and Hein (1963) demonstrated that young kittens deprived of certain visual motor experiences early in life showed impairments in the visual motor domain as adults. More startling perhaps is the research of Riesen (1965), whose studies revealed actual atrophy of visual structures in monkeys reared in environments devoid of meaningful visual stimuli and reduced levels of light. Although ethical concerns prevent researchers from conducting such experiments with human infants, there is evidence to suggest that environments that deprive infants and young children of sensory and affective experiences lead to performance deficits on tests designed to assess cognitive function (Dennis & Najarian, 1957; Kearsley, 1979; Skeels & Dye, 1939). The same studies show that remediation is possible if environments become more enriching, while continued environmental deprivation can be related to ongoing deficits in cognitive function. It should be noted, too, that it is not only the quantity of stimulation that is important for cognitive growth to take place, but also the quality of stimulation. It is certainly true that some environments—for example, noisy, disorganized, or cluttered settings— might provide too much of the wrong kind of stimulation for optimal cognitive development.

Piaget's Model of Cognition

Piaget devoted years of study to the changes in cognitive processes in young children. His research methodology consisted of extremely detailed observation of the behavior of a single child. Piaget was not content simply to observe the child's behavior as objectively as possible. Rather, his practice was to manipulate the situation in order to test the child's reaction. For example, upon observing his infant son sucking on his mother's nipple, Piaget offered him the edge of a blanket to see whether he would suck that object as vigorously. With older children, Piaget both ob-

served their approach to a learning task and carefully questioned them to understand their thinking processes. He made at least two important contributions to cognitive psychology: 1) a theory of the construction of knowledge, which has strongly influenced educational thought in the United States; and 2) a research methodology, the *méthode clinique*, that incorporates naturalistic and laboratory techniques of child study. Since research methodology is not the focus of the present discussion we confine our review to Piaget's cognitive theory.

Piaget believed that all individuals construct their knowledge of the world through a process that involves both the external environment and internal cognitive processes. According to Piaget, children construct new knowledge by a process that involves assimilating information from the environment, combining it with previously held ideas (accommodation), and constructing a new understanding.

This much of Piaget's theory is fairly widely known and understood. However, certain of his concepts are often ignored or misinterpreted and erroneously applied to educational practice. For example, Piaget believed that a state of *disequilibration*, or *disequilibrium*, was necessary in order for learning to take place. Disequilibration occurs when the child assimilates information that contradicts previously held ideas or, as Piaget would say, the existing cognitive structures. The contradiction causes the child to question the previous conclusions and perhaps to alter them to accommodate the new idea. When the child reaches a new level of understanding about the matter, equilibration is reestablished. This process of disequilibration is the means by which new information is incorporated into existing cognitive structures, expanding them and increasing the child's ability for more complex functioning. Piaget describes this process as "the spiral of knowing" (Gallagher & Reid, 1981) because the assimilation of the new knowledge depends on the existence of previous structures of knowledge into which the new ideas are incorporated. It is modification of already existing concepts through interaction with the environment that brings a child to a higher, more advanced level of knowledge.

An example may help to clarify the equilibration process. When children are presented with a problem, they try first to solve it by assimilation, that is, by using available strategies. If the strategies work, no modification of the cognitive structures will take place. For example, if children who have sorted red, blue, and yellow shapes into piles of squares and circles are then presented with a blue square, they will probably have little difficulty in placing it in the pile with the other squares. However, if they are presented with a blue triangle, the problem is not so easily solved, for there is no pile of similar shapes. The classification system breaks down; simple assimilation will not solve the problem. The contradiction represented by trying to classify the triangle with squares and circles creates a state of disequilibrium to which children may react in several ways. They may ignore the contradiction and place the triangle in the pile of squares, or place it in a new pile by itself. These solutions represent *compensations* (activities aimed at neutralizing a contradiction), which maintain the existing strategy and lead to very little accommodation or change in structure. Piaget refers to these as *alpha behaviors* (Piaget, 1977).

Instead of ignoring the problem, children may change their strategy better to accommodate the blue triangle. They may decide to group by color rather than by shape, thus compensating for the contradiction and at the same time expanding their repertoire of grouping strategies. This solution, which involves both assimilation and accommodation and, therefore, modification of existing structures, is called *beta behavior* (Piaget, 1977).

A third solution is that the children may already have anticipated the possibility of grouping by color or size or thickness before being presented with the triangle, and so experience no contradiction. This anticipation of all possibilities is known as *gamma behavior* (Piaget, 1977).

These three kinds of equilibration are important in considering the educational needs of mentally retarded children. Very young children generally use the simpler alpha behaviors described above. Children with average cognitive functioning develop independently into beta and gamma equilibrations; mentally retarded children do not. It is important for teachers to be aware of the level of responses made by young children and to encourage beta behavior as much as possible, calling attention to alternative strategies, demonstrating alternatives, and so on. Teachers should also be aware that gamma behavior is very difficult for the retarded child. If many such behaviors are observed in a child who has been labeled mentally retarded, it would be well to review the diagnosis, which may be incorrect.

Operations   Another area of misunderstanding encountered in Piagetian thought is that of operations. Piaget defines operations as actions that children perform mentally and that are reversible (Ginsburg & Opper, 1979). By reversible we mean that for each mental action, for example, addition, children can perform its opposition action, in this case, subtraction. Piaget divided children's construction of knowledge into two categories: those that involve the performance of operations and those that do not. Piagetian stages include two preoperational (sensorimotor and preoperational) and two operational (concrete operations and formal operations). These are discussed in some detail below.

Many people apparently believe that providing children with opportunities for physical manipulation of objects is the key to applying Piagetian theory to education. The concept of operations tells us that this is not correct. When he studied children's interaction with objects, Piaget concentrated on their mental manipulations. Thinking about objects and how they work, observing transformations in them (e.g., water to ice and back to water as temperature changes), and predicting what will happen to them— these mental activities are more important to the construction of new knowledge than is actual physical manipulation.

The implication for teachers is obvious. It is important to encourage children to think about the objects and events in their environment. One way to do this is to ask open-ended questions about activities in which the children are engaged. Another is to provide opportunities for each child to experiment informally with objects. Even mentally retarded preschool children can benefit from trial and error approaches to learning, particularly if they are guided along the way. Such children do require more direction from the teacher in exploring alternatives, but to assume that such children learn only by methods involving external reinforcement is to underestimate them.

Preschool children are usually in the sensorimotor period and the preoperational period. The normally developing child takes approximately 18 months to 2 years to progress through the sensorimotor stages (beginning at birth) and about the next 5 years (to age 7) to complete the preoperational stage. (For a more complete review of Piaget's stages of cognitive development, the reader is referred to Flavell [1977]; Ginsburg and Opper [1979]; and Piaget [1952].)

A child with developmental delays progresses through the same stages, in the same order as children without handicaps, but advances at a slower rate. Both the rate of progress and the ultimate level of development attained appear to depend on the severity of the retardation (Gallagher & Reid, 1981). Mildly retarded persons are usually able to perform concrete operations; moderately retarded persons generally can perform preoperations; but severely retarded persons are unable to advance beyond the sensorimotor stage (Inhelder, 1968).

The Sensorimotor Stage Piaget believed that infants are born with a neurological system of reflexes that initially operate automatically, but soon come under the infants' control. The reflexive actions cause infants to assimilate more and more information (visual, auditory, tactile) about the world and to modify their behavior accordingly. For example, infants learn to suck whatever comes in contact with their mouths. At first, this is a purely reflexive action, but it is not long before infants learn deliberately to explore new objects in this manner, and for many months they bring new objects to their mouths for examination. As infants become familiar with more and more objects, they modify their behavior to accommodate the new information. For example, they open their mouths wide for a large object such as a rubber ball, but close their mouths around a small key on a keychain.

These actions are the beginning of sensorimotor intelligence, which infants develop by exploring objects with their hands, mouth, eyes, and ears. It will be many years before they are able to learn about the world solely through mental activity. Indeed, even as adults we continue to learn many things through physical exploration.

Piaget constantly refined his theory of cognitive development. He developed the concept of the spiral of knowing only a few years before his death. Although he did not intend it to replace his stage theory, he believed that the spiral concept better describes the process by which knowledge is constructed than do the strictly separate levels of functioning implicit in a stage theory.

Piaget suggests that sensorimotor development proceeds in six distinct domains as cognitive development moves forward. These domains are object permanence, means-ends relationships, causality, spatial relationships, imitation, and play. Each of the six stages is described below. The characteristic behaviors in each of the six domains during the six stages of sensorimotor development are summarized in Table 4.2.

Stage 1—The use of reflexes (0–1 month)   At this stage the infant's reflex behaviors are modified through activity and new patterns of behavior emerge. For example, the infant is born with a strong sucking reflex and initially uses this reflex with the nipple. During Stage 1, however, the infants learns to use this reflex in other situations, such as sucking on the edge of a blanket.

Stage 2—Primary circular reactions (1–4 months)   The infant's behavior leads by chance to an interesting or advantageous result, which is then repeated through trial and error until it becomes a habit. For example, a circular reaction develops as the infant learns to bring its hand to its mouth and suck its thumb. These primary circular reactions are always centered on the infant's own body.

Stage 3—Secondary circular reactions (5–8 months)   The infant's horizons expand as it begins to crawl and manipulate objects. The circular reactions of this stage are called "secondary" because they now involve events or objects in the external environment. The secondary circular reactions are the result of the infant's ability to reproduce interesting or advantageous events that were initially discovered by chance.

Stage 4—Coordination of secondary schemes (8–12 months)   The infant's behavior is more goal directed than previously. Rather than accidentally discovering a goal, as in Stage 3, the infant has the goal in mind from the beginning. Patterns of previously learned behavior are applied to new problems in order to achieve the goal. Stage 4 is sometimes known as the application of old means to new situations.

Stage 5—Discovery of new means through active experimentation (tertiary circular reactions) (12–18 months)   Behavior loses its emphasis on what has been previously learned, and the child who has now begun to walk begins to search for novelty. The child's interest is focused less on self and those properties of an object that aid in attaining some goal. Rather, he or she seems curious about the object as an object, and desirous of learning everything about its nature. This interest in novelty for its own sake is called a tertiary circular reaction. Instead of simply repeating the behaviors that produced the interesting event, as in Stages 3 and 4, the child begins to experiment to produce variations in the event. New means to a goal are discovered through experimentation.

Stage 6—Invention of new means through mental combinations (18–24 months)   The ability to use mental symbols and words to refer to absent objects appears. This frees the child from dependence on immediate experience and introduces the world of possibilities. Rather than needing to act out solutions to problems, the child is now beginning to be able to do problem solving through thinking. Piaget believed that this is because the child is able to represent mentally an object or action that is not perceptually represented.

Until about age 7, children cannot perform mental operations correctly. One general characteristic of cognitive activity during this period is *centration*. Children tend to

Table 4.2. Major accomplishments of the sensorimotor period

Sensorimotor stage	Object permanence	Means-end	Causality	Spatial	Imitation	Play
I. Reflexes Slight modifications of initial reflexes (e.g., sucking, grasping, arm/leg movements).	No differentiation of developments in these areas. Behavior is at the level of exercising reflexes.				No imitation of new responses. May be stimulated to respond by external events (e.g., may start crying when hears other infants crying).	No evidence of play.
II. Primary circular reactions Reflexes undergo adaptations to environmental experience; coordinations between responses beginning (e.g., looking at grasped object).	No special adaptations to the vanished object. Related developments during this period include visual pursuit of a slowly moving object by following through arc of 180° and reacting to disappearance of a slowly moving object by maintaining gaze at point of disappearance.	Differentiation between means-end and causality is not possible at this stage. The following are prerequisites for both: 1) visual examination of hand, 2) visually directed grasp, 3) repetition of movements that produce environmental effect, and refinements in reach and grasp.		Infants: 1) switch gaze from one visual stimulus to another, 2) turn to localize a noise made outside the visual field, and 3) look to other end of opaque screen when object disappears at one end.	No imitation of new responses. When others imitate infants' responses, infants may repeat or intensify own responses.	Infants will repeat primary circular reactions for the pleasure of repetition (i.e., functional assimilation).
III. Secondary circular reactions Schemata are repeated. This systematically produces a change in, and effect on, the environment.	Infants: 1) move to look after a fallen object, 2) search for a partly hidden object, 3) return gaze to starting point when a slowly moving object disappears, and 4) search for object under single screen.	Infants: 1) move to object out of reach and 2) pull a support to obtain a toy attached to the support.	Infants respond to cessation of a spectacle (that they cannot reproduce) by touching the adult or the toy.	Infants: 1) follow movement of rapidly moving object, 2) rotate trunk to receive object moved behind them, and 3) examine objects by turning them over.	No imitation of new responses but infant will "imitate" model's response if that response is familiar to them. They can "imitate" in this way only responses that they can see or hear themselves perform.	Relaxed repetition of responses can be distinguished from the serious business of attempting to adapt to new experiences. Infants enjoy activity for its own sake without need for external reinforcement.

Stage						
IV. Coordination of secondary circular reactions Schemata are used together for intentional results.	Infants find an object hidden under one of two screens by searching directly under the correct screen, up to three screens.	Infants: 1) do not pull support if object is held above them, 2) expand pulling scheme to other tools, such as horizontal and vertical strings (vertical use requires object permanence, as object is not in view).	Infants respond to cessation of a spectacle, by handing the toy to the adult, but may first try to reproduce the spectacle by direct action on the toy.	Infants: 1) bring functionally related objects together (e.g., cup and spoon), 2) begin container play by taking an object out of container then placing one in at a time, building to larger numbers.	Infants overcome the limitations of Stage 3. Can imitate simple new responses, even those they cannot see or hear themselves perform.	Infants can abandon goal-directed behavior in favor of playing with actions directed at obstacle. Engage in ritualized play (e.g., infants may act out ritual of going to sleep when they come upon their pillows).
V. Tertiary circular reactions Through trial and error procedures, children discover new means to obtain desired goals. Require combination of previous chemata.	Children: 1) find an object after a single invisible displacement, 2) follow objects through a series of visible displacements and searches in correct location, and 3) find an object hidden from view and taken through successive displacements.	Children use an unattached tool, such as a rake, to get an object	Children: 1) let a toy continue activity without intervention, and 2) attempt to activate a toy after demonstration.	Children: 1) empty container by dumping, 2) move around barriers to obtain objects, and 3) build a tower of blocks	Children imitate more precisely the behaviors of a model, including more subtle or complex responses. Experiment with different ways of imitating different models.	Children rapidly convert newly acquired responses to play rituals.
VI. Invention of new means through mental combinations Children are assumed to solve problems representationally and then apply a solution to the problem situation.	Children search along a path in a complex problem when object is left in first location and the examiner's hand moves through the entire path. Children search systematically until the object is found.	Children solve problem through "foresight" (e.g., they do not attempt to stack a solid ring on a pole.)	Children display spontaneous attempt to activate a toy.	Children recognize absence of familiar persons.	Children readily imitate complex new behaviors. They imitate actions of objects as well as people.	Children engage in symbolic play (i.e., pretense or make-believe).

Adapted from Robinson, C.C., and Robinson, J.H. (1978). Sensorimotor function and cognitive development. In M.E. Snell (Ed.), *Systematic instruction of the moderately and severely handicapped*. Columbus, OH: Charles E. Merrill, reprinted by permission; and Kodera, T.L., and Garwood, S.G. (1979). The acquisition of cognitive competence. In S.G. Garwood (Ed.), *Educating young handicapped children: A developmental approach*. Rockville, MD: Aspen Systems. Reprinted by permission of Aspen Systems Corporation.

focus on a limited amount of the information available. They tend to focus on one dimension of the problem and fail to take into account other dimensions, failing to appreciate the relations among the various dimensions. They also concentrate on the static state of a situation rather than on a dynamic transformation. In addition, preoperational children's thought lacks reversibility. By this we mean that such children are unable to perform the steps of a mental operation in reverse in order to arrive at the starting point again. These limitations on their thought processes prevent preoperational children from making accurate observations about the physical world.

Between the ages of 7 and 9, children overcome the limitations characteristic of the preoperational period. They learn to decenter and take into account all dimensions of a problem; their mental operations thus become more accurate. Nevertheless, children are still bound by immediate perceptions and are not able to take into account the range of possibilities in solving a problem. Their mental operations are performed on concrete objects, which are present and observable, rather than on abstract concepts.

As children enter adolescence they are able to perform mental operations and arrive at conclusions without manipulating concrete objects. Adolescents make reality secondary to possibility. They imagine that many things might occur, that many interpretations of the data might be feasible, and that they are able to hypothesize various alternatives.

PROBLEMS IN COGNITION

Problems in cognitive development that are evident during the first years of life are usually more severe than those that appear later in life. This is because the serious problems that

are identified in children at birth tend to be biologically determined and often are not medically treatable. For example, many types of severe mental retardation are caused by abnormalities in genes or chromosomes, by birth trauma, or by the effects of low birth weight or prematurity (see Chapter 2).

In examining the problems that can occur as children progress in cognitive development through the preschool years, we must look at mental retardation, which affects cognition at a general level, and learning disability, which affects cognition at a specific level. A young child with mental retardation may have a general deficit in cognitive function, while a young child with learning disability may have a specific deficit in attention, perception, or memory.

Mental Retardation

In discussing mental retardation in children under 6, it is important to distinguish between physiological and environmental causal factors. The etiology of severe mental retardation, usually identifiable during the perinatal period, is nearly always associated with biological factors. Milder forms of mental retardation, many of which are not identified in young children until they enter a preschool program, are generally associated with environmental deprivation. Many children labeled mildly retarded in school are not considered so at home and in the community in which they live (Mercer, 1973). Children who are identified as mentally retarded before age 3 are usually severely enough impaired that there is little question about the appropriateness of the label. In children diagnosed between 3 and 5, however, there may be differences of opinion over the diagnosis. We focus here on definitions of mental retardation and on the characteristics of mentally retarded preschool children.

Definitions All definitions of mental retardation include references to the general cognitive or intellectual functioning of children. In addition, some of them include concepts such as adaptive behavior or social competence. Adaptive behavior has to do with how well individuals can adapt to and function independently in their environment. Individuals who demonstrate behavior that is adaptive may not be as retarded as a simple IQ score indicates. Adaptive behavior in young children may involve self-care skills, such as feeding, toileting, and dressing self; ability to socialize with peers; and the ability to abstain from self-destructive, stereotypical behaviors.

Both adaptive behavior and social competence are relatively more difficult to assess in preschool children, especially those below the age of 3. Thus, the term *developmental delay* rather than mental retardation is often used to describe this population.

In 1986, with the passage of PL 99-457, there was some discussion of extending downward to age 3 the diagnostic categories contained in PL 94-142. Fortunately, professionals in the early intervention field argued against this requirement as unnecessarily stigmatizing young children and resulting in possibly inaccurate labeling. It was realized that early delays do not necessarily result in later handicaps. This reasoning prevailed, and the current guidelines for preschool children under PL 99-457 use the term developmental delay. A child who is identified as developmentally delayed has an increased risk of being labeled mentally retarded later, usually upon entrance to kindergarten or first grade. Through understanding the developmental process discussed earlier in this chapter, as well as the characteristics of persons labeled mentally retarded, professionals dealing with preschool children can be more effective in facilitating a delayed child's development and may prevent the application of the label mentally retarded at some future date.

Most early definitions of mental retardation stressed the biological or genetic causes of the condition (e.g., Benoit, 1959; Ireland, 1900; Jervis, 1952; Luria, 1963; Penrose, 1949; Tredgold, 1908). It was not until the American Association on Mental Deficiency (AAMD) (renamed the American Association on Mental Retardation in 1987) first produced an official definition (Heber, 1959), which it has revised periodically, that mental retardation was defined as related to environmental factors. In 1961, the AAMD definition was revised to define mental retardation as "subaverage general intellectual functioning which originates in the developmental period and is associated with impairment in adaptive behavior" (Heber, 1961, p. 3).

In 1973, the AAMD revised the definition for the sixth time. The new definition defines mental retardation as "significantly subaverage general intellectual functioning existing concurrently with deficits in adaptive behavior, and manifested during the developmental period" (Grossman, 1973, p. 5).

The new definition was incorporated into the Education for All Handicapped Children Act of 1975 (PL 94-142) as the legal definition of mental retardation and was reaffirmed, with minor revisions, in 1977.

The significance of the 1973 revision lies first in its elimination of the borderline category, since "significantly subaverage" means at least two standard deviations below the mean, or an IQ of 70 or below. This is a much more conservative definition than Heber's, thus reducing the number of individuals who could be identified as mentally retarded. Second, the 1973 revision clearly established the place of adaptive behavior deficits in defining mental retardation. Finally, the revision clearly limited mental retardation to symptoms that are manifested during the developmental period, or before age 18.

The eighth and most current revision of Grossman's definition was published in 1983 and defines mental retardation as "significantly subaverage intellectual functioning resulting in or associated with concurrent impairments in adaptive behavior and manifested during the developmental period" (Grossman, 1983, p. 11). In this current definition, the AAMD has emphasized the importance of clinical judgment in determining whether a person should be labeled as mentally retarded (Patton et al., 1986). Instead of relying strictly on standard deviations, the concept of *standard error of measurement* is emphasized. The standard error of measurement is an estimate of the degree to which test scores would be expected to vary strictly as a result of random error (Patton et al., 1986). If, for example, the standard error of measurement on an IQ test is 3 IQ points, the clinician should report an IQ score of 70 as falling within the range from 67 to 73. The clinician would then need to look at the child's adaptive behavior before deciding whether to label the child mentally retarded. This may involve observation, informal interview, or the use of a standardized scale (Patton et al., 1986). Thus, the emphasis is placed on the clinician's judgment rather than on test scores. This current, more flexi-

ble definition and its interpretation by the American Association on Mental Retardation represent current thinking in the field of mental retardation about the labeling process.

It is interesting to note that the authors of the 1983 definition collaborated with representatives of two other major classification systems—the *International Classification of Diseases* of the World Health Organization and the *Diagnostic and Statistical Manual of Mental Disorders* of the American Psychiatric Association—as a first step in developing a worldwide classification system (Patton et al., 1986).

Table 4.3 summarizes the provisions of the 1983 AAMD definition of mental retardation.

An important aspect of the AAMD definitions (Heber, 1959, 1961; Grossman, 1973, 1983) is that they are concerned with the operationalization of mental retardation. Almost all earlier definitions had been theoretical statements about the construct of mental retardation. While they guided conceptual advancements, those definitions were not particularly useful in the actual identification and diagnosis of mentally retarded persons. Diagnosis is concerned with determining whether or not a particular in-

Table 4.3.   Provisions of the 1983 AAMD definition of mental retardation

General definition: Significantly subaverage general intellectual functioning resulting in or associated with concurrent impairments in adaptive behavior and manifested during the developmental period.

Significantly subaverage: IQ of 70 or below on standardized measures of intelligence; could be extended upward through IQ 75 or more, depending on the reliability of the intelligence test used

Developmental period: Between conception and 18th birthday

Adaptive behavior: Significant limitations in an individual's effectiveness in meeting the standards of maturation, learning, personal independence, and/or social responsibility that are expected for his or her age level and cultural group

Levels of mental retardation: Mild retardation (50–55 to approximately 70), moderate retardation (35–40 to 50–55), severe retardation (20–25 to 35–40), and profound retardation (below 20 or 25) unspecified

From Grossman, H.J. (Ed.). (1983). *Manual on terminology and classification in mental retardation.* Washington, DC: American Association of Mental Deficiency. Reprinted by permission.

dividual fits the classification identified by a definition. Such a determination is made through operational measures, such as standard intelligence tests, adaptive behavior scales, or observation.

Psychometrists encounter problems in applying the definitions to young children. The standardized intelligence tests most widely used for determining subaverage intellectual functioning are the Stanford-Binet Intelligence Scale-Revised (Terman & Merrill, 1973) or one of the Wechsler scales: Wechsler Intelligence Scale for Children-Revised (Wechsler, 1974)(WISC-R) or Wechsler Preschool and Primary Scale of Intelligence (Wechsler, 1967)(WPPSI). None of these includes norms for children below age 2. A commonly used instrument for children from birth to 2 years is the Bayley Scales of Infant Development. However, the predictive validity of this and other infant tests is very low (Bayley, 1970; McCall, 1971; Zelazo, 1979). In a sense, then, the AAMR definition is not valid for children under 2. For this reason, many practitioners prefer to use the term "developmental delay" when working with infants and toddlers.

The AAMR definition identifies four levels of severity associated with mental retardation. Each of these levels is defined by IQ ranges determined approximately by successive subtractions of standard deviations from the mean. Table 4.4 shows the differences in IQ range for the Stanford-Binet and Wechsler scales for the four levels of

mental retardation. Although this classification scheme is probably the most widely used today, at least two other major classification systems deserve some discussion. The first is the most commonly used educational classification system; the second is a medical classification system.

Educators once used a classification system that was tied to IQ levels, but was considered more useful than the raw IQ score because it gave some idea of the educability of the child with mental retardation. This practice is discouraged today as an unnecessary label placed upon a child, and most public schools have stopped it. For the reader's information, however, and because of historical interest, the following summary is offered from Gearheart (1972):

Dull/normal: IQ 76–85
Educable mentally retarded (EMR): IQ 50–75
Trainable mentally retarded (TMR): IQ 30–49
Totally dependent: IQ <30

Other categories formerly used and now abandoned for obvious reasons of offensiveness include *custodial* (similar in meaning to *totally dependent*); *severely mentally retarded* (*SMR*), or *profoundly mentally retarded* (*PMR*); *idiot* (IQ 25); *imbecile* (IQ 25–50); and *moron* (IQ 50–75). Realizing that such negative terms were in common usage less than 50 years ago helps to demonstrate how much progress we have made in accepting persons with mental retardation as people with abilities and contributions to make to

Table 4.4. IQ ranges for AAMR levels of mental retardation according to Stanford-Binet and Wechsler scores

Level	Stanford-Binet IQ range	Wechsler IQ range
Mild	68–52	69–55
Moderate	51–36	54–40
Severe	35–20	39–25
Profound	<20	<25

society. For it is certainly true that our attitudes and beliefs are reflected in our language.

As part of the definitional process, Grossman (1973) presented a classification scheme based on the medical etiology associated with the mentally retarded person. This classification system includes 10 major biological conditions including: 1) infections and intoxications, 2) trauma or physical agents, 3) metabolism and nutrition, 4) gross brain disease, 5) unknown prenatal influence, 6) chromosomal abnormalities, 7) gestational disorders, 8) following psychiatric disorder, 9) environmental influences, and 10) other conditions. Each of these major headings is subdivided further.

In general, classification systems provide guidelines for describing people with mental retardation and reveal the complex and heterogeneous nature of mental retardation. They do not, however, prove very useful as a means for planning or implementing specific program interventions. Specific information about the behavioral functioning and environmental system of a particular child is more appropriate for program planning.

Characteristics Young children with mental retardation generally display a wide variety of characteristics. They commonly have delays in all areas of development. Language, cognitive, social, and motor skills are usually delayed to some degree. Moderately to severely retarded preschool children generally lack expressive language, except for certain single-word utterances. They do not respond to verbal requests, often ignoring the adult who attempts to interact with them. Similarly, they have poor eye contact and lack the ability to tune in or attend to a person or event. They often resist social interactions with both adults and peers and are slow to initiate interactions.

Motor delays are usually apparent in severely retarded youngsters. These may be complicated by the interference of primitive reflexes in the voluntary movement patterns (see Chapter 7). Even when reflex interference is minimal, these children exhibit problems in coordination, balance, and control of movement. Severely retarded children may be completely nonambulatory, particularly if their developmental level is early sensorimotor period.

Children with mental retardation often exhibit physiological or health-related problems that result from congenital factors. These include hearing loss, poor visual acuity, heart condition, and various syndromes related to genetic abnormalities (see Chapter 2). Many children with moderate to severe mental retardation appear to be more susceptible to infection, particularly respiratory infection. As a result of these problems, they may need hospitalization or at-home care more often than nonretarded children, and are more often absent from the early intervention program.

Children with severe retardation may be prone to self-stimulating or stereotypical behaviors, some of which may be self-injurious (e.g., biting the hand until it is raw). They generally have problems with toilet training. In temperament, moderately and severely retarded youngsters vary from the docile good natured to the more stubborn and willful. In this sense they are very much like nonretarded children.

Cognitively, these children perform at a very concrete level. They have difficulty with time concepts and do better with problems in the present than with those in the past or future. Many repetitions are necessary for new learning to be truly assimilated.

Learning Disabilities

Children who exhibit unusual amounts of overactive, impulsive, or distractible behavior have been the subject of much controversy during the past 25 years. They have been variously labeled *brain damaged, brain injured, hyperactive,* or *learning disabled.* They have been described as having *minimal brain dysfunction, dyslexia,* or an *attention deficit disorder (ADD).* In terms of intervention, these children have been administered drugs such as Ritalin (methylphenadate) to calm them down; they have been put in remedial reading programs to help them catch up; and they have been taught behavior modification to make them compliant. The various diagnoses and interventions reflect the controversy among educators and psychologists that continues to surround these children.

While the term *learning disabilities* is nearly universally accepted by school personnel to describe the school age child with problems of written language (and, indeed, is incorporated into PL 94-142, the Education for All Handicapped Children Act), it does not accurately describe the preschool child who may be at risk for learning problems. Nevertheless, there are certain behaviors that, if they appear excessively or intensely, may presage a learning disability during elementary school.

Some children who exhibit this group of behaviors have been labeled attention-deficit disordered (ADD). This label originated in the neuropsychological and psychiatric communities, and is not generally recognized by behavioral psychologists. Controversy continues over whether or not such a syndrome or disorder really exists (McNellis, 1987). Nevertheless, the characteristics associated with the disorder are identifiable in the preschool child, and are, therefore, of interest to us. It should be noted that these characteristics, described below, may be seen in normally developing preschool children, as well as those with other handicapping conditions. Their occurrence does not automatically signal the presence of either ADD or a potential learning disability.

In the following discussion, the terms attention deficit disorder and learning disability are defined as separate and distinct conditions with some overlap in meaning. Learning disability is the more general term, and, like the terms mental retardation and cerebral palsy, is descriptive, lacking a precise etiology or prognosis. Attention deficit disorder is a more narrowly defined behavior syndrome (Wodrich & Joy, 1986). It is "similar to autism in that many diagnosticians assume a neurological or biochemical basis for both, but clear evidence for such is lacking" (Wodrich & Joy, 1986, p. 17).

Illustrative of the controversy surrounding the term ADD is the fact that it is defined by some as a syndrome (i.e., many behaviors occuring together in a definable pattern), and by others as simply a behavior excess (overactivity) or deficit (insufficient attention) (Wodrich & Joy, 1986). Diagnosis for ADD overlaps that of learning disability, but a child who displays the behaviors associated with ADD may not be learning disabled. Conversely, the child classified as learning disabled may not have an attention problem. This points up the importance of using caution when applying these labels, especially to young children. Misclassification can occur if children with only one or two symptoms are labeled. Because neither term provides a clear etiology or treatment, labeling the child does not offer the professional any guidelines for intervention.

Learning Disability Unlike mental retardation, learning disability has been recognized only relatively recently. Although the term learning disabilities was not coined until it was used by Kirk in the early 1960s (Johnson & Morasky, 1980), it was perhaps Strauss and his associates in the early 1940s who were most influential in beginning to study and characterize children who had specific learning problems. Strauss and Warner (1942) identified a group of children whom they referred to as having brain damage. These children were characterized as having perceptual disorders, figure-ground confusion, perseveration (inappropriate repetition of an acceptable behavior), inability to organize abstract concepts, and hyperkinesia (hyperactivity). Strauss and Lehtinen (1947) expanded these notions and prescribed educational programs for these children. Many of the characteristics suggested by Strauss are still associated with learning disabled children, and the underlying belief remains that the truly learning disabled child has some type of minimal brain dysfunction that accounts for the manifested characteristics.

Learning disabilities became formally recognized with the passage of the Learning Disabilities Act of 1969. That law defined children with learning disabilities as children who

> exhibit a disorder in one or more of the basic psychological processes involved in understanding or using spoken or written language. These may be manifested in disorders of listening, thinking, talking, reading, writing, spelling, or arithmetic. They include conditions which have been referred to as perceptual handicaps, brain injury, minimal brain dysfunction, dyslexia, developmental aphasia, etc. They *do not* include learning problems which are due primarily to visual, hearing, or motor handicaps, to mental retardation, emotional disturbance, or to environmental disadvantage.

This definition has been the mostly widely used working definition of learning disabilities and appears in PL 94-142 in a slightly more refined form. PL 94-142 requires that children classified as learning disabled show discrepancy in academic achievement or in achievement commensurate with their chronological age. In essence, this definition classifies as learning disabled those children whose achievement level is below that which would be predicted from intelligence test scores and which is not explained by the existence of another more general disability.

A problem with the definition is the fact that environmentally disadvantaged children are automatically excluded from being labeled learning disabled. As a result, learning disabilities are restricted primarily to white middle-class, mostly suburban, children. Children from lower socioeconomic backgrounds do not qualify for this label and tend to be labeled mentally retarded, with its more negative connotations.

The definition does not provide operational criteria for classifying learning disabled children. Thus, identification of children who are learning disabled depends upon the criteria established by individual agencies, school districts, and even independent practitioners. The population of children seen as learning disabled is therefore diverse, and the children's learning difficulties may be the result of repeated failure by the educational system to provide them with meaningful instructional experiences rather than the result of perceptual and/or cognitive processing problems.

The group of children with processing deficits requires more attention from professionals concerned with provision of services to preschool children. Unfortunately, many of the characteristics of learning disabled children are found, to some extent, in all 3- to 5-year-old children. The early interventionist must be concerned with whether children possess these characteristics to an excessive degree in predicting a child's future function based upon present performance (Keogh & Becker, 1973). As was discussed in Chapter 2, intervening variables can significantly change the predictive value that identified variables have for defining future conditions.

Attention Deficit Disorder The American Psychiatric Association has defined two types of ADD: attention deficit disorder with hyperactivity and attention deficit disorder without hyperactivity. The definitions of

ADD are based on behavioral descriptions, which can be summarized as follows:

A. Inattention (at least three of the following)
   1. Often fails to finish things he or she starts
   2. Often appears not to listen
   3. Easily becomes distracted
   4. Has difficulty concentrating on schoolwork or other tasks requiring sustained attention
   5. Has difficulty sticking to a play activity
B. Impulsivity (at least three of the following)
   1. Often acts before thinking
   2. Shifts excessively from one activity to another
   3. Has difficulty organizing work (despite absence of cognitive impairment)
   4. Needs a lot of supervision
   5. Frequently calls out in class
   6. Has difficulty awaiting turn in games or group situations
C. Onset before the age of 7
D. Duration of at least 6 months
E. Not due to schizophrenia, affective disorder, or severe or profound mental retardation

Attention deficit disorder with hyperactivity adds the following behaviors:

F. Hyperactivity (at least two of the following)
   1. Runs about or climbs on things excessively
   2. Has difficulty sitting still or fidgets excessively
   3. Has difficulty staying seated
   4. Moves about excessively during sleep
   5. Is always on the go or acts as if "driven by a motor" (Weiss & Hechtman, 1986, p. 16)

Characteristics of Learning Disabled or Attention Deficit Disordered Children In reviewing the characteristics of children labeled either learning disabled or ADD, it is apparent that there is much overlap between the two categories. However, as revealed by the definitions presented above, many children display only some of the possible characteristics. ADD, with its narrower definition, does not usually include perseveration or poor spatial relations as characteristics. With these exceptions, the characteristics presented below may be seen in both learning disabled and ADD children.

Children with learning disabilities or ADD reveal evidence of problems from infancy. They are likely to be irritable as babies, with colic and sleep disturbances common. Older children may be prone to bed-wetting (Wender, 1987).

Approximately half of all children labeled learning disabled or ADD exhibit problems with gross or fine motor coordination (Wodrich & Joy, 1986). They have trouble with such tasks as cutting with scissors, coloring, buttoning, and tying shoelaces. Learning to write is difficult for them, and they often dislike writing assignments.

Poor coordination is also evident in problems with balance and eye-hand coordination. ADD children may have difficulty throwing and catching a ball, riding a tricycle, or learning to walk downstairs.

Some writers have identified social interaction problems in children with learning disability or ADD. According to Wender (1987) for example, the interpersonal behavior of these children is characterized by resistance to social demands and primarily noncompliant behavior toward adults, increased independence, and domineering behavior toward other children.

Noncompliance may be manifested in such children's forgetting what they were told to do, or in outright refusal to obey. The increased independence is exhibited by children getting themselves into potentially dangerous situations. Wender's (1987) discussion includes a description of a 2-year-old who wanders 10 blocks from home and is found smiling and excited, apparently not upset by the separation from parents. At the other extreme, children may be overly dependent, immature, and clinging.

The domineering behavior of these children is expressed in teasing, bullying, and bossiness, but not necessarily in physical aggression. They have trouble making and keeping friends, and may play with younger children. An added difficulty in maintaining social relations is these children's impulsive nature; acting before thinking can hurt strained friendships.

Children with learning disabilities or ADD usually have poor self-image and low self-esteem. This is not difficult to understand, given their lack of success in interpersonal relations, motor skills, and academic achievement. These children appear to crave attention and approval, yet do not understand how to achieve either. Their oppositional behavior with adults and peers undermines their success.

Young children are by nature highly active, but there is a level of activity apparent in some children that is far beyond normal limits. Adults—especially parents—who spend time with such children know well what that level is. *Hyperactivity* (i.e., *hyperkinesis*) can be identified even in infants, when it is manifested in irregular sleeping habits, irritability during waking hours, and a high activity level. Of course, many babies outgrow these characteristics. But many children who are identified as hyperactive during middle childhood have histories of such patterns reaching back to their infancy. Children with ADD may or may not exhibit hyperactivity as noted above, but most children with learning disability have some hyperactivity.

Two other common characteristics of children with learning disabilities or ADD are *impulsivity* and *distractibility*. Both of these are also quite commonly found in normally developing children, so again, abnormality is a matter of degree. Impulsivity refers to failure to think before one acts. Distractibility refers to difficulty in attending to proper stimuli. Distractible children easily allow their attention to wander off the task. Consistent exhibition of these behaviors over time might be an indication of learning disability or attention deficit.

Perseveration, or the carrying on of an activity after it is no longer appropriate, is a fourth warning signal that might be observed in preschool children. For example, in coloring a picture of stars, a child may decide to color one star purple. Soon the entire page is purple, for the child continues to color with the purple crayon far longer than is appropriate. In the same way, a child may repeat a series of words over and over again in a meaningless way.

Difficulties with spatial relations may also characterize learning-disabled children. This difficulty might be expressed in such children's inability to find their way even in familiar surroundings; in poor body image; or in difficulty with recognizing or reproducing different shapes.

Other characteristics include poor listening ability and difficulty in following oral directions. As stated above, all of these may be considered typical behaviors in very young children. Nevertheless, some children stand out from others on the basis of the extreme forms of these behaviors. Children who display only one or two of the preceding characteristics should not be considered at risk. Unless a pattern involving several of the characteristics is observed over a considerable period of time, there is probably no reason to suspect a potential learning disability or attention disorder.

In discussing preschool children with characteristics of learning disability or ADD, we focus on physiological problems in infancy, and on problems with motor coordination, attention, and hyperactivity as the child develops. Problems in interpersonal relations and self-esteem are also significant during this period. We emphasize that not all children with attention problems exhibit all the characteristics of learning disability. Some children may have problems with hyperactivity and impulsive behaviors, others may have problems primarily with interpersonal behaviors. Moreover, some children have difficulties from infancy on, while other children experience problems only in certain developmental stages. Some children "grow out of it," while others remain learning disabled for life.

An additional word of caution is necessary for those who work with infants, toddlers, and preschool children. Many of the characteristics described above are seen in all young children. It is only when they persist beyond appropriate age levels or are extreme in nature that they may signal a learning or attention disorder.

SUMMARY

This chapter has examined the structures that account for cognitive development during the first years of life. In addition, it has stressed some of the major qualitative changes in the cognitive abilities of infants and young children, and the way these qualitative changes are linked to observable patterns of behavior in children of different ages. The basis of cognitive development is shown to be in the ability of children to relate meaningfully to their world through attention, perception, and memory processes. These processes are discussed as forming the base for the development of all higher cognitive functions. Next, Piaget's theory of cognitive development is presented. Finally, the major characteristics of mentally retarded and learning disabled children and the way in which these characteristics may be manifest during the preschool years are discussed. We conclude that cognitive problems must be relatively severe in nature to be clearly delineated in young children and that those problems that we associate with learning disabilities or ADD may not be differentially identifiable in preschool children at all.

5

The Development
of Language

1. What are the major components of language?
2. What is the relationship between language and cognition?
3. What are the major types of language disorders in children under 6?

LANGUAGE IS AN ASPECT of human development that has been the subject of lengthy and intensive investigation. Its form and function and the process by which it is acquired have long been of interest to researchers. Perhaps in no other developmental area has research produced more differences of opinion regarding the very nature of the processes under study. This reflects that language is not only extremely complex structurally, but is closely related to other equally complex developmental areas, primarily cognition and socialization. Indeed, theorists have not even been able to agree upon just what language is.

THE STUDY OF LANGUAGE

Since the 1850s, language research has focused on identifying the origins of child language. The basic issue in this research has been the disagreement concerning the nature of these origins. Some researchers have stressed a physiological approach, while others have offered psychological viewpoints.

More recently, disagreement in the United States over the nature of language has centered mainly on the ideas of three theorists in psychology. In 1957, B.F. Skinner published *Verbal Behavior,* in which he postulated that language, like any other behavior, produces a certain pattern that causes changes in the environment. These behaviors, in turn, have consequences that affect the speakers. To Skinner, verbal behavior, like all other behavior, is observable, consisting of complex muscular activities that produce noise. He rejected the association of language with thinking or other internal processes. In 1959, Noam Chomsky, one of the world's foremost students of language, published a critique of *Verbal Behavior* that brought the behavioral model into serious question. Chomsky asserted that children must have some innate knowledge of the structures of language because they acquire them so quickly and without perfect grammatical models. The Chomskian view holds that an innate biological/neurological mechanism is responsible for language acquisition. Chomsky's supporters refer to this mechanism as a *language acquisition device,* and minimize the influence of the environment on language development.

A more recent influence on the study of language acquisition is the theory of Piaget (1954), who suggested that language and cognition are two related symbol systems that depend on an underlying *symbolic function.* The symbolic function is defined as the capacity to represent reality symbolically. It develops in children through the interaction between physiological structures and environmental influences. Indeed, any discussion of language must inevitably raise cognitive issues, for the major purpose of language is the coding and expressing of ideas or thoughts. This aspect is explored in more detail later in the chapter.

Another major area of disagreement among researchers concerns the relative importance of form, function, and use of language, that is, whether grammar (syntax), content (semantics), or communicative intent (pragmatics) holds the key to unraveling the acquisition mystery.

Syntax

Syntax refers to the grammatical forms used by a speaker to express an idea. The same idea may be expressed several ways, as in the following example:

1. (a) The child rides the bicycle.
    (b) The child is riding the bicycle.
    (c) The bicycle is ridden by the child.
    (d) It's the bicycle that the child is riding.

The form the speaker chooses to express the idea is the surface structure; the underlying

idea itself is contained in the deep structure, and remains unchanged regardless of the form of linguistic expression chosen. In the above example, sentences 1.(a) and 1.(b) are expressed in simple, straightforward syntax (i.e., subject—verb—object). The difference between them occurs only in the verb form, 1.(a) encoding it in the simple present tense and 1.(b) using the present progressive. Sentence 1.(c) adopts the passive voice and sentence 1.(d) contains the subordinate clause *that the child is riding,* which modifies the predicate noun *bicycle.* Despite these differences in surface structure, the deep structure, representing the meaning of the sentence, is the same in each example.

Conversely, sentences may be expressed in the same grammatical form (surface structure) but represent different meanings. For example:

2. (a) Mary gave John the book.
        Subject—verb—indirect object—direct object
    (b) John gave Mary the book.
        Subject—verb—indirect object—direct object

Thus, grammatical structure (syntax) focuses on the forms in which the meaning is expressed, whereas the underlying meaning relates to semantics.

The process by which children acquire syntax is an interesting one. It is remarkable that children the world over learn the grammatical rules that govern their own languages with little help from adults. It has been determined that each child constructs his or her own grammar by matching new language information with previous experiences. This leads to modifications in speech in accordance with the rules inferred by the child. For example, children learning the past tense first acquire such irregular forms as *came, did,* and *went.* A few months later they begin using the regular past tense ending *-ed,* but they use it with regular and irregular verbs alike, producing such well-known examples of baby talk as *comed, doed,* and *goed.* The new information is overzealously applied to already acquired forms that give child language its endearing quality. Acquisition proceeds as children create their own grammatical rules by recognizing the patterns inherent in the language they hear and then generalizing these patterns to other situations.

By observing errors in children's early speech, investigators have been able to deduce the process by which syntax is mastered. Anisfeld (1984) has reported that children use the plural *-s* for both count nouns, such as *toys* and *spoons,* and mass nouns, such as *milk, sand,* and *sugar.* They learn that *-s* is added to words to denote more than one, and then overgeneralize the rule, producing such sentences as, *Hafta get some sands.* Another example is the inversion of subject and auxiliary verb in a question. When children first learn to ask *wh-* questions (who, what, where, when, why), they do not invert subject and verb:

What I can do?
Where Daddy's going?

Later they are able to master this inversion, but cannot manage when negation is required in the same sentence:

Why is Daddy going?
Why Daddy isn't going?

These errors demonstrate the independence of children's grammar from rote imitation. Children acquire adult grammatical forms, but filter them through their own emerging rule systems, producing ungrammatical forms that help to reveal their level of acquisition. Thus, children construct their own systems of grammar as a means for expressing their experiences and ideas.

Brown (1973) has described the child's acquisition of syntax in some detail. He divides early language into five stages, defined by the child's *mean length of utterance* (MLU). The

MLU simply expresses the average number of meaningful elements of language a child uses in an utterance. By meaningful elements we mean words such as *dog, toy,* or *mama,* or parts of words, such as the plural marker *-s,* the past tense marker *-ed,* or the progressive marker *-ing.* These smallest meaningful units of language are called *morphemes,* and children use increasingly more of them per utterance as their speech becomes more complex.

We know that chronological age is not a very satisfactory way of grouping children for language development—or for any other developmental area for that matter. In order to compare children more accurately in their acquisition of certain language functions, Brown used MLU as a more suitable index than age. For example, two children with the same MLU will have more similar language than two 3-year-olds or two 8-year-olds.

Brown defined Stage I as beginning with the child's first use of multiword sentences and continuing until MLU reaches 2.0. Other stages are defined in Table 5.1.

Brown's stages point out an obvious fact about child language: it is simpler than adult language. Sentences are shorter and less complex. Although MLU measures only length and not complexity, by the time children reach Stage V, their sentences are not only longer but also more complex.

Children achieve this simplicity by omitting unimportant words from their sentences. For example, instead of the sentence:

Table 5.1. The five stages of morpheme use

Stage	MLU
I	1.00–2.00
II	2.00–2.50
III	2.50–3.00
IV	3.00–3.50
V	3.50–4.00

From Brown, R. (1973). *A first language: The early stages* (p. 271). Cambridge, MA: Harvard University Press. Copyright © 1973 by the President and Fellows of Harvard College. Reprinted by permission.

I am going bye-bye in the car.

A young child would be more likely to say:

I go bye-bye car.

Speech characterized by this omission of prepositions, articles, and auxiliary verbs is called *telegraphic speech*. Early syntax development at Stage I is characterized by this telegraphic form of speech. The omission of these function words is found not only in spontaneous speech, but in imitations as well. Brown, Cazden, and Bellugi (1969) provide the following examples:

Mother: I see a seal.
Child: Why you see seal?
Mother: I guess I'm not looking in the right place.
Child: Why not looking right place?

As children move from two-word to three- and four-word utterances they continue to omit the less necessary function words and retain the content words.

A second syntactic characteristic of early child language is the accurate use of word order. Even at the two-word utterance level children are able to convey their meaning accurately because they order the words in a syntactically correct fashion. For example, children may say, *Daddy cookie*, the meaning of which, with the aid of context, is *Daddy is eating a cookie*. This construction reflects correct English word order, *agent—object*, which even at this early stage children use consistently. *Cookie—Daddy* is not a sentence that Stage I children would use. In fact, it is this correct ordering of words that makes it possible for adults to interpret accurately many early sentences (although context aids immensely). The classic example widely quoted from the work of Bloom (1970a) describes two identical utterances of her young subject, Kathryn: *Mommy sock*. In the first instance, Kathryn used it when she picked up her mother's sock; grammatically the sentence may be coded *possessor—possessed*. Later the same day she said the same sentence when her mother was putting Kathryn's own sock on her; in this case, Kathryn was expressing *agent—object*. In both cases, correct ordering of *mommy* and *sock* aided in the interpretation of meaning.

Stage I is also characterized by the virtual absence of *inflections*, or word endings (Anisfeld, 1984). This makes sense when we consider that the use of inflectional endings increases the number of morphemes per utterance, thereby increasing MLU. MLU at Stage I is, as we have seen, very low. Children at Stage I talk about what they observe, experience, and feel. This means they express simple ideas in the present tense, with little need for plurals, past tense endings, and other prefixes or suffixes. As MLU approaches 2.0 (sentences made up of one to three words), children begin using inflections. The increased use of inflections continues throughout childhood and accounts for both quantitative and qualitative changes in child language.

Brown (1973) has observed that English-speaking children acquire these inflections in surprisingly consistent order. He has identified 14 common morphemes that children begin to use as they enter Stage II and begin using more complex grammatical forms. The first of these grammatical morphemes to be acquired is the present progressive -*ing* form. This is followed, in orderly sequence, by the prepositions *in* and *on*, the -*s* form to denote plural, the irregular past tense, the *'s* form to denote possession, and so on. The complete list of 14 grammatical morphemes and their rank orders of acquisition is summarized in Table 5.2.

As children move into Stage II, they begin to use the full range of sentence types that are available in English. Declaratives were the first acquired; now children begin to use questions, negatives, and imperatives. In

Table 5.2. The order of acquisition of 14 grammatical morphemes in three children

Morpheme		Average rank
1.	Present progressive	2.33
2–3.	in, on	2.50
4.	Plural	3.00
5.	Past irregular	6.00
6.	Possessive	6.33
7.	Uncontractible copula	6.50
8.	Articles	7.00
9.	Past regular	9.00
10.	Third person regular	9.66
11.	Third person irregular	10.83
12.	Uncontractible auxiliary	11.66
13.	Contractible copula	12.66
14.	Contractible auxiliary	14.00

From Brown, R. (1973). *A first language: The early stages* (p. 274). Cambridge, MA: Harvard University Press. Copyright © 1973 by the President and Fellows of Harvard College. Reprinted by permission.

order to accomplish this they must learn to make certain grammatical transformations. For example, the declarative sentence, *John is eating an apple* becomes, *Is John eating an apple?* when converted to a question; the transformation involves moving the auxiliary verb *is* to the beginning of the sentence. Similar transformations are required for negatives:

John eats the apple.
John *does not* eat the apple.

and imperatives:

Don't eat the apple, *John*.

Dale (1976) has identified three stages in the development of question asking. In the first stage, children make no transformations but simply use a declarative sentence with rising intonation at the end of the sentence. Dale reports such examples as, *Mommy eggnog?, See hole?,* and *No more milk?* At this stage *wh-* questions consist primarily of *wh—noun—verb* constructions.

Where Daddy go?
What doggy eat?

The second stage involves the increased use of articles, modifiers, and inflections, but since the use of auxiliary verbs has not been mastered, no transformation is yet possible. Typical questions are:

You can't fix it?
See my doggie?

The negatives *can't* and *don't* are interesting at this stage. The first appearance of *can* and *do* in child language is with the negative elements and directly preceding the verb. Children use *can't fix, don't like, don't eat,* and so on as if they were single words, similar to the way they use *all gone* early in Stage I.

During this second stage of question asking, Dale (1976) notes that *wh-* words appear to serve as markers, or introducers, of questions rather than as true replacements for noun phrases, as they are in adult questions. For example, in the adult question, *What are you eating?, what* stands for a noun phrase, such as *apple.* But in a child's question, such as *Where put him on a chair?,* the function served by *where* is solely that of a marker. This phenomenon also produces such examples as:

Why me bent that game?
Why not you looking right place?
Why not me can't dance?

in which *why not* acts as a question marker for a negative declaration and *why* marks an affirmative declaration.

At this stage, children are able for the first time to comprehend and respond appropriately to *wh-* questions. Dale (1976, p. 109) has given us some charming examples:

Mother: What d'you hear?
Child: Hear a duck.
Mother: What do you need?
Child: Need some chocolate.
Mother: Who do you love?
Child: Mommy, you. I love fishie, too.

The third stage in question asking finds children able to use auxiliary verbs. This means that inversions placing the auxiliary at the beginning of the sentence, such as *Do you want candy?* and *Is Daddy coming home?*, are possible. Negatives are properly attached to the auxiliary verb: *Can't Annie have cookie?* In such yes-no questions the negative is inverted; in *wh-* questions it remains in declarative form: *Why the kitty can't stand up?* The *wh-* question requires more complex organization than the yes-no question; young children evidently cannot deal with both the *wh-* word and the inversion aspect simultaneously and so omit the inversion temporarily. Nevertheless, by this stage, children have achieved Brown's Stage V in syntactic development and are well on their way to using language as adults do.

The preceding discussion points up an important aspect of syntactic development. As children become more adept at using language, their sentences grow longer and more complex. This occurs by means of an orderly, predictable process that is fairly uniform across English-speaking children (and has much in common with that observed among children learning other languages, including American Sign Language). What factors account for such a well-regulated, predictable process? This question is explored later when we discuss the relationship between language and cognition.

Semantics

The study of semantics focuses on the meaning of words in sentences. As we pointed out earlier, language meaning is located in deep structure, then transformed into surface structure by means of syntactical processes. In the study of semantics, then, we must ignore the form sentences take and concentrate on their content.

Linguists who study semantics use such descriptors as *agent, action* or *state, patient,* and *beneficiary* to explain the meaning of the sentence. For example, the sentence:

John gave his bicycle to Harry.

would be coded semantically as:

agent—action—patient—beneficiary

Traditional school grammar books teach that *John* is the subject; *gave,* the verb; *bicycle,* the direct object; and *Harry,* the object of a preposition. Semantics labels differ from these parts of speech in that they more closely describe the intended meaning of the sentence.

As children acquire language they learn to express their ideas and experiences symbolically. Some of the first experiences they have as infants consist of assuming the role of agent acting upon an object. Very early, these experiences are coded into language, resulting in many first sentences of young children that consist of the simple semantic relations *agent—action, action—object,* or *agent—object.* Bloom and Lahey (1978) have noted that children talk about what they are just about to do, what they are doing or trying to do, or what they want to do. They have recorded some first sentences of children that code these early action relations: *Gia ride; Ride bike; Get truck.* Bloom (1970a) recorded children's first words at the single-word utterance level and found that they express what the children are experiencing. Rather than labeling objects, as so many language development programs emphasize, the child is expressing the following ideas, which account for about 75% of Stage I utterances. In the list that follows, the semantic relation is followed by an example.

1. Nomination: that book
2. Notice: hi, doggie
3. Recurrence: more juice
4. Nonexistence: allgone cookie

5. Attribution: big train
6. Possession: mommy sock
7. Location (state):   sweater chair
8. Location (action):   bye-bye car
9. Agent—action: Eve read
10. Agent—object: mommy sock
11. Action—object: put book, see doggie

These relations include action, state (possession and attribution), and location (both action and state). An action relation requires an agent to express the doer:

Eve   read
(agent—action)

whereas a state relation requires a patient to express who is experiencing the state:

big   train
(state—patient)

According to Bloom and Lahey (1978), children talk more about objects moving in relation to locations (*locative action*) than they do about objects already located at places (*locative state*). They apparently learn to express locative action events before they can express locative state events. For example, Bloom and Lahey (1978, pp. 137–138) quote a 2-year-old child trying to put a barrette in her hair:

Put in my hair my barrette.

which expresses locative action. By contrast, another 2-year-old expresses locative state in requesting a book from the shelf:

There's a Humpty Dumpty up there.

These relations represent the earliest events about which children talk. The developmental sequence in which these occur in child language at Stage I has been analyzed by Bloom, Lightbown, and Hood (1975), and, for the most part, confirms the sequence from Brown that is outlined above. That is, children first use single words to encode existence, nonexistence, and recurrence; they then begin using verb relations to encode action and locative events and later to encode state events; next they begin using attribution and possession. Children then learn to specify the beneficiary of an action (e.g., *Give book to Mommy*) and to specify instruments (e.g., *with a fork*). They also begin to express intention, using the forms *gonna* and *wanna* with an action verb (e.g., *I gonna eat cookie.*).

By Stage II, sentences are longer and children are combining more than one idea into a sentence. The same semantic relations are used, however; children simply learn to combine them, sometimes using a conjunction and sometimes embedding the dependent clause.

As children progress through the preschool years, their language development consists of increasing syntactic complexity (i.e., greater use of word ending, auxiliary verbs, embedded clauses, *wh-* questions, and so on, in rule-ordered sequences) and increasing variations in content. They learn to talk about increasingly abstract subjects, such as feelings, wishes, opinions, or theories. They learn to take the perspective of another person, and this is reflected in their language content. By ages 3 and 4, children are no longer tied cognitively or linguistically to their present experiences; they have learned to express past and future events that not only concern themselves but increasingly involve other people, objects, animals, and places.

Pragmatics

When we analyze any sentence linguistically, it is necessary to think not only about the form it takes—whether active, passive, interrogative, or imperative—and what meaning it conveys, but also about the context in which the sentence is spoken. The same sentence may have very different meanings and reflect different intentions on the part of the speaker in different contexts. For example, we can imagine quite different meanings for the sentence, *John loves chocolate cake* in each of these varying contexts:

1. The speaker is someone who knows John. Intended meaning: chocolate cake is a favorite of John's.
2. The speaker is John's mother. Intended meaning: John had better love the chocolate cake I baked for him.
3. The speaker is a friend of John's who has just learned that John is allergic to chocolate cake.
4. The speaker is John's wife, commenting to their hostess. Intended meaning: John will eat the too large piece of cake he has been served.

Researchers in language development formerly did not consider context an integral part of the language process. More recently, however, some psychologists have maintained that context determines meaning and is, therefore, an integral part of language. As Bates (1976a) puts it, meaning is definable in terms of context in the same way "figure" is definable only in terms of "ground." The study of language in social context is the focus of pragmatics.

Pragmatics includes the nonverbal gestures that accompany (and precede) single-word utterances. It is thus the earliest aspect of language to emerge. There is evidence to suggest that semantics emerges developmentally from pragmatics, because pragmatics has to do with the speaker's intention, and is thus closely related to cognitive development. Indeed, much of our interpretation of infants' early linguistic efforts depends upon our accurate reading of the context in which these early verbalizations occur.

In fact, a child's first words are not context-free universal signs that stand for the same referent wherever they are used, but rather are limited to mean a particular act in a specific context. Piaget (1952, 1962) calls such early communications *signals* because they are a first step in children's use of symbols and not entirely free of context. A well-known example is his daughter Jacqueline's use of the word *panama* (grandfather) for requesting something. She did not use this word with its generally accepted meaning, but rather as a means of requesting something from someone (not necessarily from grandfather). It is not difficult to surmise how such a meaning may have become attached to *panama*, given the solicitous nature of a doting grandfather. It illustrates the way children attach meanings to their early words and helps us to understand that early language develops from context.

Bates (1975) states that children's first words derive from action sequences they have learned to perform or have observed. The word often does not extend in reference beyond the particular action children associate with it. Bates provides an example from Piaget (1962) in which his daughter said *chien* as a dog passed under the balcony on which she was standing. Thereafter, she used the word *chien* for anything she observed passing beneath her balcony. From this example, we can see that children arrive at their use of words as referents through their own context-based experiences. It is this aspect of pragmatics that appears to precede the acquisition of semantics in developmental terms.

Pragmatics focuses on the communicative function of language. This means that the speaker must consider whether his message is understood by the listener. Adult speakers unconsciously take into account many nonverbal aspects of a conversation, such as whether the listener is making eye contact, whether his body posture and facial expressions give feedback, or whether he has experienced the same event as the speaker and can therefore relate to the speaker's message.

Young children do not attend to these aspects of communication as readily. Their egocentrism (see Chapter 4) prevents them from taking into account the listener's perspective, and makes them much less efficient communicators as a result. For example, young children talking on the telephone assume that because they can see an object, so can their listener, and allude to the object accordingly:

> **Child:** See Grandma? My dolly's sick.
> **Grandma:** What's the matter with your doll?
> **Child:** Well, can't you see? Her head's broken!

Maratsos (1973) conducted a study of the egocentrism of young children's speech. Six groups of 3- to 5-year-old children were shown a set of toys with easily distinguished features (color, size, etc.). They were required to request a specific toy from an adult who could see the toys only some of the time. The children had to decide how much information to provide the adult in each case in order to receive the toy they were describing. Maratsos found that the children provided more information to the adult who could not see the toys, thus demonstrating that they realized the limitation of their listener.

Like other aspects of language development, communication skills develop sequentially. A 2-year-old is not aware of the needs of a listener; however, by age 4 children are able to alter their language according to whether their listener is an adult or a younger child. By age 6 or 7 children are able to use listeners' facial expressions to gauge reactions to their message.

It should be pointed out, however, that many adults are poor communicators. The ability to tune in to another person often requires training in group process skills. This aspect of language development needs much further research in order to clarify the acquisition process.

Phonology

Phonology has to do with the sound system of language. Like other aspects of language development, it proceeds in a regular, step by step fashion. One difference between the acquisition of semantic and syntactic information and acquisition of phonological competence is that there is an anatomical aspect to phonology. The sounds of English are made by the muscles in the lips and tongue; the throat plays a part, as do the palate, teeth, and vocal cords. Neuromuscular development is, therefore, an important aspect of phonology.

Let us look briefly at the way speech sounds are produced. A good place to start is with breathing patterns. In normal breathing, air is taken in and expelled in a smooth process without interruption. In speaking, air is inhaled in the normal fashion but is restricted in some way by teeth, tongue, nose, or throat during exhalation. These restrictions cause different sounds to be made. One of the most dramatic demonstrations of the fact that speech is produced during the exhalation of air and not during inhalation is a crying baby. Babies take in great gasps of air and produce the noise of crying when they exhale. In adult speech, consonants are produced when air flows from the lungs through the throat and nasal passages in normal exhalation and is interrupted by the tongue being placed against the teeth. This is how we produce the letter *t*. Air exhaled through the mouth without a definite restriction, but only shaped by pursing the lips produces the vowel sound *o*. This is the basic difference between consonant and vowel sounds. Vowels are produced by the air flowing freely through the mouth cavity once it passes over the vocal cords, and consonants are produced by a definite obstruction in the flow of air through the mouth. The main sources of obstruction are the teeth and tongue.

Phonologists categorize vowels and consonants according to the position of tongue, teeth, and lips during their production. Vowels are categorized according to whether they are produced in the front or the back of the mouth, and whether they are high or low. Thus, we have high front vowels, such as short *i,* and low back vowels, such as *o* as in *cod.* Those consonant sounds made by stopping the flow of air completely with the tongue are called *stops.* When the air is almost but not completely closed off by the tongue we have a *fricative,* such as *f* and *v,* or *s* and *z.* Categories have been further broken down to distinguish between stops that are produced with both lips together and stops that are produced by placing the tongue behind the teeth. The former are called *bilabial stops* and include *p* and *b;* the latter are known as *alveolars,* and include *t* and *d.* Similarly, *s* and *z* are examples of *alveolar fricatives.* Many other such categories exist, but it is beyond the scope of our discussion here to describe them. The point is simply that the production of sound by the human voice has been the subject of extensive and detailed study in both English and other languages, and one of the results of such study has been an increased understanding of the developmental process involved in a child's learning to speak.

Research on early phonological development has focused on the stages through which children pass as they acquire the ability to produce more complex sounds and more complex sound combinations. Several authors (Kaplan & Kaplan, 1971; White, 1975; Willis & Ricciuti, 1975) have identified a series of stages that describe the baby's development of sound-producing abilities, without associating this phonological devel-

opment with progress in other developmental areas. Other authors (Ingram, 1976; Piaget & Inhelder, 1969) have studied phonological development as it relates to cognitive development, and have described stages in the phonological process that correspond to and depend upon the acquisition of certain cognitive skills. Let us look first at the more strictly phonological description.

Crying and Cooing Nearly everyone agrees that the first sound babies make is crying, usually during the first month of life. Dale (1976) notes that a baby's crying usually has a rising and falling variation in pitch that is sometimes helpful to parents in identifying the baby's needs. The first stage lasts for two months. Anisfeld (1984) divides the vocalizations that occur during this period into two categories: vegetative sounds, such as burping, swallowing, and spitting up; and discomfort sounds, such as crying and fussing.

By the beginning of the second month babies are able to make other vocalizations, including cooing. Cooing consists of sounds resembling back vowels. These are the easiest to produce and thus, not surprisingly, the first to appear in a baby's repertoire. White (1975) describes sounds babies make while playing with their saliva. These sounds he calls gurgling, and notes that babies appear to enjoy listening to the sounds they make. At 3¼ to 4 months, babies increasingly experiment with sounds they make. They may, for example, repeat a sound over and over as if they are practicing. However, Anisfeld (1984) states that these sounds are merely the incidental by-products of articulatory play.

Babbling At about 6 months this experimental period is followed by a babbling period. By this time vocalizations have become increasingly speech-like and are referred to as babbling. Now consonant sounds are included in combination with vowels. Variations in intonation patterns are discernible at this third stage, and these intonation patterns become increasingly similar to adult intonation patterns. This stage is characterized by the production of a wide variety of sounds, both those that are included in English and those that are not. Another characteristic is that many sounds found in English are not heard in the normal babbling of infants. Therefore, the onset of true speech requires the child both to add and delete sounds that may or may not have been used during the babbling period. Anisfeld (1984) notes that babbled syllables resemble the first meaningful words that the child will later produce. For example, these first words, as well as many babbled syllables, generally begin with stops rather than fricatives, and end with vowels. He states that both babbling and these first words are independent of the particular language community in which the child lives. Anisfeld (1984) reports research that shows that the babbling of infants from different linguistic communities is very similar, as is the phonological makeup of their first meaningful utterances. This suggests that babbling as an aspect of phonological development is independent of the linguistic environment. This information is consistent with the nativistic view of language development, for it implies that there may be an innate mechanism by which the child selects aspects of speech and language to be learned. The process by which this occurs is not fully understood.

First Words Near the end of the first year babies begin to utter their first words. Anisfeld (1984) notes that the most striking characteristic of this stage is the transition from babbling to true speech, which entails a sharp decrease in the variety of sounds produced. Babies' first words are single-syllable words consisting of simple consonant-vowel combinations. It is interesting that,

whereas they use different intonation patterns during the babbling stage, babies do not differentiate meanings by use of intonations until fairly late in their second year.

Ingram (1976) has identified six stages of phonological acquisition that correspond with Piaget's stages of cognitive development (Table 5.3). The first two of Ingram's stages correspond to Piaget's sensorimotor period, that is, from birth to about 18 months of age. Ingram's first stage spans the first year of life and consists of preverbal vocalizations (babbling) and the development of early perceptual abilities. Ingram notes that infants as young as 1 month of age have the ability to make fine perceptual distinctions both visually and auditorally. Around their first birthday, children begin to utter their first words, placing them in Ingram's second stage, the phonology of first 50 words. This stage corresponds to the single-word utterance level that is Brown's Stage I of language development and ends when the child's vocabulary reaches about 50 words. This 6-month period corresponds to the last part of the sensorimotor period identified by Piaget, just before the child acquires the ability to represent ideas symbolically. Ingram's research indicates that children do not have the ability to use multiword sentences and engage in syntax until they have achieved Stage VI of the sensorimotor period, when this ability to think representationally emerges. For this reason, neither Ingram nor Piaget would consider these first 50 words as representing true linguistic development. That is, children use these words not as context-free, socially accepted signs, but rather as personal symbols very much tied to and dependent upon their direct experiences.

It is not until Stage III, the phonology of simple morphemes, which begins around 18 months and continues until age 4, that the child's system of speech sounds is based on

Table 5.3.   A comparison of Piaget's stages of cognitive development with six major stages of phonological development

Piaget's stages	Phonological stages
Sensorimotor period (birth–18 mos.) Children develop sense and motor ability; actively explore their environments until the achievement of the notion of object permanence.	I. Preverbal vocalization and perception (birth–1 yr.) II. Phonology of first 50 words (12–18 mos.)
Period of concrete operations (18 mos.–12 yrs.) Preconcept subperiod (18 mos.–4 yrs.) Onset of symbolic representation Children can use a system of social signs to refer to the past and future, although they live primarily in the present.	III. Phonology of simple morphemes (18 mos.–4 yrs.) Vocabulary increases rapidly as children develop a system of speech sounds. Children use a variety of phonological processes to simplify speech. Most words consist of simple morphemes.
Intuitional subperiod (4–7 yrs.) Children's play begins to mirror reality rather than changing reality to fit their own structures. Children begin to solve tasks such as the conservation of liquids by use of perception.	IV. Completion of phonetic inventory (4–7 yrs.) Most speech sounds are acquired by the end of this period. Simple words are by and large pronounced correctly. First appearance of more complex words, which are pronounced poorly.
Subperiod of concrete operations (7–12 yrs.) Ability to solve tasks of conservation is developed as children can now perform reversible operations. Children no longer need to rely on perception.	V. Morphophonemic development (7–12 yrs.) More complex derivational morphology of language is acquired. Rules such as vowel shift become productive. VI. Acquisition of spelling Ability to spell complex words is developed. Linguistic intuitions are developed.
Period of formal operations (12–16 yrs.) Ability to reflect abstractly. Children can now solve problems through reflection.	

true representational behavior. Ingram notes that this stage is initially marked by two abrupt linguistic changes: a rapid increase in vocabulary and the first use of two-word utterances. At this stage most words consist of consonant-vowel or consonant-vowel-consonant syllables. These accomplishments correspond to parallel progress in cognitive development, from sensorimotor to preoperational abilities. A major advancement in cognitive development beginning about age 2 is the ability to understand past and future. Children then begin to represent these concepts in their language, and we see morphemes to mark past and future tense begin to appear in their speech. During the next 2 years, phonological development concentrates on, first, mastery of vowel sounds and, second, various processes of consonant acquisition. The first words used during this period have the consonant in the initial position, but children soon learn to use consonants in the medial and final positions as well. Also at this stage consonant clusters emerge, nearly always in the initial position. Early consonant clusters include *st,* as in *story* or *stop; pl,* as in *play;* and *cl,* as in *clap.* Initial clusters are used first, followed by clusters at the end of a word, as in *apple* or *noodle.*

Ingram (1976) has identified some interesting processes young children use at this stage to simplify their phonological productions. Table 5.4 provides a summary of Ingram's data. He identifies three processes that children commonly use. Most young children appear to simplify their speech in very similar ways, possibly because some sounds are physiologically easier to produce

than others. For example, *for* is easier to say than *floor,* and so a young child is likely to omit the *l* in the consonant cluster, retreating to a consonant-vowel-consonant pattern. In a similar way *step* becomes *dep.* It is easier to utter consonant-vowel-consonant words in which both consonants are made in the same part of the mouth. For example, children will find *coat* difficult to say because the *c* is produced in the back of the mouth and the *t* is produced in the front of the mouth. A common substitution for *coat* is

Table 5.4. Common phonological processes found in the speech of young children

Syllabic structure processes

1. Deletion of final consonant (e.g., out [æw], bike [bay])
2. Reduction of clusters (reduction of a consonant cluster to a single consonant, e.g., floor [fər], step [dəp]
3. Deletion of unstressed syllables (e.g., banana [næna]
4. Reduplication (e.g, rabbit [wæwæ], noodle [nunu])

Assimilatory processes

5. Prevocalic voicing of consonants (consonants tend to be voiced when preceding a vowel, e.g., pen [bɛn], teac [di])
6. Devoicing of final consonants (e.g., bed [bɛt], big [bɪk])
7. Nasalization of vowels (e.g., friend [frɛ̃])
8. Velar assimilation (apical consonants tend to assimilate to a following velar consonant, e.g., duck [gək̞], tongue [gəŋ])
9. Labial assimilation (e.g., top [bap])
10. Progressive vowel assimilation (an unstressed vowel will assimilate to a preceding stressed vowel, e.g., apple [ʔaba])

Substitution processes

11. Stopping (fricatives and occasionally other sounds are replaced with a stop consonant, e.g., seat [tit], soup [dup])
12. Fronting of velars (velar consonants tend to be replaced with alveolar ones, e.g., book [but], coat [towt]
13. Fronting of palatals (similar to above, e.g., shoe [su], juice [dzus])
14. Denasalization (replacement of a nasal consonant with an oral one, e.g., no [dow], home [hub])
15. Gliding (substitution of a glide [w] or [y] for a liquid sound, i.e., [l], [r]; e.g., rock [wak], lap [yæp])
16. Vocalization (replacement of a syllabic consonant with a vowel, e.g., apple [æpo], flower [fawo])
17. Vowel neutralization (reduction of vowels to a central [a] or [ə], e.g., bath [bat], book [ba])

something like *tote*. A similar example is an assimilatory process; the word *top* is pronounced *bop*, with a labial initial consonant to match the labial final consonant. Other interesting examples may be gleaned from Table 5.4.

It is apparent from Ingram's work and that of other researchers that the period from 18 months to 4 years, which parallels Piaget's preoperational period, is an important one in children's acquisition of the sounds of their language. Although they emerge from this stage with an incomplete phonetic inventory, they make important progress in their ability to use the more difficult sounds of their language. Meanwhile, their neuromuscular growth is continuing and they become more efficient in their physiological ability to produce these sounds. Ingram's fourth stage also coincides with Piaget's preoperational or intuitive stage, and is the last of the six stages he outlines to describe the development of the preschool child. This stage marks the completion of children's phonetic inventory, and characterizes the years from 4 to 7. An important accomplishment of this stage is the mastery of the fricatives *s, z,* and *sh,* and *f* and *v,* and the affricates *ch* and *j*.

By age 7 children can pronounce most words in their vocabulary correctly. However, long words continue to be mispronounced. Children seem to be able to pronounce the initial portion of the word correctly, but have difficulty with endings. It is during this stage that children begin to use the correct morphemes *-s, -z,* and *-az* for the plural, for the possessive, and to mark the present tense.

A phonological ability that develops quite late is the use of stress to differentiate words. For example, compound words such as *redhead* and *highchair* are stressed on the initial word, and *red head* and *high chair* have their accent on the final word. Ingram asserts that in order to differentiate words like this, children need to be able to perform a reversible mental operation. For this reason, Ingram believes that this particular phonological ability is not developed until children are well into Piaget's cognitive stage of concrete operations.

Several issues remain unresolved in the study of child phonology. One of the most interesting and most significant has to do with children's use of contrast. Do children consciously use a different sound in a word in their primitive vocabulary in order to differentiate it from another similar word? Some linguists (e.g., Jakobson, 1968) believe that children use contrast to clarify their meaning from the earliest stages as in the following examples from Ingram (1976, p. 20):

(a)	plane	me
	plate	pe
(b)	Mark	mək
	milk	nək

In each of the examples the child has differentiated the initial consonant with a contrasting sound. Jakobson and others who believe in an innate theory of language development would argue that these examples show that children develop their own phonological system independent of adult language. Others would argue that children's use of contrast is taken from and depends upon the adult system. This issue is currently under study by investigators of child phonology. It shows how much remains to be learned about the acquisition process in language development.

The evidence presented above shows that phonological acquisition is similar to the acquisition process involved in semantics and syntax in that children go through an orderly, predictable sequence of development that is common to nearly all language-learning children.

Learning Languages Other Than English   A recent model proposed by Pye, Ingram, and List (1987) claims that children learn the phonology of a given language fairly uniformly, but that each language is learned somewhat differently phonologically by its native speakers. In other words, children acquiring different languages develop different phonological systems. Research data indicate that children very quickly develop an organization in their phonologies that is highly predictable within a given language. For example, children learning English tend to substitute *w* for *r*, whereas children learning the Mayan language Quiche use *l* as the substitute (Pye et al., 1987).

This evidence brings into question the idea that children choose the sounds that are physiologically easiest to produce when they are learning their native language. If that were the case, all children would learn and use the same sounds first, no matter what language they were learning. Thus, the work of Ingram and others calls into question the purely nativistic hypothesis developed by Jakobson (1968).

Research in child language acquisition is refining existing theories to show that language learning principles proposed for one language are not the same for all other languages. Each language seems to have its own acquisition patterns.

COGNITIVE DEVELOPMENT AND LANGUAGE DEVELOPMENT

The first studies of child language that adopted Chomsky's linguistic theory (e.g., Brown & Bellugi, 1964; Brown & Fraser, 1963; Menyuk, 1964; Miller & Erwin, 1964) emphasized syntactic structures, with little attention devoted to underlying semantic meanings. The distinction between surface structure and deep structure was not made clearly, nor was emphasis given to semantics as an important aspect of sentence structure. However, these pioneer studies did contribute enormously to our knowledge of how children learn language, create their own grammars with structural rules, and follow an invariant non-age-related order in acquiring these grammars.

In the 1970s, psychologists and psycholinguists began to emphasize the semantic base of deep structure. Language came to be viewed as based on the child's experiences with objects and people, a means of coding these experiences. Language thus depended on the child's level of cognitive development. Schlesinger (1971), for example, showed that the structural relationships in children's utterances are semantic ones (agent, action, patient) that are merely encoded by syntactic devices into surface structure.

Brown (1973) summarizes the semantic point of view in his discussion of the work of Bloom (1970b), Fillmore (1968), and Schlesinger (1971).

> Evidence and argument in the past decade have moved us . . . from the earlier nonsemantic characterizations of Stage I speech as telegraphic or as governed by pivot grammar. The direction of the movement is toward a richer interpretation assigning a limited set of semantic relations or roles to the Stage I child's intentions . . . . (p. 147)

Cognitive Bases of Language

The move from syntactic to semantic emphasis in language acquisition theory paved the way for researchers to consider language as a correlate of cognitive development. Much evidence suggests that children use language as a means of coding their experiences. This coding ability depends upon prior development of cognitive abilities that make it possible to organize or process information in verbal form.

Bowerman (1973), for example, notes that children's earliest efforts at word combinations result from their discovery of ways to express various semantic relationships. These relationships are similar across languages because they originate in the way human cognitive abilities process nonlinguistic experiences common to children everywhere. Bowerman proposes that the concept *initiator of action* may be one of the easiest to grasp, and so appears early in child language. Less easy to understand is *person affected by stimulus,* and so this appears later. Gradually the child acquires the concepts of *agent* and *subject.* These steps reflect the increasingly abstract cognitive abilities of the child.

Controversy exists concerning the nature of the relationship between cognitive development and language development. Vygotsky (1962), one of the leaders in this area, believed that preverbal intelligence and preintelligent speech join only when the child's utterances are comprehensible to an adult. He theorized that language stems from totally different roots from those of sensorimotor intelligence.

According to Chomsky and the *learnability theorists* (Wexler & Culicover, 1980), language acquisition is the result of maturation of an innate language learning capacity that is highly specific and not related to more general cognitive abilities.

Pinker (1984) proposes a *continuity assumption* that children have innate cognitive and language acquisition mechanisms similar to adults. He rejects both the notion that children develop cognitive and language abilities in an interactive concurrent process, as suggested by Piaget, and the notion that children's language ability changes qualitatively as a result of neural maturation, as suggested by Chomsky.

To Sinclair (1969, 1970, 1971, 1973), the primary psycholinguistic interpreter of Piagetian thought, language is a cognitive ability. She notes that the child's growing awareness of self as agent acting upon the environment is related to the learning of the semantic functions of agent-action and action-object.

In her studies applying Piagetian theory to child language, Sinclair has concluded that thought has its roots in action. She traces infants' progress through the sensorimotor period, noting that their activity is aimed at successful manipulations (cognitive) and personal satisfaction (affective). As babies overcome their perceptual and motor egocentrism through decentration, their goals become less immediate and they gain a knowledge of objects and events that they wish to communicate. Language is thus a means for babies to symbolize their activity and to encode their experiences.

According to Sinclair (1969), both language and representational thought depend on a more general symbolic function, which Piaget has defined as the capacity to represent reality symbolically through signifiers that are distant from what they signify. Sinclair distinguishes among *signals,* which are spatially and temporally bound; *symbols,* which have personal rather than universal meanings (e.g., a child using a cereal box as a pretend train); and *signs,* which are distinct signifiers for objects or events, are abstract, and are socially agreed upon. Adult words fall into the latter category. Children's first words, still context-bound and without universal meaning, qualify as signals or symbols. The general symbolic function emerges at the end of the sensorimotor period and can be observed, for example, in symbolic play, drawing, and language. The first acts that require mental imagery are preverbal acts of imitation. Later, verbal imitations are produced. The roots of language, therefore, are found in the sensorimotor period.

Sinclair has reported several experiments that show how the child's language is structured by logic. Since this logic is slowly constructed by the child through interactions with objects and people, it follows that language depends not on innate structures, but rather on the development of universal symbolic structures. These structures are developed during the sensorimotor period, and are also responsible for the development of sensorimotor intelligence. Thus, in Piagetian terms, language and cognition are interdependent. Both are based on an underlying symbolic structure that develops through operative knowledge.

Piaget's theory, then, is useful in defining the initial set of linguistic universals used by children. Acting upon the environment is the source of knowledge, and language is one way to represent knowledge.

Representation of objects can take place only after a child understands that a given object exists whether or not the child is acting upon it. Gradually, children come to realize that they are only one agent among many. First other persons and later objects are understood to act upon objects. This experience enables children to develop the semantic relations necessary to express these concepts in language.

Bloom (1970a) adapted Piagetian theory to her conceptual framework of language development. She believes that knowledge of the substance and process of language development can be a major source of insight into the development of thought. She theorizes that what children are able to say is related to what they know about language. The emergence of syntactic structure in children's speech therefore depends on the prior development of the ability to organize experience cognitively so that it may be coded into language.

Since the late 1970s, attempts have been made to relate language development more specifically to Piaget's six stages of sensorimotor development (see Table 4.2). Studies linking language development and cognitive development have focused on Stages V

and VI of the sensorimotor period. For example, Bloom and Lahey (1978) believe that until object permanence is achieved at the end of Stage VI, children cannot learn the names of many objects. The achievement of object permanence means that children realize that objects exist independently of their actions upon them and independently of the time and space context in which they appear. Bloom and Lahey thus imply that Stage VI is a prerequisite for language development. Other studies, by Bates (1976), Edmonds (1976), and Ingram (1976), indicate that imitation at Stage V and symbolic play and means-end differentiation at Stage VI are prerequisites for the development of language as a context-free sign system.

Support for this point of view comes from Snyder (1975), who examined cognitive development in both normal and language-delayed children and found that only the means-end scale of the Uzgiris-Hunt scales distinguished the two populations. It is interesting that children's first words reflect their own actions in the events in which they are participating, and are strongly context bound. For example, *ball, no, more,* and *all gone* are among many children's first words (Bloom & Lahey, 1978). Such words express the conditions of existence, nonexistence, recurrence, and disappearance, as noted above. Children are able to express these concepts with one-word phrases. Earliest words record children's actions. For example, Edmonds (1976) reports a child saying *going* as he walked out of the room, and *fall* as he fell down. Bloom and Lahey (1978) have noted that success in learning to talk depends on the ability to perceive and organize one's environment. This is consistent with the cognitivist view of language development discussed above.

More recently, other authors have questioned this view. Gopnik and Meltzoff (1987), for example, note that at around 18 months children will often suddenly start to use many new names, a phenomenon that has been called "the naming explosion." It is during this time that children seem to learn that every object has a name. This period seems to be linked to the development of categorization, for at about the same time, children learn that objects can be placed into categories (Gopnik & Meltzoff, 1987).

Gopnik and Meltzoff question the general dependence of language emergence and Stage VI sensorimotor development, and suggest that the relationship is more limited and more specific, as manifested in the following relationships in skill attainment:

1. Attainment of Stage VI object permanence is linked with the use of words denoting disappearance.
2. Attainment of Stage VI means-ends skills is linked with the use of words denoting success-failure.
3. Attainment of Stage VI categorization skills is linked with the naming explosion.

Children can use words productively and symbolically before they attain these Stage VI behaviors. But certain language skills, including those listed above, appear to require the attainment of Stage VI. The early one-word phrases of Stages IV and V may be explained by the child's need for social interactions, rather than by cognitive prerequisites. Gopnik and Meltzoff suggest that at around 18 months children stop using language exclusively to communicate with other people and begin to use language as a way of sorting out their own cognitive problems. This would account for the use of language before Stage VI, but would maintain the links between cognition and language described by other authors, including Piaget.

The Child's Linguistic Environment

In tracing the roots of language acquisition, it is important not to overemphasize cog-
nitive prerequisites at the expense of linguistic input. It is certainly true that the child's environment, and particularly the adults in that environment, has a great impact on the child's language-learning ability.

Early in the first year of life, mother-infant interactions prepare the baby for later language learning. The most interesting aspect of this early communication between infant and caregiver is the ritualized turn taking that characterizes it. Like a true conversation, the interactions between mother and baby consist of a series of activities in which first the mother and then the baby takes the initiative. These interactions appear to be rule-governed, sequential, and orderly. Even though the infant cannot speak, the mother interprets its nonverbal behavior (smiles, cries, coos, and gestures) as attempts to communicate, and comments upon them as if the baby were engaging in a true conversation. The following example of a mother talking to her 6-month-old infant (Widerstrom, 1982a) illustrates the conversational nature of the interchange.

> Oh, sucking your thumb in the bath tub. (Infant is lying in tub with thumb in mouth.) My goodness, you *are* comfortable. You are comfortable, aren't ya? Yeah. Yeah. (Infant reaches for washcloth.) Hey! What are ya doin' with that washcloth? We'll have to get you some more soap. We'll have to get you some more soap. Right? Ah ah ah! Talk to me. Talk to me. What are ya doin' with your thumb in your mouth all the time? Huh? Kinda hard to talk with your thumb in your mouth all the time? Don't talk with your thumb in your mouth. Oh what? Oh what? (Infant puts washcloth in mouth.) Want that finger or do you want the washcloth?

Bruner (1975) believes that this dialogue between infant and mother is crucial for the development of later language. He has identified certain rituals that mother and child carry on during play that teach the child that conversation requires reciprocal responses. Such activities as playing peek-a-boo or reading picture books together are examples. According to Bruner, the dialogue also teaches the child early semantic relations. He suggests that the child learns role shifting from agent of action to recipient of action when the mother gives the baby an object or holds out her hand in order for the baby to give her an object.

These early interactions are basically pragmatic in nature, for they rely heavily on contextual information provided by means of gestures, smiles, and physical contact, as well as words. At this early pragmatic level, communication consists of perceptual information provided to the infant. These interactions appear to pave the way for the development of semantic and later syntactic knowledge on the part of the infant.

One area of interest to researchers that has generated much controversy concerns the role imitation plays in the child's learning of language. The behavioral viewpoint has placed heavy emphasis on imitation, going so far as to maintain that children learn all of their language by imitating adults. This point of view has been refuted by evidence that parents do not provide correct and complete language samples to their young children, nor do they correct errors in grammar when they talk to their young children (Chomsky, 1965; Moerk, 1975). Rather, adults appear to monitor the content of their children's language, but ignore grammatical errors or idiosyncrasies. An example of this process comes from Bloom and Lahey (1978, p. 281):

(Mother gave Gia a bottle of milk for lunch; milk was fresh; Gia pushing bottle away)
Gia: it old
Mother: It's old?
Gia: yes
Mother: It's not old
Gia: it old
Mother: It's not old (Mother picks up Gia's bib; starts to put it on her; bib is soiled)
Gia: that old

Mother: It's not old/Well if you didn't spill all your food over it it wouldn't be old.

Nevertheless, it is obvious that imitation must play some role in child language acquisition, for the nativist position that the language acquisition device accounts for nearly all language learning does not account for all the facts. Let us look for a moment at the research on mothers' speech to young children, most of which was published in the 1970s. Some characteristics that aid children in developing language were identified. Ferguson (1977), Garnica (1977), Gleason (1973), and Sachs (1977) noted that mothers use higher pitch when talking to their infants than they do in normal speech. They use special intonation patterns (Sachs) and prolong the duration of stressed words (Garnica). Their vocabulary is less varied and more concrete than that of nonmothers and their sentences are syntactically less complex (Phillips, 1973; Ringler, 1975). Snow (1972) found many questions in mothers' speech and much redundancy, and Phillips noticed the presence of many affirmatives, all of which would encourage communication. Both Phillips and Snow found that mothers limit the semantic content of their speech to the constructions that the child has mastered, talking about the here and now rather than the past or future, and limiting their conversation to what the child is experiencing. Thus, it appears that linguistic input to children learning language is neither too complex nor confusing.

Nevertheless, Dale (1976) has noted that mothers' speech is always found to be more complex than children's. He believes that imitation aids children in extracting what they are developmentally capable of processing. Bloom (1970b) concurs with this analysis, for she found significant differences in the way children use imitation. Her research confirmed that children imitate the words and grammatical structures that they are in the process of mastering.

Nelson's (1987) theory of the rare event states that the crux of language growth lies in rarely occurring instances in which potentially challenging and useful input strings are actually seized by the child's system and put into storage and compared with previously stored similar forms. Nelson notes that only about 10% of adult utterances to children are selected by the children and used in language learning. This 10% represents adult language that expands on the child's previous utterance and is at the child's current level of language learning. Thus, the pertinent adult utterances are useful and challenging.

If Dale, Bloom, and Nelson are correct, children use imitation selectively to help them in mastering new grammatical forms, new semantic relations, and new vocabulary.

Bootstrapping and Scaffolding The idea that children construct their own knowledge base in language acquisition by using what they already know to learn more advanced forms is known as *bootstrapping* (Shatz, 1987). An early example of bootstrapping is Bruner's (1975) observation that children learn agent-action-object semantic relations through their interactions with objects during spontaneous play. Early notions of bootstrapping were used to explain the acquisition of syntax. It was thought that the more abstract forms of syntax or grammar were first learned by the child at a more basic semantic or pragmatic level.

More recently, researchers (Pinker, 1984; Shatz, 1987) have expanded the idea of bootstrapping to include children's knowledge of communication in general. That is, children use whatever knowledge of language they have to gain an understanding of new forms, content, and uses. Shatz (1987) maintains that it is not a linear process of building syntax on top of semantics on top of pragmatics, but rather a case of children

using whatever they know about language, communication, and interaction to learn more. Children elicit language from the adults around them, through the use of gestures, smiles, and vocalizations, in order to facilitate their learning. They use various strategies for maintaining discourse, storing and analyzing language information, and generally taking an active role in their own language learning (Shatz, 1987). The idea of bootstrapping is very important for understanding the child as an active learner.

Scaffolding refers to the process by which the adult models utterances or phrases that children can imitate and incorporate into their own lexicon (Snow, Perlmann, & Nathan, 1987). Children often imitate adult words that they have not fully understood. The process provides a boost to children from the adult in learning new words. Thus, scaffolded utterances are less demanding to produce than spontaneous utterances.

Problems in Language Development

To intervene successfully with children who are not developing adequate language spontaneously, it is necessary to understand the nature of language disorders. Are language-disordered children delayed in their acquisition of normal forms, or are they deviant? Do they learn best through imitation or do they need to base language on their own experiences? For what purposes do they need language skills? Answers to these questions will help us to develop a sound intervention program based on a consistent theory.

Research indicates that children with language disorders learn language the same way that normally developing children do, but at a slower pace. That is they are not deviant in their acquisition, but merely delayed (Johnston & Schery, 1976; Menyuk & Looney, 1972; Morehead & Ingram, 1973).

Evidence from normal acquisition research also tells us that while children do imitate adult language, they are very selective about what they imitate, choosing only those aspects that they are in the process of acquiring (Nelson & Van Kleek, 1987). They do not imitate forms that are either too easy (already acquired) or too difficult (beyond their competence). More importantly, their acquisition of new forms is based on their current experiences, rather than on what they hear adults talking about (Bryen, 1982). This would favor an experiential approach to intervention, with emphasis on developing the cognitive concepts and social interactions underlying the language expression.

Finally, language acquisition studies have determined that nonhandicapped children use language to express their experiences and their understanding of the world (Bates, 1976a; Bloom & Lahey, 1978). This is also true of children with language disorders (Bricker, Dennison, & Bricker, 1976; Widerstrom, 1979).

Specific Language Impairment Leonard (1987) has questioned whether specific language impairment is a useful construct for making decisions about children's intervention programs. He points out that children who exhibit delays in other developmental areas, such as musical ability or spatial relations, are not considered to be "disordered." Our culture highly values abilities in language and logical thinking, and uses them as indicators of intelligence. Yet many children who exhibit delays in language are otherwise developmentally average and demonstrate average intelligence.

Leonard concludes that children with specific language impairments that are not due to neurological dysfunction are not delayed solely in language development. They do not resemble younger normally developing children exactly. Their problems appear to be related to difficulties in using their own language environments to develop their rules of communication. Leonard cites the following areas of difficulty:

1. Extracting regularities in heard speech
2. Registering the conversational contexts in which regularities occur
3. Examining regularities for word-referent associations and evidence of grammatical and phonological rules
4. Using associations and rules to formulate utterances

While Leonard acknowledges that language-impaired children often exhibit limitations in nonlinguistic skills, such as symbolic play, imagery, or auditory processing, he points out that the identification of such deficits does not aid our understanding of the child who has problems with language, nor does it point us in the right direction for intervention. Rather, the focus of intervention should be language.

Linguistic Competence Another approach to language disorders is to look at specific populations that experience difficulties with language development, such as hearing-impaired or mentally retarded children. In their review of the literature on the communication of mentally retarded children and adults, Abbeduto and Rosenberg (1987) identified specific skills with which this population has difficulty. They note that poor performance on these skills limits the linguistic communicative competence of the child or adult. They have thus focused their approach on the development of pragmatics.

The skills identified by Abbeduto and Rosenberg as critical to communicative competence include turn taking; producing and understanding illocutionary acts; keeping the conversation going through topic maintenance, discourse ties, and conversational repairs; and fulfilling the roles of both speaker and listener as necessary. Let us examine each of these skills more closely, in order better to understand the idea of communicative competence.

Turn Taking   Most adults follow the convention of conversation that dictates that only one person speak at a time. Both listener and speaker observe conventions in giving up and taking over the role of speaker, a process that allows the conversation to proceed smoothly with equal participation by both parties.

Children lacking in communicative competence do not recognize the rules governing turn taking, and tend either to dominate conversations or, more commonly, to fail to understand how to enter a conversation and take the role of speaker. Such children either hang back and merely observe others conversing, or they fail to respond to questions directed to them. In either case, the result is a one-sided conversation, unsatisfactory to both speaker and listener.

Illocutionary Acts   An illocutionary act is the function an utterance is intended to perform in the communicative interaction (Austin, 1962; Searle, 1969). It is the speaker's job to make sure that the intention of the illocutionary act is understandable; the listener's job is to decide which of the range of possible illocutionary acts the speaker intends by an utterance. Obviously, if either party to the conversation fails, the conversation is unsuccessful. Abbeduto and Rosenberg (1987) have provided the following examples of illocutionary acts. The utterance is followed by the intended function.

I promise that I'll return: promise
Move over: request for action
This is a dog: assertion
What time is it?:   request for information

The problem with illocutionary acts is that the intended meaning is not always clear, and often the listener must infer what the speaker actually intends. In the statement, *Where is my coat?*, the speaker may be performing a simple request for information or, more likely, a request for action (*Please get me my coat.*). It is the speaker's duty to make the intended meaning clear according to pragmatic rules.

Young children who are developing language normally may have difficulty with illocutionary acts, both as speaker and listener. Sometimes utterances are too subtle for them to catch. Children with communication disorders seem especially prone to missing the connection in conversations. Such children appear unable to use the context of the communicative interaction to provide them with clues to the speaker's intended meaning. Moreover, they are unable to make their own meanings clear when they speak.

Topic Maintenance   Communicative interaction is more than a series of unrelated speaking turns. Utterances must respond to prior statements or questions. The listener must recognize when he or she must respond to an utterance. The speaker has the obligation to demand a response that furthers the conversation and to allow the listener adequate time to respond.

At the topic level, both parties are obliged to restrict their utterances to the topic under discussion. The speaker selects utterances appropriate for the proper development of the topic, and the listener keeps track, so that he or she is able to respond appropriately.

An important aspect of this process is identifying accurately what the speaker means by his or her intended referents. The listener must determine to what objects, persons, events, or places an expression refers. Often this depends on the context of the conversation, because the speaker may assume the listener knows what the speaker is talking about. Young children often take for granted that the adult knows what their statements refer to, without realizing that they have not provided sufficient information. For example:

Child: I want that one.
Adult: Which one?
Child: That one.
Adult: The red one or the blue one?
Child: That one.
Adult: I can't tell which one you are talking about.

Similarly, older children with language disorders often seem unable to put themselves in their listener's position. Children with mental retardation may lack the cognitive ability to take another's perspective well enough to be a good conversationalist.

Discourse Ties A successful conversation is linked not only by conversational obligations of speaker and listener, but also by certain grammatical devices that make the conversation smoother and more cohesive. These are referred to as discourse ties, because they help the listener tie the current utterance to the speaker's previous utterances.

Examples of discourse ties are adverbial phrases, such as *moreover, nevertheless,* or *as a matter of fact;* pronouns, such as *his, hers, it, these,* or *those;* and the definite article *the.* In the statement, *Bring me the yellow box,* the listener has enough information to know what is being requested. If the speaker were then to say, *The yellow box is on the table in the hall,* the interaction would become choppy. *It* suffices for the referent *yellow box. It's on the table in the hall* makes for a smoother, more cohesive interaction.

Children with mental retardation sometimes do not understand unspecified referents, and need to have the information stated more concretely. They have more difficulty inferring what the speaker means. This is also common in children with other communication disorders.

Conversational Repairs Even highly competent adults occasionally make mistakes in their attempts at communication, requiring repairs to be made to get their meanings across. *What did you say?* or *What do you mean by that?* represent examples of conversational repairs. A competent listener must recognize breakdowns in the communication process, request a repair, and let the speaker know what the problem is. The speaker must recognize and respond to the request as soon as possible.

Young children are usually quite adept at letting the adult know when they do not understand something. Children with communication disorders or mental retardation may be less successful than other children. Often they are unaware that anything is wrong. At other times they do not know what to do about the problem and opt to let the conversation die.

Speaker and Listener It should be apparent from the above examples that speaking and listening are inherently connected in the conversation process and are highly interdependent. It takes two to make a conversation, and each makes a different but equally necessary contribution. If either speaker or listener fails to fulfill his or her obligations, the conversation fails. This is very often the case when one of the roles is taken by a child with communication problems. Most of the pragmatic skills discussed here require cognitive as well as linguistic skills. This means that children with cognitive delays will also exhibit these problems.

Communicative interaction depends on the speaker and listener being finely tuned to each other's needs and intentions. Young children develop this sensitivity gradually. Apparently those with communicative disorders fail to develop the sensitivity to others' needs required for successful communicative interactions.

Form, Content, and Use According to Bloom and Lahey (1978), a language disorder may involve difficulty in conceptualizing ideas about the world, coding those ideas into language, or using the code for speaking or understanding.

In the developmental-cognitive approach, language skills are divided into three areas in order to assess delays and plan interventions. Traditionally, speech therapists have focused their remedial programs on disorders of form or syntax. We now realize that disorders of content (semantics) and use (pragmatics) are more serious and demand at least equal attention. Let us examine each area in order to provide background for planning intervention.

Disorders of form include problems with lexicon (vocabulary) and grammar. The most common problem young children exhibit in this area is the substitution of earlier, simpler forms for more advanced, more complex ones. These are usually representative of the child's developmental level. For example, an older child with language delays might use such younger forms as

> I falled down and hurted myself.
> I going school now.
> Please more milk.

The omission of auxiliary verbs and prepositions and the substitution of improper past tense forms are normal for the 3- or 4-year-old, but not for the 5- or 6-year-old. An analysis of the grammatical forms a child uses is a first step in diagnosing language disorders.

Disorders of content or meaning are generally more serious than disorders of form, since they usually indicate a lack of concept development. To remediate content disorders, it is necessary to teach the concepts underlying the linguistic expression. An example of disordered content from Schwartz (1974) appears below. The speaker is a 6-year-old hydrocephalic child, who does not understand the concept of a button and its use.

> this is a button . . . it has two holes in it . . . it's like a lady has . . . it has a shape . . . it is round . . . this is a button . . . you put it on your blouse or an apron in case an apron has a button . . . that's big like this . . . you can roll it and throw it but you never smash a window . . . because if you have a button or a shape that goes on the wall or if you take it and hang it on the dress that would be very nice . . . would you do that for me? . . . if you have a dress or a coat you can hang it on or you can keep it out to take it to the store

In planning an effective intervention for this child we must consider his cognitive deficits. Before we can expect the child to code ideas into correct language we must help him to become familiar with many objects and understand that different objects have different uses.

Disorders of use also depend on the child's level of cognitive development. We use language to communicate; where this is not possible for a child, as below, it represents a serious problem. The 10-year-old child in this example from Bloom and Lahey (1978) reveals an inability to process prior utterances, to focus on a relevant subject, and to take into account the needs of his listener. These represent cognitive, rather than linguistic, deficits. Communication is a thinking process as well as a linguistic one, and so intervention must be designed to develop such cognitive concepts as decentration, representational thinking, and memory.

> (Mark and his teacher are talking)
> **Mark:** Mom used to take me to McDonalds February 1974, she used to put me up in the— at 1:30 . . . and I went to the doctors' office at 2:45
> **Teacher:** What kind of things do you eat when you go to McDonalds?
> **Mark:** a hamburger, a Big Mac quarter pounder, soft drinks, and french fries . . . I never go to McDonalds for breakfast you know . . .

Teacher: Why not?
Mark: why well you know . . . I used to sleep in New York, in the Catskill Mountain . . . I used to go to a motel . . . I don't know where I ate breakfast . . . you know RD's roast beef sandwich . . . that restaurant was in Pennsylvania but it's in New Jersey, . . . it's now in New York, on the way to New York City, Manhattan

Studies of child language have revealed that children talk better in context than when they are imitating adults and that they use more advanced forms when they talk about what they are doing. Intervention in disorders of language use should be experimentally based to allow children to develop the concepts necessary for accurate communication of their ideas.

Hearing impairment may affect the language development of preschool children. The term covers the entire range of auditory impairment, from mild hearing loss to deafness (Moores, 1982). *Deafness* is defined as the threshold below which human speech cannot be understood (Hallahan & Kauffman, 1982). Other levels of hearing impairment are defined in terms of decibels of hearing loss. Children are usually diagnosed as having mild, moderate, severe, or profound loss according to the range of pitch (frequency, measured in Hertz, or Hz) and loudness (intensity, measured in decibels, or db) they can hear. The pitch of the human voice in normal speech falls within a range of 500 to 2,000 Hz, the range within which hearing tests are conducted. Levels of hearing loss within that Hertz range are determined by the ability to hear various decibel levels:

Normal hearing: 1–25 decibels
Mild hearing loss: 26–54 decibels
Moderate hearing loss: 55–69 decibels
Severe hearing loss: 70–89 decibels
Profound hearing loss: 90 decibels or
    more

A child with mild hearing loss can understand speech when spoken face to face, but has some difficulty with normal conversations. The child with moderate loss has difficulty with normal conversations, especially if there is background noise, but can understand amplified speech. The child with severe loss will have difficulty even with amplified speech and will probably require some type of augmented communication. If the hearing loss is profound, there will be little if any ability to hear speech sounds, even if amplified (Peterson, 1987).

Whether a hearing loss is mild or severe is often related to the type of loss experienced by the child. Hearing losses are categorized by their location in the ear. If the outer or middle ear is damaged, the result is a *conductive hearing loss*. These are often caused by infections in the middle ear, known as *otitis media*. Such infections cause an excess of fluid to accumulate in the eustachian tube, which blocks sounds from traveling to the inner ear and the auditory nerve. Conductive hearing losses are the easiest to treat, and both medical and surgical procedures, including draining fluids from the eustachian tubes, may be indicated. Children with conductive loss usually respond well to hearing aids, and hearing can often be restored to nearly normal ranges.

Children with *sensorineural hearing loss* have more serious problems. This type of loss occurs in the inner ear and/or the auditory nerve, which connects the ear to the brain. The function of the inner ear is to transform sound waves received from the outer and middle ear into electrochemical impulses capable of being processed by the brain. These are sent to the brain by way of the auditory nerve. Sensorineural damage may be caused by illness, high fever, drugs, or congenital defects. Such losses do not respond to hearing aids, and damage is usually permanent and difficult to treat.

Recently a surgical procedure has been developed, however, that offers hope to children with sensorineural hearing losses. *Cochlear implants* are now available to both children and adults who suffer damage to the cochlea, the part of the inner ear where sound waves are transformed to electrochemical impulses. An artificial cochlea is implanted in the inner ear, replacing the damaged one. Initial reports on this procedure have been favorable.

The greater a child's hearing loss, the greater the potential language deficits. Because of their inability to imitate speech sounds, children with severe or profound hearing loss have little or no intelligible speech. Children with mild or moderate loss may have some articulation problems. The greatest disability is in the area of normal language development; that is, learning the correct form, content, and uses of language. Because learning oral language is so difficult for many hearing-impaired children, many speech and language professionals advocate teaching children sign language as part of a total communication program (Ling, 1984).

Hallahan and Kauffman (1982) suggest that hearing-impaired children have three obvious disadvantages in learning to speak. First, they receive inadequate auditory feedback when they make sounds. Second, they do not receive adequate verbal reinforcement from adults. Third, they are unable to hear adult speech adequately and thus cannot use adult speech as a model.

While they are clearly at a disadvantage in learning to speak, deaf children are capable of learning language and communication skills. In fact, most deaf children become proficient in the use of American Sign Language (ASL). The linguistic structure of ASL is as complex as that of spoken English and, in fact, is able to show some relationships that spoken English cannot (Moores, 1982). In short, it is important to recognize that preschool children with

hearing impairments can and do learn language. They are, however, not particularly well equipped to communicate in the oral-aural modes of English.

Preschool education of hearing-impaired children has become more and more commonplace. These programs have been developed and housed largely outside of the public schools, and have been affiliated with private schools, universities, or speech and hearing centers. Early intervention programs for hearing-impaired children have sparked debate about the most effective type of communication system to use in educating them. As Moores (1982) suggests, "some educators firmly believe that the use of any kind of manual communication will prevent children from developing speech and language and doom them to lifelong existence in a mute subculture. Others just as firmly believe that depriving children of such a system will cause them irreparable linguistic, educational, and emotional damage" (p. 240). In an attempt to resolve these dichotomous positions, Moores concludes that, "if there is any chance that a child will have difficulty through sole reliance on auditory-vocal communication, oral-manual communication should be initiated immediately. The use of oral and manual communication can facilitate development" (p. 252). This type of approach, called *total communication* because it combines oral and manual approaches, became popular in the late 1960s, when studies began to reveal that manual communication facilitated language development and academic achievement in deaf children (see Stuckless & Birch, 1966; Vernon & Koh, 1970). Moores, Weiss, and Goodwin (1976) have suggested that preschool programs for hearing-impaired children should put strong emphasis on cognitive-academic activities, and that math should receive as much attention as reading and language from the beginning of instruction.

In the final analysis, early interventionists must provide young children with hearing impairments with opportunities to develop language, communication, academic, and social skills. Because of the relatively low incidence of deafness, this has not always been the case for hearing-impaired children in infancy and early childhood.

Aphasia Aphasia is the inability to use or understand spoken language in the absence of hearing impairment or mental retardation. Two forms of aphasia are recognized. In *expressive*, or *motor*, aphasia children have difficulty using words. Children with expressive aphasia may be able to show or even tell how a common object is used, but may be unable to name it. In *receptive*, or *sensory*, aphasia, children appear to hear what is being said to them, but are unable to process it meaningfully. According to Adler (1983), both expressive and receptive aphasia occur in the left hemisphere of the brain, but in different locations. They are generally the result of brain damage, which may also affect the child's written language in the guise of a learning disability.

In a sense, aphasia is analogous to a learning disability of language function. It is linked to central nervous system dysfunction that is either congenitally based or the result of later central nervous system damage. Young aphasic children can manifest characteristics similar to those of hearing-impaired children and careful assessment is often necessary to distinguish between them. Fortunately, aphasia occurs only rarely in children. It presents a particular challenge for early interventionists, however, since it can significantly interfere with the early development of language and related cognitive abilities in young children.

Speech Disorders Speech disorders interfere with the ability to speak clearly. They may cause social problems if children are teased and ridiculed, but these disorders cause language problems only when they interfere with effective communication. It is difficult to classify children under the age of 5 or 6 as speech disordered, since many speech characteristics of very young children mimic those of older speech-disordered children. Early interventionists should keep these problems in mind so that facilitation and remediation programs can be designed for children whose difficulties do not improve as they reach kindergarten or first grade. Three basic types of speech problems can be seen in children: problems of articulation, voice, and stuttering.

Articulation problems are characterized by imperfect sound production. These imperfections can be in the form of sound distortions, sound substitutions, or sound omissions. These imperfections occur naturally within the normal speech development of 2- to 6-year-old children. If, however, they persist to any degree into the first grade, speech and language therapists should be consulted and interventions designed. Correct speech models should be provided for young children. However, caution should be used in directly calling attention to children's errors. Attention may increase children's anxiety about speaking and thus reduce their verbal output.

Voice disorders include excessively loud, soft, and hoarse voices and are usually associated with imperfect vocal cord structures. Preschool children need to learn to control their voices in an acceptable fashion. Constant yelling and screaming, for example, can lead to vocal cord strain and eventual damage. Loud speaking may also be a sign of hearing loss in young children. Excessive hoarseness in children should be thoroughly investigated if it is persistent, since hoarseness is often related to nodules on the vocal cords, which may require surgical removal. Speech and language therapists are often the best resources for remediating these problems.

Stuttering is defined as excessive disfluency in speech and is characterized by the absence of meaningful repetition of sounds, words, or phrases while speaking. It may also be characterized by repeated and frequent hesitation during speech. The causes of stuttering have not clearly been established and theories suggest both biological and psychoemotional causation. Everyone, especially young children, whose speech is emerging, has disfluencies when speaking. Like articulation errors, disfluencies are a natural part of speech development and become a problem only when they persist after age 5 or 6 and are of a severe enough nature to interfere with effective communication.

Parents and early interventionists should be patient with preschool children when they experience disfluencies. Urging children to slow down or start again merely calls attention to the disfluency and may result in anxiety. This anxiety can provide the basis for becoming a stutterer, and may actually increase anxiety. Because stuttering can be difficult to remediate in older children and adults, early intervention is important.

THE DEVELOPMENT OF LITERACY

For many years, it was thought that children should not be taught to read before the age of 6. It was believed that a mental age of 6.6 years was necessary for the child to profit from reading instruction (Pflaum, 1986). Many states prohibited the teaching of reading in kindergarten because of the widely held belief that it was harmful to children. Speaking, reading, and writing were believed to develop in hierarchal fashion, with oral language beginning at age 1, reading at age 6, and writing at age 7 or 8. The earlier skills were considered to be prerequisites for those that followed (Johnson & Myklebust, 1967).

Recent research has shown that literacy development begins much earlier than first grade (Pflaum, 1986). Many children show an interest in books and writing materials at 2 or 3. Early readers have not been found to have more difficulties than other learners later in their school careers. Nor are they necessarily gifted. What they share with other early readers is a strong interest in words: the sounds of words, how words look on a printed page, and so on. Children who become early readers usually like to be read to from a very early age, and have favorite books and stories as toddlers.

Several researchers have identified similarities between language and literacy. Snow (1983), for example, has noted that during the preschool years, children learn both to talk and to read and write through spontaneous practice and through social interactions with adults and peers. Both oral and written language develop in young children through scaffolding and bootstrapping (see p. 102). Both require decontextualization as the child develops, since children's early verbal and written communications consist primarily of labels understood only in context.

Goodman (1986) stresses the naturalness of the writing and reading process developmentally. She advocates allowing children to experiment with words and pictures, books and pencils as they learn to talk and increase their vocabularies in the preschool years. She maintains that reading, writing, and speaking develop in an interdependent manner rather than hierarchically. Oral language is not a prerequisite for written language; one complements and aids the other as the learner progresses through childhood.

The Beginnings of Reading

This new approach to children's literacy has implications for preschool children identified as at risk for handicaps. Since the majority of preschool children with handicaps are identified as language delayed, it is important to take account of written language as well as oral language in planning their individual educational programs. Early childhood special educators must be knowledgeable about the early roots of literacy, and promote the development of literacy in young preschool children with handicaps who are developing oral language.

According to Pflaum (1986) young children are aware of literacy-related facts such as the different functions of print and pictures. Such awareness is the precursor to learning to read. Many children become aware of these facts through their own investigations; others need to be made aware of them by teachers or parents. Children with delays need special assistance with reading readiness, and early childhood special educators should plan activities to promote literacy development. Some guidelines are presented below.

To develop *awareness of print:*

- Encourage the child to look at picture books.
- Help the child tell the story from the pictures.
- Read stories to the child, showing the pictures.
- Show the child the printed words and explain their meanings in the story.
- Help the child to understand that print and pictures have different functions.
- Ask the child to help predict what will happen next in the story.
- Ask the child to identify letters in the words found in the stories.
- Point out that letters may be used over and over in different words.
- Trace the words as you read aloud to the child, moving in a left-right direction.
- Write the child's name and point out the letters and how they sound.
- Use periods and question marks in writ-

ing examples for the child, and explain their use in writing and in texts.
- When reading to the child, take some time to stress the letters in the words and the sounds they stand for. (Pflaum, 1986)

Studies of young children's development of reading ability show that children initially think that the text represents simply the names of the objects pictured. Later they realize that the text represents all the words read by the reader. Finally, they learn that text is really just talking written down (Goodman, 1988). When this happens they have made the cognitive link between speaking, reading, and writing.

In Goodman's (1988) recent study of 3-, 4-, and 5-year-olds' reading ability, she found that most of the children in all age groups could read some words in context. All 3-year-olds could handle books properly, and many of the children could name the parts of a book. Five-year-olds understood that print carries a message. Many of them had a concept of story and understood that a sequence of events was required.

All of these understandings, which typically develop during the preschool years, are precursors of reading and should be fostered in children with language or other delays.

The Beginnings of Writing

Recent research has not determined whether reading develops before writing (Pflaum, 1986), but experts in the field of children's literacy believe this is not important. Pflaum (1986) has identified five stages in the process of learning to write. Beginning with drawing and scribbling and proceeding to the use of conventional spelling, the stages are as follows:

1. The use of straight or curved lines that only the writer can interpret and even then not for long

2. After some letters are learned, the writing of letters in different combinations to represent words

3. The attempt to assign a sound value to these "letters"

4. The combining of letters to represent sounds rather than the use of single letters to stand for syllables

5. The use of invented spelling, gradually replaced by conventional spelling

Preschool and primary teachers who use the whole language approach stress the spontaneous aspects of learning to write (Rhodes & Dudley-Marling, 1988; Temple, Nathan, Burris, & Temple, 1988). They warn against the inhibitory effects of too much correcting of errors. In such programs, children are encouraged to express themselves without worrying about breaking rules of convention. In fact, writing words as they sound helps children understand sound/symbol relationships and eventually become more accurate readers and spellers. The results of this learning process are often charming and make for delightful reading.

For example, Matthew (age 5) presented his mother with the following testimony during his first month in kindergarten:

(Mom, I love you because you're nice, you're nice because you share. Love, Matt)

Other examples of invented spelling and early writing follow. Both examples are from 6-year-olds (Temple et al., 1988).

O L ABt. ESKiMOS
ESKiMO. MES. ruL
MEtrS. i. NO.A. Let.
A. Bot. ESKiMOS. bECUS.
i. SUdyEdthM. iNSOL
thE. acl

(All about Eskimos
Eskimo means raw meat eater. I know a lot about Eskimos because I studied them in school.)

Sant PdTriks
day is cumeing in
to weeks. My
Teachr hdsdnt
Got a chance
To PuT up The
Pichers for it.
I Like it
Becose We Get
To edT Goas
and Turky BuT
The BesT ParT
is. You GeT To
GeT FdT.

A

Boy is this
boring.
S.t. Paterics
ddy is in two
Months if You
Thank thdts
not Boring
Tell Me Whdt is.

B

No Geting
To eat turcky.
No Pillgrims.
No indeins
No inethang.
Like I say
if you Dont thdnk
thdts Not Boring
C

Whdt
is

SUMMARY

This chapter begins with a description of the major components of language—syntax, semantics, pragmatics, and phonology—and then reviews the links between cognition and language. Next, the child's linguistic environment is examined, with emphasis on the role adults play in language learning. Then follows a section on early literacy. The remainder of the chapter discusses language disorders in terms of form, content, and use, with special attention to problems such as hearing impairment, aphasia, and stuttering.

Social and Emotional Development

1. How do temperament and play affect social development?
2. How can the development of self be affected by a disability in a young child?
3. How can social development be distinguished from cognitive development?
4. What may be the relationship between deviance and problems in social development?

ANY BEHAVIOR BY AN individual that takes place in the presence of another individual may be considered social behavior if that behavior is in some way reacted to by the second individual. The interaction between parent and infant is therefore a social interaction. Data presented by Brazelton, Koslowski, and Main (1974), for example, suggest that infants have a repertoire of social behavior at birth. Their definition of social behavior is oversimplified, since it is through social behavior that the young child achieves awareness of self, feelings of emotion, feelings of trust and security, and social role identification. In essence, as Anastasiow (1981) has suggested:

> socioemotional development seems to mean a lot of different things to different people . . . . [It] means the development of emotions, the ability to get along with peers, the development of ego and superego, the ability to control emotions, the ability to work and love, the

ability to form attachments and affiliations with caregivers and peers, and the ability to grow and develop as a person—in other words it is a confusing puzzle. (p. 2)

In this chapter we discuss social and emotional development in young children and address some specific problems that children can have in their social-emotional development. As Anastasiow's statement suggests, social and emotional development covers a spectrum of behavioral and intrapsychic states. We have space to discuss here only those areas of social-emotional development judged to be most important in the lives of young children with handicaps. These areas are the role of temperament and play in social development, attachment, and development of self. Problems of social and emotional development including autism, childhood psychosis, oppositional behavior, hostile and aggressive behavior, shyness, and fears are also discussed.

115

Social and emotional development progresses through the first 3 years of life in a series of relatively discrete and identifiable steps. Sroufe (1979) calls these steps "stages," although he adds the proviso that "these 'stages' are not proposed as a necessary, invariant sequence, but rather as normatively descriptive" (p. 475). These stages are of heuristic value in helping to understand the unfolding of social and emotional behavior during the first three years of life. Table 6.1 outlines the stages of social and affective development and reveals a relationship between cognitive and social development stages. The cognitive and social domains facilitate each other. While we can and do study the various domains of development separately, they are clearly interrelated. What a child is doing in one developmental domain (e.g., cognition) affects what he or she is doing in another developmental domain (e.g., social) and vice versa.

During the preschool years, children begin to develop additional awareness of sex roles. Sex roles are learned through identification with and imitation of parents and other primary adults in the environment. It is also during this period that children learn to seek social functions from appropriate social agents in the environment, such as turning to a parent for caregiving.

Two important factors that play a role in the social and emotional development of children are temperament and play. Temperament is measurable in the infant at birth and throughout early childhood (Simeonsson, 1986). Play is a social function that is critical in the development of social and affective behavior. While they are clearly not the only determinants of social development in young children, we focus on these factors because they are typical of the kinds of factors that lead to social development. Moreover, a good deal of attention has been given to both temperament and play in the literature concerning social development.

TEMPERAMENT

The pioneering work on temperament was done by Thomas and colleagues (1963) as part of the New York Longitudinal Study (Beckwith, 1979). These researchers were concerned with the "how" of behavior—the nonmotivational and stylistic ways in which infants and young children behave. From this interest the construct of temperament emerged. Temperament can be defined as the underlying style or pattern of a person's behavior that sets the stage for his or her reactions to the world. Thomas, Chess, and Birch (1968) identified 10 categories that can be used in assessing the temperament of infants and young children. These categories are defined in Table 6.2. Carey (1970) and Buss and Plomin (1975) have used similar categories to codify infant temperament.

Temperament is important in the social and affective development of the child because it is responsible, in part, for how others in the environment react to the child. This issue is particularly important in dyadic interaction between infant or child and the primary caregivers. A mother responds differently to children of different temperaments, and these responses may lead to different social developmental outcomes. Furthermore, some evidence suggests that infants and children with certain temperamental patterns are more likely to display behavior disorders later in childhood (Thomas, Chess, & Birch, 1968). But, as was discussed in Chapter 2, the probability of exhibiting a particular characteristic in the future is based on a multitude of risk factors. Thus, while the premise of Thomas, Chess, and Birch has some validity, it is also important to note that what may be considered a difficult temperament by one caregiver would not necessarily be considered a difficult temperament by another caregiver. The prediction of behavior disorders is probably

Table 6.1. Stages of cognitive, affective, and social development, birth to 18 months

Cognitive development	Affective development	Social development
0–1 month Use of reflexes Minimal generalization/accommodation of inborn behaviors	*0–1 month Absolute stimulus barrier* Built-in protection	*0–1 month Initial regulation* Sleeping, feeding, quieting arousal Beginning preferential responsiveness to caregiver
1–4 months Primary circular reactions First acquired adaptations (centered on body) Anticipation based on visual cues Beginning coordination of schemes	*1–3 months Turning toward* Orientation to external world Relative vulnerability to stimulation Exogenous (social) smile	
4–8 months Secondary circular reactions Behavior directed toward external world (sensorimotor "classes" and recognition) Beginning goal orientation (procedures for making interest sights last; deferred circular reactions)	*3–6 months Positive affect* Content-meditaed affect (pleasurable assimilation, failure to assimilate, disappointment frustration) Pleasure as an excitatory process (laughter, social responsivity) Active stimulus barrier (investment and divestment of effort)	*4–6 months Reciprocal exchange* Mother and child coordinate feeding, caretaking activities Affective, vocal, and motor play
	7–9 months Active participation Joy at being a cause (mastery initiation of social games) Failure of intended acts (experience of interruption) Differentiation of emotional reactions (initial hesitancy, positive and negative social responses, and categories)	*7–9 months Initiative* Early directed activity (infant initiates social exchange, preferred activities) Experience of success or interference in achieving goals
8–12 months Coordination of secondary schemes and application to new situations Objectification of the world (interest in object qualities and relations; search for hidden objects) True intentionality (mean-end differentiation, tool using) Imitation of novel responses Beginning appreciation of caused relations (others seen as agents, anticipation of consequences)	*9–12 months Attachment* Affectively toned schemes (specific affective bond, categorical reactions) Integration and coordination of emotional reactions (context-mediated responses, including evaluation and beginning coping functions)	*10–13 months Focalization* Mother's availability and responsivity tested (demands focused on mother) Exploration from secure base Reciprocity dependent on contextual information

(continued)

Table 6.1. (continued)

Cognitive development	Affective development	Social development
12–18 months Tertiary circular reactions Pursuit of novelty (active experimentation to produce new effects) Trial and error problem-solving (invention of new means) Physical causality spatialized and detached from child's actions	*12–18 months Practicing* Mother the secure base for exploration Elation in mastery Affect as part of context (moods, stored or delayed feelings) Control of emotional expression	*14–20 months Self-assertion* Broadened initiative Success and gratification achieved apart from other
18–24 months Invention of new means through mental combination Symbolic representation (language, deferred imitation, symbolic play) Problem-solving without overt action (novel combinations of schemes)	*18–36 months Emergence of self-concept* Sense of self as actor (active coping, positive self-evaluation, shame) Sense of separateness (affection, ambivalence, conflict of wills, defiance)	

From Sroufe, L.A. (1979). Socioemotional development. In J.D. Osofsky (Ed.), *The handbook of infant development.* New York: John Wiley & Sons. Copyright 1979. Reprinted by permission.

more closely associated with the interaction of the temperaments of caregivers and their children than it is a function of the individual temperamental characteristics of one or the other (see Sameroff & Chandler, 1975).

While there is evidence that temperament has a genetic component, it is also true that temperament characteristics may change as a result of the social environment (Simeonsson, 1986). Recent research on child temperament has emphasized measurement

Table 6.2. Definitions of temperament characteristics

Characteristic	Definition
Activity level	Degree of activity, either active or passive
Rhythmicity	Regularity of behavior patterns (e.g., eating, sleeping)
Approach/withdrawal	Tendency to approach or withdraw from new situation (e.g., how outgoing child is)
Adaptability	Ability to adjust to new situations
Intensity of reaction	Level of response to environmental events (e.g., vigor, furor)
Quality of mood	General disposition
Persistence	Tendency to stick with task despite obstacles to its completion
Distractibility	Degree to which environmental stimulation can divert child's attention
Attention span	Ability to keep attention focused on task at hand
Threshold of responsiveness	Amount of stimulation necessary to evoke child's response

of temperament characteristics in young children (Fullard, McDevitt, & Carey, 1984; Persson-Blennow & McNeil, 1982). Typically, the variability of characteristics such as activity level, impulsivity, mood intensity, and rhythm is rated on a Lickert-type scale. The resulting profile is labeled either "difficult," "easy," or "slow to warm up" (Simeonsson, 1986). The complete list of diagnostic clusters is presented in Figure 6.1.

PLAY

Play is one of the important functions of childhood and is essential in facilitating a child's development. Bruner (Bruner, 1972; Bruner, Jolly, & Sylva, 1976) has suggested that play is particularly important as a means for children to learn the social function of their behavior in a safe and nonthreatening situation. In discussing the role of play in the development of symbolic processes, Piaget (1951) suggests that "play emphasizes assimilation rather than accommodation [because] play need not fit the demands of reality" (Baldwin, 1968, p. 232). This suggestion underscores Bruner's point that play provides a safe situation in which to explore social as well as cognitive schema.

Play has traditionally been considered an important part of the curriculum in preschool programs. This is because play was thought to promote development in all growth areas—intellectual, social, language, and motor skills. Spontaneous play was encouraged in traditional nursery school programs, for example, simply by allowing some time in the schedule each day for free play. Teachers generally believed that they need not teach children to play, but rather that the learnings to be gained from play would accrue indirectly from the experience.

	High activity	Arrhythmic	Withdrawal	Slow adaptation	Intense	Negative mood	Low persistence	Low distractibility	Low threshold
6			Slow to warm up	Slow to warm up		Slow to warm up			
5		Difficult	Difficult	Difficult	Difficult	Difficult			
4									
3		Easy	Easy	Easy	Easy	Easy			
2					Slow to warm up				
1	Slow to warm up								
	Low activity	Rhythmic	Approach	Very adaptive	Mild	Positive mood	High persistence	High distractibility	High threshold

Figure 6.1. Defining diagnostic clusters of temperament tracts. (From Simeonsson, R. J. [1986]. *Psychological and developmental assessment of special children.* Boston: Allyn & Bacon; reprinted by permission.)

As preschool programs for handicapped children became more numerous as a result of the ascendancy of the philosophy of early intervention, emphasis came to be placed on the direct teaching of skills to the young child, and teachers were less willing to trust in the seemingly haphazard benefits of play to promote learning. The purpose of such programs was to help at-risk children and children with handicaps to catch up with their peers, and direct instruction seemed a faster method of ensuring progress. In addition, because early intervention programs were generally funded through federal grants and many were experimental in nature, a strong emphasis was placed on testable results. Teaching of specific skills, therefore, was and continues to be a major focus of most preschool programs for the handicapped. The traditional nursery school emphasis on play has been rejected as too nondirective and too haphazard.

As a result of this trend, the benefits of spontaneous play as a means for cognitive, social, language, and motor development have been temporarily lost, or at least underexploited. There is a strong case to be made for the inclusion of play in the curriculum of children with handicaps, for there is compelling evidence that play is necessary for a child's optimum development.

In the following discussion we examine some issues related to play and learning in general, including the implications of research in this area, and then relate these to what we know about the play of children with handicaps. Finally, we discuss the role of parents in helping children with handicaps achieve optimal development through play.

Let us begin with a definition of play. Sylva (1977), drawing on the work of several other writers, defines play as active, persistent, manipulative or locomotor experimentation with objects, with the environment, with one's own body, and/or with other organisms. It is self-initiated and lacks apparent immediate survival purpose. Bower, Bersamin, Fine, and Carlson (1974) add that it is enjoyable, serious, and voluntary. According to Tizard and Harvey (1977), it is orderly and not goal oriented. The lack of a goal in play distinguishes it from problem solving (Sylva, 1977). Nevertheless, it is a primary vehicle for communicative, cognitive, and social-emotional development (Rogers, Herbison, Lewis, Pantone, & Reis, 1986).

In summary, play is an enjoyable activity that the child engages in voluntarily for the fun of it. The child has no particular goal in mind but nevertheless pursues the activity in an orderly fashion and is serious about the activity. As we shall see in the following section, there seem to be serious consequences of a child's play experiences.

Play and Learning

In studies of animals other than humans, play has been found to be biologically useful (Lorenz, 1972). Many animals have an inborn curiosity that encourages them to explore their environment. Through play, they learn about new objects, experience a greater variety of events, and become more adaptable to new situations. They are at home in a variety of environments as a result and are therefore better survivors.

Through play, animals also learn flexibility. The playing animal uses behaviors from survival patterns, such as feeding or fleeing, and combines them into novel approaches. This combinatorial aspect is considered by some researchers to be the very essence of play; it trains the animals to string together bits of previously acquired behavior to form novel solutions to problems. In this sense playing is important training for problem solving.

In a similar fashion, play emerges in children as a result of curiosity about their environment. Because it is self-initiated and relatively tension-free (one cannot fail in play because there is no goal), it is an excellent means for a child to practice problem solving.

Studies of children's play and its effect on learning have shown that there is indeed a close relationship between the two. A classic study by Smilansky (1968) associated deficits in dramatic play with cognitive deficiencies in disadvantaged preschool children. Smilansky used the following definitions of cognitive play:

1. *Functional play* involves simple, repetitive muscle movements with or without objects.
2. *Constructive play* is goal directed and consists of educational activities, such as building with blocks or tinker toys, and working with puzzles. Objects are necessary.
3. *Dramatic play* involves make-believe activities, role playing, and symbolic play. Dressing up, dramatizing stories, and playing house are examples.
4. *Games* are formal, usually highly organized and rule-bound. They vary from simple circle games or chase games to more complex team games.

In an experiment with 3-, 4-, and 5-year-old children without handicaps involving a problem-solving task, Sylva (1977) found that children who played with test materials solved the problem as well as those who observed an adult solve the problem and then attempted it themselves. The play group progressed from simple to complex means in completing the task, showing they learned as they progressed. By contrast, the observer group immediately used the most complex means, demonstrated by the adult, to solve the problem. These children did not

try to work the problem out gradually, and so less learning took place. In another study, Feitelson and Ross (1973) reported increases in originality and exploration as measured by a test of creativity for 5-year-olds who were trained in symbolic play.

Another study of the relationship between play and problem solving involved groups of disadvantaged children who were taught to expand their play into more symbolic activities through adult modeling (Rosen, 1974). These children showed significant improvement in post-test problem-solving behavior. In a similar experiment, Dansky (1980) examined three groups of low SES children on their performance on cognitive tasks following experiences in sociodramatic play, exploration, and free play. The first two groups received training; the third acted as controls. Only those trained in sociodramatic (symbolic) play demonstrated improvement in cognitive performance. Finally, Saltz, Dixon, and Johnson (1977) found that fantasy play (e.g., acting out fairy tales) increased the cognitive performance of disadvantaged preschool children, whereas activities such as cutting, pasting, and listening to stories had no such measurable effect.

Studies with young children with handicaps have yielded similar results. Newcomer and Morrison (1974) used play therapy with institutionalized mentally retarded children and found increases in their scores on the Denver Developmental Screening Test. Both group and individual play therapy seemed to promote cognitive and social development. Fraiberg and Adelson (1973) found that play helps the blind child develop the capacity for symbolic representation, as evidenced, for example, in use of the pronouns "me" and "I."

In summary, there appears to be a strong link between the type of play variously described as symbolic, sociodramatic, or fantasy and the development of cognitive abilities.

Play and Social Development

Although it depends upon cognitive structures, play can also be viewed as a social phenomenon, since it also depends to a large degree on a child's interaction with other people. Early forms of play are solitary and may be based on the child making variations on a theme in a similar manner to tertiary circular responses (see Chapter 4). Vocal play may not even depend upon a social object, but may result from the child making voice adaptations. These early solitary play behaviors are important in social development in that they help the child to establish and differentiate self from other. It is only as the child's cognitive development becomes less egocentric that he or she can begin to play cooperatively with others. Cooperative play relies upon a child's ability to take the perspective of the playmate, setting the stage for the development of prosocial behaviors, such as sharing, helping, and cooperating.

It should not be inferred, however, that solitary play is by definition a lower level of play than cooperative play. Rubin, Maioni, and Hornung (1976) suggested that parallel, not solitary, play is indicative of the least mature level of a social play hierarchy for 3- and 4-year-olds. Children who play by themselves may simply wish to "get away from it all," they suggest, and the children's activities—such as painting, clay modeling, or writing a story—may be at a very high level indeed. However, children who exhibit parallel play, that is, playing beside other children rather than with them, may actually want to play with the other children but lack the ability to do so.

Researchers have identified several types of play, some based on interactions with people and others based on exploration or use of objects. The best known and most widely used category system for social play

is probably that of Parten (1932). By observing nonhandicapped nursery school children during free play, she identified six categories of play in which children typically engage. These are summarized below.

1. *Unoccupied behavior.* Child engages in random behavior, such as watching something of momentary interest, following the teacher, or engaging in play limited to his or her own body.
2. *Onlooker.* Child watches others play, often talking to the children being observed, making suggestions, or asking questions, but not entering into play.
3. *Solitary independent play.* Child plays alone and independently, with toys different from those used by children within speaking distance and makes no effort to get close to other children.
4. *Parallel activity.* Child plays independently but chooses an activity that will naturally bring him or her close to other children. The child is beside rather than with other children; uses toys similar to those of children nearby.
5. *Associative play.* Child plays with other children in a common activity, forming a group that excludes other children. Each child acts as he or she wishes; there is no subordination to the needs of the group. All children engage in similar if not identical activity; there is no division of labor.
6. *Cooperative, or organized, supplementary play.* Child plays in a group organized for some play purpose (product, drama, competition, or game). There is division of labor, with children taking different roles. One or two children dominate, become leaders, and exclude some other children from the group.

Parten found that all the children she observed, who ranged in age from 2 to 5, participated in all the types of play described except onlooker behavior, which was observed only in children younger than 3, and cooperative play, which was not seen in the youngest children. She noted that onlooker behavior was most common at 2½ to 3½; solitary play was most common among 4- and 5-year-olds; and cooperative play was most common among older children with the highest IQ levels. There was also a positive correlation found between group play and IQ level in 3-year-olds. That is, only the 3-year-olds with higher IQ levels engaged in group play. By age 4, all the children engaged in associative or cooperative play. Parten speculated that language development facilitated group play.

Parten considered solitary play a lower, or younger, form of play, but it should be noted that her purpose was to measure social (group) participation. This would automatically relegate solitary play to a less favored position. As we have noted above, her results have been questioned. In an early study of the play of educable and trainable mentally retarded children based on Parten's categories, Capobianco and Cole (1960) found that the play abilities of those children assigned to Parten's solitary category had been underestimated. More recently, Shugar and Bokus (1986) concluded that "self activity in the peer situation, shown to be often cognitively rich and task-oriented, may have been misrepresented in the early peer research literature. . . . How much children play on their own and how much they interact with other children when playing with them [have] turned out to be separate issues" (p. 191). Research does not support the notion of a hierarchy of play from solitary to group activity.

A recent addition to the play repertoire of the young child is the microcomputer. If used as a tool for exploring, the microcomputer can be considered an object of play, for it can elicit experimentation and problem solving in a noncompetitive environment. For this reason, it has attracted the interest of researchers in child development. In a comparison of the effects of a microcomputer activity and toy play on the social and communicative behavior of a group of five preschool children, some of whom had handicaps, McCormick (1987) found that the computer activity was at least as effective as the toys in stimulating vocalizations and social play among the children. She found higher levels of both communication and play when the children without handicaps played together in dyads than when a child with a handicap was paired with a nonhandicapped peer. This would suggest that when used as a creative or exploratory toy, a microcomputer can effectively stimulate play in preschool children with handicaps.

Play of Children with Handicaps

Does the play of children with handicaps differ from that of nonhandicapped children? Do children with handicaps play in a manner expected for their mental age? Or are their play habits qualitatively different from those of other children? The answers to these questions are important in helping us to understand the educational needs of children with handicaps. In addition, we need to know whether children with handicaps play spontaneously, or whether they need to be taught to do so. Can or should they be taught to play at higher levels than they choose spontaneously? A great deal of research has been done on these issues. Although the results are mixed, there are some definite trends. Let us examine the evidence.

As Rogers (1988) and Li (1981) point out, many studies of the play of children with handicaps involve institutionalized children. The effects of institutional life are difficult to separate from the effects of the handicapping condition on the children's play abilities. Other confounding variables are socioeconomic status and the subject's degree of emotional adjustment. These variables sometimes affect the child's play more than the handicapping condition does. Taking these variables into consideration, few differences are found between the play of children with handicaps and that of children without handicaps.

Children with Mental Retardation In an early study, Tizard (1964) found that mentally retarded children play at a level commensurate with mental age, and that they engage in spontaneous free play. In a study involving relatively well adjusted, noninstitutionalized mentally retarded children, Hulme and Lunzer (1966) found that the play behavior of these children was not easily distinguishable from that of nonretarded children of comparable mental age. In a similar study, Weiner and Weiner (1974) analyzed the toy-play behavior of noninstitutionalized mentally retarded children and compared it to that of nonretarded children. They found some types of play to be primarily related to chronological age, and other types to mental age. Only a few play behaviors seemed to be found exclusively among nonretarded children. Throwing and pounding of toys, for example, was observed only in a group of nonhandicapped 3-year-olds, and not among 6-year-old mentally retarded children whose mental age was 3. And only the nonhandicapped 3-year-olds and 6-year-olds combined toys into more complex forms. Using push-pull toys, manipulating toy parts, and orally exploring toys, however, were associated with mental age, for both nonhandicapped 3-year-olds and mentally retarded 6-year-olds (whose mental age was 3) demonstrated these.

Several of these early studies involve institutionalized children and suffer from the problem described above. More recent work has reported that severely and profoundly mentally retarded children demonstrate early symbolic play skills when their mental age is at least 20 months (Rogers, 1988; Whittaker, 1980). Whittaker (1980) found the appropriate use of spoons and cups to be a precursor to doll-related play in both retarded and nonretarded preschool children. He reported that doll-related play emerges at the same time as one-word utterances and the understanding of simple, novel instructions.

As Rogers (1988) points out, the occurrence of symbolic play appears to distinguish children with retardation from children with both retardation and autism. In their study of the symbolic play of severely retarded and autistic children, Wing, Gould, Yeates, and Brierley (1977) found that both the type of handicap and the environmental setting (homes, school, residential care) affected the child's level of play. The autistic children in their sample did not engage in symbolic play, even when their mental age was greater than 2, the age at which children typically emerge from the sensorimotor period and begin using symbols. Wing and her colleagues also observed that children who did not engage in symbolic play were more likely to be in residential care than living at home. This group included children with autism as well as children with severe retardation, some of whom had mental ages over 2. The group who tended to play symbolically most often were the children with Down syndrome.

Children with Autism Autistic children demonstrate significant deficits in symbolic play compared to children of equivalent mental age (Rogers, 1988). They spend more of their time in less mature forms of play than do nonhandicapped children or children with mental retardation. This is thought to be because children with autism have specific impairments in all areas of symbolic functioning: play, language, and concept formation (Mundy, Sigman, Sherman & Ungerer, 1984).

Nevertheless, recent intervention with autistic children to promote the development of symbolic thought and communication has proven effective (Rogers et al., 1986). Using a play-based approach, Rogers and her colleagues demonstrated significant improvement in the cognitive, perceptual/motor, social/emotional, and communicative skills of preschool children with autism.

Children with Hearing Impairment Hearing-impaired children follow typical patterns of development in their emerging play skills, but the rate of development has been found to vary with socioeconomic level, age at which hearing aids are first introduced, and availability of early language training (Mogford, 1977; Rogers, 1988). As with other developmental variables, socioeconomic status and language competence appear to be critical factors underlining the association between symbolic play and language. Mogford (1977) reported that deaf children have been observed to have imaginary playmates despite serious expressive and receptive language deficits. The play of these children was less social and more solitary than that of hearing children.

Children with Visual Impairment Children with severe visual impairment demonstrate significant delays in the development of symbolic play. In a study involving very young (18 to 38 months) visually-impaired children, Rogers and Puchalski (1984) observed symbolic behavior in half the children at a mean age of 25.9 months, considerably earlier than previous literature suggests and much closer to the 20 months found in children without handicaps. The emergence of symbolic behavior was associated with the use of the word "no" and with general sensorimotor development.

Children with Language Impairment Given the association between language and symbolic play, one would expect children with language impairment to be slower in developing more mature forms of play. Research confirms this to be partly true. When a group of these children was compared to a group of nonhandicapped children of the same chronological and mental age, their level of symbolic play was found to be lower (Udwin & Yule, 1982). However, when language-impaired children were compared with younger nonhandicapped children who had a similar expressive language level, the language-impaired children demonstrated higher levels of symbolic play (Terrell, Schwartz, Prelock, & Messick, 1984).

The Purposes of Play for Young Children

Play is a basic component for young children's development, and, as such, is necessary for the optimal development of all children. Most early childhood education programs emphasize play as a primary means of learning for children without handicaps. Early childhood special education professionals have begun to recognize the value of spontaneous play for children with handicaps as well. Although some children with severe handicaps may need to be taught or encouraged to engage in exploratory or dramatic play, or their learning environments especially arranged to encourage play, there are benefits from play that all children can enjoy (Widerstrom, 1984).

In summary, research shows that although some children with handicaps are very much like other children in the quality and spontaneity of their play, others need encouragement, assistance, or training. Sheridan (1975) expresses the consensus of several authors (Li, 1981; Mogford, 1977; Wehman, 1977) in stating that some disabled children learn slowly and sometimes lack drive and powers of concentration. Having once achieved a basic skill, these children may fail to elaborate on it, remaining stuck at an elementary level. To progress they need "prolonged, patient, individual, step-by-step instruction and must be stimulated to constant practice" (p. 118).

Children try out new roles, experiment with their environment, and test their limits in physical and mental activity through play. Play also provides a safe forum in which to experiment with aggression and sexual arousal as a means of learning how to handle these feelings without fear of adult antagonism. Hartup (1983) points out that play is a uniquely child-child activity, and that peer interaction is therefore a better means of eliciting play behavior than adult-child interaction. In play activity with peers, children encounter an equalitarian environment with fewer constraints than adult-child relationships typically encompass, and this environment facilitates many kinds of learning: social, cognitive, moral, language, and motor. Indeed, inadequate peer relations are prognostic indicators of social and emotional trouble in young children, for loners more often end up as delinquents or develop adjustment difficulties in adulthood.

In the final analysis, play is important in the development of cognitive, social, and affective communicative, and motor skills. It facilitates the adequate development of both self and interpersonal social behavior. Play should be an integral part of any program designed to maximize the development of preschool children with handicaps.

Attachment

Members of a species tend to affiliate or attach themselves to each other. Lorenz (1957) described an early form of attachment he identified as *imprinting*. This phenomenon, which is most notable in birds, is characterized by what appears to be an automatic attachment between newly hatched birds and their mothers. Phenomena such as imprinting support the supposition that attachment within a species is an innate function. However, Lorenz (1957) also demonstrated that young birds tend to imprint not only to their mothers, but also to the first large, seemingly animate object in their environment. Lorenz even demonstrated that these young birds would imprint to him.

Research by Gottlieb (1965) indicates that imprinting may be affected by auditory stimulation during the prenatal period. Gottlieb demonstrated that birds of one species are more likely to imprint to birds of another species than to their own if the singing of the latter species is predominant in the environment during the gestation period. This work on the basic animal process of imprinting led to the development of an ethologically based theory of attachment, as suggested by Bowlby (1969).

According to Bowlby, attachment begins with the infant's instinctual tie to the mother, maintained and increased by the mother's responsiveness to the infant. Bowlby believed that attachment (or "bonding," as it is sometimes used in reference to animals) served the adaptive purpose in earlier evolution of protecting the young from predators. His theory develops from that of Freud (1915, 1926), who suggested that the mother provides the source of all pleasure for the infant by satisfying its instinctual needs (e.g., eating). Attachment results as the mother becomes a greater and greater source of satisfaction.

Over the years the attachment between mother and infant has received much attention from researchers. The attachment process is now recognized as an important aspect of mother-child interaction, upon which the child's welfare depends. Researchers have studied both typical and atypical patterns of attachment, and have examined predictive aspects of the quality of attachment. The importance of the quality of this attachment is now well established by an extensive body of research.

Perhaps of greatest interest to clinical psychologists, early interventionists, and others who work with infants is the emerging emphasis on providing early intervention to at-risk mother-infant dyads with a view to improving maladaptive and potentially harmful parent-child interactions. Some recent studies (Cassidy, 1986; Main, 1983; Olson, Bates, & Bayles, 1986) suggest that insecure attachments during the early months of life can impair academic and behavioral functioning in later childhood and well into adulthood. If taken early enough, preventive measures might mean the difference between academic failure and success, emotional well-being and behavior disorder.

The Strange Situation

Psychologists who study the quality of the attachment between mother and child generally base their observations on the technique developed by Ainsworth and her colleagues (Ainsworth & Wittig, 1969; Ainsworth, Blehar, Water, & Walls, 1978) known as the Strange Situation. This laboratory procedure was designed to examine the quality of an infant's attachment to its mother during separation and reunion. Individual differences in infant responses to the situation (temporarily being left with a stranger) allow for the classification of infants into one of three major attachment categories: insecure-avoidant (Group A), secure (Group B), or insecure-ambivalent-resistant (Group C).

Infants are usually tested at 12 months of age. They are classified as secure (Group B) if they demonstrate mild distress following separation and respond positively to reu-

nion with the mother. Group A babies actively avoid the parent upon reunion, and Group C babies resist parent overtures during reunion. Insecure infants generally display a high level of distress during the separation and are unable to be settled by their mother upon her return.

More recently, a fourth attachment category has been described by Main and Solomon (1986): the insecure-disorganized/disoriented infant whose behavior is unpredictable, and who often has a mother who is, herself, disturbed.

Factors Affecting the Quality of Attachment

Over time, research on attachment has moved from simple descriptions of the characteristics of securely or insecurely attached infants to attempts to isolate various factors that influence the quality of the attachment. Belsky, Rovine, and Taylor (1984) identified three influences on attachment: marital quality and similar environmental influences, infant temperament, and mother's personality.

Infant temperament was considered important because some infants are easier to bond with than others. Belsky and his colleagues considered the mother's interpersonal affect and ego strength to be critical in determining quality of attachment. These factors can be measured prenatally.

External influences included parenting skills of the mother and father, both parents' employment situations, the family's social network, and the quality of the marriage. Noting that all marriages tend to deteriorate following the birth of a baby, Belsky and his colleagues (1984) found that both secure and insecure mothers are rated about the same on marriage quality at 3 months after birth (down from prenatal ratings), but by 9 months, ratings of mothers of securely attached infants have stabilized while those of insecurely attached mothers continue to decline.

The work of Sroufe and his colleagues (Erickson, Sroufe, & Egeland, 1985; Sroufe, 1979, 1983, 1985; Sroufe & Fleeson, 1986) has added a great deal to our knowledge about attachment and its effect on later development. Sroufe views attachment as an ongoing process of active construction that is continually changing as a result of external and internal forces. In his view, there is no critical period for this process in the biological sense; however, since the factors that determine attachment are relatively stable (infant temperament, mother's affect, marriage quality), it is difficult for an insecurely attached infant to become attached later.

Sroufe found quality of attachment as measured by the Ainsworth Strange Situation to predict social/emotional well-being at 3 years and quality and content of fantasy play in preschool. For example, insecurely attached children tended to have no people in their fantasy play, and to use more conflict themes with fewer happy resolutions than securely attached children.

Sroufe also found that insecurely attached children (both avoidant and resistant-attached groups) were more likely to be victimized by other children than securely attached children, and that resistant-attached children were more likely to victimize other children.

In examining the teacher-child interaction, Sroufe found teachers to control more, to reject more, and to display more anger toward insecurely attached children, especially avoidant children. Teachers seemed to expect more mature behavior from the securely attached children. These conclusions imply that a secure attachment will probably mean a child who is better at coping with stress, whereas an insecure attachment may mean a child who cannot cope

well with stress and who lacks self-control. It is clear, then, why an insecure attachment is considered to be a risk factor in predicting later school performance.

In examining attachment as an aspect of developmental psychopathology, Cicchetti and Schneider-Rosen (Cicchetti, 1984; Cicchetti & Schneider-Rosen, 1984; Gersten, Coster, Schneider-Rosen, Carlson, & Cicchetti, 1987; Schneider-Rosen & Cicchetti, 1984; Schneider-Rosen, Braunwald, Carlson, & Cicchetti, 1985) focused on two groups of at-risk infants and infants with handicaps: reproductive casualties (infants with Down syndrome), and caretaker casualties (abused or maltreated infants). Cicchetti and Schneider-Rosen found mothers of infants with Down syndrome to be securely attached to their babies as a rule, despite the fact that these babies tend to be hard to read because of their hypotonicity, lack of eye contact, and biochemically passive temperament. Down syndrome babies are more difficult to rouse to smile or laugh, and more difficult to calm. Nevertheless, they are as likely to be as securely attached as normal infants, because their mothers tend to be more intrusive and work harder on the attachment than other mothers. Cicchetti notes that as a result of the secure attachment, they tend to perform language and other symbolic tasks at developmentally appropriate levels; many Down syndrome children also develop mastery, self-esteem, and trust at appropriate mental age levels. Many are currently integrated into regular classrooms in elementary school (Widerstrom & Goodwin, 1987).

Caretaker casualties, however, are far less likely to develop secure attachments with their mothers. Cicchetti (1984) estimates that 70% of these infants are insecurely attached at 12, 18, and 24 months and that there is a continuity of maladaptation that leads to increasingly delayed development. Noting that quality of attachment predicts the development of self, mastery, and language, Cicchetti states that it is not surprising that maltreated infants experience increasing delays in these areas.

The evidence suggests that while some infants' adaptation can be altered as the result of environmental changes in the infant's life that might lower risk factors, the prognosis for caretaker casualties is poor. Psychologically unavailable mothers produce infants who begin life with full mental capacities but are retarded by 15 months of age. Cicchetti attributes this decline to the increasingly insecure (anxious-avoidant) attachment that develops between mother and infant. He notes that even when the infant is premature—a factor that places the infant at biological risk—the greater risk comes from the insecure attachment.

As Tronick, Ricks, and Cohn (1982) have pointed out, the mother-infant interaction requires both mother and infant to perform. The infant must engage the mother by signaling to her with smiles, eye contact, and touching. The mother must respond by looking, talking, smiling, as well as by engaging in such caregiving activities as feeding and diapering. If either infant or mother fails to perform, there is a lack of synchrony in the interaction and a mismatch occurs.

Tronick states that mismatches can be repaired and the interaction can become a successful one. If this occurs, the infant feels the success and goes on to develop good coping skills. If, however, the infant fails to engage the mother, it substitutes other, noninteractive, behaviors in its repertoire: gaze avoidance (withdrawal); focusing on objects instead of on mother; and self-regulatory behaviors such as putting its fist in its mouth to calm itself. Over the long run, these behaviors lead to psychopathology in the child.

Depressed mothers, according to Tronick's research, do not look at or play with their infants as much as other mothers do. Their infants look at and play with objects less than other infants, and they look at their mothers less. The mismatched interaction thus causes the infant to withdraw from exploration of the external world; this in turn adversely affects the infant's development of cognitive, social, communicative, and motor skills.

In a study that dramatically illustrates this point, Cassidy (1986) examined the exploratory behavior of securely and insecurely attached infants. Using the Ainsworth Strange Situation, she identified three groups of infants: those with avoidant (Group A), secure (Group B), or resistant (Group C) attachments. She then coded the infants' behaviors as they attempted to negotiate their environments, playing with toys, exploring by crawling, and examining novel objects. The coding identified those behaviors designated as failures to negotiate the environment: losing balance, tripping, or falling; accidentally banging or knocking a toy or mother; sitting or stepping on a toy; dropping a toy unintentionally; or allowing a toy to hit or fall on himself.

The insecurely attached infants were significantly more likely to fail to negotiate the environment than the securely attached infants were. This would suggest that more securely attached babies are better able to explore their environments and thus to engage in more activities that promote cognitive development.

Quality of Attachment as a Predictor of Later Performance

It seems clear from the preceding review of the literature that the quality of attachment may be critical to the child's future development. That the mother-child interaction is predictive not only of future psychological well-being but also of later academic performance should not be surprising, since the former dictates the latter. Until recently, however, evidence of this relationship was lacking. A recent study by Olson, Bates, and Bayles (1984) provides interesting evidence of these links between attachment in infancy and academic performance in first grade.

In a longitudinal study of mother-infant interaction, Olson and his colleagues measured attachment factors at 6, 13, and 24 months and then tested the children's social and cognitive competence at 6 years. Interaction measures at 6 months included amount of close physical contact (cuddling) and object stimulation (offering and demonstrating toys). At 13 months the measures included the amount and quality of the mother's teaching, her management style (directive versus punitive), amount and quality of affection she demonstrated, and her style of responding to her infant's speech (corrective versus positive). At 24 months the interaction measures included the amount and quality of the mother's affection and verbal stimulation, and whether the mother used positive or negative methods of control. In addition to the interaction measures administered at 13 months, each infant was rated on quality of attachment using the Ainsworth Strange Situation procedure.

These data were correlated with scores at 6 years on tests of self-control, motor inhibition, problem solving, and IQ, and teacher ratings of aggression, social competence, and academic performance. Significant correlations were found between interaction factors at 6 and 13 months (close contact, object stimulation, affection, and response to infant's speech) and teacher ratings of aggression, social skills, and academic performance at 6 years. Quality of attachment at 13 months predicted impulse inhibition.

However, the most predictive intervention measures were those administered at 24 months: mother's quality of verbal stim-

ulation at that age was highly positively correlated with the infant's IQ, delay of gratification, quality of peer interactions, and positive teacher ratings of social skills and behavioral competence. It was negatively correlated with aggression. Mother's negative control at 24 months was negatively correlated with IQ, impulse control, and academic performance at 6 years. Mother's positive control at 24 months was positively correlated with academic performance at age 6.

These results tell us that the mother-infant relationship can be predictive as early as 6 months, but is most accurate at 13 and 24 months. It appears that because early security of attachment influences a child's developing sense of security, it helps to determine his or her level of self-control. Good impulse control, the ability to delay gratification, and inhibition prepare the child to perform well in school and to be a good playmate.

Summary

The preceding discussion has illustrated the growing interest in attachment theory as an important factor in child development. It is part of a more general interest in the interactions between parent and child that may facilitate or hinder the child's optimal development. Study of the atypical or maltreated child has aided our understanding of the attachment process, and has demonstrated that insecure attachments may have long-term consequences in behavior and performance.

DEVELOPMENT OF SELF

An important psychological achievement for the human infant is the awareness of being a separate entity (or "self") from the mother.

Mahler, Bergman, and Pine (1975) have described this process, called individuation, in some detail. They describe several stages of the process, beginning with autism and ending with the emergence of self. These stages are summarized in Table 6.3.

Another view of this process is based on the infant's contingency experiences that result from interactions with the environment (Lewis & Brooks, 1978; Thurman, 1978). In this view, the awareness of existence separate from other depends on the feedback mechanism that provides the infant with basic contingency information from its own actions; it is this kinesthetic feedback that forms the basis for the development of self.

In infancy, circular reactions, as discussed in Chapter 4, provide a major avenue for children to test their effectiveness on the inanimate world. Interaction with parents and other social beings provides young children another major means of developing self. This human interaction can be critical in determining the types of perceptions and feelings young children have about themselves. These early feelings and perceptions of self form the basis of the way individuals feel about themselves later in life. For example, in discussing the vivid case of John Merrick, the Elephant Man, who was horribly disfigured by neurofibromatosis, Montagu (1971) speculates that Merrick must have

Table 6.3. Stages of individuation in infants

I. Forerunners of the separation-individuation process

Normal autistic phase (birth–1 month): Infant sleeps most of the time, waking principally when hungry; achieves homeostatic equilibrium.

Normal symbiotic phase (1–4 months): Infant cannot differentiate self from mother; understands mother as needs satisfier.

II. First subphase: Differentiation and the development of body image (4–10 months)

Infant's smile signifies development of mother-infant bond.

Infant becomes aware of surroundings (hatching).

Infant visually scans environment, but interest quickly returns to mother (checking back).

Infant begins seeking distance to learn "mother" versus "other."

Infant experiences stranger anxiety (8 months).

Infant begins to differentiate self from mother.

III. Second subphase: Practicing (10–18 months)

Infant learns to walk, explore on own.

Infant practices mastery of skills and autonomy.

Infant desires independence from other.

IV. Third subphase: Rapprochement (18–24 months)

Infant begins use of symbolic language.

Infant becomes aware of separateness from mother, seeks interaction with her.

Mother-infant attachment is solidly formed.

Infant experiences second phase of stranger anxiety; fears separation from mother.

V. Fourth subphase: Consolidation of individuality and beginnings of emotional constancy (24 months onward)

Infant establishes emotional object constancy, built on trust developed with mother.

Adapted from Mahler, Bergman, and Pine (1975).

received "a great deal of love from his mother [during his early childhood and that] . . . on any other assumption it would be difficult . . . to account for the strength, health, integrity, and amiability of John Merrick's personality" (p. 7). Each of these traits was developed by Merrick in spite of the mistreatment and exploitation he underwent during his later childhood, adolescence, and young adult years.

The development of a positive self-image depends largely on the child's feeling that the primary caregivers are trusting and accepting. A feeling of trust provides the infant with a general sense of well-being and sets the stage for the infant to take the risks necessary to try out new forms of behavior. Testing new forms of behavior is not only necessary for the development of cognitive abilities, as was seen in Chapter 4, but is also important for the child's development of self. It is through these new behavior patterns that the child learns to behave autonomously and to exert self-control. Commenting on Erikson's (1963) second stage of psychosocial development, Suran and Rizzo (1979) suggest that when the child is 18- to 36-months-old, "the main focus is on the integration of self as an autonomous unit able to exist in an independent fashion" (p. 33).

Unfortunately, it is difficult for some parents to trust and accept a child who is developmentally delayed. A parent's acceptance is often based on the child's ability to meet the parent's expectations. When the child is unable to meet parental expectations because of developmental problems, deficits in the child's self-concept and overall social and emotional development can occur. Thus, a child experiencing a physical or cognitive problem may develop a concomitant social or emotional problem. Professionals providing services to young children with developmental delays must be aware of the

needs of both the child and the family in dealing with the child. It is often necessary to make a difficult decision about whether the child or the family should come first. It is possible that the trust and acceptance necessary for the child's ultimate development of self and general well-being may be created only by shifts in and even dissolution of existing family units. Chapter 12 provides a more complete discussion of families with young children with handicaps and how to deal effectively with such families.

PROBLEMS OF SOCIAL AND EMOTIONAL DEVELOPMENT

As Samuels (1981) has pointed out, "there is no question that children with exceptionalities are at a greater risk of developing maladaptive behavior [i.e., social and emotional problems]" (p. 153). It follows from Samuels' statement that there are two classes of emotionally disturbed or behavior-disordered children. One class consists of those children who have as their only disability some impairment in social and/or emotional development. The other class of children are those to whom Samuels is alluding, those who, because of a disabling condition, such as cerebral palsy, mental retardation, or chronic illness, develop problems in social and emotional development. As was suggested in Chapter 2, one of the primary purposes of early intervention programs for developmentally disabled children is to reduce the degree of risk they experience during their development. Early interventionists must strive to create environments that minimize the development of concomitant social and emotional problems. The remainder of this chapter is devoted to the various types of social and emotional disabilities present in preschool children. Our emphasis is on preschool children because only rarely, and only in the most severe cases, do social and emotional disabilities manifest themselves prior to the age of 3.

It is difficult to begin any discussion of problems in social-emotional development without talking first about social deviancy. *Deviance* can be defined as difference with a negative connotation. In a sense, deviancy is inherent in the label. In a classic essay, Simmons (1969) suggested that no human behavior is inherently deviant. According to his reasoning, only those behaviors labeled as such are deviant. While Simmons' notion can be applied to the labeling of any disabling condition, it is particularly relevant to social and emotional disabilities. These disabilities are more often defined in terms of adherence to social norms. In fact, most young children engage in some behavior patterns that could be labeled socially deviant. Almost all young children, for example, express fears, are oppositional, and even display autistic-like behavior. But it is only when these behavior patterns are seen as being outside of the accepted range that children are labeled phobic, oppositional, or autistic. It is often possible to reduce the degree and severity of these behavior patterns, concomitantly reducing the probability of the child being labeled in the future. Here again we see an avenue by which early intervention can decrease risk to the child.

The concept of deviance is discussed more fully in Chapters 10 and 11 in the context of intervention. It is mentioned here so that the reader will be mindful of its implications in the definition and labeling of problems in social-emotional development.

Autism

Perhaps the most severe type of social and emotional disorder of early childhood is autism. In its classic form, *early infantile autism*, the child begins to show symptoms of the condition prior to the second year of life. Kanner (1943), who first identified the parameters of infantile autism, suggested that autistic infants would not mold to their mothers' bodies when held, would not anticipate or seek human contact, and felt strange to their mothers when held. Rogers and her colleagues (1986) report that in the United States there are between 5,000 and 10,000 children between the ages of 2 and 5 with the diagnosis of autism or pervasive developmental disorder (PDD), a related disorder causing severe disturbances of language, cognition, and social relationships.

Children with autism have specific impairments in all areas of symbolic thought: symbolic play, symbolic language, and conceptual thought (Rogers et al., 1986). According to Kanner (1943) and Rutter (1985), the classic characteristics of autism include the following:

1. Onset of condition at birth or at about 2 years of age after apparently normal development
2. Impaired or complete lack of appropriate social interactions with parents, other adults, and children
3. Severely impaired or complete lack of language ability
4. Lack of intellectual development, or retardation in certain areas, accompanied by normal or superior abilities in other areas
5. Self-stimulating behavior, such as repetitive and peculiar use of objects and toys, or repetitive and peculiar body motions, such as rocking or spinning
6. Little or no eye contact with others
7. Compulsive behaviors and extremely negative reactions to changes in the environment
8. Extreme distress for no discernible reason
9. Hyperactivity (excessively active) or

hypoactivity (inactive), often accompanied by erratic sleep patterns

10. Inability to perform certain gross and fine motor activities, such as walking with a normal gait

11. Unusual reaction to sights and sounds, for example, seeming not to hear certain sounds and overreacting to others by holding hands over ears

12. Apparent insensitivity to pain, frequently resulting in self-abusive behaviors

According to Rutter, it is necessary to differentiate between disorders arising during infancy involving serious abnormality in the developmental process itself (autism and pervasive developmental disorder), and psychoses arising in later childhood involving a loss of reality in individuals who previously functioned normally. The latter is labeled *childhood schizophrenia* and is discussed below.

Rutter (1986) cites five characteristics that distinguish autism from childhood schizophrenia:

1. Onset before 30 months
2. Deviant language development
3. Deviant social development
4. Stereotypical behavior
5. Absence of delusions, hallucinations, or thought disorders

In most cases the developmental pattern is abnormal from birth, but in approximately 20% of cases there is a period of normal development during the first 2 years.

The etiology of autism is not precisely known, but most experts today agree that it is a form of organic brain dysfunction (Schopler & Mesibov, 1986; Rutter, 1984, 1986), probably involving a deficit in information processing (Rutter, 1985). According to Dawson (1983) it is associated with cerebral lateralization. In a study of autistic children, 7 out of 10 were found to have right hemisphere dominance. Several authors have suggested a physiological cause. Fein, Skoff, and Mirsky (1981) found irregular patterns of auditory-evoked responses. Ornitz and Ritvo (1977) found elevated levels of seratonin in the blood of autistic subjects. Unfortunately, the studies that have purported to define the causes of autism have been difficult to replicate, leaving the question of etiology essentially unanswered (Rutter, 1986).

Effective intervention for autistic children has been limited. In the 1950s and 1960s psychodynamic approaches were tried; in the 1970s there was a movement toward operant conditioning. None of these proved entirely effective, and recent authors (Rogers et al., 1986; Schopler & Mesibov, 1986) have adopted more eclectic approaches, incorporating developmental, behavioral, and psychoanalytic theories. These recent approaches to intervention emphasize the teaching of social and communication skills to the autistic child, since these are the primary deficits characterizing the disorder. For example, the TEACCH curriculum, developed at the University of North Carolina (Wooten & Mesibov, 1986; Olley, 1986), is a structured program that includes behavioral objectives, a social systems perspective for involving the child's family, and individualized learning activities.

An intervention approach based on play and emphasizing the development of symbolic thought has also achieved some success (Rogers et al., 1986). Providing for experiences to enhance symbolic play, social/communicative play skills, and parent-child interactions, the approach has resulted in increased symbolic functioning and improved communicative and interpersonal skills. This approach is especially encouraging because, as noted earlier, poor ability to perform symbolic activities differentiates autistic children from children with other handicapping conditions.

Regardless of the intervention methods adopted, the prognosis for autistic children is not good. In almost all instances, symptoms persist to some degree throughout an affected child's life. Autism remains one of the least understood conditions and represents one of the most difficult conditions for interventionists.

Childhood Psychosis

Unlike autism, childhood psychosis first manifests itself in preschool children. These children often have shown patterns of development within the normal range prior to the time at which psychotic symptoms first appear. The onset of symptoms is usually gradual, and, as a result, symptoms often go unnoticed for a period of time.

Childhood schizophrenia is the most widely recognized form of childhood psychosis. It is characterized by the same types of symptoms associated with adult psychosis. Psychotic children may exhibit disturbed patterns of thought. They may become withdrawn or disoriented, and suffer from hallucinations. They may suffer a decrease in their language ability. They may also exhibit inappropriate mood shifts and affective states. The incidence and severity of symptoms varies greatly from case to case. Rutter (1985) has suggested that schizophrenic children have more varied symptoms than autistic children and that the former are more likely to have contact with other people.

While the factors accounting for childhood psychosis and schizophrenia appear to be as varied as those associated with autism, there is a notable difference. There is a clear family relationship in childhood schizophrenia. Gianascol (1973) found that 16% of families with one schizophrenic parent also had schizophrenic children. When both parents were schizophrenic the figure rises to about 40% (Erlenmeyer-Kimling, 1968). Although these authors have tended to make a case for genetic causation of schizophrenia, it must be pointed out that children may just as likely exhibit schizophrenic patterns of behavior because of the models provided and the childrearing practices adopted by their schizophrenic parents. In their study of children of schizophrenic mothers, Sameroff and Zax (1978) suggested just such a transactional model and were unwilling to link schizophrenia in these children solely to genetic mechanisms.

Phobias

Another problem in social-emotional development that sometimes manifests itself in children is fears, or phobias. A fear may be defined as a persistent behavioral overreaction to some aspect of the environment, the result of which is often anxiety and withdrawal. Generally, the fearful individual will make every attempt to avoid the fear-inducing situation. Infants and young children display fear and wariness in certain situations (e.g., an 8- or 9-month infant will usually show wariness of an unfamiliar adult). It is important to recognize that such fear responses may be appropriate and adaptive for the young child and that these responses should not be discouraged. These fear responses, most of which have a physiological basis, are the basis for the development of fears. Thus, while fear responses are important and necessary for the individual survival and developmental progress, when these same responses are converted into generalized fears they can become a major hindrance to maximum social and emotional development.

Bijou and Baer (1961) suggest that fears develop when naturally occurring fear responses are classically conditioned to other stimuli and then brought under operant control. *Classical conditioning* derives from Pavlov's (1927) early work with dogs. His paradigm suggests that certain stimuli will bring about certain physiological responses. The link between a particular stimulus and the subsequent response that occurs is an unlearned or *unconditioned stimulus (UCS)* and elicits an *unconditioned response (UCR)*. Pavlov demonstrated that if a UCS was presented simultaneously with a neutral stimulus (i.e., one that does not automatically elicit a certain physiological response), the neutral stimulus would eventually elicit a response of the type elicited by the UCS. At this point the neutral stimulus becomes a *conditioned stimulus (CS)* and the response to it a *conditioned response (CR)*. In Pavlov's experiments with dogs he used meat powder as a UCS, which was followed by salivation as a UCR. After pairing meat powder with a buzzer (neutral stimulus) for a number of trials, the buzzer became a conditioned stimulus that elicited salivation. Figure 6.2 shows Pavlov's experiment schematically.

Fears, according to Bijou and Baer, can originate in a similar manner. Suppose, for example, that a 3-year-old child is sleeping in a dark room and is suddenly awakened by a clap of thunder. This loud noise acts as a UCS for fear responses. This UCS is paired with the neutral stimulus of darkness. If this experience is frightening enough, or if it occurs several times in rather close succession, then darkness can become a CS for the same types of fear responses that are automatically elicited by the loud sound of the thunder. Herein would lie the basis of a child's fear of the dark.

This fear could become even more firmly established if the parents became overly attentive to the child's fearful responses, thus providing positive reinforcement. Bijou and Baer have suggested that fear responses come under operant control in this way. That is, the responses become, in part, a function of their reinforcing consequences. It is often difficult for parents and other caregivers to know how much attention to provide to children when they exhibit fear. Too much attention can contribute to a maladaptive, long-standing fear, while not enough attention may make the child feel isolated and insecure.

Oppositional Behavior

Oppositional behavior is behavior that is negative and uncooperative. Oppositional children often refuse to obey requests by

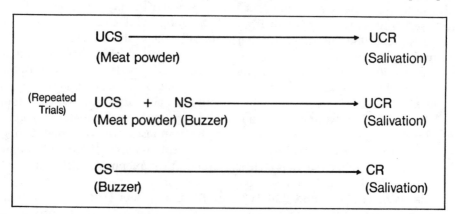

Figure 6.2. A schematic representation of classical (Pavlovian) conditioning.

caretakers and have violent and prolonged temper tantrums when made to do something they do not want to do. The basis for oppositional behavior in preschool children often resides in the pattern of interaction between the child and the parent(s). Typically, oppositional children receive a good deal of parental attention when they behave in undesirable ways. However, parents of these children will seldom, if ever, attend to them when they are behaving in more appropriate ways. Thus, the child learns that negative and uncooperative behavior brings about parental attention. Since parental attention is so important to young children, they will continue to behave in inappropriate ways even when the attention they receive from their parents is negative. The negative attention they receive becomes even more rewarding to them because their parents pay them no attention for desired behavior.

As long as the same pattern of interaction is maintained the oppositional behavior will continue. This builds up feelings of frustration in the parents and often causes them to have negative feelings toward their child. These feelings may affect the parents' ability to make the child feel wanted and secure, and thus further impede the child's social and emotional development.

The most effective means of changing an oppositional child is to modify the pattern of interaction between child and parents. The parent can be taught to direct more positive attention to the child when he or she behaves in an appropriate or cooperative way and to pay no attention to the child's inappropriate behavior (unless, of course, a dangerous situation exists). In this way the pattern of interaction between the parent and child is reversed. What had been attended to is now ignored and what had been ignored is now attended to. Some of the means by which parents can be effectively taught are discussed later in Chapter 12.

Aggression

Aggressive behavior is any behavior designed to hurt people or property. Aggression, or hostility, can interfere significantly with a child's social acceptance by both adults and peers. This often leads to further aggressive behavior, as the child attempts to gain attention and recognition from others. It is important to deal effectively with aggressive behavior in children at its onset, since it can not only hinder the child's social development, but can also cause injury to others.

There are several potential bases for aggressive behavior. Some authors (e.g., Rutter, 1975) have suggested that brain damage brings about increases in aggressive behavior. While this may be true, it is often difficult to demonstrate, since aggression itself may be used by clinicians as a means of suggesting that brain damage exists in a child. The argument becomes circular: children are defined as brain damaged because they are aggressive, and their presumed brain damage is then used as a basis for explaining their aggressive behavior.

Aggression has also been related to frustration. This point of view suggests that children work through their frustration by being aggressive toward others.

Children may become aggressive because of aggressive models in their environments. Parents who use physical punishment as a primary means of child management provide aggressive models for their children. Kazdin (1975) has suggested that punishment leads to aggression in children precisely for this reason. Of course, television also provides a myriad of aggressive models for children to imitate. Even the typical Bugs Bunny or Roadrunner cartoon is full of aggressive models. Like oppositional children, aggressive children often receive parental attention through their aggressive behavior and only through it. It is therefore not un-common to find children who are simul-taneously aggressive and oppositional.

Like oppositional children, aggressive children must be given much attention and social praise for acting in appropriate ways. At the same time, they must be taught more adaptive ways of behaving, since they have learned that their primary means of getting what they want is through hostile and ag-gressive acts. This aggressive form of in-teraction often becomes so firmly estab-lished that these children never engage in more prosocial behavior, such as helping, sharing, and cooperating. Moderating their aggressive tendencies deprives them of their primary means of social interaction, unless these other more desirable patterns of be-havior are specifically taught to them.

Isolation

Some children tend to isolate themselves from others. This isolation may be because of shyness, or it may be related to patterns of withdrawal associated with the more severe forms of impairment in social and emotional development (e.g., autism, childhood schi-zophrenia).

Shyness is a function of the child's tem-peramental makeup and is characterized by hesitancy and/or lack of ability to interact socially. Because of the highly competitive nature of our society and our basic belief that human interaction is necessary, shy children are often viewed by parents and teachers as having a social problem. The as-sumption is that if children are shy their social development will be impeded. These attitudes often make shy children feel unac-cepted and may even promote a tendency to withdraw further from others. Shy children get the message that it is not all right to be shy. It then becomes more difficult for them to become assertive because their self-con-cept becomes negative as they are pushed to become more assertive or outgoing.

Interventions designed to help children overcome shyness should be implemented in such a way as to keep such children from feeling strange because of their shyness. It is important to keep in mind that there is noth-ing inherently wrong with being shy; it is our cultural norms that do not tolerate shyness. Perhaps if early interventionists were more concerned with the development of good self-feelings and less concerned with shyness per se, this norm might begin to reverse itself. Self-acceptance, after all, ought to be one of the major objectives of activities designed to facilitate social and emotional development.

Withdrawal is distinct from shyness in that withdrawn children not only fail to make and maintain social contact with oth-ers, but they also withdraw when others make social contact with them. While shy children may avoid social contact, they will not usually withdraw from it. Withdrawn children neither seek nor want social contact and behave as if they abhor such contact.

Withdrawal is often one of several symp-toms of severe social or emotional disability. As was suggested above, it is one of the characteristics noted in both autistic and schizophrenic children. Strain and his col-leagues (Strain, Kerr, & Ragland, 1981; Strain & Timm, 1974) have demonstrated methods for dealing with socially with-drawn children. These methods generally depend on the use of peer models and rein-forcement techniques. However, interven-tionists of a more psychodynamic orienta-tion question whether such techniques treat a symptom of a more deep-seated emotional disability rather than the disability itself. Strain's techniques can reduce the amount of social withdrawal exhibited by preschool children. Whether this decrease in social withdrawal then makes these children less autistic or schizophrenic depends on how one views the problem (i.e., whether one is of a psychodynamic or a behavioral persuasion).

SUMMARY

This chapter first discusses some of the major features of the social and emotional development of infants and young children. Specifically, it looks at temperament, attachment, and play, and the role each plays in the social and emotional development of a child. Next, the development of self and self-concept are discussed. Finally, attention is then given to various problems in social-emotional development as well as some of the means by which these problems are believed to develop. Theories and research relevant to infants' and young children's social and emotional development are presented throughout the chapter.

7

Physical Development

---

1. What is the role of reflexes in the motor development of infants?
2. What are the major features of motor development during the first five years of life?
3. What are the major characteristics of children with cerebral palsy and muscular dystrophy?
4. What are some other physical impairments that may be found in young children?

OF THE MAIN AREAS of development—physical, cognitive, social, and language—physical development is the least influenced by environmental factors. It progresses in more predictable stages than do the other areas, and so we tend to pay less attention to it in educational programs than we do the other developmental areas. Non-handicapped children generally attain the milestones of physical development with minimal assistance from teachers, parents, or specialists. This fact is probably more descriptive of educational programs in the United States than it is for some other countries that place greater emphasis on physical fitness and prowess. Our culture values cognitive and social skills more highly, and therefore gives these skills greater emphasis in school programs.

Physical development is nevertheless an important consideration for many disabled children. Goals for improving gross and fine motor functioning are often the primary focus of the disabled child's individualized education program (IEP). This would be true, for example, for a child with spina bifida or cerebral palsy. In addition, many children with multiple disabilities have educational goals established in all areas, with goals for motor functioning sharing equal importance with cognitive, social, or language goals. The special knowledge of the physical or occupational therapist is often sought for designing strategies to promote motor development.

In this chapter we discuss normal development, including the difference between gross and fine motor. Next we look at normal neurophysiological development in order to gain an understanding of the neuromotor functions underlying motor development. We pay special attention to the nervous system and its importance in achieving adequate motor functioning. We then briefly discuss early reflexes and their role in early motor development and examine early sensory development. Next, we review the normal developmental milestones in gross and fine motor from birth to age 5. The rest of the chapter is then devoted to a review of problems in physical development that may be encountered in young children with handicaps.

MOTOR DEVELOPMENT

Gross motor development refers to the development of the large muscle groups of the arms and legs; *fine motor development* involves the small muscles of the hands. Because motor development is a *proximodistal* process, with growth occurring from the trunk to the extremities, children gain control of the large arm and leg muscles before they achieve good coordination of the hands and fingers. Motor development is also *cephalocaudal,* progressing from head downward, which explains why infants achieve head control and the ability to sit before they can walk.

These facts reveal that motor development is primarily a maturational process. According to Zaichkowsky, Zaichkowsky, and Martinek (1980), motor development is the product of growth, maturation, heredity, and learning. Growth refers to increases in size, while maturation refers to increases in complexity, organization, or control. Although motor development is probably less affected by environmental factors than is intellectual or language development, and, as previously noted, is strongly influenced by maturational factors, such aspects of the environment as nutrition, physical activity, and illness can cause differences in the rate and quality of motor development. Perhaps it would be most accurate to state that given an adequate environment, physical development is primarily a maturational process.

Neurophysiological Processes

Motor functioning depends on bones, muscles, and nerves working together. The bones of the body originate as soft cartilage tissue and then ossify, or harden. The ossification process begins during the prenatal period and continues through late adolescence. Girls generally have a more fully developed skeleton at birth than do boys (Zaichkowsky, Zaichkowsky, & Martinek, 1980), a difference that increases with age. Girls appear to be more stable in skeletal development than boys, that is, the rate of bone ossification is less variable in girls than in boys.

The level of motor functioning depends to a great extent on the tone, control, and strength of a child's muscles (Johnston & Magrab, 1976). The ability to flex or extend a muscle smoothly depends partly on the tone of the muscle. For muscles to perform smoothly, muscle tone must be neither too high (hypertonicity) nor too low (hypotonicity). Hypertonic muscles are tense, rigid, and resistant to movement. Hypotonic muscles lack tone, appear limp and weak, and do not provide adequate support. Both hypertonicity and hypotonicity are seen in cerebral palsied children.

Muscle control is centered in several areas of the brain. Voluntary motor activity is controlled by upper brain centers located in the cerebral cortex. Involuntary, or unconscious, muscle movement (e.g., digestion of food, eye blinking, reflex movements) is controlled by lower brain centers, that is, the cerebellum and parts of the brain stem (see Figure 4.5).

Although muscle strength is related to muscle size, it depends more on coordination of muscles, or how well muscles work together in a group. This in turn is determined by the quality of the signals that the muscles receive from the brain. Proper stimulation is necessary for a muscle to work effectively, no matter how large it is.

Muscles are attached to bones at the joints and work in pairs. If you bend your arm at the elbow, for example, the muscles in your inner arm flex and the muscles along your outer arm extend. This complementary process of flexion and extension is the basis for all muscle movement. A newborn baby is normally in a state of flexion, with arms, legs, and head drawn in toward the body. As the infant grows, muscles learn to extend for reaching and bending, and then to alternate flexion and extension for crawling, walking, and running.

Muscles and bones work only when they are connected to the central nervous system by means of nerves. In fact, the nervous system is basic to all physical activity; nearly all problems in motor functioning in young children involve some dysfunction of the nervous system.

The brain controls all bodily activity through the nerves of the peripheral nervous system, that is, the spinal cord and the networks of nerves that reach to every part of the body. Muscle activity depends on electrical impulses that originate in the brain and travel from the spinal cord through peripheral nerves to specific muscle groups (Johnston & Magrab, 1976). Muscle control is the result of electrical impulses traveling back and forth between the brain and the muscles. When the brain or some part of the peripheral nervous system is damaged, the messages are incomplete and poor muscle tone, control, or strength result. Cerebral palsy, for example, results from damage in the motor area of the brain rather than in the muscles of the arms and legs, where the dysfunction is most apparent. Spina bifida is caused by a damaged spinal cord and results in the inability to use the lower parts of the body.

Changes in muscle tone cause movement (see Figure 7.1). These changes, from a relaxed to a tight muscle, are dictated by the nervous system stimulating or inhibiting the muscle through neural impulses. The former cause the muscle to contract and the latter cause it to relax.

Figure 7.1 shows how this works, with muscles working in pairs. In the top diagram (a) the arm is at rest, with both flexor (F) and extensor (E) muscles in a neutral position. To bend the arm at the elbow (b), the muscle located along the upper side of the arm (the flexor) must contract (F), and the muscle along the lower side of the arm (the extensor) must stretch (E). To straighten the arm in full extension (c), the flexor muscle must extend or stretch out (F), and the extensor must contract (E).

It is thus apparent that muscle tone, control, and strength depend on a well-functioning brain and peripheral nervous system. For a more complete and highly readable description of the muscular, skeletal, and neuromotor systems, the reader is referred to Johnston and Magrab (1976).

Perceptual-Motor Function

Consider for a moment a young child's everyday motor activity. The muscles move to reach, grasp, run, stoop, or stretch in response to a stimulus of some sort: a desired toy, the teacher's voice calling to come eat lunch, Daddy appearing in the doorway. Motor responses are closely tied to the sensory stimulation that triggers them. These stimuli are received by the brain, which coordinates the sensory information it receives and the appropriate motor responses. Motor development, therefore, is one part of sensorimotor activity.

For optimal motor functioning to occur, the sensory systems that supply information

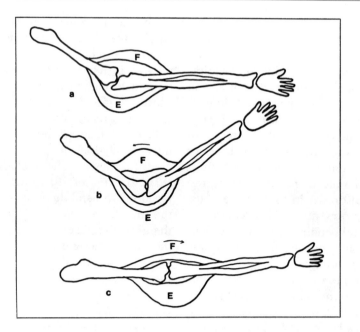

Figure 7.1.	Musculoskeletal interaction. From Johnson, R., and Magrab, P. (1976). *Developmental disorders: Assessment, treatment, education.* Austin, TX: PRO-ED. Copyright 1976. Reprinted by permission.

to the brain must be well functioning. Ayres (1972) has identified six sensory systems: visual, auditory, tactile, vestibular (balance), proprioceptive (movement), and olfactory (smell). While all six provide the brain with environmental information, the vestibular and tactile systems are of particular interest to teachers and specialists working with motor-impaired children.

The vestibular system controls balance and is centered in the inner ear. Other lower brain functions are influenced by vestibular input. Reduced input can be dangerous to a child, causing decreased respiration and heart rate, nausea, or perspiration (Lerner, Mardell-Czudnowski, & Goldenberg, 1981).

Touch is important to infants as a communication system. A major reason for delayed development in institutional babies is infrequent handling. Babies seem to respond best to a quiet, soothing touch administered with

firm, steady pressure, as in swaddling, the age-old remedy for a fussing baby. The young infant's crying is often triggered by the Moro reflex. A sudden change in position will cause the baby's head to go back and the baby will start to cry. Crying in turn causes the baby to throw its head back, triggering a second Moro response, followed by more crying. In this way a circle of behaviors is established unless the Moro reflex is inhibited by touching the baby. Firm, steady restraint soothes the infant by interfering with the circle of responses (Brazelton, 1969).

Tactile stimulation is thus basic to a child's early development, creating a sense of comfort and well-being or discomfort, aversion, or fear. The tactile system, like the vestibular, functions prenatally. Much of the intervention for children with problems in motor development is concerned with proper tactile stimulation. Many children with multiple handicaps who function at retarded levels have an aversion to being touched or touching other people and objects. Occupational therapists must spend a good deal of time helping such children adapt to tactile stimulation in order to promote normal sensorimotor integration.

Early Motor Development

Early motor activity is primarily involuntary and is expressed through primitive reflexes. Like sensory receptors, several reflexes are present in the fetus and continue after birth. Others appear at or soon after birth and prepare the infant for later, more complex movement.

Early research concluded that early primitive reflexes were centered primarily in the lower parts of the brain, gradually became integrated into more complex mechanisms as the brain developed and higher centers took control of movement. Reflex development was seen as a hierarchy beginning with the earlier developed spinal cord and brain stem, and gradually including the midbrain and cerebral cortex as the fetus and neonate developed (Ayres, 1972; Fiorentino, 1972). If damage to the cerebral cortex occurred in the adult, it was thought, these primitive reflexes again took control of movement.

Recent research has refuted both the idea that reflex development is hierarchical and the belief that abnormal motor performance in an adult or older child is similar to the motor performance of a healthy infant. Studies of the neurological functioning of healthy infants, for example, have provided evidence of the qualitatively different organization of the young nervous system from that of the adult (Willis & Widerstrom, 1986). Prechtl (1981) pointed out that, contrary to earlier views of the infant as dominated by involuntary, rigid motor patterns, the infant's behavior is complex, variable, and graceful. He concludes, "At the onset of extrauterine life the neural mechanisms for vital functions such as breathing, rooting, sucking, and swallowing, crying, spatial orientation, sleeping, and waking are fully developed as very complex control systems and not as simple reflexes" (p. 198).

Based on systems analysis of the brain, Prechtl rejected as imprecise the view that early or primitive reflexes come under increasingly voluntary control as the infant nervous system develops. There are important implications of this new understanding of reflex development for the intervention programs designed for preschool children with motor delays. Most programs currently offered are based on the sensory integration model developed by Ayres (1972). This model, based on the hierarchical theory of reflex development, may not be as appropriate as was once believed.

In addition to primitive reflexes, human beings rely on a system of automatic reflexes. These are not present at birth, but develop during the first two years of life. They remain an important part of the involuntary and largely unconscious nervous system that monitors daily functioning. An example is the reflexive thrusting out of arms to protect one from a fall when one trips. These reflexes, too, are located in the lower brain.

All reflexes are elicited by a stimulus of some sort. When the proper stimulus is present, the reflex is triggered independent of any conscious decision by the child. Because of this fact and because the primitive reflexes normally are integrated at about 6 months of age, these reflexes are used as the basis for diagnosing neurological dysfunction in infants.

Primitive Reflexes In the normally developing fetus and neonate, early reflexes follow an orderly sequence of development. Early work conducted with human embryos and fetuses from artificially terminated pregnancies have demonstrated that the human infant is capable of movement as early as the fifth week of pregnancy. The fetus first responds to tactile stimulation during the eighth week, and the mother can usually feel fetal movements by the twelfth week. Prenatal primitive reflexes include *swallowing, sucking, crying,* and the *positive support reflex* (Willis & Widerstrom, 1986).

The *Moro reflex* is present before and at birth. In a normal infant, it disappears at approximately 3 to 5 months of age. Its absence at birth or its presence beyond 5 months is indicative of neurological dysfunction.

The Moro reflex is elicited by striking the surface on which the baby is lying or by shaking its head rapidly. The baby first extends its arms in an embracing position, then returns its arms and legs to a flexed position close to the body. Unlike the startle response, the Moro reflex is not an auditory reflex. It has two stages, extension followed by flexion, whereas the startle response is simply a flexion movement. The Moro reflex can interfere with normal motor functioning if it does not disappear on schedule, since the protective extensor reaction that normally replaces the reflex at about 6 months of age is suppressed if the Moro reflex is too strong. When this happens, the baby's arms extend to either side, rather than downward, a movement that is not useful in preventing a fall. In addition, a sudden change of position continues to elicit the response, upsetting balance and interfering with voluntary movement.

The *asymmetrical tonic neck reflex (ATNR)* is evident when the infant's head is turned to one side. If the infant's head is turned, the stretch of the neck muscles causes an extension of the arm and leg on the side of the body toward which the head is facing. The opposite arm and leg remain in a flexed position.

This reflex is seen in nearly all premature infants and in about half of all normal infants during the first week of life (Willis & Widerstrom, 1986). It normally disappears by the fifth month, although it may last until the ninth month during sleep. Maintenance of this reflex beyond the normal limit interferes with voluntary reaching and self-feeding. The teaching of feeding skills to severely retarded or cerebral palsied children can be frustrating if the ATNR is not sufficiently suppressed to allow voluntary bringing of the hand to the mouth. When it is not suppressed, the ATNR also prevents the learning of many important gross motor movements, such as turning from back to stomach, crossing the midline, and crawling on hands and knees. However, in the very young infant, this reflex encourages extension of the arms to prepare for reaching and grasping.

The *Landau reflex* does not appear at birth, but is usually present by 6 months of age and lasts until the second year of life. In a prone (on stomach) position, the infant extends its arms and legs when the head is raised, and flexes these limbs when the head is lowered. This reflex encourages the extension of hips and legs that is necessary for crawling and standing.

The *crossed extension reflex* is present at birth and normally disappears at 3 to 4 months of age. When stimulated on the sole of the foot, the infant extends that leg; the opposite leg remains in flexion. This reflex interferes with crawling if it is not suppressed at the proper time, since the baby cannot make reciprocal movements, extending one leg after the other.

The *positive supporting reflex* is present at birth and lasts until 6 to 8 weeks of age. It then reappears as early as 3 months of age and finally is suppressed at about 10 months in normal babies. The reflex is elicited by touching the soles of the feet on a hard surface, causing extensor tone in the hips and knees so that the legs straighten and support the body's weight. The child has the tendency to stand on the toes, bringing the legs together. While this reflex encourages extension patterns in the young infant to prepare for standing, it interferes with learning to walk if it continues after 10 months of age, for reciprocal movement of the legs is blocked. Balance and coordinated bending of the knee and ankle joints are also inhibited by the increased tone in the leg muscles.

By 6 months of age a normal infant has broken the early patterns of total extension or flexion as seen in the Moro or Landau reflexes and has learned to extend some muscles while flexing others. For example, a baby this age will be able to extend head and trunk muscles while flexing the hips, a necessary combination for sitting.

Automatic Reflexes   Three major categories of reflexes are not present at birth but develop during the first 2 years of life. These reflexes maintain the child in an upright position (righting reactions), maintain equilibrium (equilibrium reactions), and protect the child during a fall (protective reactions). We briefly examine two examples of these reflexes.

The *labyrinthine righting of the head* is an important reflex for the promotion of head control. Seldom present at birth, it is first seen at about 2 months, and is a strong influence on the child at 6 to 8 months, when sitting and crawling are first learned. The reflex is evident when the child is tipped downward, to one side, or backward. The tendency is for the head to maintain an upright position. This reflex does not disappear but continues to offer protection throughout life by maintaining the head in an upright position.

The *protective extensor reaction* (parachute) emerges at about 6 months and replaces the Moro reflex. Whereas the Moro reflex causes the child to throw his or her arms out to the sides—a useless movement for protecting the head during a fall—the parachute reaction causes the arms to extend above the head so that the hands, not the head, bear the brunt of the fall. This is an excellent example of an automatic reflex taking over or suppressing a primitive one as the child's needs change, for while the Moro reflex is useful to the very young child in developing extensor muscles, the parachute reaction better meets the needs of the older, more active infant, who needs protection from falls.

It is thus apparent that the primitive reflexes serve useful purposes in the very young infant, but that their maintenance beyond the first year of life interferes with higher development. This is not true of the automatic reflexes, which emerge as the baby begins to crawl, stand, and walk, for they complement rather than inhibit voluntary movement.

In children with motor delays, these automatic responses do not develop at the normal rate and so are not available to the child for facilitating motor development.

Early Sensory Development

Prenatal Sensory Function   Research studies have demonstrated that, in contrast to motor development, human sensory development is so rapid that all sensory systems are capable of functioning at birth. In the fetus, the *tactile* system is the first to develop. Sensation is first noted in the oral region, spreading over the facial region and then over the entire body.

Next to develop are the *proprioceptive* and *vestibular* systems, which account for movement and balance. Proprioceptive receptors are located throughout the body, buried deep in muscle tissue. They are responsible for early fetal movements associated with breathing, sucking, and locomotion (Willis & Widerstrom, 1986). Vestibular neurons form a large complex in the brain stem and are connected to the semicircular canals located in the inner ear by means of the auditory nerve. They are responsible for balance.

The senses of *taste, smell, hearing,* and *vision* develop in that order. Studies of preterm infants have determined that all of these systems are capable of functioning prenatally, but that the visual and auditory systems are not well formed until well after the first postnatal year (Aslin, Pisoni, & Jusczyk, 1983).

Sensory Function in Infancy and Early Childhood Young children do not develop full auditory functioning until they are about 12-months-old, when they are able to hear lower frequency sounds as well as less intense noises (Aslin et al., 1983).

Since the visual system develops late in pregnancy (during the ninth month), it is not surprising that the young infant does not see as well as the older child. In fact, it is not until age 4 that most children have visual acuity comparable to that of an adult. As discussed in Chapter 4, visual recognition memory also develops more slowly than other sensory processes.

Autonomic Responses The nervous system coordinates the interplay of numerous physiological systems that are necessary to the child's optimum physical functioning. Two of these systems—the *sympathetic* and the *parasympathetic* nervous systems—are important in understanding the behavior of many children with physical disabilities and are worth some discussion here. The sympathetic system, which is responsible for arousal (e.g., fight or flight during danger, crying during hunger), develops prenatally as part of the developing infant's survival repertoire.

The parasympathetic system is responsible for the inhibition of responses, and grad-ually develops during the first two years of life. This maturation results in the infant's growing ability to inhibit its behavior. By measuring this inhibitory capacity, an indirect measure of central nervous system maturation is obtained (Willis & Widerstrom, 1986). At-risk infants have been identified by their less controlled parasympathetic functions (Brazelton, 1973), which results in their greater difficulties in calming themselves.

DEVELOPMENTAL MILESTONES

The First Year (0–12 months)

In nonhandicapped infants, the first year of life is a period of tremendous growth and development. Although rapid progress is apparent in nonmotor developmental areas, as demonstrated by recent research in cognitive development, for example, motor growth from birth to 12 months is the most striking area of change. During the first 12 months, infants develop the ability to hold their heads up, walk without support, arise from a back-lying position to standing without assistance, and stack one block atop another with precision.

What specific events take place during the first year of motor development? Cratty's (1986) summary chart of motor behaviors is useful for outlining these events (see Table 7.1).

During the first 4 months or so, infants concentrate on development of head control: raising, turning, and maintaining an upright position. The Landau and Moro reflexes and the emerging righting reactions promote the extension of arm and neck muscles to aid in this process. At the same time, babies begin to use their forearms to help lift their heads while in a prone position. Arms and legs extend, at first unilaterally and by 6

Table 7.1. Milestones in motor development during the first year of life

Approximate time behavior occurs	Behavior
Gestation	Moro reflex appears
	Fetal activity prior to birth indicative of later motor competency and vigor
Birth	Birth reflexes, including Moro, startle, palmar grasp, rooting, sucking, crawling reflex, and so on, appear
	Novel stimuli sought, variable activity levels evidenced
	Walking reflex appears
1 month	Arm-supporting reflex appears
2 months	Labyrinthine righting reflex appears
	Separate perceptual-motor and cognitive traits identifiable
3 months	Pull-up reactions in the arm (reflex) appear
	Walking reflex disappears
	Infant can turn over from back to stomach
6 months	Moro reflex disappears
	Voluntary creeping appears
	Swimming reflex disappears
	Voluntary crawling appears
	Crawling reflex disappears
9 months	Supporting reflex in the legs seen
	Palmar and plantar grasp reflexes disappear
	Righting reflexes of the head and body disappear
12 months	Supported walking appears
	Infant can move from lying on back to standing; independent locomotion

Adapted from Cratty, B.J. (1986). *Perceptual and motor development in infants and children* (3rd ed., p. 132). Englewood Cliffs, NJ: Prentice-Hall. Copyright 1986. Reprinted by permission.

months bilaterally, that is, with both arms and both legs extending at the same time.

During the next 2 months, infants learn to reach for objects, bring objects to their mouths, bring their hands together, and bring their feet to their mouths. By 6 months they can roll over from back to stomach and crawl forward and backward on their abdomens. They can sit up with minimal support, putting them in a better position to examine objects that they find. They do this by grasping the objects radially and then shaking or mouthing them. The radial grasp uses primarily the thumb, index, and second fingers, an improvement over the earlier palmar

grasp, in which the object is grasped by the middle fingers and palm of the hand (Wickstrom, 1983).

From 8 to 12 months, babies continue to gain increased control over movements. Arms and legs move independently (one at a time) or reciprocally, as in crawling. Older babies can rotate their trunks, moving from a supine (lying on back) position to sitting upright, and can then pull themselves to a standing position without assistance. They can often walk with support (cruising). In hand movement, they have developed the pincer grasp as well as the ability voluntarily to release an object they pick up. This important new skill allows babies to stack one block atop another by the time they are about 1-year-old. The ability to release with precision develops rather slowly, so that one year later, at age 2, children can stack only six or seven blocks.

The Second Year (12–24 months)

Walking and its various refinements represent the major gross motor accomplishments of 2-year-olds. Walking forward without support is generally accomplished by 18 months. The second half of the year is devoted to walking up and down stairs with assistance, one step at a time; standing up from a sitting position; and rolling over. Fine motor development progresses to the greater control needed for such activities as throwing a ball overhand (using both hands), pouring objects from a container, or finger feeding.

The Third Year (24–36 months)

By 3, children have learned to walk up and down stairs, although they still cannot alternate their feet and still need to hold on some of the time (Bayley, 1935). Three-year olds can pedal a tricycle, run, jump holding on, and hop on one foot. Walking, they swing their arms alternately with their feet. They are learning to master buttons, zippers, and buckles, and can generally dress themselves independently. They have begun to use tools such as pencils, paste applicators, and scissors. They can string beads, place puzzle pieces, and do other similar preschool tasks with ease and apparent pleasure. They can throw a ball 4 to 5 feet. They can build a tower of 10 cubes and copy a circle (Gesell, 1949).

The Fourth Year (36–48 months)

During the fourth year, children refine those skills learned at 2, including running, jumping, and hopping. They improve in balance and coordination so that they can walk a balance beam, jump down from a step, hop from foot to foot, and walk downstairs using alternate feet.

It is interesting to note that in learning to use stairs children follow a predetermined sequence based on increasing demands for balance and coordination. Just as a young puppy who crawls upstairs is unable to descend, very young children can creep upstairs before they learn to creep down because less balance and coordination are required to perform the former. At each level of difficulty—walking with support, walking without support, and alternating feet—children master the skill while ascending before they demonstrate it while descending.

In fine motor coordination children just under 4 refine the eye-hand coordination skills mentioned above, such as ball throwing, buttoning, drawing, and so on. They are not ready to catch a ball or tie their shoes with much success.

The Fifth Year (48–60 months)

During this final year before kindergarten children learn to skip (this task has been used as an indicator of readiness for kindergarten), to improve ball skills, and to improve their balance, coordination, and strength, a process that continues throughout the childhood years and into early adulthood. By age 5 most children can dance to music, climb ladders and trees, and walk backward, and are learning to jump rope and even to roller skate (Wickstrom, 1983).

In terms of fine motor skills, children can draw simple houses, print the capital initials of their names; copy circles, squares, and crosses (Gesell, 1940); dress and undress; lace their shoes; do their own buttons; and cut with a knife (Sanford, 1974).

In summary, although there is wide variation in individual motor accomplishments, the average child entering kindergarten is very competent in physical activities and able to perform most motor acts independently. Table 7.2 summarizes this progress.

DISORDERS OF MOTOR DEVELOPMENT

In order to function optimally, the entire motor system must be intact. Problems occur when any part—bones, muscles, joints, or nerves —malfunctions. Motor delays may be the primary developmental problem in certain conditions, such as cerebral palsy, or they may be one problem among several, as in severe mental retardation, where serious delays in cognition and language are of equal concern.

Motor Disorders Due to Brain Damage

Cerebral Palsy The most commonly occurring condition resulting from brain damage is cerebral palsy. According to Johnston and Magrab (1976), one prominent dysfunctioning element usually affects the cerebral palsied child more than others,

Table 7.2. Gross motor attributes in early childhood

Approximate time of appearance	Behavior
1 year	Walking unaided
	A rapid, running-like walk
	Ability to step off low objects
2 years	Walking rhythm becomes even
	Crude jumping with 2-foot take-off
	Ability to throw small ball 4–5 feet
	True running
	Ability to walk sideward and backward
3 years	Ability to walk a 10-foot long line, heel to toe
	Ability to hop from two to three steps, on preferred foot
	Ability to walk balance beam for short distances
	Ability to throw a ball about 10 feet
4 years	Running with good form; leg-arm coordination apparent; ability to walk a line around periphery of a circle
	Skillful jumping
	Ability to walk balance beam
5 years	Ability to broad-jump from 2 to 3 feet
	Ability to hop 50 feet in about 11 seconds
	Ability to balance on one foot for 4–6 seconds
	Ability to catch large playground ball bounced to him

Adapted from Cratty, B.J. (1986). *Perceptual and motor development in infants and children* (3d ed., p. 132). Englewood Cliffs, NJ: Prentice-Hall. Copyright 1986 by Prentice-Hall, Inc. Reprinted by permission.

and this element gives its name to the type of cerebral palsy from which the child suffers. The elements that may be dysfunctioning are tone and control, and these, in turn, affect muscle strength. When the primary deficit is too much muscle tone, the child is labeled *rigid* or *spastic;* if there is too little tone, the label is *atonic* or *hypotonic.* Defects in control are labeled *choreoathetoid, tremor,* or, when poor balance results, *ataxic.* Defects in strength are labeled *paresis* (weakness) or *plegia* (paralysis). Several prefixes are used with the term *plegia* to describe the parts of the body that are paralyzed. *Paraplegia,* for example, refers to paralysis of the legs; *quadriplegia* refers to paralysis of both arms and legs; and *hemiplegia* refers to paralysis of one side of the body.

As noted earlier, hypertonicity results in either spasticity or rigidity. A spastic muscle is initially very resistant to movement, but then quickly collapses; a rigid muscle maintains a strong resistance to change of position throughout the movement.

Problems with control of movement usually manifest themselves as involuntary movement disorders. When any of the major cortical motor areas of the brain are damaged, there is a lack of inhibition of involuntary movements originating in the lower brain. This causes the child to become dominated by movements over which he or she has no control. *Chorea* involves rapid, jerky movements of the arms and legs; *athetosis* involves slower, more writhing movements of the hands, feet, or face (Johnston & Magrab, 1976). *Choreoathetosis* describes the condition in which both types of movement are present.

Problems with balance characterize the child with ataxic cerebral palsy. Such a child has difficulty with all gross motor tasks, including walking. Fine motor tasks are more readily mastered, unless there are serious problems with muscle tone.

Cerebral palsy is caused by injury to the brain before, during, or after birth. According to Hart (1979) conditions that may cause a brain lesion include the following:

1. Anoxia (lack of oxygen) during prenatal development or birth
2. Birth trauma
3. Heavy use of alcohol by the mother during pregnancy
4. Hyperbilirubinemia, a condition involving excessive destruction of red blood cells or an interference with bile excretion
5. Chromosomal abnormalities
6. Rh blood incompatibilities
7. Complications of twin pregnancy delivery
8. Prenatal conditions, such as rubella
9. Complications of the placenta
10. Thyroid disease
11. Kidney infection or diabetes in the mother

Because cerebral palsy is caused by a nonprogressive brain lesion, the motor performance of an affected child does not deteriorate, and the child is often able to improve his or her condition through physical or occupational therapy.

It is now the practice to begin working with cerebral palsied babies from birth, since methods for diagnosing the condition at birth are now available. The therapist works to encourage voluntary movement, to minimize the effect of involuntary reflexes, and to encourage spastic or rigid muscles to work smoothly.

Children who are born prematurely are at the greatest risk for cerebral palsy because they have less resistance to problems that may occur during and after birth. Prematurity may also be an indication of problems that occurred prenatally. The incidence of cerebral palsy is directly related to low birth weight, a condition usually accompanying prematurity. About 15% of infants who weigh between 1,000 and 1,500 grams at birth have damaged nervous systems; for those weighing less than 1,000 grams the rate is 33%. The more premature the child, the greater the risk of cerebral palsy. Improved care of premature newborns during the past 20 years has caused the incidence of cerebral palsy to decline by about one-half (Hart, 1979).

About one-third of children with cerebral palsy are mentally retarded, and a substantial number have seizure disorders, hearing and vision problems, and language problems. These problems vary with the severity of the cerebral palsy. About 35% of severely impaired cerebral palsied children die by age 5. The life expectancy for those who live past age 5 is 40 to 45 years.

Treatment   Since the brain lesion responsible for cerebral palsy is not progressive, the child can improve with treatment. This consists of physical therapy to increase voluntary, normal movement while at the same time suppressing involuntary, reflex-based movement.

In recent years, children with cerebral palsy have commonly been treated with *neurodevelopmental treatment* (NDT), first developed by Karl and Berta Bobath (1975) in Britain and now widely practiced in the United States as well. The basic principle of NDT is that the child is an active participant in the therapy, with the therapist following the child's lead. This is in contrast to other therapy methods, which place the child in a passive role and the therapist in a dominant one. The emphasis is on facilitating the child's normal, natural movement so that he or she can experience what it feels like to move normally. The child is then more highly motivated to practice normal movement patterns.

Handling   An important part of the daily treatment of children with cerebral palsy involves proper handling. Caretakers must be taught how to promote normal movement and inhibit abnormal reactions, and how to position the child for sitting or lying down so that he or she is comfortable, but does not develop abnormal patterns.

When observing the motor development of children with cerebral palsy, it is obvious that head control is delayed. Moreover, the abnormal reaction patterns that dominate their movement are centered in the head, neck, and spine. It follows, therefore, that a basic principle of positioning and handling these children is to control the abnormal patterns from key points, consisting of the head, shoulders, and hips. These and other handling principles are more thoroughly described in Finnie (1975).

Muscular Dystrophy   Muscular dystrophy is another condition of early childhood resulting from brain lesion. Unlike cerebral palsy, muscular dystrophy involves a progressive lesion, so that the child's condition deteriorates over time, often resulting in death before the teen years. The cause of muscular dystrophy is unknown, but the disease is thought to be an inherited recessive metabolic disorder. It affects three times as many males as females.

The most common form of the disease is *Duchenne juvenile muscular dystrophy*, which is usually diagnosed at the time the child would normally begin to walk, about the second year. The disease gradually destroys the voluntary muscles of the body, replacing them with fat cells and fibrous tissue.

Children with Duchenne muscular dystrophy may exhibit a swelling in the calf area, as fat cells replace muscle cells, and they may display some or all of the following characteristics:

1.   Running with an awkward, flat-footed gait
2.   Tiptoeing, as a result of muscle weakness

3. Walking with a sway back (lordosis), as a result of weakness in the abdominal wall
4. Difficulty getting up from a lying or sitting position on the floor (Cratty, 1986)

As the disease progresses, the child loses the ability to walk, appears to gain weight, and becomes increasingly weak and immobilized. Confinement to bed is eventually necessary, and death usually follows an attack of infection.

There is currently no cure for muscular dystrophy. Treatment consists of postural drainage, physical therapy for contracted muscles, and the administration of antibiotics to combat infection. The services of a specialist in motor development and physical therapy are necessary for effective treatment. Often this professional can improve the child's functioning and thus lengthen the time the child can remain in the classroom.

Motor Disorders
Due to Other Causes

Bone Disorders   *Osteogenesis imperfecta* is a congenital condition involving bones that break easily causing abnormal skeletal development and sometimes shortened height. Deafness may also result from this condition.

Osteomyelitis is an infection of the bones that causes crippling. Treatment with antibiotics and sometimes surgery have proved successful in reducing the incidence of this condition.

Hip dysplasia is a congenital condition involving dislocation of the hip. It can be diagnosed soon after birth. It is more commonly found in girls than boys. Treatment may involve braces or surgery; if untreated, the child is unable to walk normally. Early treatment is usually very successful.

Spinal Cord Disorders   *Scoliosis* is a malformation of the spine involving lateral curvature. It is treated orthopedically so that children with the condition do not require special educational programming.

Spina bifida is a congenital condition that develops prenatally while the spinal cord is being formed. A normal spinal column consists of the spinal cord and its protective covering, the *meninges*, completely surrounded by bone. In infants with spina bifida, there is an opening in the bones of the lower spinal column, exposing the spinal cord and meninges. Sometimes part of the meninges will protrude through the opening and form a sac on the child's back. This sac, known as a *meningocele*, is filled with cerebrospinal fluid and covered with skin, so that it appears as a bulge on the child's back. A more serious form of spina bifida, *myelomeningocele*, occurs when a portion of the spinal cord itself protrudes through the opening and is not completely covered with skin, thus exposing the child to loss of cerebrospinal fluid, as well as to bacterial infection.

If there is no protrusion, treatment is usually not required. For myelomeningocele, surgery is required, and is usually performed a few hours after birth. Since the condition can be identified prenatally through amniocentesis (Hart, 1979), treatment can begin very early. The surgery consists of replacing the protruding cord and membrane within the spinal column. Some damage to nerves usually remains, however, so the child usually has problems with walking, bladder and bowel control, sitting, and standing. Because spina bifida only affects the lower part of the body, children with the condition are of normal intelligence, although some children with spina bifida have language delays and require the assistance of a speech and language therapist (Anastasiow, 1986).

Educational programming for children with spina bifida is usually limited to a physical therapy regimen to improve muscle tone in lower extremities and to learn to use artificial ambulatory aids, such as wheel-chairs, braces, or canes. If their physical problems can be managed, children with spina bifida generally perform very well in regular classrooms.

Hydrocephalus is a condition encountered in spina bifida children that results from an accumulation in the brain of cerebrospinal fluid, the fluid normally found circulating through the brain and spinal cord. The fluid is prevented from normal circulation by the meningocele. A buildup of fluid in the brain causes swelling and enlarging of the head that may result in damage to the brain and the optic and auditory nerves.

Formerly, many children with spina bifida were mentally retarded because of brain damage caused by hydrocephalus. New surgical techniques, performed at birth or soon thereafter, now make it possible to prevent the accumulation of fluid and the resulting damage to brain tissue. Through a surgical procedure, a shunt is inserted in the brain ventricles to drain the excess fluid from the skull to another part of the body, where it is eliminated with other body wastes. It was formerly necessary to replace these shunts frequently as the child increased in size; recent advances in technique have produced shunts that expand as the child grows.

Congenital Conditions   *Sickle cell anemia* is carried by a recessive gene and is found almost exclusively among black children. The disease causes the red blood cells to change shape (to look like sickles) and lose their ability to carry their normal supply of oxygen. When this oxygen deprivation occurs, the child is subject to extreme pain, dizziness, and weakness. Swelling of fingers and toes is noticeable. These bouts of severe pain, known as sickle cell crises, usually begin in children before the age of 2 and are common during the preschool years. They decrease in frequency as the child approaches adulthood.

Carriers of sickle cell anemia can be detected through laboratory tests. There is currently no cure for the disease, and treatment consists of blood transfusions, pain relievers, and bed rest.

Cystic fibrosis is a metabolic disorder that results in the lack of an enzyme necessary for production of saliva, sweat, and mucus. The result is production of a sticky mucus that interferes with normal digestive and respiratory processes. The disease is inherited through a recessive gene. Because infants can now be identified as suffering from cystic fibrosis earlier than previously, more children now survive the disease. However, most do not live beyond age 20, even with the more intensive care available in recent years. There is currently no cure for the disease.

Rheumatoid arthritis involves the deterioration of the linings of the body's joints, which causes painful swelling and deformity in hands, arms, or legs. The cause of childhood arthritis is unknown. Treatment focuses on relief from pain, infection, and swelling (Wyne & O'Connor, 1979).

Infections   *Meningitis* and *encephalitis* are the result of damage to the brain or spinal cord from infection. If the meninges is infected it is known as meningitis; if the brain itself is infected, the result is encephalitis. These conditions were once fatal, but are now controlled by antibiotics. Some children suffer brain damage that remains after the infection has been treated.

Seizure Disorders (Epilepsy)   The most commonly encountered seizure disorder (epilepsy) in young children is the *akinetic*, or *minor motor, seizure*. During an akinetic seizure, the child may fall forward or backward, resulting in head injuries unless the child wears a helmet for protection. Akinetic seizures may occur hundreds of times a day and are less responsive to drugs than are other types of epilepsy. Many infants and children with minor motor seizures must be institutionalized.

Psychomotor, petit mal, and *grand mal seizures* are rarely seen in children younger than 2. *Psychomotor seizures* may occur as early as age 2. They are manifested by high pulse rate, perspiration, salivation, repetitive motor behavior, and, sometimes, visual or auditory hallucinations. Momentary loss of consciousness may occur.

Petitt mal and *grand mal seizures* rarely occur before age 5. Petit mal seizures are most common between the ages of 5 and 18; grand mal seizures are most commonly found in adults. Both involve loss of consciousness and various other symptoms.

About 85% of seizure disorders are controllable by means of medication, so that the child or adult may lead a normal life (Hart, 1979). The remaining 15% are less responsive. Many young children with minor motor epilepsy fall into the latter group.

The causes of epilepsy are not well understood. Heredity appears to play a role in some cases, although 65% of those with seizures have no family history of epilepsy. Some seizure disorders are related to other disabling conditions, such as cerebral palsy; others are related to high fevers in infancy. These latter, known as febrile seizures, may lead to epilepsy if not treated. The administration of anticonvulsant drugs over a long period of time is effective in preventing febrile seizures (Carter, 1975).

VISUAL IMPAIRMENTS

The development of the visual system is presented in detail in various standard texts on disabled children (Peterson, 1987). The present discussion is thus limited to a brief overview.

Normal Visual Development

The eyes develop from outgrowths of the forebrain, differentiating prenatally into very specialized sensory organs that, in the non-handicapped, full-term infant, are almost fully developed at the time of birth. Because the eyes develop from the brain, their growth and development in early childhood parallel that of the brain, resulting in an enormous increase in size during the first three years of life (Buncic, 1980). By age 15, the child's eyes have tripled in size from birth, with three-fourths of this growth occurring in the first 3 years.

By 6 weeks of age, an infant's eyes are able to move in unison or symmetrically, whereas at birth they move somewhat independently. By 2 months, the infant can fixate and follow a bright light. Although the optic nerve is fully myelinated at term, it is not until 4 months that the eyes have anatomically reached a reasonable state for function, with full differentiation of the visual cortex and complete myelination of the rest of the neural optic system.

By 6 months the development of stereoscopic binocular (three-dimensional) vision has begun. The cerebral reflexes that control three-dimensional vision continue maturing until the child is about 8-years-old. Straightness of the eyes during the act of vision is maintained by the binocular reflex, which must be strong enough to prevent involuntary movement (nystagmus).

Research on infants' visual abilities has found infants to be more adept at visual discrimination and visual/motor coordination than was once thought to be the case (Willis & Widerstrom, 1986).

Definitions of Normal Visual Acuity

Visual acuity is defined in terms of the better performing eye and is measured with corrective glasses or lenses. According to the National Society for the Prevention of Blindness, a person with visual acuity of 20/70 or better in the better eye after correction is considered to be within the average range. The two legally recognized categories for visual impairment in the United States are blind and partially sighted. *Blindness* is defined as visual acuity for distance vision of 20/200 or less in the better eye after correction, or visual acuity of more than 20/200 if the widest diameter of field vision substends an angle no greater than 20 degrees. *Partially sighted* is defined as visual acuity greater than 20/200 but no greater than 20/70 in the better eye with correction (National Society for the Prevention of Blindness, 1966, p. 10). Partially seeing children have sufficient vision to allow vision to be used as the primary modality for their education.

Vision Testing

According to Buncic (1980), the clinical assessment of visual acuity in infants is indirect at best, consisting as it does of observation by the physician of constrictions of the baby's pupils to direct light and observation of whether the infant fixates on the light. Nevertheless, using such optokinetic techniques, researchers have been able to measure the visual acuity of infants soon after birth. Numerous researchers have determined that the neonate's visual acuity is poor in comparison to the adult's, but improves significantly during the first six months of life (Banks & Salapatek, 1983).

In older children, visual acuity is usually screened initially by means of the Snellen chart, which consists of rows of letters descending in size or, alternatively, rows of capital Es pointing in various directions. Standing at a distance of 20 feet, the child identifies the letters or their direction. A reading of 20/50 Snellen means that the child can see at 20 feet what a person with normal vision can see at 50 feet. Although Snellen charts are merely screening instruments, the Snellen method of indicating acuity (20/x) is widely used by those in-

volved in vision testing. For example, the research on infant vision referred to above reported acuity of 20/280 Snellen in a group of premature infants and of 20/670 Snellen in a group of babies less than 5-days-old. The average 2-month-old is thought to have visual acuity of about 20/200.

For testing near point and far point vision and for assessing other aspects of vision, such as muscle balance and fusion, more elaborate equipment is required. The Keystone Telebinocular or the Bausch and Lomb Orthorater are examples of instruments used for these purposes.

Disorders of Vision

Several conditions may cause visual problems for infants and preschool children. Symptoms may include redness, swelling, or watering of the eyes, extreme sensitivity to light, or squinting or frowning. Children suffering from such symptoms may be inattentive to visual stimuli, neglect to make eye contact, hold books and toys too close, or be unresponsive to interactions with adults or other children (Peterson, 1987).

Most infants and young children are mildly *hyperopic* (farsighted), a condition that worsens to about age 3 and then gradually improves after age 7. About 25% of infants are *myopic* (nearsighted); these infants' visual acuity must be monitored for possible fitting of glasses or contact lenses, which can be fitted in early childhood. The initial fitting of contact lenses is often done under general anesthesia, and parents must be prepared to cope with the stress of the child's adjustment period.

The other refractive error commonly seen in young children is *astigmatism*, which prevents the accurate focusing of the retinal image. Astigmatism may be either hyperopic or myopic.

Other conditions affecting infants and young children include amblyopia, strabismus, leukokoria, retrolental fibroplasia, glaucoma, and cataracts. *Amblyopia* may be defined as a reduction in visual acuity by at least two lines on the Snellen chart. It is commonly referred to as a lazy eye, because the amblyopia interferes with the eye's fusional reflexes, causing that eye to turn, or "cross," so that the child's eyes no longer focus together. The condition is usually corrected by patching the good eye, forcing the amblyopic eye into use.

Strabismus is caused by the imbalance of the eye muscles, and causes the eyes not to focus together. Forms of childhood strabismus include *pseudostrabismus*, an apparent crossing of the eyes in infancy that disappears with age, and *manifest strabismus*, a misalignment of the eyes that results in either *esotropia* (cross eye, or turning in of the eyes) or *exotropia* (wall eye, or turning out of the eyes). Exotropia, the most common type of childhood strabismus, should be identified by 6 months so that corrective lenses, or in some cases surgery, may be prescribed as early as possible. Sometimes strabismus is associated with conditions such as Down or Turner syndrome. In such cases, the eyes are often severely crossed, do not respond well to glasses, and require early surgery. Strabismus and amblyopia often occur together and one often causes the other.

Leukokoria refers to the presence of a white pupil in the child's eye. It can be caused by several factors, including cataracts and retrolental fibroplasia (see below), or it can indicate the presence of a malignant retinal tumor, known as *retinoblastoma.*

Retinoblastomas usually occur in only one eye. A small number of these tumors are genetic in origin. Treatment consists of removal of the tumor, followed by radiation or chemotherapy. With early detection, the prognosis for unilateral cases is good.

Retrolental fibroplasia, or retinopathy of prematurity, results in visual impairment caused by toxicity from the administration of oxygen to premature infants. The incidence of the condition has greatly decreased as hospital staff have learned carefully to monitor the amounts of oxygen administered to high-risk infants. Sometimes, however, the physician must choose between the baby's life and possible blindness. The physician then tries to administer the least amount of oxygen possible in the hope of preventing total blindness.

Like strabismus, *glaucoma* occurs in many forms in young children. The most serious is congenital, and causes blindness through overaccumulation of intraocular fluid, resulting in pressure on the eyeball. *Primary congenital glaucoma* responds well to treatment, in which the excess fluid is drained from the eye by means of a surgically created drainage channel. It is usually diagnosed early in infancy.

Other forms of glaucoma in childhood are found in association with such conditions as neurofibromatosis, juvenile rheumatoid arthritis, and retrolental fibroplasia.

A *cataract* is any opacity in the lens. It may or may not lower visual acuity, depending on its size and location. Several types of cataracts are hereditary, usually autosomal dominant. Cataracts may also be associated with other medical problems, such as maternal rubella, galactosemia, diabetes mellitus, and Down syndrome, and may be acquired through trauma to the lens resulting from radiation, inflammation, or long-term drug use.

Recent improvements in surgical techniques have made possible early removal of cataracts in children as young as 4- to 6-months-old. The infant is then fitted with contact lenses. Some physicians favor postponing cataract surgery until the child is older and visual disability requires it.

Effect on Cognitive and Language Development

Visual disorders rarely cause serious enough delays in cognitive or language development to warrant the child's isolation from the educational mainstream. Although infants blind from birth experience significant developmental delays (Fraiberg, 1975), children whose visual impairment occurs later in childhood generally experience only mild delays, if any. Both groups can profit from association with seeing children. The primary educational needs of blind and visually-impaired children are gross motor training in infancy (Adelson & Fraiberg, 1975) and orientation and mobility training in early childhood (Kirk & Gallagher, 1983). For a discussion of educational programming for the visually impaired, the reader is referred to the many excellent materials available from the American Foundation for the Blind, the National Society for the Prevention of Blindness, and National Aid to the Visually Handicapped.

SUMMARY

This chapter first reviews muscles, bones, and nerves, and the role they play in motor development. A review of typical sensorimotor development follows, with information presented on early motor development, including primitive and automatic reflexes, and early sensory development. The developmental milestones in early childhood are discussed, followed by information on problems and treatment of physical development that can occur in infants and young children, including cerebral palsy, spina bifida, and muscular dystrophy. Finally, a section on visual function and visual impairments is presented.

11

AN
ECOLOGICAL
PERSPECTIVE

Assessment

8

Screening and Assessment of Infants, Children, and Families

1. How are screening and assessment used in identifying young children with special needs?
2. Is it possible to develop tests that are not culturally biased?
3. What are the advantages of using standardized tests?
4. What are the advantages of using informal assessment methods?
5. What is the importance of reliability and validity?

INTEREST IN IDENTIFYING INFANTS and young children at risk for developmental delays has been growing over the last 15 years. Major impetuses for this trend were the Education for All Handicapped Children Act (PL 94-142) of 1975 and the 1986 amendments, PL 99-457, which provided for a diagnostic/prescriptive approach to service delivery for handicapped children from birth to age 21. The individualized education program (IEP) that law prescribed for each child with a handicap forced all professionals working with children with handicaps to become involved in some way in the diagnostic process.

An important part of PL 99-457 is the requirement that families of infants served un-

der the law must receive an *individualized family service plan* (IFSP) that includes a description of the functioning of both the child and the family, and a statement of the primary goals to be achieved by each. These must be based on accurate assessment data that delineate both strengths and needs related to enhancing the child's development.

As a result of these laws, and the state laws that complement them, demand has grown for diagnostic instruments appropriate for the birth to 5 population. In particular, professionals are seeking effective, nonintrusive methods for assessing families.

Identification of young children with handicaps begins with screening, followed, when appropriate, by more comprehensive assessment. The purpose of this chapter is to discuss screening and developmental assessment of children from birth to age 5 and their families, as well as certain issues related to these processes. Table 8.1 defines some of the basic terms used in this chapter. The reader is urged to become familiar with them before reading the rest of the chapter.

SCREENING

Screening involves examining the population at large to determine which individuals are most likely to manifest a particular condition. Screening is not a positive identification procedure, and further assessment is typically necessary to determine with any certainty that a problem indeed exists.

Infants and young children may be screened for developmental delays or abnormalities, for emotional problems, for hearing and vision difficulties, for learning problems, and for specific medical problems. Screening ranges from inexpensive procedures such as routine tests for phenylketonuria or pediatrician-administered developmental checklists to complex tissue examination of fetal development. Given the scope of current medical and developmental screening efforts, certain guidelines must be followed to ensure that procedures are appropriate and serve the needs of infants and young children and their families. These assumptions include the following:

1. Screening for a particular disorder should be done only if intervention is available to the child and family.
2. Screening should be only the first step to further diagnosis and treatment, if such steps prove necessary.
3. Intervention or treatment following screening should improve the condition of or outcome for the child.

4. The disorder being screened for should be relatively prevalent or, if not relatively prevalent, the consequences of not discovering and treating the rare problem should be severe.
5. The screening devices should be accurate, rapid to administer, cost effective, and acceptable to the population being screened and should require a minimum of professional time.
6. Early intervention should be superior to later intervention for the condition for which screening is being performed.

The need for systematic screening increases with the mildness of the disorder, regardless of age. The child with a severe handicap is more readily identifiable and more quickly receives services. The child with a mild but significant handicap is more likely to go undetected.

Prenatal and Perinatal Screening

The screening of children for potential problems begins before birth. Routine physical examinations during pregnancy check the growth of the developing fetus. Special procedures, such as sonography, ultrasound, fetal biopsy, and amniocentesis, are available to detect deficits in the fetus if difficulties are suspected. Twenty-seven or more neurological disorders involving severe mental retardation can now be identified and diagnosed during the fourth and fifth months of pregnancy (O'Brien, 1971). *Amniocentesis*, which has become quite common in the past decade, plays a major role in this identification process. In amniocentesis, a small amount of amniotic fluid is drawn out of the embryonic sac for biochemical analysis. The fluid contains fetal cells that can be analyzed to determine chromosomal or other genetic abnormalities. The procedure is usually performed during the four-

Table 8.1.   Glossary of screening and assessment terms

Screening: a large-scale, one-time procedure designed to determine the presence or absence of developmental problems. Screening is done to identify those infants or children considered at risk, that is, who will probably need special services to aid their normal development. Screening is usually quick and inexpensive.

Assessment: the process by which children are identified as handicapped and in need of special education services. Testing is not synonymous with assessment, for a test may yield only a score, whereas a good assessment will yield much information useful for educational programming. Assessment is not so much a process as part of a process; the other part is intervention, without which the assessment is useless.

Standardized tests: tests that include fixed administration and scoring procedures, empirical testing of items, standard apparatuses or format, and tables of norms. They most often yield a score or set of scores that may be used to compare a child's performance with those of others in his or her age group. Standardized tests may be either *norm referenced* or *criterion referenced.* Most tests are norm referenced.

Norm-referenced tests: tests that provide tables of scores describing the test performance of a reference group of children, usually from various parts of the country and from different socioeconomic backgrounds, against which a particular child's score may be compared. The tabled scores are usually expressed as grade- or age-equivalents, standard scores, or percentile equivalents.

Criterion-referenced tests: tests that consist of series of skills in academic or developmental areas, grouped by age level. They compare the child's performance on each test item against a standard or criterion that must be met if the child is to receive credit for that item. The child is measured against the criterion rather than against norms established by other children's performance. Often informal teacher assessmennts are based on criterion-referenced techniques. Some standardized tests, nonetheless, are criterion referenced.

Ordinal scales: scales that contain items arranged in the order in which they emerge developmentally. Many standardized tests use a cluster of items at each level that are typical of development at that level and that are arranged in order of increasing difficulty. However, within each age level, the items simply represent development at that level and do not emerge sequentially as items in ordinal scales do. For example, on the Uzgiris-Hunt ordinal scales a baby must have mastered reaching before grasping, whereas on the Binet standardized scale a child may pass some items at the 4-year-old level before mastering all 3-year-old items.

Validity: whether a test measures what it purports to measure. This may be assessed by investigating its content validity (the actual items on the test), construct validity (the underlying construct, such as intelligence or creativity, that is being tested), or predictive validity (how well the test predicts future performance in the same or a related area).

Reliability: a measure of how accurate and consistent a test is. This is usually ascertained by administering the test to the same person more than once and comparing scores (test-retest reliability), or by administering first the odd items and then the even items on the test to the same person and comparing the two resulting scores (split-half reliability). Standardized norm-referenced tests usually have more extensive information available concerning their validity and reliability than do criterion-referenced tests. However, this does not necessarily mean that the former are superior to or more useful than the latter.

teenth to sixteenth week of pregnancy. A major screening use of amniocentesis is the detection of Down syndrome, a chromosomal disorder whose risk increases with parental age. Other problems identifiable through aminocentesis include Tay-Sachs disease, PKU, and spina bifida. Prenatal detection procedures should be combined with genetic counseling that informs the prospective parents about the risks of the procedure to the developing fetus, the probability of the risk of occurrence or recurrence, and the possible options available. Genetic counselors should provide support to prospective parents in deciding whether to continue or to terminate the pregnancy. Follow-up support should be available once the parents have made their decision.

Prenatal screening of high risk pregnancies serves three major functions:

1. Negative results relieve parental anxiety and concern over possible difficulties
2. Positive results may confirm suspected difficulties and allow parents to prepare for dealing with the difficulties the infant may present
3. Positive results may provide parents with the information necessary to decide to terminate the pregnancy

Hansen (1978) reported that abortion reform in New York state has been associated with a decline in the number of children born with Down syndrome.

More common screening procedures begin at birth. The Apgar test of vital signs (Apgar, 1953) is perhaps the most commonly used screening technique for young infants. It is routinely used throughout the United States and other countries. Developed by Dr. Virginia Apgar, the procedure measures the physiological functioning of the newborn infant in five areas immediately at birth and 5 minutes after birth (see Table 8.2). Each area of functioning—respiration, circulation, color, tone, reflex response—is rated with a 0, 1, or 2, for a total of 10 possible points. Healthy infants score 8, 9, or 10 on one or both evaluations. Infants who earn a score of 6 points or less are considered to be at risk.

Another routine screening procedure undertaken at birth is the analysis of newborn blood and urine samples to detect phe-

Table 8.2. Scoring system for the Apgar Test of Vital Signs

Vital sign and status	Score	60 sec.	5 min.
Heart rate			
Absent	0		
Less than 100	1		
100–140	2		
Respiratory effort			
Apneic	0		
Shallow, irregular	1		
Lusty cry and breathing	2		
Response to catheter stimulation			
No response	0		
Grimace	1		
Cough or sneeze	2		
Muscle tone			
Flaccid	0		
Some flexim of extremities	1		
Flexion resisting extension	2		
Color			
Pale, blue	0		
Body pink, extremities blue	1		
Pink all over	2		
Total			

nylketonuria (PKU). While this procedure is widely practiced in the United States (all but two states required it in 1975), only eight states routinely screen for six other metabolic disorders that also cause retardation (Heward & Orlansky, 1980). Although the incidence of these disorders is low, such procedures are well worth the expenditure of time and money and should be expanded.

Postnatal Screening

No nationally coordinated effort to screen all children in infancy for developmental delays currently exists. One screening effort that has met with limited success is the Early and Periodic Screening, Diagnosis, and Treatment (EPSDT) program required by the Social Security Amendments of 1967. This program is required by law for the purpose of identifying child health problems and developmental disabilities in preschool children. The screening effort is far from universal, however; until 1981 it involved only those children receiving Aid to Families with Dependent Children (AFDC) who were eligible for Medicaid. The guidelines have now been expanded to include all children eligible for Medicaid, but the program still cannot be considered a national screening effort involving all young children, nor is any such program currently recommended by federal or state governments. Given the current trend toward cutting back social services, it is unlikely that such an effort will be undertaken in the foreseeable future, however cost effective it might prove to be.

Screening Instruments One difficulty encountered in instituting a comprehensive screening program has been the lack of appropriate test instruments. Recent revision of the Denver Developmental Screening Test (Frankenburg, Dodds, & Fandal, 1982) and the Developmental Indicators for the Assess-

ment of Learning (Mardell-Czudnowski & Goldenberg, 1984), and the publication of the Miller Assessment for Preschoolers (Miller, 1982) represent positive steps toward a solution of this problem.

Several screening tests for preschool children are based on the Gesell Developmental Schedules, first used in the 1930s to identify developmentally delayed infants (Knoblock & Passamanick, 1974). These schedules include tasks designed by Gesell for his study of normal development and have been adapted for use in many tests, both standardized formal tests such as the Bayley (1969) and McCarthy (1972) scales and less formal procedures such as the Brigance Diagnostic Inventory of Early Development (Brigance, 1978), the Learning Accomplishment Profile (Sanford & Zelman, 1981), and the Portage Guide to Early Education (Shearer & Shearer, 1976). Several assessment instruments are described later in the chapter.

An interesting approach to screening is the Developmental Indicators for the Assessment of Learning (DIAL, Mardell-Czudnowski & Goldenberg, 1984). The DIAL represents an interdisciplinary approach to screening that makes it possible for a group of children to be evaluated simultaneously in gross and fine motor development, concepts, and communication. The classroom teacher plays a major role in the DIAL screening process, thus eliminating one problem involving interdisciplinary teams, namely, the assessment specialist who is too far removed from the daily process of intervention in the preschool classroom.

The Role of the Early Childhood Specialist in the Screening Process As we have seen, screening procedures may be medical, psychological, or developmental. The early childhood specialist plays an important role in the latter. Working with infants and young children on a daily basis, this professional has valuable knowledge and experience of typical and atypical performance in all the developmental areas. A good early interventionist can help the interdisciplinary screening team by communicating with parents and siblings in a non-threatening, supportive manner.

ASSESSMENT

Screening infants and young children for developmental delays is an attempt to identify those children who are suspected of having a problem serious enough to require intervention. Assessment is typically a process of confirming or denying the existence of a problem and locating its etiology. In a medical context, assessment often leads to diagnosis—the process that determines the specific cause or etiology of the disorder and delay. By contrast, assessment in special education generally refers to the use of medical, psychometric, educational, and clinical techniques to place a child in one or more classification categories (e.g., retarded).

The assessment process is an attempt to determine a child's strengths and weaknesses so that a specific program of intervention can be planned and implemented. Harbin (1977) views assessment as a systematic process of collecting information on both a child's level of functioning in specific areas of development and his or her learning characteristics, and carefully interpreting the collected information to provide direction in the day-to-day management of the child.

Limitations in the Assessment Process

The major goals of the assessment process include diagnosis, documentation of status or progress, and planning intervention (Simeonsson, 1986). Without accurate doc-umentation and a direct link to intervention, the process loses its purpose. Basic to the process is the assumption that the instruments used are valid, accurately documenting the strengths and needs of the child and family. However, as Simeonsson has pointed out, a variety of factors may limit that assumption in the assessment of young children with special needs. These factors include definitional problems and limitations of the child, the examiner, the measurement, and the setting. These limitations are summarized in Table 8.3.

The most pertinent of these for the early interventionist are limitations introduced by the child, the examiner, or the measurement instrument.

Children at risk for handicapping conditions tend to be less predictable than other children in terms of responsiveness and reactivity. This may result in inconsistent performance of assessment tasks from one session to the next, making it difficult to describe the child's levels of functioning accurately. Additionally, impairments of sensory and motor functioning may limit the child's experiences and therefore his or her acquisition of skills and knowledge.

Limitations of the examiner include lack of experience or skill in assessing infants and young children with severe handicaps; the possibility that instruments chosen may be unreliable or invalid; and the inaccurate interpretation of results. Examiners may also have biases against certain handicapping conditions that lower their expectations of the children they are testing.

The suitability of standardized instruments for use with young children with special needs has been extensively debated. As Simeonsson (1986) has pointed out, the limitations of young children with handicaps discussed above may make it inappropriate to assess them with instruments that are standardized on children without

Table 8.3. Limitations in the assessment of young children

Source of limitation	Key issues considered
Definitional issues	Lack of agreement on definitions of basic terms
	Need for designations that will reflect both presence of handicap and degree of impairment
Child	Impaired function in more than one area
	Performance and functioning affected by medication and state
	Presence of idiosyncratic behaviors
	Variability in rate of development across areas
Examiner	Lack of knowledge/experience with special children
	Personal biases and expectations
	Invalid assumptions concerning effects of the handicap
	Difficulty interpreting a child's response
	Lack of special communication skills (i.e., signing skills)
Measurement	Standardization populations exclude handicapped
	Extreme normative values cannot be derived
	Test assumptions violated when used with handicapped
	Difficult to compare results from different tests
	Insufficient data base for the various handicapping conditions
Setting	Inadequate or inappropriate setting in terms of ambient light, sound, other physical features
	Artificial nature of setting
	Failure to consider positioning needs of child

From Simeonsson, R. (1986). *Psychological and developmental assessment of special children.* Boston: Allyn & Bacon. Copyright 1986. Reprinted by permission.

handicaps. Problems include inability of the child with sensory or motor impairments to respond; restriction on making accurate inferences and generalizations from the results; and truncated normative tables that do not permit the derivation of extreme values.

Current Issues in Assessment

Four issues currently affect intervention programs for preschool children with handicaps. These include the issues of cultural bias; standardized testing versus other alternatives; the implications of early intervention for assessment; and the predictive validity and reliability of early childhood assessment instruments.

Cultural Bias The Education for All Handicapped Children Act of 1975 (PL 94-142) established the principle of non-discriminatory testing to determine the existence and extent of handicapping conditions in children. The principle has not been put into practice effectively, however, for several reasons. Attitudes of psychometricians have been difficult to change, and traditional methods of standardized testing have proved hard to replace. Additionally, few available assessment instruments have been successful in avoiding cultural bias (for an excellent discussion of this issue, see Goodwin and Driscoll, 1980, pp. 14–15). It is probably true that no instrument can ever be culturally unbiased, since every test tends to favor the cultural group used in its development (Anastasi, 1976). Nevertheless, there is evidence to suggest that a commitment to making testing less discriminatory is lacking and that only the fear of federal scrutiny motivates many testers to reduce cultural bias in assessment (Bernal, 1977).

Cultural bias in testing has come to mean the use of standardized tests. PL 94-142 specifically prohibits the classification of a child as handicapped on the basis of one criterion or test score. Impetus for this stipulation came in the 1970s from the work of several people interested in the education of children with handicaps, notably Mercer and Hobbs. Mercer's (1973) study of mentally retarded children in Riverside, California, revealed that a disproportionate number of black and Hispanic children were labeled mentally retarded on the basis of standardized tests and placed in segregated classes. Mercer concluded that such tests as the Stanford-Binet Intelligence Scales are culturally biased and, therefore, underestimate the potential ability of children who are not from white, English-speaking (Anglo), middle-class families. Her response to this problem is the System of Multicultural and Pluralistic Assessment (SOMPA), which is based on the belief that multiple criteria give a more accurate estimate of potential ability.

The SOMPA consists of a series of assessment instruments, both norm-referenced and criterion-referenced, and is intended for children between 5 and 11. The instruments include identification of the socialization milieu in which the child is being reared, evaluation of the child's general academic readiness, assessment of the child's adaptive behavior in nonacademic activities, an inventory of the child's health history, and screening for physical impairments (Mercer, 1973). Academic readiness is measured by the Wechsler Intelligence Scale for Children-Revised (WISC-R) or the Wechsler Preschool and Primary Scale of Intelligence (WPPSI) and the Bender Visual-Motor Gestalt Test. Except for the physical screening, all assessment data are secured in interviews with the child's primary caregiver. These include the

Sociocultural Scales, which identify the social, cultural, and economic characteristics of the child's home environment and compare them with the predominant school culture; the Adaptive Behavior Inventory for Children (ABIC); and the Health History Inventory. The assessment system yields an Estimated Learning Potential instead of an IQ score; this is derived from the WISC-R score adjusted for the child's sociocultural background.

In arguing for pluralistic assessment, Mercer states:

> By developing multiple normative frameworks to describe children from different sociocultural settings, pluralistic assessment will recognize the child's right to be evaluated within an appropriate sociocultural framework. Assessing a child's performance in relation to that of other children from similar backgrounds will free evaluation from the single normal curve, adjust definitions of "normal-abnormal" for differences in sociocultural background and take into account sociocultural differences within ethnic/racial groups. (1973, p. 155)

Underlying the standardized testing movements in the United States was the melting pot theory, with its prescription that all culturally different people adapt to the majority culture. Cultural pluralism challenges this assumption and promotes a recognition and appreciation of difference. While it is true that standardized tests do measure accurately how well a minority child will perform in a white, Anglo, middle-class educational setting, and while this information may be important and necessary, it nevertheless also remains true that cultural difference is often translated by these tests into deficit (Cole & Bruner, 1971), which results in minority children being erroneously diagnosed as needing special services to overcome their "handicap."

Alternatives to Standardized Testing
With the increasing criticism of standardized tests voiced by the courts and by children's

advocacy groups, as well as by parents of children with handicaps and by professional educators, interest in identifying alternative procedures has developed.

A second concern with standardized testing is that it is often substituted for a complete program of assessment. Such a program should include the following functions (Wodrich, 1986):

1. Facilitation of remediation
2. Planning for prescriptive intervention
3. Provision of information to parents and professionals

The score yielded by the standardized test is not useful for any of these functions. The score might be included as part of the information on which classification decisions are based, but since PL 94-142 specifically forbids labeling children as handicapped on the basis of a single test score, it cannot substitute for a broader, more comprehensive assessment.

Wodrich (1986) believes that, in order to facilitate remediation, assessment data should provide as much information as possible about the way the child learns, so that the remedial program can be individualized to his or her special needs. Through *dynamic assessment,* this can be accomplished in an educational setting. Dynamic assessment emphasizes observation of the manner in which the child performs a task, with attention to both accurate performance and errors. Much valuable information about a child's method of information processing can be gained from observing the errors he or she makes in problem solving.

Wodrich (1986) believes that all assessment should facilitate the planning of treatment and should help those adults who live or work with the child to understand that child's strengths and needs better. Labels such as mental retardation, which result from standardized testing, accomplish neither purpose.

Laosa (1977) has suggested four alternatives to standardized testing. First, criterion-referenced tests that measure the child against his or her own previous performance, rather than against the majority, may be less biased. However, Laosa cautions, criterion-referenced tests must be evaluated in terms of who determines what the objective will be and who establishes the criteria. This type of test may also be culturally biased if the objectives and criteria reflect majority standards or values. One advantage of the criterion-referenced test is that it yields specific information regarding skills that the child can or cannot perform. This information is more useful for educational programming than is the numerical score yielded by the standardized test.

A second alternative is to test the child's ability to perform Piagetian tasks. Stages associated with these tasks occur across cultures and, therefore, tests associated with them are less likely to be biased. Although several such tests have been developed, none has achieved wide acceptance among psychometricians and they are used mainly for research (Keogh & Kopp, 1978). The best known of these, and the most appropriate for preschool children, is the Ordinal Scales of Psychological Development, developed by Uzgiris and Hunt (1975). Studies have revealed some positive correlation between performance on these Piagetian-based scales and more traditional tests of intelligence (Goodwin & Driscoll, 1980).

As a third alternative, Laosa suggests using diagnostic tests. While many of these are standardized, they test specific areas, such as visual-motor coordination, rather than general ability. The information they yield is therefore less likely to be culturally biased and less likely to be used to label children. However, few standardized diagnostic tests are available for use with children under 4; more commonly, instruments designed for very young children are criterion-referenced skill assessments.

Finally, Laosa recommends using informal observational techniques to assess the child's behavior. This approach is appropriate for infants and preschool children, since they are less inhibited by adult observers than older children, and thus can provide much valuable information to the trained observer. This approach, discussed in greater detail in Chapter 9, is gaining wide acceptance among preschool educators of both children with and children without handicaps. Of course, the information gleaned from informal observation is only as biased as the observer who records it, suggesting that no assessment method may be entirely free of bias.

Early Intervention and Educational Assessment Keogh and Kopp (1978) have noted the lack of assessment procedures designed to provide information for differentiated program planning. As a result, most programs for infants and preschool children with handicaps are broad-based and non-specific, providing enrichment activities that may or may not address the child's deficits.

According to Keogh and Kopp (1978), early intervention programs for both handicapped and disadvantaged (potentially handicapped) preschool children reflect the lack of assessment instruments specific enough to identify fundamental developmental processes. Weak assessment procedures at entry into these programs, designed primarily to label the handicapping condition, result in all children receiving similar interventions, regardless of symptoms. This produces inconclusive outcomes, reflected in data that may not show rehabilitative results. Keogh and Kopp summarize their position:

> Where assessment provides description and delineation of the developmental sequence of behaviors, and when antecedent and outcome developmental events are identified, there is an increased probability that assessment data

will lead to appropriate and selective interventions and that program outcomes can be objectively evaluated. (p. 537)

Keogh and Kopp maintain that a good assessment instrument will not only describe the developmental sequence and specify where the child is functioning within the sequence, but will also identify desired developmental outcomes for an individual child. Antecedent experiences that underlie a particular skill should also be identified, so that these may be taught as prerequisites for the developmental skill to be learned. This process requires very specific task analysis and is evident in few assessment instruments currently in use. Exceptions are the ordinal scales of sensorimotor development (Escalona & Corman, 1969; Uzgiris & Hunt, 1975), which require extensive training to administer.

An alternative to commercial instruments is to develop informal procedures for use with children in a particular program. An example of this process is the early intervention program for blind infants developed by Fraiberg and colleagues (Fraiberg, 1971; Fraiberg, Smith, & Adelson, 1969), in which a thorough developmental sequence of sensorimotor skills was constructed through observation of the infants. The researchers noted, for example, that because blind babies fail to develop midline hand play at 4 to 5 months, they experience delays in developing object permanence and sensorimotor schemes. Object permanence is not achieved by blind infants until age 3 or later (Fraiberg, Smith, & Adelson, 1969). Further observation of the development of hand play in blind infants revealed that delays in reaching for objects on sound cue interfered with progress in learning to creep. The importance of adaptive hand behavior to later locomotive and cognitive learnings thus became apparent; without such careful observation the existence of such links might not have been discovered. The result was a sequence of components and antecedent experiences that underlie such developmental accomplishments as head and trunk control, reaching and grasping, crawling, and object permanence. These sequences then became the basis for definitive, specific assessment procedures that led to meaningful intervention programming for the infants.

This approach appears to be more effective than the approach founded on the beliefs that early interventions of any type aid development and lead to positive outcomes; that stimulation should concentrate on cognitive and language abilities; and that children at risk for a variety of conditions, both medical and socioeconomic, benefit from global enrichment activities.

Reliability and Predictive Validity of Early Childhood Assessment Instruments

When assessment is conducted for the purpose of planning effective intervention, the most useful procedures are behavioral observation and criterion-referenced skills inventories. However, a second purpose of assessment—to identify children with potential handicaps—requires instruments that predict well which children are at developmental risk. For this purpose, the validity and reliability of the assessment instruments are crucial.

Evaluation of the predictive validity of infant assessment instruments indicates that the most commonly used instruments are not very good predictors. Perhaps the best known summary of these studies is by Bayley (1970), who concluded that her scales of infant intelligence are not predictive of later IQ. Holden (1972) also used the Bayley scales and found that they did not predict mental retardation.

Even the Apgar rating of neonatal physiological functioning has not been found to predict later neurological dysfunction (Drage et al., 1966). Infants who had low (0–5) Apgar scores at birth had significantly more indicators of neurological dysfunction at age

1 than did infants whose Apgar scores at birth fell from 7 to 10, but these differences in central nervous system functioning had disappeared by age 7.

In reviewing the predictive validity research conducted in the 1960s, Lewis (1976a) found little predictive validity between early infant IQ scores and later measures of intelligence. Indeed, within the first two years of life, little consistency in IQ performance was demonstrated. In a longitudinal study involving retarded and nonretarded infants, Werner, Honzik, and Smith (1968) found the correlation between IQ at 20 months measured on the Cattell Infant Intelligence Scale (Cattell, 1960) and IQ at 10 years measured on the SRA Primary Mental Ability Test (Thurstone & Thurstone, 1954) to be 49; if only those children who scored below 80 at 20 months were included, the correlation rose to 72. Similarly, Share, Koch, Webb, and Graliker (1964) found significant correlations between Gesell scores at infancy and IQ scores (Stanford-Binet) at 5 years for children with Down syndrome. These studies suggest that predictive validity for standardized infant tests is adequate only when the instruments are used with children at the low end of the normal distribution.

According to Parmelee, Kopp, and Sigman (1976), identifying infants at developmental risk by using only one factor (e.g., test score, prematurity, low SES) is not accurate. They recommend instead a cumulative risk score (see Chapter 2) that takes into account biological, behavioral, and sociological factors, such as nutrition, quality of caregiving, and the cognitive environment of the home. This approach is an attractive alternative to the current practice of identifying infants at risk on the basis of a Bayley or Gesell score.

The reliability of standardized early assessment instruments is generally considered to be adequate. Such tests have good validity in part because test constructors have borrowed items from each other, giving those items a high validity (Goodwin & Driscoll, 1980). Sigel (1979) has cautioned that using standardized tests with high-risk children may not yield the same level of reliability as that obtained with average children. He attributes this to the fact that high-risk children tend to be moodier and more easily fatigued and to have higher activity levels and lower attention levels than other children. All of these factors may adversely influence their test performance.

Multidisciplinary Assessment of Development

Because of the provisions of PL 99-457, multidisciplinary assessment has become the accepted practice for evaluating children with special needs. Whereas formerly each specialist evaluated the child in isolation and shared information with other professionals through written reports, today a multidisciplinary team evaluates the child, with several professionals working simultaneously with a child and family, sharing information and observations. The result is a more holistic, less reductionist view of the child, with consideration given to the environment in which the child lives and attends school. In short, the assessment process has become more ecologically focused in recent years. (See also the discussion in Chapter 9.)

While members of the multidisciplinary team have learned to work more closely together in both the assessment and intervention provided for young children with special needs—causing some to label this collaboration "transdisciplinary"—it is convenient when describing the assessment process to consider separately each discipline and its contribution to the total picture of the child and family.

For members of the team who work with the child and family on a regular basis, the assessment process is an ongoing one, with "every treatment session . . . an evaluation" (Short-DeGraff, 1986, p. 165). This makes possible the continual updating of intervention goals and the development of new objectives as the child progresses.

Pediatric Assessment of Development

With the current trend toward interagency collaboration for service delivery—demonstrated by planning and intervention carried out cooperatively among educational, health, and social service providers—the role of the developmental pediatrician has gained added importance. This is particularly true in the case of infants at risk for handicaps and their families. The pediatrician or pediatric nurse is often involved in the assessment process as a member of the multidisciplinary team, and therefore also participates in the decision making and planning leading to the individualized plan.

In addition to background and experience related to the child's medical or health condition, the developmental pediatrician brings to the team special training in developmental disabilities. The pediatric assessment of development generally consists of a general medical assessment, a developmental history, and a neurodevelopmental examination (Msall & Ichord, 1986).

In assessing the child's general state of health, the pediatrician looks at diet, nutrition, and physical growth; the immunization record; and any concerns expressed by the parents. In addition, a physical examination and laboratory tests are administered to identify syndromes; chromosome anomalies; heart, lung, or kidney disorders; hydrocephalus; seizure; or other disorders. The child's medical history is examined for evidence of recurrent illness and the family's access to health care services is determined.

The developmental history forms the basis for developmental diagnosis (Msall & Ichord, 1986). The history examines the child's progress in four areas of development: cognitive, communication, social-emotional, and motor. In the case of infants and young children at risk, the pediatrician may concentrate on the development of gross and fine motor skills, while taking into account progress in the other areas as well. A record of developmental milestones is an important part of the history. In addition, a developmental screening or assessment instrument, such as the Denver Developmental Screening Test (Frankenburg, Dodds, & Fandal, 1982) or the Revised Gesell Developmental Schedules (Knoblock, Stevens, & Malone, 1980) may be administered.

A neurodevelopmental examination is given to provide a measure of the integrity of the child's central nervous system (Msall & Ichord, 1986). The primary areas of examination and the specific focus of each are presented in Table 8.4.

The developmental pediatrician arrives at a diagnosis of the child based on a synthesis of the information provided by the three types of assessment.

Psychological Assessment of Development The psychologist has the primary responsibility for evaluating the child's intellectual ability, adaptive behavior, emotional and social behavior, personality traits, and temperament (Witt & Cavell, 1986).

Intelligence Testing For testing intellectual ability an IQ test is used. For many years the Stanford-Binet Intelligence Scale (Terman & Merrill, 1973) was the most popular tool for this purpose. That instrument was criticized, however, for placing too much emphasis on verbal skills, which put very young children and children from different cultural backgrounds at a disadvantage. The scales developed by David Wechsler (Wechsler Intelligence Scale for Children, WISC-R, Wechsler, 1974, and Wechsler Preschool and Primary Scale of Intelligence, WPPSI, Wechsler, 1967) gained popularity in the 1970s, partly

Table 8.4. An expanded neurodevelopmental examination

Exam item	Developmental focus
Behavior	Assess level of arousal, activity, and social competence.
Cranial nerves, general	Observe specific localizing signs and oromotor dysfunction.
Cranial nerves, special nerves	Assess vision and hearing, with attention to perceptual maturation.
Gross motor function	Define developmental level and deviancies in posture, mobility, and tone.
Fine motor function	Define developmental levels and deviancies in reach, grasp, and eye-hand movements.
Cerebellar function	Describe abnormalities in balance and coordination.
Peripheral senses	Describe deficits in touch, position sense, and pain (to assist in localizing dysfunction).
Deep tendon reflexes	Describe abnormalities, including pathological reflexes (to assist with localization).
Primitive reflexes	Describe abnormal persistence and localization.
Abnormal movements	Identify presence of chorea, athetosis, and ballismus.

From Msall, M.E., and Ichord, R. (1986). Developmental pediatric assessment. In D.L. Wodrich & J.E. Joy (Eds.), *Multidisciplinary assessment of children with learning disabilities and mental retardation* (p. 217). Baltimore: Paul H. Brookes Publishing Co. Copyright 1986 by Paul H. Brookes Publishing Co. Reprinted by permission.

because they consisted of both verbal and nonverbal scales. The WPPSI is normed for children between 4 and 6½; the WISC-R is appropriate for older children. Like the Binet, the Wechsler scales have been criticized for their lack of a theoretical base.

Much interest has been generated by the Kaufman Assessment Battery for Children (K-ABC) (Kaufman & Kaufman, 1983), which is based on a theory of information processing. Appropriate for children between 2½ and 12, the K-ABC tests the child's ability to process information in both sequential and simultaneous modes, which the authors claim parallels the functioning of the two hemispheres of the brain. Questions have been raised concerning the validity of such a theoretical base (Kieth, 1985), but the K-ABC remains an important psychological assessment tool at present.

For children under 5, two standardized tests are widely used by psychologists and other professionals: the Bayley Scales of Infant Development (Bayley, 1969) for infants 2- to 30- months, and the McCarthy Scales of Children's Abilities (McCarthy, 1972) for ages 2½ to 8½. All six of these intelligence tests have well established reliability and validity.

Adaptive Behavior The most widely used test of adaptive behavior is the AAMD Adaptive Behavior Scale (Lambert, Windmiller, Tharinger, & Cole, 1981). This test has the sponsorship of the American Association for Mental Retardation and is comprehensive in scope and well standardized. The ABS tests adaptive behaviors of children from age 3 in five categories, listed below with examples.

Personal self-sufficiency This cluster of items reflects the degree to which a child is able to handle his or her basic needs such as eating, drinking, and toileting.
Community self-sufficiency This factor assesses the extent to which a child can function appro-

priately in common, everyday situations such as traveling about the neighborhood, communicating with others, and performing economic activities.
Personal-social responsibility Items within this factor reflect relatively high-level social interaction skills including getting to school or work on time, showing initiative in school or job settings, interacting cooperatively with others, and assuming responsibility for one's own actions.
Social adjustment This factor comprises items from Part Two of the ABS. The inappropriate behaviors assessed include those in which a child is interacting inappropriately with other individuals (e.g., the child is aggressive, lies, cheats, steals). Such behaviors are characteristic of children who act-out or have behavior disorders. (Witt & Cavell, 1986, p. 50).

A second useful instrument for infants and young children is the updated and revised version of the Vineland Adaptive Behavior Scale (Sparrow, Balla, & Cicchetti, 1984). Because it is appropriate for infants from birth, it may eventually replace the AAMR scale.

In order for a child to be classified as mentally retarded, he or she must demonstrate below average functioning in adaptive behavior as well as in intelligence.

Emotional and Social Behavior The psychologist is trained to administer projective tests to assist in understanding the child's emotional development. For young children, these might include projective art, in which they are asked to draw a person, a member of their family, or themself. The interpretation is subjective relative to standardized, norm-referenced instruments, and such tests are therefore not used universally.

Personality and Temperament An objective test of personality that yields a norm-based score may be administered by the psychologist. An example is the Personality Inventory for Children (Lachar, 1982), which is completed by the child's parents. It is designed to assess children's emotional and behavioral status, and to screen for intellectual delays.

In addition, tests of temperament have been developed for infants and very young children that are usually administered by the psychologist. Examples include the Infant Temperament Questionnaire (ITQ) (Carey & McDevitt, 1978) and the Toddler Temperament Scale (TTS) (Fullard, McDevitt, & Carey, 1984), which have been used extensively in research and are appropriate for children to age 3. Both are well-developed instruments with good reliability and validity.

However, most psychologists who work with very young children rely on informal observation to determine the emotional and social status of the child. For the observations to yield useful information, they must be carried out in the child's home, school, or child care environment so that the psychologist can note the quality of the child's interactions with parents, other adults, and peers.

Audiological Assessment It has been estimated that approximately 10% of all children experience some degree of hearing impairment between birth and age 11 (Hayes, 1986). This includes both children with and children without other handicaps. Given that hearing impairment often accompanies other handicaps, and usually leads to delays in language development, it is important that young children at risk for handicaps receive audiological evaluation early in life.

Recent advances in technology have made it possible to test the hearing of infants and very young children without language. Many neonatal intensive care units currently test all children immediately prior to discharge (Hayes, 1986). If hearing loss is detected, rehabilitation can begin as early as 1 month. Such procedures greatly reduce the risk of language delay in very young children.

A combination of behavioral and physiological measures are used to ensure accurate audiological assessment of infants and young children (Hayes, 1986). To test *behavioral audiometry*, the audiologist observes responses to both noise signals and speech. For the infant under 6 months of age, a simple observation of responses to sound is made and recorded on an audiogram. For infants and children between 6 months and 3 years, some form of conditioned audiometry is used, in which the child is reinforced visually or with food for responding to test items. For children over 3, the audiometry examination might incorporate play. In each case it is possible to plot an audiogram without requiring the child to wear earphones. Several examples of audiograms plotted for infants and young children are presented in Figure 8.1.

Physiological techniques include acoustic immittance measures and auditory evoked potentials. *Acoustic immittance measures* assess middle ear and cochlear function by means of a probe tube sealed into the external ear canal that emits sound that is reflected by the tympannic membrane. The degree of reflection is measured. For the *auditory evoked potential*, changes in the child's electroencephalogram (EEG) are measured in response to sound. The most useful type of auditory evoked potential is the auditory brain stem response (ABR), in which a pair of electrodes is attached to the child's scalp and the responses to sound measured. For infants, this may be the only accurate method of assessment; for older children, it affords a useful method of confirming the behavioral assessment.

Speech-Language Assessment The speech-language pathologist is responsible for assessing the development of communication skills and oral-motor functioning. Assessment of the latter, which includes speech, may be shared with the occupational thera-

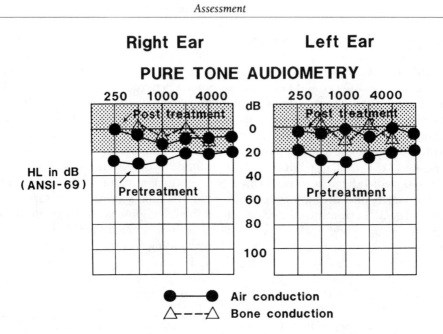

Figure 8.1.   Pre- and posttreatment behavioral audiogram from a 6-year-old boy with recurrent otitis media with effusion. This audiogram was obtained by conditioned play audiometry. Pretreatment audiogram shows mild bilateral conductive hearing loss. Following treatment (insertion of pressure-equalizing tubes in the tympanic membrane) the pure tone audiogram is normal (ANS)-69: American National Standards Institute 1969 standard for audiometric normal hearing). (From Hayes, D. [1986]. *Multidisciplinary assessment of children with learning disabilities and mental retardation* [p. 123]. Baltimore: Paul H. Brookes Publishing Co. Reprinted by permission.)

pist, particularly in the case of a child with severe oral-motor problems that affect speech and feeding. The assessment consists of tests of expressive and receptive language, articulation, and, sometimes, auditory processing.

Several tests of receptive and expressive language exist for use with young children. One of the most widely used for children under 3 is the Receptive and Expressive Emergent Language Scale (REEL) (Bzoch & League, 1971), which is based on parent report and begins at birth. For preschool children two companion tests are the Test of Early Language Development (TELD) (Reid, Hresko, & Hammill, 1983) and the Test of Early Reading Ability (TERA) (Hresko, Reid, & Hammill, 1984; see Widerstrom, 1987 a & b for a review). A comprehensive test of communication skills is the Sequenced Inventory of Communication Development (SICD) (Hedrick, Prather, & Tobin, 1975), which yields information on receptive and expressive skills from 4 months to 4 years. It is one of the few scales currently available with norms for children under 3.

While speech-language pathologists now give more attention to problems of language development and less to articulation problems than formerly, the child's speech patterns nevertheless receive a thorough evaluation. Methods vary for this procedure, but in the case of very young children, informal observation techniques are probably the most useful. Articulation skills are always developed in terms of developmental expectations (Norman-Murch & Bashir, 1986).

Occupational Therapy Assessment The assessment performed by the occupational therapist varies according to the nature and extent of the child's disability, the child's age and reason for referral, and the environment in which assessment and intervention are carried out, including the extent of communication among team members evaluating the child (Short-DeGraff, 1986). Of primary interest are the child's motor abilities, including gross and fine motor, and perceptual motor, oral-motor, and neuromotor skills. If a physical therapist serves on the multidisciplinary assessment team, both therapists work together in conducting the motor assessment. In addition, the occupational therapist may assess the ways in which motor skills are carried out in activities of daily living, such as feeding and self-care. The child's play skills and interactions with other children may be observed. The parents' interactions with the child, such as their ability to handle and position, feed, and play with the child may be evaluated. The assessment might also include measures of sensation, balance, muscle tone, coordination, joint range of motion, postures, and reflexes. Usually the occupational therapist will also evaluate the child's need for adaptive equipment to enhance motor functions such as walking, standing, toileting, feeding, and dressing.

Occupational therapists use a variety of evaluation methods, including informal observation of movement and standardized testing. One standardized instrument is the Miller Assessment for Preschoolers (MAP) (Miller, 1982), developed by an occupational therapist to screen preschool children for potential handicapping conditions in five areas: basic motor and sensory abilities; fine motor and oral-motor abilities; visual-motor integration; language; and cognitive abilities. The MAP was designed for children 2 years, 9 months to 5 years, 8 months. It has good reliability and validity data, and was standardized on a large number of subjects.

The Movement Assessment of Infants (MAI) (Harris et al., 1984) was also developed by occupational therapists, together with physical therapists. It asesses muscle tone, reflexes, automatic reactions, and voluntary movement in infants up to age 1. Reliability and validity studies for the MAI are currently being conducted; preliminary results are positive.

The Peabody Developmental Motor Scales (PDMS) (Folio & Fewell, 1983) were developed by educators, and do not require specialized training as a therapist to administer. They are used by both educators and therapists for children from birth to age 6 years, 11 months, and have gained wide acceptance in the early intervention field. The PDMS consists of two scales, one for gross and one for fine motor skills, and measures reflexes, balance, grasp, hand use, eye-hand coordination, manual dexterity, locomotion, and receipt and propulsion of objects. The test authors report good validity and reliability (Folio & Fewell, 1983).

Southern California Sensory Integration Tests (Ayres, 1986), a battery of tests designed to measure sensory integration, are widely used by occupational therapists to assess the child's ability to integrate sensory information and use it effectively. The tests remain popular despite criticisms over the past decade that they are psychometrically weak and lacking in theoretical construct (Ottenbacher & Short, 1985).

In addition to standardized instruments, the occupational therapist uses a variety of informal measures of feeding and oral-motor function, and other activities of daily living. Informal observation yields information on range of motion, posture, and parent-child and peer interactions.

Physical Therapy Assessment The physical therapist is an important member of the assessment team if the child exhibits any type of motor dysfunction. Working under the supervision of a medical doctor, the physical therapist takes responsibility for the child's general motor functioning. The physical therapist's functions often closely overlap with those of the occupational therapist. The assessment focuses on the child's posture, muscle tone, motor coordination, and voluntary movement. While the physical therapy assessment consists primarily of informed observation, some published tests, such as the Milani-Comparetti Motor Development Screening Test (Trembath, 1978), may be administered to assess abnormal reflexes. Both the physical therapist and the occupational therapist make invaluable contributions to the assessment of infants and young children.

Special Education Assessment The specialist in the education of infants and young children with special needs plays a unique role in the multidisciplinary assessment. Because this professional sees the child and the family more frequently than do other team members—often on a daily basis—he or she has greater opportunity to become familiar with any special problems experienced by the child or family. Often the special educator and the family develop a special relationship, which may prove helpful during both assessment and intervention. For this reason, the early childhood specialist often leads the team during the intervention phase, taking overall responsibility for ensuring that assessment data are translated into appropriate intervention objectives. The early childhood specialist is seen as the member of the team with the most generalist point of view, and thus best suited to oversee the overall development of the child.

The special education assessment examines the process by which the child learns and the products (performance) of the

learning (Hannafin, 1986). These include an assessment of skill levels in the developmental areas (cognition, communication, motor, social, and self-help) to determine where deficits exist, and observation of the behaviors used by the child to perform various skills. These behaviors provide insight into the child's learning style.

According to Neisworth and Bagnato (1988), assessment instruments currently available to the early childhood specialist may be classified into eight categories: curriculum-based, adaptive-to-handicap, process, norm-based, judgment-based, ecological, interactive, and systematic observation. The type of instrument used depends on the purpose of the assessment. Instruments in each of these categories have certain unique advantages. For example, if the goal is to link assessment data to curriculum objectives, a curriculum-based instrument might be chosen. If the purpose is to assess the effect of a handicapping condition on measurement outcomes, an adaptive-to-handicap instrument would be appropriate. If the early childhood specialist seeks to assess the child's interactions with his or her environment, an ecological or interactive approach could be taken. (See Chapter 9 for a more extensive discussion of conducting ecological assessments.) For direct intervention, where assessment ideally leads to an appropriate curriculum based on individual objectives for each child, curriculum-based or adaptive-to-handicap instruments have proven particularly useful.

These eight categories, together with some examples of each, are presented in Table 8.5.

For curriculum-based assessment, the Learning Accomplishment Profile (LAP) (Sanford & Zelman, 1981) and the Early Learning Accomplishment Profile (ELAP) (Glover, Preminger, & Sanford, 1978) were developed for children from birth to 72 months. These profiles are criterion refer-

Table 8.5. Categories of early intervention assessment

Category	Definition	Instruments	Purpose
Curriculum based	Child mastery of objectives within a continuum of objectives	Learning Accomplishment Profile (Sanford & Zelman, 1981) HICOMP Preschool Curriculum (Willoughby-Herb & Neisworth, 1983)	Identify individual treatment objectives. Track child progress and provide feedback for instructional changes. Offer common base for interdisciplinary diagnosis and treatment
Adaptive-to-handicap	Modification of assessment content to include or permit alternative sensory or response modes	Oregon Project Curriculum (Brown, Simmons, & Methvin, 1979) Uniform Performance Assessment System (White, Edgar, Haring, Affleck, Hayden, & Bendersky, 1981) Early Intervention Developmental Profile (Rogers, D'Eugenio, Brown, Donovan, & Lynch, 1981) Carolina Curriculum (Johnson-Martin, Jens, & Attermeier, 1986)	Obtain valid assessment by circumventing handicap Identify goals for instruction Specify strategies for learning
Process	Detection of changes in child related to changes in stimulus events; qualitative changes in cognitive status	Information Processing Approach (Zelazo, 1982) Infant Learning (Dunst, 1981)	Probe possible capabilities when more direct conventional assessment is not feasible
Norm-based	Comparison of a child's skills and characteristics relative to an appropriate referent group	Battelle Developmental Inventory (Newborg, Stock, Wnek, Guidubaldi, & Svinicki, 1984) McCarthy Scales of Children's Abilities (McCarthy, 1972)	Describe child characteristics relative to peers
Judgment-based	Impressions of developmental/behavioral traits (e.g., reactivity, motivation, normalcy)	Carolina Record of Individual Behavior (Simeonsson et al., 1982) Perceptions of Devel-	Detect perceptions and bias. Estimate nebulous/difficult to observe processes. Enhance

(continued)

Table 8.5.   (continued)

Category	Definition	Instruments	Purpose
		opmental Status (Bagnato & Neisworth, 1987)	scope of assessment battery
Ecological	Evaluation of the physical, social, and psychological features of a child's developmental context	Early Childhood Environment Rating Scale (Harms & Clifford, 1980) Home Observation for Measurement of the Environment (Caldwell & Bradley, 1978)	Describe nature of reciprocal interactives. Identify environmental variables that suggest needed changes in interactions
Interactive	Examination of social capabilities of the infant and caregiver and the content and extent of synchrony between them	Brazelton Neonatal Behavioral Assessment Scale (Brazelton, 1984) Parent Behavior Progression (Bromwich, 1978)	Appraise parent-child reciprocity, discover match between child competencies and tasks presented
Systematic observation	Structured procedures for collecting objective and quantifiable data on ongoing behavior	Pla-Check (Doke & Risley, 1972) Mapping (Ruggles, 1982)	Analyze functional relations among antecedents, child behavior, and consequences. Provide close-ups of strengths and weaknesses, and detect small changes

Adapted from Neisworth and Bagnato (1988).

enced, and are scored on a pass/fail basis for each item. They yield age-equivalent scores in each of six developmental areas. Items failed by a particular child become the basis for the teaching curriculum.

Another popular curriculum-based instrument is the Brigance Diagnostic Inventory of Early Development (Brigance, 1978), which presents task analyses of skills in 11 domains. It is a criterion-referenced instrument intended for children from birth to 84 months. A fully developed accompanying curriculum is available.

An assessment instrument that is very closely linked to curriculum is the Track Record, which accompanies the HICOMP Preschool Curriculum (Willoughby-Herb & Neisworth, 1983), a behaviorally-based system of 800 objectives in 4 developmental areas. The instrument is appropriate for children from birth to 5. It is particularly useful for children with severe handicaps, because it breaks skills into very small steps for both assessment and learning.

One of the soundest adaptive-to-handicap instruments is Developmental Programming for Infants and Young Children (DPIYC) (Schaefer & Moerch, 1981). The DPIYC consists of the Early Intervention Developmental Profile (EIDP) (Rogers et al., 1981) for ages birth to 3, and the Preschool Developmental Profile (PDP) (Brown et al., 1981) for ages 3 to 6. Together with a Stimulation Activities guide of intervention activities matched to the assessment, with suggestions for modifying activities according to the child's handicapping condition, the EIDP and PDP provide a comprehensive survey of developmental skills in six domains. They are intended for use by the multidisciplinary assessment team.

A practical instrument using the process approach is Infant Learning (Dunst, 1981), which combines assessment with intervention based on the Piagetian Uzgiris-Hunt scales of sensorimotor development. Infant Learning presents goals and treatment methods in the developmental range of birth to 30 months, using the domains identified by Uzgiris and Hunt (1975), such as object permanence, imitation, and means-ends causality.

A relative newcomer to the field in the category of norm-based instruments is the Battelle Developmental Inventory (BDI) (Newborg, Stock, Wnek, Guidubaldi, & Svinicki, 1984), which has recently found favor among both researchers and interventionists. The BDI is comprehensive in scope, assessing 341 developmental skills in 5 domains. It includes guidelines for adapting the test to children with sensorimotor impairments and diverse developmental disabilities. It represents the only current example of a standardized norm-based instrument that includes curriculum-based features. Although data on the validity and reliability of the instrument are incomplete, the BDI shows promise of becoming a standard tool in early childhood assessment.

In addition to the instruments discussed above, numerous rating scales have become available in recent years to measure such diverse variables as the child's developmental behaviors, home environment, temperament, interactions with parents, and play. Several of these scales are discussed in greater detail later in this chapter or in Chapter 9.

Assessing Children with Specific Handicapping Conditions

Certain children present special problems to the professional conducting an assessment. Children with visual or hearing impairments, for example, cannot be administered the most commonly used standardized tests, because their handicaps prevent them from optimum performance. Adaptations have been developed for these children and children with motor delays, autism, and other special conditions. Simeonsson (1986) has summarized test instruments appropriate for use with young children with hearing or visual impairments (Table 8.6). This work (Simeonsson, 1986) provides excellent background information for assessing the child with sensory impairments.

The child with autism presents special problems because of the severe communication deficits, deficits in attention, perception, and memory, and problems with social interactions commonly found among this population. Several recommendations for facilitating assessment of autistic children are presented by Marcus and Baker (1986). They include the following:

1. Take the child's viewpoint and understand the reality the child has constructed because of limitations of cognition, communication, and/or perception. The implication here is that the child will be given the benefit of the doubt rather than engaged in a battle of wills.

2. Use appropriate instruments and provide flexibility in test procedure. This

Table 8.6. Selected measures for assessing children with sensory impairments

Measure	Age	Format of results	Psychometric properties
Child Behavior Checklist (Achenbach & Edelbrock, 1981)	4–16 years	*T* scores for internalizing, externalizing, and total problem score	Interrater and test-retest reliabilities in *r* = .90s
Behavior Problem Checklist (Quay & Peterson, 1967)	Kindergarten–6th grade	Scores for conduct problems, personality problems, inadequate-immature behavior, socialized delinquent behavior, psychotic behavior	Interrater reliability *r* = .75–.77; test-related *r* =.74–.91 (Taylor, 1984)
Reynell-Zinkin Developmental Scales for Young Visually Handicapped Children (Reynell, 1979)	0–15 years	Six age scales for cognitive and linguistic development	Information not found
Test of Basic Concepts (Boehm, 1971)	Kindergarten–2nd grade	Assessment of 50 basic concepts	Information not found
Blind Learning Aptitude Test (Newland, 1971)	6–20 years	Learning aptitude test—age and test quotient	Internal consistency, *r* = .93; test-retest reliability, *r* = .87 (Newland, 1971)
Perkins-Binet Intelligence Scale (Davis, 1980)	3–18 years	Two forms: U = usable vision; N = nonusable vision; scores for mental age and IQ	Information not found
Socio-Emotional Assessment Inventory (Meadow, 1983)	3 to 6–11; 7–21 years	Preschool inventory—five subscales; school age inventory—three subscales	Interrater reliability for subscales *r* = .58–.93, test-retest reliability *r* = .79–.86 (school-age inventory)
Matching Familiar Figures Test (Kagan, Rosman, Day, & Phillips, 1964)	Preschool and elementary age	Error score, latency score	Correlations of .44 and .34 between MFF and other measures (Johnson & Bommarito, 1971)
Empathy Task (Borke, 1971)	3–8 years	Scores reflecting child awareness of others' feelings	Not reported

(continued)

Table 8.6.   *(continued)*

Measure	Age	Format of results	Psychometric properties
Modification of Rotter IELC Scale & Piers-Harris Self Concept Scale (Koelle & Convey, 1982)	Children and adolescents	Internal/external score, self-concept score	Correlation of Rotter IES with modified form $r = .17$; self-concept with original $r = .82$
Modification of AAMD Adaptive Behavior Scale (Suess et al., 1983)	3–30 years	Profile	Interrater reliability $r = 73–96$

From Simeonsson, R.J. (1986). *Psychological and developmental assessment of special children* (pp. 211, 233). Boston: Allyn & Bacon. Copyright 1986. Reprinted by permission.

would include modifying instructions to make tasks clearly understandable, altering the sequence of items presented to balance language with visual motor tasks, and simplifying a task to give the child a successful experience.

3. Conduct the assessment in a highly structured environment, with clearly stated rules and an absence of distracting stimuli.

4. Realize that administering a standardized test to a child with autism will not yield valid information about that child.

Marcus and Baker (1986) have summarized the most useful diagnostic/behavior rating scales for use with autistic children (Table 8.7).

The child with motor delays presents unique problems for the early interventionist. The occupational or physical therapist can offer valuable assistance to the examiner in adapting the instruments, positioning the child, and interpreting the test results. The prescriptive checklist for positioning (Stephens & Lattimore, 1983) may also be useful. The following points should also be kept in mind:

1. Caution must be exercised in the use of norms, since many standardized tests

have not included children with motor impairments in their norming samples.

2. An informal evaluation of the child's vision, communication, hearing, and postural control should be obtained before beginning the assessment. This will ensure that the child is not asked to perform unreasonable tasks.

3. Evaluation of the motor-impaired child, like that of any other child with handicaps, should include assessment of intelligence, adaptive behavior, communication skills, self-concept, and social behavior, as well as a thorough evaluation of motor functioning (Wilhelm, Johnson, & Eisert, 1986).

For assessing the neuromotor status of infants, the Movement Assessment of Infants (Harris et al., 1984) is recommended. For infants and young children from birth to age 7 the Peabody Developmental Motor Scales (Folio & Fewell, 1983) are recommended. These instruments are more fully described on p. 181.

Play-Based Assessment

In recent years early interventionists and researchers have become interested in assessing young children in play settings. Because

Table 8.7.   Characteristics of diagnostic/behavior rating scales for autistic children

Scale	Age range	Domains	Mode of administration	Scoring
Autism Screening Instrument for Educational Planning	18 months	Sensory; relating; body and object use; language; social; and self-help	Checklist	57 items, sums of weighted items
Behavior Observation Scale	30–60 months	General language; language; response to stimuli; attending response; response to being helped; response to ball play; inappropriate response to pain; motility disturbances to stimuli	Observation in nine 3-minute intervals; combination of structured and unstructured; checklist	67 items, frequency count
Behavior Rating Instrument for Austistic and Atypical Children	Up to 54 months	Relationship to adult; communication; drive for mastery; vocalization and expressive speech; sound and speech reception; social responsiveness; body movement; psychobiological development	Descriptive ratings based on observations	10-scale score from severe autism to normal 3½–4 year level; cumulative score and profile
Childhood Autism Rating Scale	All ages; has been mostly used with pre-adolescents	Relationship with people; imitation; affect; body awareness; relation to nonhuman objects; adaptation to environmental change; visual responsiveness; near receptor responsiveness; anxiety reaction; verbal communication; nonverbal communication; activity level; intellectual functioning; general impressions	7-point rating scale based on observation of testing	Scale scores (1–7) and total score (15–60); 3 categories identified: no autism, mild to moderate autism, severe autism
E-2 Checklist	Up to 7 years	Social interaction and affect; speech-motor manipulative ability; intelligence and reaction to sensory stimuli; family characteristics; illness development; physiological-biological data	Checklist based on parental report, including retrospective recall	Multiple choice; items scored + or −; autism score the difference be-

(continued)

Table 8.7.   (continued)

Scale	Age range	Domains	Mode of administration	Scoring
E-2 Checklist (continued)				tween pluses and minuses; +20 considered cutoff for Kanner syndrome

From Marcus, L.M., & Baker, A. (1986). Assessment of autistic children. In R.J. Simeonsson (Ed.), *Psychological and developmental assessment of special children* (p. 300). Boston: Allyn & Bacon. Copyright 1986. Reprinted by permission.

play follows a regular developmental sequence from infancy through childhood, it lends itself to providing a measure of maturity and competence that is useful for planning intervention (Fewell & Kaminski, 1988).

The assessment takes the form of observing play behaviors in nondelayed children, then arranging the behaviors sequentially from earlier to later, based on the play research literature. Several researchers have developed scales using this information that may be used in assessing children with developmental delays. The most widely known of these scales include the Peer Play Scale (Howes, 1980), the Symbolic Play Scale Checklist (Westby, 1980), the Play Assessment Checklist for Infants (Bromwich, Fust, Khokha, & Walden, 1981), and the Play Assessment Scale (Fewell, 1986b). The last two are available only in experimental editions from the authors. All of the scales described below are currently used primarily in research studies, and none are available commercially (Fewell & Kaminski, 1988).

Peer Play Scale (Howes, 1980) measures five levels of interactive play: parallel, parallel with mutual regard, simple social play, reciprocal and complementary action, and reciprocal social play.

Symbolic Play Scale Checklist (Westby, 1980) measures the development of symbolic behavior by means of observations of both play and symbolic language beginning at 9 months of age and continuing through age 5. It requires observation of both symbolic and nonsymbolic behaviors.

Play Assessment Checklist for Infants (Bromwich et al., 1981) requires videotaping infants as they interact with sets of toys. The videotape is then reviewed and scored. The instrument was designed to be used in conjunction with the infant development scales developed by Bromwich and Parmelee (1979).

Play Assessment Scale (Fewell, 1986b) also requires observations of children interacting with specific sets of toys. The play behaviors are then scored, and a play age calculated. Fewell's scale includes scores for both spontaneous and elicited play.

Play assessment is a useful means for determining the developmental levels at which early intervention should begin. Although not available commercially at this time, the assessment scales described here have been thoroughly researched and tested on adequate numbers of infants and young children. They can be very useful in providing a basis for developing instructional objectives related to play.

SUMMARY

This chapter begins with a discussion of differences between screening and assessment, and lists some of their limitations. Current issues of importance to professionals who conduct screenings and assessment of infants and young children are also discussed, including issues related to cultural bias in testing, norm-referenced versus criterion-referenced testing, and special considerations for using assessment in early intervention. Next, a discussion of multidisciplinary assessment is presented, with an overview of assessment from the viewpoint of the various professionals involved in serving infants and young children and their families. Finally, special problems in assessment and special means of assessment (i.e., assessment through play) are discussed.

9

Ecological Assessment of Infants, Young Children, and Their Families

1. What information might be obtained from observing a child and his or her family at home?
2. How might a family interview serve to build rapport with a family?
3. Why is it important to assess a family's needs as well as strengths?
4. What aspects of the early intervention center environment are useful to assess?

A NUMBER OF ISSUES AND techniques for assessment and evaluation were discussed in the previous chapter that focused on assessment of infants and young children. The focus here is somewhat different in that this chapter includes techniques for assessing the children's environments and families, as well as the infants and children themselves.

Ecological assessment has been defined by Neisworth and Bagnato (1988) as "the examination and recording of the physical, social, and psychological features of a child's developmental context" (p. 39). Ecological assessment is also concerned with interaction between the individual and the physical, social, and psychological environment. This chapter focuses on the assessment of chil-

dren and their environments; Chapter 10 provides a model through which the interaction and fit between individual children and their environments can be assessed. Both chapters stress the importance of an ecological approach to assessment and program planning.

Ecological assessment involves assessing individuals in their natural settings and assessing the settings themselves. The settings of primary concern in early intervention are the settings in which intervention takes place (e.g., classrooms, centers, hospitals) and the home and family setting. To be valid and complete, ecological assessment must consider the relationship between the child and a variety of different settings and activities. It

191

must employ techniques that take into account the culture, socioeconomic status, and value system of the child and family (Bailey & Wolery, 1989). Many of the techniques discussed in this chapter are naturalistic and observational because such approaches enhance the validity of an ecological assessment.

OBSERVATIONAL TECHNIQUES

As reliance on standardized tests as the sole source of assessment information decreases, observation of young children becomes more important. Observation can take place in the home or center (naturalistic) or in a more controlled laboratory-like setting (clinical). The nature of the setting is determined by the type of information sought. A language specialist may wish to observe children individually in conversation with their mothers; such a session could be conducted in a clinic or office. However, to obtain information regarding children's social interactions with peers and adults, informal language with peers, or interactions with other family members, observation must take place in the home or preschool center.

Several strategies for observing children have been developed during the past 50 years. Some of these techniques come to preschool education from the field of ethology, the study of animals in their natural environment. Others, such as the keeping of anecdotal records, have been used by preschool teachers for many years.

Narrative Descriptions

Narrative descriptions include anecdotal records, running records, and specimen descriptions. Anecdotal records have been used by classroom teachers for years to record the be-

havior of children about whom they are especially concerned. Such a record is simply a collection of descriptions about a child gathered whenever there is something of interest or importance to record. It usually reflects the writer's biases, since there are no built-in protections against them. Nevertheless, anecdotal records can help teachers gain specific information about a child's behavior patterns and what conditions might be reinforcing them. For example, a child considered to be aggressive may react to provocation by certain other children, a fact which may not become apparent until a series of provocative episodes have been recorded and analyzed.

Anecdotal records may also be used to find out what children have learned from a particular curriculum unit or presentation (Irwin & Bushnell, 1980). This is especially true for younger children, whose informal play is very spontaneous and who readily incorporate new experiences into play situations.

It is useful to reproduce here some guidelines developed by Brandt (1972) for researchers using anecdotal records. As Irwin and Bushnell note, these guidelines are also useful for teachers. They have been adapted from the original.

1. Record the anecdote as soon as possible after it occurs. It is important to have as accurate information as possible, since fresh information tends to be more accurate. Because of the demands on teachers' time, this guideline is sometimes difficult to follow.
2. Identify the basic action of the key person and what was said. It is important to try to record word for word what was said by the child. It may be necessary to paraphrase what was said by other people involved. The flavor of the conversation should be preserved.
3. Include a statement that identifies the setting, time of day, and basic activity.

This statement should be recorded at the beginning of each anecdote. If the child did something different from what he or she was expected to do, the expected behavior should be recorded as well.

4. Preserve the sequence of the episode. The anecdote should have a beginning, middle, and end.

5. Include three levels of actions in the anecdote; molar, subordinate molar, and molecular. The molar level describes the main activity of the anecdote: Jack was playing the piano. The subordinate molar level records more specific information about the main activity: Jack was playing the same four notes over and over again on the piano. The molecular level provides a qualitative description of the activity: Jack smiled and hummed to himself as he noisily banged away on the piano.

Running records provide more complete information than anecdotal records because they continue over extended periods of time. Whereas anecdotal records are kept intermittently, running records must be maintained at scheduled times, say, every hour or every day, at predetermined intervals. The more detail included, the more useful is the record for understanding the child's behavior. The following excerpts from a running record written in 1941 give an idea of what kind of information this type of observation can provide.

> Frances slid, bumped herself, and cried. Mary, watching, said, "What did Frances doing? What did Frances do?" to recorder, who explained.
> Mary: "Frances broke that hand," holding up her own right hand. Recorder repeated the remark to make sure she had heard correctly and Mary answered, "Yeh."
> (Ten minutes later) Mary: "I didn't bump my finger," holding up her hand with fingers spread.
> Adult: "You *did?*"

> Mary said, "I didn'. Frances bumped it."
> Polly, coming out into the hall and finding Mary there, said, "Oh, here's two Barb'ras. 'Is is a Barb'ra," touching Mary, "an' '*is* is a Barb'ra," indicating herself.
> Mary looked at her solemnly and replied, "'*Is* me."
> Polly, smiling and affable, repeated, "Here's two Barb'ras. Here's a Barb'ra and here's udder Barb'ra," touching each of them as before.
> Mary let her finish her sentence, then repeated stoutly without a smile, "'*Is me.*"
> Polly started to repeat her story, but may have sensed Mary's disapproval, for this time she called herself a "Barb'ra," then said, "An' 'is is Ma'y."
> Mary looked mollified and nodded saying again, "'Is is *me.*" (Woodcock, 1941, pp. 186, 191)

Running records are generally more complete than anecdotal records, but both forms of recording are easy to do and require little preparation or training. They are time consuming if done effectively, however.

Specimen descriptions were first used by researchers in the field of ecological psychology to record behavior of children or animals in their natural environment. Barker (1955) first used them in his study of midwestern children. Specimen descriptions differ from anecdotal and running records in the following ways:

1. Specimen descriptions are more formal, requiring that subject, setting, time, and episode be identified at the beginning of each narrative.

2. Specimen descriptions are limited to a series of episodes. Each description must contain only one episode or event.

3. To record a specimen description the observer must be able to sit uninterrupted and record events during an entire episode. This is not difficult for a professional researcher, but is impossible for a classroom teacher working with a group of children.

4. The specimen description contains more

objective reporting. The observer is supposedly less involved with the subject(s) and makes fewer inferences regarding their feelings, thoughts, and intentions than do writers of anecdotal or running records.

In their excellent review of running records and specimen descriptions Irwin and Bushnell (1980) include guidelines developed by Barker's associate, Herbert Wright. These are summarized in Table 9.1.

As stated above, the major advantage of the narrative description techniques discussed here is the ease with which they can be carried out. For this reason, they are widely used by classroom teachers and researchers interested in obtaining information informally about children as they go about their daily business of exploring and learning. These techniques can provide the teacher with information for program planning that cannot be gleaned from other sources such as testing or parent interview. For this reason, they remain an essential ingredient in a good assessment program.

Nevertheless, narrative descriptions have a major flaw, namely, observer bias. Since only one person observes the child and his or her interactions, the record is inevitably

Table 9.1. Guidelines for recording running records and specimen descriptions

1. Describe the scene as it is when the observer begins the description
2. Focus on the subject's behavior and whatever in the situation itself affects this behavior. Events or conditions removed from the subject need to be considered when:
    a. an action or circumstance would normally impinge on the subject but does not do so
    b. an action or circumstance leads to a change in the subject's situation, even though the subject is not initially aware of the change
3. Be as accurate and complete as possible about what the subject says, does, and responds to within the situation
4. Put brackets around all interpretive material generated by the observer so that the description itself stands out clearly and completely
5. Include the "how" for whatever the subject does
6. Give the "how" for everything done by anyone interacting with the subject
7. For every action report all the main steps in their proper order
8. Describe behavior positively, rather than in terms of what was not done
9. Put no more than one unit of molar behavior in each sentence
10. Put no more than one thing done by a person other than the subject into a single sentence
11. Do not report observations in terms of the time an event happened, but do mark off predetermined time intervals (eg., 1-minute intervals)
12. Write in everyday language
13. Use observational tools (tape recorders, cameras, or video tape) whenever possible and transcribe notes on the typewriter. Barker and Wright (1955) used a system of observe-dictate-interrogate-revise in making their observations for *Midwest and Its Children*. This procedure calls for an initial observation period followed by dictation of the observation. A colleague then listens to the dictated narration of the observation and asks questions or interrogrates the observer to correct inconsistencies, ambiguities, unclear or incomplete information, and so on. The observer then transcribes the dictation and revises the observation. Barker and Wright find it helpful to have the interrogator look at the revised transcription once more before it is submitted for final typing. Time, purpose, and budget will determine what, if any, observational tools you will be able to use and what steps you will take in preparing a final copy of your anecdotal observations.

From Irwin, D.M., and Bushnell, M.M. (1980). *Observational strategies for child study* (p. 106). New York: Holt, Rinehart & Winston. Copyright 1980. Reprinted by permission.

biased by the interpretations, perceptions, and inferences of this one recorder. In addition, the very nature of the narrative style encourages the imputing of intentions, feelings, and thoughts to the subject that may not actually exist (Thurman & Widerstrom, 1979). An example, taken from one of our students' classroom observations, makes the point clearer.

> Michael eyed the plate of cookies *as if he wanted to take one*. He looked around *to make sure no one was looking at him*.

Note the inferences contained in the italicized portions. These impart quite negative conclusions about Michael's intentions. Since the observer cannot read Michael's mind, however, the inference may not be correct. This kind of interpretation of a child's intentions or feelings is very common among classroom teachers and may be very detrimental to a child. It subverts the purpose of informal observation and may result in the child being inaccurately and unfairly labeled. In its way, the narrative description may be just as biased as the standardized test. It is important for this aspect of the assessment program to be as fair and objective as possible; teachers thus have a responsibility to obtain narrative observational data that do not reflect their own culture, values, or expectations of the children they teach.

Sampling Techniques

One major disadvantage of narrative recording procedures is the time required to carry them out effectively. By contrast, sampling techniques offer a means of obtaining information about a child by concentrating only on certain behaviors, or certain time periods for observation. For example, we may be interested only in the problem-solving ability of a child and so need only record instances relating to that ability. Or we may wish to learn more about how a child behaves in a free play situation; only that time period then needs to be observed. Although the information gathered using sampling techniques is not as comprehensive as that from anecdotal records, it is easier for a busy classroom teacher to obtain. Sampling techniques are most appropriate for center-based classrooms, but may also be adapted for home-based program use. Although to date they have been used mostly in research (Irwin & Bushnell, 1980), they offer much to teachers as an assessment tool to aid in program planning.

In time sampling the observer chooses specific behaviors that are easily observable and occur with some frequency. These might be negative behaviors, such as spitting or hitting, or positive ones, such as sharing a toy or showing affection. A small number of behaviors are chosen and their occurrence is recorded during short, regularly scheduled observation periods. A behavior (e.g., hitting) is operationally defined and then recorded each time it occurs during the observation period (frequency). Some behaviors, such as crying, are more appropriately measured by the length of time they continue (duration). The sample time periods are assumed accurately to reflect the child's behavior.

The behaviors in question are generally recorded on a special recording sheet, which simplifies the process. An alternative to the recording sheet is the wrist counter, on which the wearer pushes a button to record instances of the behavior observed during a given time period.

Unlike time sampling, event sampling is not restricted to specific preplanned time intervals but takes place whenever the targeted behavior occurs. An observer studying a child's temper tantrums, for example, records information whenever a tantrum occurs. There may be many hours or days in between recording periods. Thus, event sam-

Effective assessment of preschool children with handicaps can take place informally in the preschool classroom.

pling is more appropriate for infrequently occurring behaviors and the behaviors of one or several children may be recorded concurrently.

Event sampling is very time consuming for researchers, who may be forced to spend hours waiting for a behavior to occur, but it is well suited for classroom teachers, who can simply go about their daily business between recording sessions. Event sampling has the advantage of not isolating the target behaviors and interrupting the sequence in which they occur as does time sampling. It preserves the context in which the behaviors occur, making it possible to analyze causal relationships, getting at the why as well as the what of the behavior (Wright, 1960). Whereas time sampling is a method for quantifying behavior, event sampling allows us to examine it in qualitative terms as well. Which method to use in a given situation depends on the kind of information desired and the amount of time available for obtaining it.

Checklists and Rating Scales

Checklists provide a more structured form of observational data. They are useful for gathering information on development of specific skill areas. While narrative and sampling techniques seem best suited for assessing a child's social or emotional development, the checklist is useful for assessing academic needs. Good commercial checklists are available, but checklists are also simple to construct.

If we placed all of our assessment techniques on a continuum from informal and unstructured to formal and structured, the checklist would fall somewhere in the middle. Anecdotal and specimen records would fall at the informal, unstructured end of the continuum and standardized tests would be placed at the structured and formal end. The checklist moves us down the continuum toward formal testing, because it requires the observer to participate in the assessment process by presenting the child with specific tasks to perform rather than merely recording whatever the child happens to do. The checklist remains informal, however, in that there is not a prescribed way in which tasks must be presented.

Additionally, many items on checklists—such as using a pincer grasp, speaking in complete sentences, or sharing toys with others—may be assessed by observing the child during his or her daily routine.

A checklist is simply a list of skills, usually arranged in developmental sequence and sometimes with normative age levels noted for each skill, that is presented to the child in sequence and graded on a pass/fail basis. The checklist may be either criterion- or norm-referenced or both. In the sense that it measures the child's performance against a written criterion it is criterion-referenced; in the sense that it provides normative age levels against which to measure the child's performance it is norm-referenced.

Generally, the child either passes or fails an item without consideration for the quality of his performance. However, a good checklist provides a clear criterion for each task so that the observer can decide on an objective basis whether or not the child can perform the task in question. This is the most important requirement for a good checklist, for clearly spelled out mastery criteria increase the reliability of the instrument and make it easier to administer.

Two well known and commonly used skills checklists are the Learning Accomplishment Profile (Sanford, 1974) and the Portage Guide to Early Education (Bluma, Shearer, Frohman, & Hillard, 1976). (See further discussion in Chapter 8.) These instruments list tasks in each developmental area—cognitive, language, motor, social development, and self-help skills—and provide a column for recording pass/fail. A second column is used for recording the date at which mastery was achieved. The checklist thus shares another characteristic with the informal narrative description: it is meant to be part of an ongoing process rather than administered only once or twice, as are formal tests. This greatly increases its usefulness as a tool for program planning, since new information regarding the child's skill levels is constantly available for incorporating into individualized plans.

Many early childhood educators feel that commercially available checklists do not break skills down into small enough components to be useful for lesson planning. For that reason, they often prefer to develop their own checklists. This can be done by proceeding as follows:

1. Choose a developmental area in which the child needs special instruction. Pick a specific skill from this area to assess.
2. Observe several older children or children without handicaps to determine the specific components of the skill. Use a commercial checklist to get started, then fill in the gaps through observations.
3. List the developmental steps in sequence.
4. Transfer the skill sequence to a checklist format, with columns for recording date of first assessment, date of mastery, and comments
5. Develop a criterion for each step to deter-

mine whether or not the child has mastered the skill at that step

Skills checklists are among the most widely used assessment instruments in educational programs for both children with and children without disabilities, because they are easy to administer, provide information that is useful for program planning, and are relatively reliable and free of bias. However, checklists are only one part of a good assessment program. Without information from both ends of the continuum as well as from the middle, we do not have a complete picture of the child.

Rating scales are used to make judgments about a child's behavior or environment. They are not as useful as checklists, for they are not well suited for assessing academic performance. In addition, because they require a judgment to be made yet rarely provide criteria on which to base such a judgment, such scales tend to contain a great deal of bias. Nevertheless, a rating scale may be a useful time saver. Take, for example, the Pupil Behavior Rating Scale, developed for assessing the emotional behavior of young children. This instrument allows the observer to rate a child in terms of attention span, activity level, and distractibility in order to identify possible learning disabilities. The rating scale can be based on knowledge previously gained about the child, or can be determined through current observation. Either way, little time needs to be spent in direct observation compared to narrative or sampling techniques.

A portion of the Pupil Behavior Rating Scale is reproduced in Table 9.2 to illustrate the general format such scales take. Usually the observer is asked to rate the subject on a particular behavior on a numerical scale (e.g., 1 to 5). Sometimes the scale is descriptive, ranging from "Never" through "Sometimes" to "Always." The information gained may be useful in identifying areas for further

testing, but it is usually too general to be very helpful in program planning. For this reason, rating scales are more useful during the screening process than they are for assessment.

ASSESSING FAMILIES

Recognizing that family provides a major context within which the child develops, early intervention programs have been concerned for many years with family involvement and with a family's ability to facilitate the child's development. More recently, programs have become more family focused inasmuch as they have begun to center on both the needs of the family and those of the child. To some extent this family focus grows out of the provisions of PL 99-457, which call for the development of Individualized Family Service Plans (IFSPs). Development of these plans, which must include statements about family strengths and needs (see Chapter 10) necessitates the assessment of families. Examples of family-focused programs are discussed in Chapter 13.

Interviews

One means of gathering information from a family is through an interview. Interviews are useful because they are often informal and provide the family members and the professional conducting the interview the opportunity to build rapport with each other. Interviews can provide a good deal of information in a relatively short period of time. Often the interviewer will have a specified set of questions to which families may provide answers. For example, the interviewer may ask specific questions concerning the family structure, the child's developmental progress, or the nature of the family's social support system (Winton & Bailey, 1988). At the

Table 9.2. Pupil behavior rating scale

Name_____ School_____ Grade_____

Sex_____ Date_____ Teacher_____

I. Auditory comprehension and listening

Ability to follow directions

(1)	(2)	(3)	(4)	(5)
Always confused; cannot or is unable to follow directions	Usually follows simple oral directions but often needs individual help	Follows directions that are familiar and/or not complex	Remembers and follows extended directions	Unusually skillful in remembering and following directions

Comprehension of class discussion

(1)	(2)	(3)	(4)	(5)
Always inattentive and/or unable to follow and understand discussions	Listens but rarely comprehends well; mind often wanders from discussion	Listens and follows discussions adequately for age and grade	Understands well and benefits from discussions	Becomes involved and shows unusual understanding of material discussed

Ability to retain orally given information

(1)	(2)	(3)	(4)	(5)
Almost total lack of recall: poor memory	Retains simple ideas and procedures if repeated often	Average retention of materials; adequate memory for age and grade	Remembers procedures and information from various sources; good immediate and delayed recall	Superior memory for both details and content

Comprehension of word meanings

(1)	(2)	(3)	(4)	(5)
Extremely immature level of understanding	Fails to grasp simple word meanings; misunderstands words at grade level	Good grasp of grade level vocabulary for age and grade	Understands all grade level vocabulary as well as higher level word meanings	Superior understanding of vocabulary; understands many abstract words

II. Spoken language

Ability to speak in complete sentences using accurate sentence structure

(1)	(2)	(3)	(4)	(5)
Always uses incomplete sentences with grammatical errors	Frequently uses incomplete sentences and/or numerous grammatical errors	Uses correct grammar; few errors of omission or incorrect use of prepositions, verb tense, pronouns	Above-average oral language; rarely makes grammatical errors	Always speaks in grammatically correct sentences

Adapted from a project developed under Research Grant, U.S. Public Health Service Contract 108-65-42, Bureau of Neurological and Sensory Diseases.

same time the interview may give family members the opportunity to bring out and discuss issues that are important to them.

In discussing the family-focused interview, Winton and Bailey have suggested that these interviews may be used to assess family resources and perceptions and collaboratively to set goals. They suggest that the family-focused interview be conducted in four phases. The introductory phase should be used to explain the purpose and structure of the interview, and assure confidentiality. In essence this phase should be used to put family members at ease and reduce their anxiety.

The inventory phase represents the major portion of the interview. Family members should do most of the talking. The interviewer should make an opening statement and ask open-ended questions. The interviewer should convey that he or she is there to listen, not to lecture or to judge. This will allow family members to begin with topics and concerns that they feel comfortable discussing.

The third phase is summary, priority, and goal setting. During this phase the thoughts and feelings of the family members are summarized and the needs of the family are listed in order of priority. The goals identified should be seen as the family's goals and the family should be given responsibility for achieving them. The professional should be cast in the role of helper. This approach helps empower the family to a greater degree. Such empowerment is the centerpiece of a family-focused service delivery system.

The closure phase ends the interview. During this phase, the family's contributions are acknowledged and they are given the opportunity to share any other ideas or concerns. This last point should be remembered since, as Winton and Bailey (1988) point out, "during closure, family members may share critical information that had not emerged during the more formal part of the interview" (p. 201).

In conducting family-focused interviews, interviewers should also keep in mind the following guidelines:

1. Be flexible. Let the family take the lead and set the agenda.
2. Treat family members as equals. Approach families in a noncondescending manner.
3. Be accepting. Accept what the family has to say without being judgmental or negative.
4. Consider cultural differences and family values. Accept the culture of the family and the values that they bring to the interview even though they may differ from those commonly shared by other families.
5. Avoid the use of jargon. Make certain that family members are spoken to in understandable terms. If technical terms are needed during the interview be sure they are adequately explained.

Use of these guidelines, coupled with the structure provided by Winton and Bailey (1988), should help ensure that family interviews are successful data gathering opportunities. More importantly, following these guidelines can help in building family-professional partnerships.

Other Family Assessment Instruments

In addition to interviews a number of paper and pencil instruments have been developed that can be used to obtain information from families. These instruments, discussed below, measure areas of family functioning such as social support, coping, stress, cohesion, and needs. For a more complete overview of family measures, see Dunst and Trivette (1985), Fewell (1986a), and Bailey and Simeonsson (1988).

Tools to Measure Social Support Social support has been shown to be a significant mediator of stress. Typically, the greater the social support available to a family, the lower the degree of stress the family experiences (Cohen & Syme, 1985). Measures of social support can provide useful information to early intervention professionals and can help them determine what kinds of social support a family may require. Dunst, Trivette, and Jenkins (1988) developed the Family Support Scale for such a purpose. The scale consists of 18 items, which can be completed by family members in about 5 minutes. The scale identifies 18 possible sources of support (e.g., parents, spouse, co-workers, early childhood intervention program) and asks respondents to rate how helpful each has been in terms of raising their child(ren). Dunst and colleagues (Dunst, Jenkins, & Trivette, 1984; Dunst, Trivette, & Jenkins, 1988) report that the scale has good reliability.

Trivette and Dunst (1988) have developed the Inventory of Social Support. This scale can be used in conjunction with the Family Support Scale, and provides information about how often a person has contact with various individuals and agencies that can provide support. The list of individuals and agencies is identical to that on the Family Support Scale. A second part of the Inventory of Social Support includes 12 questions about Social Support (e.g., Who do you go to for help or to talk with? Who loans you money when you need it? Who takes time to do things with your child? Who encourages or keeps you going when things get hard?). Respondents then indicate where they go for these social support functions. As Trivette and Dunst (1988) suggest "a complete matrix provides a graphic display of the respondent's personal network in terms of both source and type of support" (p. 159).

Another commonly used measure of social support is the Family Environment Scale (Moos, 1974). Not all of the items on this scale measure social support. One group of items does address interpersonal relation-ships within the family. Thus, the scale provides some measure of intrafamily support. Adequate internal consistency and test-retest reliabilities have been reported for this scale (Fewell, 1986a). The scale includes 90 statements (e.g., family members really help and support each other; family members almost always rely on themselves when a problem comes up; we tell each other about personal problems; friends often come over for dinner or to visit), which respondents must identify as true or false.

Tools to Measure Coping   It is often useful to understand how a family copes so that, where necessary, alternative coping strategies can be developed by the professional. One instrument that can be particularly useful is the Coping-Health Inventory for Parents (CHIP) (McCubbin, McCubbin, Nevin, & Cauble, 1979). The CHIP lists 45 coping behaviors (e.g., believing in god; eating; allowing myself to get angry; getting away by myself) and asks respondents to indicate how helpful each behavior is in helping them cope. The CHIP was specifically designed for use with families who have a member requiring medical care. The definition of coping provided by the authors on the test form states that "coping is defined as personal or collective (with other individuals, programs) efforts to manage hardships associated with health problems in the family."

Another measure of coping is the Ways of Coping Inventory, developed by Folkman and Lazarus (1980; 1985; Folkman, Lazarus, Dunkel-Shetter, DeLorgis, & Gruen, 1986). The inventory provides eight scales: confrontive coping (e.g., stood my ground and fought for what I wanted); distancing (e.g., made light of the situation; refused to get too serious about it); self-controlling (e.g., I try to keep my feelings to myself); seeking social support (e.g., talked to someone to find out more about the situation); accepting responsibility (e.g., criticized or lectured myself); seeking social support (e.g., talked to someone to find out more about the situation); accepting responsibility (e.g., criticized or lectured myself); escape-avoidance (e.g., wished that the situation would go away or somehow be over with); effortful, planful problem-solving (e.g., I knew what had to be done, so I doubled my efforts to make things work); perceiving growth (e.g., changed or grew as a person in a good way). The Ways of Coping Inventory includes 66 items, which respondents rate using a 4-point scale that reflects the degree to which each strategy was employed in coping with a stressful event.

Tools to Measure Stress Families with infants and young children with special needs often experience stress (Beckman, 1983). The amount of stress in caring for a child with special needs may be related to the family's ability to deal effectively with the child. Thus, it is useful for the early interventionist to know the degree of stress a family experiences. Recognizing this, Holroyd (1974) developed the Questionnaire on Resources and Stress (QRS). The QRS has been useful in research studies for distinguishing among families of children with different handicaps (Fewell, 1986a). The length of the original QRS (285 items) made it less useful in the clinical setting. Friedrich, Greenberg, and Crnic (1983) developed a short form of the QRS, which has only 52 items but which correlates very favorably with the longer version. The short form measures parent and family problems; pessimism; child characteristics; and physical incapacitation. Items are responded to as either true or false.

The Parenting Stress Index (PSI) (Abidin, 1983) is a 101-item questionnaire on which parents use a 1 to 5 rating scale to indicate how well statements describe their feelings. The parent domain includes the following subscales: depression, attachment, restriction of role, competence, social isolation, relationship with spouse, and health. The child domain includes adaptability, acceptability, demandingness, mood, distractibility, and reinforcement of parents. Fewell (1986a) reports that the PSI has been used in a number of research studies to discriminate groups of parents of children with disabilities from normative groups. She also reports that the scale has a high degree of internal consistency. "The extensive developmental work on the PSI suggests that this scale may be an important contribution to the assessment of stress in families, particularly those who have children with special needs" (Fewell, 1986a, p. 285).

Tools to Measure Cohesion and Adaptability Probably the most widely used measure of family cohesion and adaptability is the Family Adaptability and Cohesion Evaluation Scale III (FACES III) (Olson, Portner, & Lavee, 1985). The FACES III includes 20 items, to which various members of the family may respond. Two forms of the scale have been developed, one for any family member, and one for parents. Each of these has two versions, one on which respondents are asked to describe their family as it is, and a second in which they are asked to describe their family as they would like it to be. Each item is responded to on a 5-point scale, with 1 representing "almost never" and 5 representing "almost always." Cohesion items include the following: family members ask each other for help; we approve of each others' friends; and members feel very close to each other. Adaptability items include the following: children have a say in their discipline; rules change in our family; and it is hard to tell who does which household chores. FACES III is based on the circumplex model, which identifies 16 types of family systems ranging from those that are low in both cohesion and adaptability to those that are high on both dimensions. Olson and his colleagues suggest that balanced families are those that fall within the mid range on both the cohesion and the adaptability dimension. Scoring of the FACES III allows the researcher or clinician to determine where a family fits into the circumplex model. Although it is useful in classifying families, this approach carries with it the risk of labeling a family and creating a judgmental posture. Olson and his colleagues do point out the necessity of examining the degree of discrepancy between various family members' scores. The scale has been used extensively among families of children without handicaps and its authors report extensive data on its reliability. It has not been used much with families of young children with disabilities.

Tools to Measure Family Needs and Strengths The necessity to develop IFSPs requires that early intervention professionals assess the needs and strengths of families. Dunst, Cooper, Weeldreyer, Snyder, & Chase (1988) have described the Family Needs Scale (FNS). The FNS consists of 41 items representing various family needs, such as "feeding my child," "saving money for the future," "getting a place to live," and "exploring future educational opportunities for my child." Each item on the scale is either marked as not applicable or rated on a 5-point scale, with 1 representing "almost never" and 5 representing "almost always." The authors report a high degree of internal consistency for the scale, as well as a high level of split-half reliability. The authors report that a factor analysis yielded the following factors: basic resources (e.g., furniture, clothing, child care), specialized child care (e.g., respite care, dental and medical services), personal and family growth items (e.g., educational opportunities, family travel, saving money), financial and medical resources (e.g., money for special child necessities, adequacy of family health care), child education (e.g., child therapy, current and future educational placements), meal preparation (e.g., time to cook, help with feeding), future

child care (e.g., respite care, child's vocational future), financial budgeting, and household support. The authors conclude:

> the Family Needs Scale was specifically developed for intervention purposes. The scale is used to elicit family-identified needs, and the responses on the scale are used to prompt descriptions of the conditions that influence a respondent's assessment of his or her needs. The discussions that center around the responses on the scale help clarify concerns and help define the precise nature of the family's needs. (p. 150)

Another measure of family needs is the Parent Needs Inventory (PNI) (Robinson & De Rosa, 1980). The PNI consists of 25 statements, which respondents are asked to sort twice. The first sort represents the parents' present situation; the second sort represents their ideal situation. The PNI assesses the grief process, knowledge of child development, and knowledge of local resources. The scale takes about three hours to complete. Fewell (1986a) reports that the PNI has adequate reliability.

Trivette, Dunst, and Deal (1988) report on the Family Strengths Profile, which can be used to record family strengths and behavioral exemplars of each strength. The profile provides a useful format and can be used by interviewers to cover a number of family strengths. The profile includes the following listing of strengths: commitment, appreciation, time, sense of purpose, congruence, communication, role expectations, coping strategies, problem solving, positivism, flexibility, and balance. The instructions for the Family Strengths Profile state:

> The Family Strengths Profile provides a way of recording family behaviors and noting the particular strengths and resources that the behaviors reflect. Space is provided down the left-hand column of the recording form for listing behavior exemplars. For each behavior listed, the interviewer simply checks which particular qualities are characterized by the family behavior. (Space is also provided to record other

qualities not listed.) The interviewer also notes whether the behavior is viewed as mobilizing intrafamily or extrafamily resources, or both. A complete matrix provides a graphic display of a family's unique functioning style.

Tools for Measuring Parent-Child Interaction　　Few people question the importance of parent-child interaction in child development. Earlier chapters in this book point out how parent-child relationships can facilitate or interfere with cognitive, language, social, and physical development. In addition, it has become universally accepted that parents and families are an integral part of early intervention programs. Thus, it is important to be able to assess the nature of the parent-child interactive systems so as to aid parents in facilitating the development of their children.

Systems for assessing parent-child interactions are usually observational in nature and define categories of behavior for both children and parents. Rosenberg and Robinson (1986) have suggested that

> to be useful, observational measures of parent-child interaction should (1) permit reliable assessment of dyads containing young children whose patterns of behavior may be ambiguous due to a handicap that limits the child's ability to interact; (2) offer a system that is efficient and that can be easily incorporated into an intervention program; and (3) identify strategies that foster effective interactions between parents and their children. (pp. 35–36)

Thus, assessment of parent-child interaction should provide the basis for intervention to improve the interactive system. In observing the interaction, professionals should also be afforded the opportunity for teaching and instructing parents.

Systems of parent-child interaction have been classified as *molar* or *molecular* (Rosenberg & Robinson, 1986, 1988). Molar systems are those that are based on large classes of behavior, such as responsivity or enjoy-

ment. Molecular systems define a number of discreet behavioral categories, such as smiling, touching, vocalizing, and level of infant arousal. Molar systems are more often used to categorize the style of interaction between parents and children, whereas molecular systems tend to be more descriptive and are used to examine the specific responses used during interaction and how those responses are related to each other.

Molar Scales　　The Maternal Behavior Rating Scale (Mahoney, Powell, & Finger, 1986) consists of 18 maternal behaviors and 4 categories of child behavior. Based on behavioral observations, each of these items is rated on a 5-point scale. The scale provides assessment of child-oriented maternal pleasure, quantity of stimulation, and control. The authors report interrater reliabilities based on correlations in the .80 range. Rosenberg and Robinson (1988) suggest that the scales should have adequate internal consistency, but report that Mahoney and colleagues do not report these data.

Rosenberg and Robinson (1985) developed a molar system to assess parent-child interaction. The Teaching Skills Inventory (TSI), Version 2, contains 15 items that are rated on a 7-point scale. The items on the scale measure the structure of the mother-child interaction, maternal responsivity, maternal instructional skills, and child interest. The authors report an interrater percentage of agreement of 86 and a high degree of internal consistency. They have also demonstrated that the scale is sensitive to changes in maternal behavior when those areas measured by the scale are targeted for intervention.

Molecular Systems　　Descriptions of molecular coding systems abound in the literature. Most of these systems have been developed for specific programs or for specific research purposes. The Social Interactions Assessment/Intervention (SIAI) model, described by McCollum and Stayton (1985), provides a useful illustration of the application of a molecular observations system to early intervention. The system targets specific child behaviors that parents would like to see become more frequent. Observations are then made to determine what parental behaviors may be affecting the occurrence of the targeted child behaviors. Intervention sessions are videotaped and assessed by coding the targeted behaviors and assessing changes in them. The authors report a high degree of interobserver reliability using SIAI.

ASSESSING ENVIRONMENTS

Ecological assessment depends not only on assessment of the individual child, but also on assessment of the child's environment. The two environments that determine the child's ecology are the early intervention center and the home.

Assessing the Early Intervention Center

Perhaps the best known tool for assessing an early intervention center is the Early Childhood Environment Rating Scale (ECERS) (Harms & Clifford, 1980). Although the ECERS was designed to be used in environments serving children without handicaps, its applicability to centers serving children with handicaps has been demonstrated (Bailey, Clifford, & Harms, 1982). The ECERS consists of 37 items that assess personal care routines, furnishings and displays, language-reasoning experiences, fine and gross motor activities, creative activities, social development, and adult needs. Scoring is on a 7-point scale (7 representing "excellent" and 1 representing "inadequate"). To be evaluated by the ECERS, a center must be observed for several hours and the staff must be inter-

viewed. Harms and Clifford (1983) report that interrater reliability based on correlation was .88 and that the test-retest reliability of the instrument was quite high.

Using the same format as the ECERS, Harms and Clifford have developed two additional environmental rating scales that target specific environments. The Infant/Toddler Environmental Rating Scale (ITERS) (Harms, Cryer, & Clifford, in press) can be used to assess environments serving children under 30 months. The Family Day Care Rating Scale (FDCRS) (Harms & Clifford, in press) can be used to assess care provided in a family day-care home. All three of these measures can provide useful information about the quality of the care and intervention environments of infants and young children.

Moore (1982) developed the Early Childhood Physical Environment Scales. One scale focuses on the entire center and assesses visual connection between spaces, closure of spaces, spatial separation, mixture of large and small spaces, separation of staff and children's areas, separation of functional versus activity areas, separation of age groups, and connection between indoor and outdoor spaces. The second scale assesses individual classrooms, and focuses on spatial definition of activity centers, visual connections to other centers, size, storage and work space, concentration of same-use resources, softness, flexibility, variety of seating and working positions, amount of resources, and separation of activity centers from circulation paths. Each dimension is rated on a 5-point scale.

Smith, Neisworth, and Greer (1978) have offered a number of suggestions related to the evaluation of educational environments. Many of these suggestions are applicable to environments serving young children with special needs. The reader is also referred to Chapter 11 for a discussion of how the environment may be considered in implementing programs for infants and young children with special needs.

Assessing the Home

The Home Observation for Measurement of the Environment (HOME) Inventory was developed by Cadwell and Bradley in 1972 and has since become the most widely used tool for assessing home environments. The most recent version of the HOME includes a scale for infants (birth to 36 months) and preschool children. The infant version consists of 45 items, divided into the following subscales: maternal responsiveness, physical organization, maternal acceptance, availability of play materials, maternal involvement, and variety of stimulation. The preschool version contains 55 items, divided into the following subscales: stimulation through toys and games; language stimulation; physical environment; warmth and affection; stimulation of academic behavior; encouragement of social maturity; variety of stimulation; and level of physical punishment. Although the overall reliability of the HOME is good, some of the subscales tend to be less reliable (Bailey & Wolery, 1989; Rosenberg & Robinson, 1988). Thus, as Rosenberg and Robinson suggest, "it may be advisable to use only the total HOME score, which has an acceptable level of internal consistency, when making decisions . . . about individual children" (p. 168). To be evaluated by the HOME, a home must be visited by professionals who interview and observe the family members. The HOME can be used to gain valuable information about the home environment that can be used to provide feedback to parents. However, as Bailey and Wolery (1989) point out, care should be taken "to communicate a positive impression of parenting skills" (p. 108) and the early interventionist should understand that "there is considerable variability in the importance of individual items" (p. 108) for different families.

SUMMARY

This chapter has reviewed a number of instruments and techniques that can be useful in carrying out an ecological assessment. These techniques and tools recognize the importance of the interaction between the young child with special needs and his or her environment. These techniques include informal observational methods of assessment as well as more formalized checklist approaches. Assessment of families is given emphasis not only because of the family provisions in PL 99-457, but also because of the significant interrelationship between the child and the family. Family assessments can be carried out through the use of family-focused interviews as well as through the use of questionnaires designed to measure social support, coping, stress, adaptability, and family needs and strengths. Several techniques used to assess early intervention environments were also discussed. These assessment tools focus on both the physical and the affective dimensions of these settings. Attention was also given to the assessment of the home environment.

IIB

Program Planning and Intervention

10

Individualized
Program Planning

---

1. What is the major premise of the ecological congruence model?
2. How is the ecological congruence model compatible with a developmental approach?
3. What is the importance of task analysis in program planning?
4. What are the three components of a well constructed instructional objective?
5. Why is a team approach important when implementing the ecological congruence model?

SINCE THE PASSAGE OF PL 94-142, the Education for All Handicapped Children Act, in 1975, there has been a legal mandate to develop individualized education programs (IEPs) for all children classified by the public schools as requiring special services. PL 94-142 required that public school systems that provide services to any children between the ages of 3 and 5 must provide the same services to all children ages 3 to 5 regardless of handicapping condition.

PL 99-457, the Education of the Handicapped Amendments of 1986, extends the provisions of PL 94-142 to children between 3 and 5 with handicaps. In addition, it provides states with funds to serve at-risk infants and infants with handicaps between birth and age 2. The provisions of the law call for multidisciplinary approaches to assessment and require the development of Individualized Family Service Plans (IFSPs) for all in-

fants served. These plans include the provisions of the IEPs, and also require that the needs and strengths of families be included. Thus, the law recognizes that both children with handicaps and their families are important in the development of individual plans. Many states have also mandated services to these populations. The National Association of State Directors of Special Education reported in October, 1988, that 5 states had mandated services to birth; 1 state had mandated services to age 2; 18 states had mandated services to age 3; and 3 states had mandated services to age 4. Clearly, then, legislative mandates apply to a large number of children who fall within the birth to 5 range.

As a result of these mandates, educational technology has been applied to the development of individualized educational services. In this chapter, we examine how educational technology facilitates the individual development of young children with handicaps. Specifically, task analysis, development of instructional objectives, and data recording systems are examined.

THE ECOLOGICAL CONGRUENCE MODEL

Before we can consider the technology of education, we must establish a context for that technology. Several years ago, Thurman (1977) devised the ecological congruence model for providing special educational services. His model is concerned with both the development of the child and the fit between the characteristics of the child and the environment. He suggests that educational in-

terventions must be concerned not only with changing the child to fit the environment, but also with changing the environment to fit the child. When the child and the environment are in harmony, a state of ecological congruence exists.

According to Thurman, the ecological congruence model has three critical dimensions: deviancy, competency, and tolerance for difference. These dimensions are illustrated in Figure 10.1 and are explained below.

According to the ecological congruence model, deviancy is a function of the label placed on individuals and/or their behavior. Essentially, the model accepts Simmons' (1969) suggestion that no human behavior is inherently deviant as a valid basis for the conceptualization of deviancy.

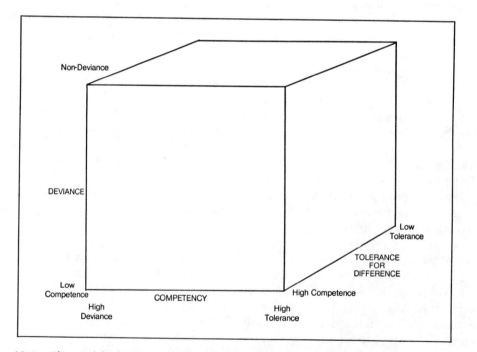

Figure 10.1. The model of ecological congruence. (Adapted from Thurman, S.K. [1977]. The congruence of behavioral ecologies: A model for special education programming. *Journal of Special Education, II,* 329–333. Reprinted by permission.)

The judgment made about a particular behavior or set of characteristics can be made relative only to the social context in which it has occurred. Thus, those conditions accounting for the label placed upon a behavior and, subsequently the individual himself, lie within the environmental context in which the behavior occurs. (Thurman, 1977, p. 330)

Competency can be defined, in the simplest terms, as functional behavior.

Just as every social setting defines parameters for deviance, so does it define a certain set of functional behaviors, or behaviors that lead to the completion of a task or job, within that setting. Competency/incompetency, unlike deviance, is an attribute of the individual, since given a specific task a person either has or does not have the necessary behavior repertoire to perform the task. (Thurman, 1977, p. 330)

Incompetence cannot be inferred solely from nonperformance, since performance of a task is a function of internal and external motivational factors, as well as competence. Lack of performance does not necessarily mean lack of competence.

Tolerance for difference is the dimension of the ecological congruence model that determines the goodness of fit between the individual and the environmental/social context. Within every social system there is a range of tolerance for difference. Each system defines its own range of what is or is not acceptable. Individuals viewed as excessively different, either because of their assigned degree of deviancy or their lack of competence in performing tasks within the system, are not tolerated by the system. Lack of tolerance by the system establishes an incongruent ecology.

Although not discussed in the original description of the ecological congruence model, incongruence in an ecology may result from intolerance by individuals of the system. If, in fact, individuals perceive systemic attributes they cannot tolerate, then a lack of ecological congruence results. For ecological congruence to be maximized, mutual tolerance of individuals for systems and systems for individuals must be brought about. Most often, human service interventions change individuals to make them more tolerable to social systems, and thus create more congruent ecologies. Interventions are rarely designed to make systems more tolerant of individual differences, be they in levels of competence or degree of perceived deviance. Somewhat more frequent, although still rare, are interventions designed to increase individuals' tolerance of social systems.

Individual approaches to educational programming have dealt almost exclusively with the application of educational technology to changing individuals. Individualized educational approaches designed to increase ecological congruence must have three objectives: 1) to change individual patterns of behavior, 2) to change the tolerance for systemic difference of these individuals, and 3) to change the tolerance of the system for individual differences in competence and perceived deviancy. This approach does not alter the usefulness of the technology to be discussed, but rather modifies the way it is applied.

When an individual's ecology is congruent, the stage has been set for maximization of his function and adjustment. Competent function brings along with it human dignity acceptance within the setting, and provides the basis for developing higher levels of competency. Congruence along the deviancy/nondeviancy dimension results in greater acceptance of the individual within the setting. [This coupled with the individual's tolerance for the setting leads to a feeling of security and nurturance.]

Congruence results in (a) the individual's expression of his maximum competence . . . (b) the acceptance of him with his individual differences [and (c) his feelings of security and comfort]. Congruence does not necessarily mean "normal," rather it can be seen as maximal adaptation [between the individual and the environment]. To borrow a term from biology, a homeostatic relationship exists between the individual and the environmental setting. As with all homeostatic situations, congruent behavioral ecologies will be in a state of dynamic equilibrium. . . . Such dynamic states are the basis of further adaptation and development of [both] the individual *and* his environment [and their continued interaction with each other]. (Thurman, 1977, pp. 332–333)

The ends inherent in the ecological congruence model are particularly relevant to disabled and at risk preschool children whose perception of the environment and whose environments' perception of them may significantly alter their developmental course (Sameroff, 1979; Sameroff & Chandler, 1975; cf. Kearsley, 1979; Thurman & Lewis, 1979) and the ultimate nature of the ecological system of which they are part. In individualized program planning for young children with handicaps, the assumption is that program plans will improve ecological congruence rather than change individual patterns of behavior in order to increase individual levels of competence.

While the ecological congruence model suggests interventions that are designed to improve ecologies, it simultaneously recognizes the importance of individual development within the ecology. In fact, as will be seen in the ensuing discussion on program planning, assessment of a particular child within an ecological system depends upon adequate knowledge of a child's developmental progress and the various factors that account for it. Competence, in the ecological congruence model, represents the developmental status of the individual. Ability to perform a particular task or behavior (i.e., express competency) is clearly a function of a child's developmental status. It is the interrelationship between the individual's developmental status and degree of competency, and the setting's reaction to them that is important within the context of the ecological con-

gruence model. Essentially, the program planning strategy to be discussed is both developmental and ecological in nature, and recognizes the unique contribution of each approach to the other.

Using the Ecological Congruence Model in Educational Planning

Thurman (1977) has suggested a 9-step process to assess degree of ecological congruence. The following steps are a modification of the original process.

1. Identify the major environmental settings that are important in the child's life.
2. Develop an inventory of critical tasks in those settings (i.e., those tasks that make the setting function).
3. Assess the child's competence to perform those tasks.
4. Assess motivational variables (i.e., contingency structures) and other factors that affect the child's ability to perform tasks.
5. Assess the child's tolerance of the environment.
6. Determine which of the child's behaviors and/or characteristics are outside of the level of tolerance of the system. (Note: These behaviors and/or characteristics may be those labeled as deviant, or they may be the result of insufficient development of the child to perform necessary tasks.)
7. Identify objectives for each component of the ecology (i.e., child and system) that, when accomplished, will lead to increased ecological congruence.
8. Identify strategies for accomplishment of the objectives.
9. Establish a means by which interventions are to be monitored and their effectiveness assessed.

Smith, Neisworth, and Greer (1978) suggest that there is a range of educational environments, each of which has a role in the total education of the child. In discussing these environments, they suggest that "psychological and educational research [have] strongly documented the powerful influence of the environment on learning. Yet very little attention [has been] given to assessing the characteristics of the environment" (p. iv). They conclude that "astute diagnosticians are presently well beyond the point of focusing their assessment efforts exclusively on the child" (p. iii). The implementation of the ecological congruence model takes into account the points made by Smith and his colleagues and provides a useful context within which to examine existing aspects of educational technology. The remainder of this section elucidates the educational planning process as it is influenced by the ecological congruence model. Various aspects of educational technology are examined.

Identification of Major Environmental Settings   Each of us operates in a number of environmental settings each day. Only some of these settings, such as the daily family meal or weekly church service, have a major influence on one's life. Other settings are generally much less influential (e.g., the busy street corner or the shopping mall). The relative importance of any setting depends on the individual and his or her overall ecology. The shopping mall, for example, may hold great importance for a blind 3-year-old who is just developing independent mobility skills.

To determine the most important environmental settings for any child, it is first necessary to identify the settings the child frequents. Although one should not assume *a priori* that an infrequently entered setting is not significant, as a rule those settings that young children occupy most frequently are generally the ones of greatest significance.

Barker (1968) has provided a means for identifying individual units of the environment, which he terms *behavior settings*. Behavior settings can be used to define an individual's behavioral ecology and the way in which setting characteristics influence an individual's behavior. For our present purpose, it is most useful to apply Barker's strategy to identify environmental settings within which child setting congruence can then be determined.

Behavior settings, according to Barker (1968), have a standing pattern of behavior and a specific milieu. The standing pattern of behavior and milieu remain constant regardless of the individuals occupying the setting. For example, in the behavior setting *family dinner,* the standing pattern of behavior includes eating, sitting, passing food, and some degree of conversation. The milieu includes the physical features of the setting (i.e., the table, chairs, plates, utensils). The behavior setting is defined when the standing pattern of behavior and milieu come together in a functional manner at a given point in time. The behavior setting *family dinner* could not exist without all necessary utensils or enough chairs for all members of the family to be seated. Nor could it exist if people were sitting at the table but not engaging in eating, a critical aspect of the standing pattern of behavior. Thus, while the milieu is always present in space and time, it becomes part of a behavior setting only when it is surrounded by the proper standing pattern of behavior.

The identification of behavior settings begins with interviews with parents or primary caregivers of young children with handicaps. Parents are asked to describe a typical day in their family and to describe where they go and what they do. Settings entered by older siblings, especially those closest in age to the child in question, may be of particular importance. These settings may provide useful insights into what the target child will be expected to do in the future. Interviews with parents can also include questions about the frequency of certain activities. Parents and other caregivers can also be asked to keep simple logs or diaries for a week or two to gain additional insights into the behavior settings that the target child enters. A visit to the home can be useful in determining the milieu of those behavior settings occurring there. If the child has already entered a day program of some kind, visits can be made to the program and staff there can be asked about daily activities. Parents, teachers, and other caregivers can be asked to rate the importance of each setting identified for the child. For example, one family may view *Sunday morning church service* as a very important behavior setting and one with which they seek congruence for their child. Another family may be more concerned with ecological congruence during mealtimes, or when visiting relatives.

Most families inhabit fairly standard behavior settings. As a result, some may question spending time on interviews, diaries, and home visits. Each family is unique, however, and each may exhibit a different profile in the frequency of different behavioral settings. Moreover, interviews, diaries, and home visits reveal the relative importance of different behavior settings. Keep in mind that individualized program planning is the impetus for ecological congruence for ecologies that include preschool children with handicaps.

Inventory of Critical Tasks   Each behavior setting is defined in part by a series of behavioral tasks. Once the most important settings have been identified, further analysis of these settings may be necessary. Since the ecological congruence model is concerned with competence in those settings that make up a child's ecology, it is important to identify the competencies required for independent function of the individual within the setting. Using the earlier example of family dinner, one necessary task for independent function is self-feeding. Self-feeding, however, may not be necessary for ecological congruence. The milieu and the behavior of other members of the setting often provide the individual modifications necessary to bring about congruence for the 9-month-old child who has not yet acquired independent feeding skills. Such modifications include high chairs, bibs, down-size utensils, and help from other members of the family. This example shows how naturally occurring systems modifications can bring about ecological congruence. The family system may or may not be as ready to make the necessary environmental modifications for a disabled 3-year-old who possesses the same level of competence in self-feeding as a nonhandicapped 9-month-old.

Critical competencies exist in most settings. If the same 9-month-old had developmental problems that did not permit independent sitting in a high chair, achieving congruence with the environment might be more difficult. Again, interviews with parents and caregivers, as well as systematic observations of behavior settings, can be useful for identification of task competencies for various levels of function. Further individualization is possible by assessing the individual level of competence that the target child has in displaying these competencies. In a sense, the tasks included in the task inventory of the major behavior settings form the basic curriculum targets for the child's further development. This statement should not be taken to mean that certain systems modifications may not be necessary so that the child can express his or her maximum level of competence. Forgetting to examine and implement the necessary systems modifications would be to abandon the ecological congruence model.

Assessing the Child's Competencies A number of tools, both standardized and informal, can be used in assessing the competency of young children with handicaps (see Chapters 8 and 9). These tools may be useful in getting a general picture of the child's level of competence and development. They may also provide information about the child's ability to perform tasks within given behavior settings. None of these assessment devices, however, is tied directly to competencies required in specific behavior settings. *Task analysis* is a way to assess a child's competence to perform specific tasks in a given behavior setting.

Task analysis can be defined as breaking down a complex task into its component parts or behavioral steps. It is a way of developing instructional sequences, and has been used extensively in educational and vocational programming for both severely and profoundly retarded individuals (cf. Gold, 1976; Smith & Snell, 1978; Van Etten, Arkell, & Van Etten, 1980) and preschool children with handicaps. Within the context of the ecological congruence model, task analysis can be applied to specific tasks that are critical to function within a particular setting. These task analyses may then be used to assess the competency of an individual child.

For example, a critical skill in a preschool classroom is a child's ability to enter the room, take off his or her coat, and hang it on a hook. A task analysis of this skill (competency) might read as follows:

Step 1: Child removes coat
Step 2: Child locates hook
Step 3: Child hangs coat on hook

These three steps are necessary to accomplish the critical competency and are indeed a task analysis of sorts. To be useful for assessment and instructional purposes, a greater degree of precision is necessary, however. These rather large steps must be broken into small-

er, more discrete steps. A better task analysis of the skill might read as follows:

Step 1: Child grabs one edge of coat at the chest.
Step 2: Child extends arm holding coat and lifts coat off of one shoulder.
Step 3: Child grabs other edge of coat at the chest with other hand.
Step 4: Child extends other arm lifting coat off at other shoulder.
Step 5: While still holding coat with one hand, child pulls one arm out of the sleeve.
Step 6: With arm free of sleeve, child reaches across body and grabs top of collar.
Step 7: While continuing to hold collar, child pulls other arm from sleeve.
Step 8: Child continues to hold coat by collar and locates hook.
Step 9: Child places inside of collar over the hook.
Step 10: Child releases coat from hand.

This task analysis breaks down the task into much smaller and more discrete steps than did the previous one. As a result, it can be used to assess much more precisely a child's competence in taking off a coat. Even this task analysis could be broken down into finer steps. For example, Step 1 could be further broken down as follows:

Step 1: Child bends arm at elbow at 90°.
Step 2: Child rotates arm so it is against the body.
Step 3: Child extends fingers.
Step 4: Child places fingers on the edge of the coat.
Step 5: Child flexes fingers around edge of coat.

This task analysis breaks the skill of grabbing the edge of the coat into its specific components. The degree of detail (i.e., the number of steps) in a task analysis depends upon the general nature of the task as well as the functioning level of the child. In the examples above, the second task analysis represents the level of detail necessary for most children. The steps in the first task analysis are clearly too large; those in the third analysis are more detailed than is needed for most children. The third analysis probably would be of use for a child with particular difficulties in motor function or hand-eye coordination.

Task analyses for critical tasks in a setting can be used to determine a child's degree of competence. Suppose a new child entered a program and the teacher wanted to find out whether or not the child could take off his or her coat. By employing the task analysis developed above, the teacher may find that the child can perform each step of the task, that the child can perform some but not all of the steps, or that the child cannot perform the task at all. To increase the level of ecological congruence, the teacher would probably want to develop an instructional program to increase the child's ability to take off his or her coat. If the other children in the class had already achieved this competency, they might not be tolerant of the child who was just learning the skill. In that case, the teacher might have to develop a means by which the other children could become more tolerant of differences. The teacher might have to be tolerant of the extra time necessary to instruct the child and get the coat off and hung up.

Assessing Motivational Variables An assessment may reveal that a child has the competency to perform a particular task, although observation may reveal that the child rarely performs the task spontaneously and independently. In this case, the child's performance deficits can be accounted for by lack of motivation. Motivation may be defined as a person's tendency to perform tasks and may be intrinsic (come from inside the individual) or extrinsic (come from outside the individual). Intrinsic motivation involves performing a task because it is expected, or because it leads to a feeling of doing right. Extrinsic motivation involves performing a task because it leads to a compliment, or because it leads to a reward, such as food, money, or special considerations. Although almost no one is exclusively intrinsically or

extrinsically motivated, children, especially those who are delayed cognitively, tend to be extrinsically motivated. Thus, our emphasis in this section is on identifying variables related to extrinsic motivation.

Extrinsic motivation is inherent in the environment. Put another way, children tend to behave (i.e., perform tasks) because their behavior results in certain consequences in the external environment. These consequences may be arranged so that children are more likely to behave in one way than another (see Chapter 11). Such arrangement of learning environments increases motivation, and concomitant increases in task performance (i.e., expression of competency) and learning (i.e., acquisition of new competency) come about.

Lack of ecological congruence may be a result of lack of performance, due either to lack of motivation or lack of competence. In developing individual plans for the establishment of ecological congruence, it is important to assess how a child is best motivated. What environment increases the child's tendency to perform critical tasks? To determine the optimum environment, both the child and the environment must be observed.

Such observations should be structured to determine what consequences children experience as a result of their behavior. Behavior that is followed by positive environmental consequences is probably desirable behavior; that which is followed by negative environmental consequences is probably undesirable behavior. By the same means, the consequences desired by particular children can be identified. When children are observed in a free environment without any planned intervention on their behavior, it can be assumed that they are behaving in the manner in which they are motivated to behave. Thus, if children enter the room and spontaneously hang up their coats, it can be assumed that they are motivated to perform in this manner. At the same time, if the behavior is followed consistently by verbal praise from the teacher, it is likely that the teacher's verbal approval is contributing to the children's motivation. Children whose coat hanging performance is not consistently followed by teacher praise and who continue to perform this task can be assumed to be motivated by other factors, which are probably more intrinsic in nature.

Consequences of behavior that increase a child's tendency to behave in a certain manner are referred to as *positively reinforcing consequences*, or *positive reinforcers*. As suggested above, the activities in which a child freely engages are activities reinforcing to that child. To increase the performance of certain tasks by the child (assuming, of course, such intervention is necessary for ecological congruence), it is important to establish a reinforcement hierarchy for the child. A *reinforcement hierarchy* is a list of consequences available in the environment that the child values. The more a particular consequence is valued by a child the higher that consequence appears in the hierarchy.

A reinforcement hierarchy can also be determined by asking parents what their children like best. Of course, children, too, can be asked to describe what they like, providing they have the necessary language skills to communicate likes and dislikes. Another means of finding effective reinforcers for children is to test the effect of various consequences on their behavior. This can be done relatively simply by having children perform a simple task (e.g., finger tapping, hand clapping, jumping up and down), and counting the number of times they perform the task in a minute. Several of these one-minute sessions can be followed by a particular consequence. Several more performances can be rewarded by another consequence, and so on until five or six different consequences have been employed. Those sessions in which the greatest number of behaviors (e.g., taps, jumping) occurred are assumed to be the sessions that were followed by the more reinforcing consequences. These consequences probably appear near the top of the reinforcement hierarchy.

An understanding of motivational factors is necessary for establishment of ecological congruence. The techniques discussed in this section are used to acquire information about the motivational structure of the child's environment and the specific factors that are important for motivating a particular child. More will be said in Chapter 11 about the way the learning environment can be organized to make maximum use of motivational variables. Suffice it to say at this point that it is necessary to assess both competence in performing critical tasks, and response to various motivational variables. From the perspective of ecological congruence, the motivational aspects of the environment should maximize the child's expression of competence and support the learning of new critical competencies.

Assessing the Child's Tolerance of the Environment   Systematic observation is a major source of data about young children's tolerance of their environments. Children should be observed in a number of different settings and during various activities within each setting. It is important to determine to what degree they spontaneously interact with people and objects in the environment. For example, is a particular child observed to make frequent or infrequent contacts with other children in the setting? How frequently the child makes contacts with adults in the environment also provides important information about the child's level of tolerance. Data may indicate that the child is more likely to approach and interact with some people in the environment than with others, thus indicating a higher degree of tolerance of some people by the child.

Another key to the child's tolerance of a particular environmental setting is the ease with which the child enters the setting. For example, a child who comes to the classroom reluctantly or protestingly suggests a low level of tolerance for the classroom setting. Such behavior is a primary source of incongruence between the child and the environment and requires an intervention designed to increase ecological congruence. Another child may enter the classroom freely, but throw a tantrum at lunch time. This child tolerates the classroom environment generally, but would appear to have a low level of tolerance for lunch. Some intervention to increase ecological congruence is probably necessary.

A child who displays a low level of tolerance for the system will, in most cases, become more tolerant over time. This is particularly true if the system is tolerant and responsive to the child's needs and if a trusting and nurturing environment is provided. Of course, educational interventions may be specifically designed to increase a child's tolerance for the environment. The common procedure of ignoring a child's temper tantrums is a case in point. Although ignoring a child helps ensure that undesirable behavior is not being positively reinforced (at least in the classroom), it may be interpreted by the child as a sign of tolerance. Ignoring the child during a temper tantrum requires that the people in the environment tolerate the child's yelling and screaming until the child stops. Confrontation with the child increases the intensity of the tantrum, not only because the child receives attention for his or her behavior, but also because the people in the system are not being tolerant of the child's behavior. This confrontation often results in mutual intolerance, which creates an even greater level of incongruence in the ecology.

Assessing Tolerance of the Child in the Environment The degree of tolerance in any environment is defined by the people in the setting, both individually and collectively. For example, in a family setting, one parent may tolerate a 5-year-old cerebral palsied child's inability to go to the bathroom independently while the other parent may not tolerate it at all and refuse to interact with the child during toileting times. In another family, both parents may tolerate the child's inability to toilet independently. In still a third, neither parent may tolerate it. In the case of intolerance by both parents, it is likely that the child will be placed outside of the family.

In program planning for ecological congruence, it is important to assess the degree of tolerance in the social system for the preschool child with a handicap. This assessment can be made by observing how various individuals in the social system interact with the child. Do people approach the child, and if so under what circumstances? What behavior on the part of the child is followed by negative, or aversive, consequences? Negative consequences of a behavior suggest that the behavior is not desired or tolerated in a particular setting. Negative feedback suggests that the child is expected to behave differently in order to be tolerated in the setting. This is not to suggest that negative consequences are necessarily effective in changing the child's behavior. Nor is it to suggest that the individual who provides the negative consequence to the child cannot become more tolerant of the child's level of functioning.

People's expectations also measure their limits of tolerance. Through interviews, it is often possible to determine different people's expectations for a particular child. This is especially true for parents, siblings, teachers, and other caregivers who have regular opportunities to be with the child. The primary concern is the current expectations for a particular child. In addition, some understanding of general expectations and limits of tolerance may also be determined through observation and interview techniques. These more general expectations and toleration limits may be important in maintaining ecological congruence over time. They are also important in developing long-term objectives for interventions.

Identifying Program Objectives Interventions must be planned when there is incongruence between a preschool child with a handicap and his or her environment. This lack of congruence can come either from the system's intolerance of the child because of perceived deviancy or incompetence, and/or from the child's intolerance of the system. Before program objectives can be identified, the sources of incongruence and the specific settings or situations in which incongruence exists must be discovered. These data and the characteristics of the child are the basis of objectives.

Well-articulated objectives underpin any successful intervention program. Objectives delineate what behaviors, values, attitudes, and physical modification must be brought about to establish ecological congruence. In addition, a well-formulated objective can be used to gauge the effectiveness of a particular intervention.

Program objectives should be established by a team of professionals and parents. This team should identify which areas of incongruence are most important, so that increased congruence can be developed in these areas first. These priorities will be the result of the team's discussion of the assessment data gathered, as well as of the perceptions of each member of the team. The role of the team in program planning is discussed more fully later in this chapter.

The important thing to remember in constructing objectives is that program planning must address both changes in the child and changes in the child's environment and social system. More traditional approaches to program planning have placed almost total emphasis on changes in the child. Some approaches have addressed certain interventions to parents (see Chapter 13), but these interventions have usually been designed to make parents more effective change agents for their children. Parent-oriented programs have not usually been concerned with increasing parental tolerance except as it is affected by the child's increased behavioral functioning.

The passage of PL 94-142, the Education for All Handicapped Children Act, provided an unprecedented impetus to individualized program planning. The mandate of PL 94-142, however, has clearly been to develop individualized objectives to change the behavior of individual handicapped children. Although PL 94-142 has been important, it has substantially ignored the need for both the child and his or her environment to change. If ecologically sound interventions are to be carried out, objectives that address both changes in the child's environment and changes in the child must be developed. The provisions for Individualized Family Service Plans (IFSPs) found in PL 99-457 help set the stage for the development of more ecologically sound interventions.

In the early 1960s, Mager (1962) introduced a way to prepare clearly stated, operationally defined instructional objectives. Mager's system has weathered the test of time and is still being advocated by researchers and practitioners involved with special education instruction (cf. Berdine & Cegelka, 1980; Safford, 1978; Van Etten, Arkell, & Van Etten, 1980). This system is, in fact, inherent in the requirements found in

PL 94-142 and 99-457 for establishing individualized objectives. Mager suggests that a well-constructed instructional objective has three essential characteristics. First, it stipulates the specific behavior expected. Second, it delineates the conditions under which the child is to emit the specified behavior. Third, it provides a criterion by which the accomplishment of learning the specified behavior can be assessed.

Consider the following examples of objectives.

> Susie will identify her coat while it is hanging with four other coats.
> Susie will take her coat off its hook.
> Susie will identify her coat five out of five times for 3 consecutive days.

Each of these objectives meets a different one of Mager's criteria. The first example does not specify the behavior clearly enough, since "identify" could mean pick up, verbally label "that's mine," point to, or take the coat from its hook. This objective also does not include a criterion for acceptable learning performance. It does, however, express the conditions under which Susie must "identify" her coat, namely, while it is hanging with four other coats. The second example provides an observable behavior by stipulating that Susie will take her coat off its hook. This example, however, fails to identify the conditions under which the behavior will be performed. The third example provides a criterion, but does not meet the other two conditions. The following objective meets all of Mager's criteria.

> Susie will take her coat off the hook while it is hanging with four others, five out of five times for 3 consecutive days.

This objective is well constructed because it is based on an observable behavior, provides the conditions under which the behavior must be performed, and gives a criterion by which learning can be assessed.

Task analyses can also be a basis for developing instructional objectives for a child. In our earlier example of task analysis the ability of the child to take off a coat was viewed as a critical competency for a particular preschool classroom. Suppose that through the assessment process we discover that Susie cannot take off her coat and that this is a skill that the team agrees she should learn. The accomplishment of that skill represents a terminal objective for Susie that could be stated as follows:

> Given Susie with her coat on, and the verbal command, "Take off your coat" (conditions), she will remove her coat and hang it on a hook (behavior) within 2 minutes five out of five times for 3 consecutive days (criterion).

A terminal objective represents the learning of a complete task rather than any specific step in a task. Each step in a task can be expressed as an en route objective; that is, one that takes the child closer to some terminal point. Thus, the first en route objective for Susie in learning to take off her coat and hang it up might be as follows:

> Given Susie with her coat on, and the verbal command, "Take off your coat," Susie will grab one edge of the coat at the chest within 10 seconds five out of five times for 3 consecutive days.

The next en route objective might then be as follows:

> Given Susie with her coat on, holding one edge of the coat at the chest, and given the verbal command, "Take off your coat," Susie will extend her arm lifting the coat off of one shoulder within 10 seconds five out of five times for 3 consecutive days.

The rest of the en route objectives would be developed from the next eight steps of the task analysis using a similar strategy.

The ecological congruence model mandates that objectives also be developed to change the setting to bring about congruence. The structure of these objectives can be essentially the same as that used for the development of objectives for individual children. Of course, the content of objectives for settings is different from that of objectives for children. Suppose we return to our earlier example of the father who was intolerant of his daughter's inability to toilet independently. Recall also that this child had cerebral palsy and lacked the physiological control to be completely independent in toileting skills. Since she was toilet trained to the maximum extent possible, increasing her competence for independent toileting was not possible. To increase the ecological congruence in the family setting, the parent lacking tolerance must become more tolerant of the child's level of competence. An objective for the parent might read:

> Mr. Ray will take Ann to the bathroom, when she asks to go, three times during the day for 8 consecutive days.

Another objective might read:

> Given Ann's lack of independent toileting behavior, Mr. Ray will make positive statements about Ann's ability at least four times a day for 4 consecutive days.

In this objective the positive statements might have to be further defined with specific examples. These positive statements would be assumed to stem from increased acceptance of Ann's ability and more good feelings toward her on the part of her father. Notice, too, that an objective does not necessarily express the means for intervention, but merely the proposed outcome of intervention.

So far we have considered examples of objectives either to change the child, or to change aspects of the child's environment to establish congruence in the ecology. On many occasions, both child and environment will have to change for congruence to increase. In that case, complementary objectives are necessary—some that address child change and others that address system

change. Suppose a 4-year-old, developmentally delayed child has acquired only rudimentary eating skills, that is, he can eat certain foods with his fingers but not with his utensils. His older brothers would like to have friends come to dinner but are embarrassed by their younger sibling's lack of competence in eating. An objective could be developed to increase the child's eating competence. Such an objective might state:

> Given meal time and a plate of cut up food in front of him, Bobby will use a spoon to complete his meal for six consecutive meals.

At the same time, objectives might be developed that would help Bobby's brothers deal more effectively with their embarrassment over his behavior. For example, an objective for them might read as follows:

> Given Bobby's poor eating behavior, his brothers will be able to express their feelings verbally about it at least once a week for 4 consecutive weeks.

In addition, the boys might be taught strategies to explain Bobby's behavior to their friends, should the need arise. An objective for this ability might read as follows:

> Given their friends at dinner and Bobby eating with his fingers, Bobby's brothers will be able to answer questions about his behavior if asked.

The reader should be aware by now of the importance that the ecological congruence model places on changing not only the child, but the child's environment.

Identifying Strategies for Accomplishing Objectives Chapter 11 deals with program implementation. At least a word should be said here, however, about the way potential change strategies can be identified. In general, it is necessary to understand the particular characteristics of the individual or the system and the conditions accounting for the incongruence in the ecology in order to identify change strategies. The reader is reminded of the earlier discussion of conditions accounting for cognition in Chapter 4. The format of Figure 4.1 can easily be adapted for use in determining conditions that may account for the characteristics of a particular child, as well as the characteristics of the systems with which the child interacts. The same model is also applicable to identifying the conditions accounting for incongruence in the ecology.

Identifying Means for Monitoring Progress In the planning process, some thought should also be given to how to monitor progress toward congruence. The planning process should establish the frequency of and guidelines for monitoring activities. As was suggested earlier, in and of themselves properly constructed objectives are a means of program monitoring. Whether a particular objective has been met can be judged by whether the behavior specified in the objective is occurring at the level specified in the criterion.

One additional aspect of program monitoring that can take place as part of the planning process is the establishment of time lines for the accomplishment of objectives. For example, it may be decided that a particular terminal objective should be met in 6 months while another may require only 3 months. Time targets can be useful, but they must be flexible, since a number of different factors affect how quickly objectives are met.

THE TEAM APPROACH TO PROGRAM PLANNING

The ecologies of infants and preschool children with handicaps is complex. Both the children and their environments are multifaceted. To program for ecological congruence effectively, as many aspects as possible of the child/ environment system must be identified. Thus, a holistic approach to program planning must be adopted. Since no single individual possesses the professional expertise to analyze the entire child/environment system, a team approach to program planning and implementation is necessary. As discussed earlier in Chapter 8, using a team approach increases the chances of considering all aspects of the child/environment system. Each professional can bring a particular expertise and perspective to the program planning process. Minimally, a program planning team for young children with handicaps should include representatives from special education, nursing, social work, psychology, and speech-language therapy. Teams may also include physicians, physical and occupational therapists, audiologists, and nutritionists. The more professionals represented on the team, the more complete a picture can be obtained of the child and his or her ecology. In addition, the program team should include the parent or guardian or other advocates for the child and family. Each professional must be concerned with assessing the status of the child, the child's environment, and the interaction between the two. Each professional has unique skills to bring to the evaluation and planning process as well as to program implementation. At the same time, each professional must be open to suggestions and negotiations that bring about the best individualized program for the ecology being served.

Team function has been characterized as occurring on three levels (Copeland & Kimmel, 1989). The first level is *multidisciplinary*. On a multidisciplinary team each professional is responsible for assessing the child and/or family of concern. These assessments are specific to each professional's discipline. Multidisciplinary teams often spend little time discussing clients and may assign the responsibility of summarizing information to a single member of the group. Typically, multidisciplinary approaches do not provide means for professionals to come to consensus, or to provide each other with feedback on the results of their assessments. It has been suggested that the multidisciplinary approach can result in professional contradictions and client frustration (Sparling, 1980). As Peterson (1987) suggests, the multidisciplinary approach has a number of weaknesses that limit its application. It is interesting to note, however, that the language in both PL 94-142 and PL 99-457 makes reference to the use of multidisciplinary teams.

Teams also function at the *interdisciplinary* level. In interdisciplinary team function greater emphasis is placed on communication among team members. As with the multidisciplinary approach each professional may assess the child and family independently. Here, however, team members then attend a team meeting at which they report and discuss their individual findings. All team members are given the opportunity to provide other members of the team with feedback. Team members are given the chance both to agree and disagree with each other. A final set of recommendations is formulated through team consensus. The individualized plan that is developed as a result of interdisciplinary team function integrates the findings and recommendations of all the members of the team. After implementation of the plan the team continues to meet and to make recommendations based on the progress of the child and family. Of course, it requires more time and communication to bring about effective interdisciplinary team function than it does to operate on a multidisciplinary basis.

The third level on which a team can operate is the *transdisciplinary* level. Transdisciplinary team function requires even more commitment to effective communication than interdisciplinary function. In a transdiciplinary approach, professionals from several dis-

ciplines work together in carrying out assessments. For example, a social worker and psychologist may interview a family together, or a speech-language therapist may observe a child being assessed by a physical therapist to determine how well the child is using language.

Another approach used by transdisciplinary teams is *arena assessment*. This approach requires all members of the team to be available for the assessment session. Although only one team member may interact with the child, this person elicits responses from the child that let other professionals draw conclusions about the child's function from their own disciplinary perspectives. Parents are included as participants in the arena assessment. The transdisciplinary approach depends upon the designation of one individual from the team as the leader for a particular child and family. This person might conduct the arena assessment and would be responsible for the ongoing services for the child and family. A transdisciplinary approach requires that each member of the team can share this lead role equally. Thus, for this approach to be effective it is necessary for each member of the team to participate in *role release* and *role exchange*. Role release means giving up one's traditional role; role exchange means taking on the role of another. On a transdisciplinary team, therefore, a physical therapist might have to incorporate the role of a psychologist in implementing a program plan. The transdisciplinary approach requires that members of the team are willing to provide information and training to each other so that role release and role exchange can be effective. As Peterson (1987) suggests, "the transdisciplinary approach was conceived in an attempt to reduce the compartmentalization and fragmentation of services that sometimes occur when many professionals are working simultaneously, yet separately, with a child [and her family]" (p. 487). As suggested above, this type of approach requires significant teamwork and communication to be ultimately effective.

The advantages and disadvantages of multi-, inter-, and transdisciplinary approaches are summarized in Table 10.1. Regardless of the level of team function, each team member brings a unique perspective and contribution to the team. The contribution of individual team members may be affected by the ecology being assessed and may thus vary from case to case. To help the reader understand the contributions that each member of the team can make, we briefly examine the roles of professionals from the major disciplines involved in early intervention services.

The Role of the Special Educator

The main goal of special education is to ensure that the environments of infants and young children with handicaps facilitate their development and increase their competence. Thus, special educators must become aware of both the educational needs of the child and the opportunities the child's environment provides. They must assess the child's competence within the various settings in which the child operates and analyze those settings to discover ways in which the child's competence can better be expressed. For example, an educational assessment may reveal that a child with spastic quadriplegia is not only able to complete but enjoys the challenge of wooden puzzles. However, if the classroom environment has only tables with slick tops that allow the puzzle boards to slide around when knocked by the child's uncoordinated movements, an opportunity for the child to express competence may be lost. A special educator should recommend and implement the necessary environmental modifications. In this case, that might mean placing a rubber mat on the table, attaching a

suction cup to the puzzle board, or placing the puzzle board in a frame that is firmly attached to the table.

Special educators may also be important in assessing and identifying specific educational strategies for behavior change in both the child and in other individuals in the child's environment. Special educators should also be responsible for formulating specific educational and developmental objectives for the child and for planning and implementing the strategies necessary to achieve those objectives. In this regard it may be necessary for special educators to incorporate and integrate the suggestions of other team members, especially speech-language, physical, and occupational therapists. Finally, special educators must be prepared and have in place a means to assess the effectiveness of the intervention strategies being employed. This assessment plan must be in keeping with the overall evaluation plan being used by the team. This last point actually applies to the ongoing assessment activities being carried out by any professional on the team and thus is not unique to the special educator.

The Role of the Nurse

The main focus of nursing is on the health status of the child and the family, and promotion of the highest possible degree of health in the child's ecology. Nurses conduct health assessments aimed at basic health care needs especially those related to the child's handicap. They might also be concerned with assessing the physiological status of the child.

Through assessment, for example, a nurse might discover that a 3-year-old with an orthopedic handicap has poor hygiene and is generally unkempt in appearance. Further investigation might indicate that the child's mother had not been taught proper lifting techniques and so finds it difficult to bathe

Table 10.1. Summary of various levels of team approach

	Description	Advantages	Disadvantages
Multidisciplinary Approach	Professionals work independently evaluating and serving the client in their own domains. Each applies the expertise and techniques of his or her discipline in isolation of what professionals in other disciplines are doing concurrently with a child or parent. Little or no interaction or ongoing communication occurs among professionals dealing with the same client.	• Child is evaluated and given therapeutic intervention by several disciplines that provide more in-depth assessment and treatment than a single professional could provide. • May be more convenient for professionals involved in that no extra time demands are imposed for coordination and planning with members of other disciplines. Each is free to apply his or her own style of service delivery without compromise with others who may advocate other ways of dealing with the client.	• Does not facilitate an integrated, synthesized approach to assessment and early intervention programming. Practitioners do not gain benefits of feedback from other professionals; thus, the client does not get full advantage of the potential expertise that could be tapped if all professionals synchronized their efforts toward common goals. • Chances are increased that techniques used with the child by each discipline will be incompatible. The child is treated in pieces rather than holistically, promoting fragmentation of treatment and reduction of the power of intervention to impact upon child's total development.
Interdisciplinary Approach	Professionals from various disciplines work together cooperatively in both planning and delivering services to the child or parent. Emphasis is upon teamwork and interaction among team members, who help and rely upon each other to provide well-coordinated, integrated services for the individual, although each discipline ultimately delivers the services in its own domain. Role definitions and modes of serving the client are relaxed in that staff does not necessarily work under its personal styles for implementing programs but, rather, adheres to a common system under which all team members agree to work.	• Services are planned and delivered with an orientation to the whole child and are better integrated to ensure compatibility of treatment techniques across disciplines. • Provides a more enriching, stimulating context for professionals. The expertise and input of other disciplines offers a means for team members to discuss their perspectives, to learn and expand their own skills, to gain support in their work, and to have access to other sources that can aid them in treatment of the child.	• Requires experienced administrative, communication, and leadership skills among team members if they are to work effectively as a team. • Places heavy time demands on team members to participate in meetings for purposes of joint planning and coordination. Quality and quantity of teamwork can be restricted by heavy caseloads or simply in synchronizing schedules of team members. • Places a premium on personal qualities of professionals that make for good team effort and coordination. Chances for staff conflict increase when individuals are

(continued)

Table 10.1. *(continued)*

	Description	Advantages	Disadvantages
Interdisciplinary Approach			protective of professional turf, lack respect for expertise of colleagues, or thwart common effort toward mutual goals.
Transdisciplinary Approach	Professionals from various disciplines work together cooperatively by educating one another in the skills and practice of their disciplines so that one team member can act as the single agent for carrying out services with a designated child or parent. This "role exchange" means that in working with a given child, a team member assumes the roles and responsibilities of other disciplines by delivering the treatment program based upon program prescriptions and instructions provided by joint planning of the total team.	• With one person working with a single client and synthesizing the treatment program, the burden for coordinating several separate therapy programs is lifted. Parents and child relate to only one person instead of many, making communication between client and interventionists less complicated. • Offers a means for delivering diverse services to children in rural areas or areas understaffed by various disciplines. Also a useful approach with severely multiply handicapped populations in which training requires simultaneous attention to many handicapping conditions. • Enhances the professional skills of the classroom teacher, who is often the pivotal or focal point of this approach.	• Places considerable responsibility upon each team member to master the skills and methodologies of other disciplines sufficiently to deliver quality programming to the child or parent. May be viewed as an unnecessary investment of time, given the presence of already trained, skilled personnel on the team. • Requires considerable time for cross-sharing, planning, coordination, and training of the member designated to deliver the treatment program. Also necessitates a high level of cooperation and trust among disciplines. • Role release may be difficult to operationalize if professionals take a formal, legalistic view of their respective professional role. State licensing may prohibit some aspects of role release.

Adapted from Peterson, N.L. (1987). *Early intervention for handicapped and at-risk children: An introduction to early childhood-special education.* Denver: Love Publishing Co. Reprinted by permission.

the child as often as she would like. The nurse might then teach the mother how to lift the child properly, something that would result in a higher level of congruence in the ecology.

Nurses may also be important to the team for assessing the status of health maintenance measures in the child's ecology. Sick-

ness often leads to a lack of congruence in the ecology, making the prevention of health problems a major factor in the continued maintenance of ecological congruence. Nurses are critical for identifying techniques to reduce the spread of infection and sickness among both children and adults. Nurses are also important in providing care for and consultation about children with special health problems, such as those requiring assisted ventilation, special feeding tubes, or frequent medication. Nurses may also be useful in providing health care expertise to professional staff and family members.

The Role of the Social Worker

Social workers probably understand family systems better than members of any other single profession. They are thus in a position to build a partnership with families and to assess families' needs. Their expertise can be particularly valuable in defining the degree of congruence within the family ecology. Social workers can provide insight into family attitudes, expectations, and practices that are of critical importance in defining the degree of ecological congruence within the family. Social workers are also able to identify the conditions that account for the lack of congruence in the family. They are essential when the level of congruence in the family is so low that physical, emotional, or psychological abuse is manifest toward any children, whether handicapped or not. They are often skilled in identifying factors that are the precursors to abuse and may be able to create higher levels of congruence between parents and children, thus preventing an abusive situation from developing.

The Role of the Psychologist

Psychologists assess the child's functioning levels and psychological status. In addition, they can identify the psychological needs of family members and the need for psychological supports to teachers and other service delivery personnel. Psychologists often can gain insight into parents' feelings by interviewing them individually. These data can be used in conjunction with those gained by social workers to assess and plan for changes in individual patterns of child/environment interactions.

Another important skill of psychologists is the ability to suggest how to approach a child or family to achieve the desired outcome. Many school psychologists are skillful in dealing with teachers and with agencies that might be involved in program planning and implementation. Many psychologists also have expertise in designing and implementing evaluation schemes to assess the effectiveness of various interventions, as well as the overall effectiveness of services to be provided to children and families.

Recall the earlier example of Ann and her father. It might well have been a psychologist who would have discovered Mr. Ray's inability to deal with Ann's lack of independent toileting and the lack of congruence it created. The team psychologist would have been instrumental in developing the objectives for Mr. Ray and might also have had primary responsibility for developing and implementing the necessary interventions. Such activities would be in keeping with the primary mission of the psychologist to derive a comprehensive picture of child and family functioning and to identify, implement, and/or evaluate psychological interventions.

The Role of the Speech-Language Therapist

Speech-language therapists play the primary role in determining a child's communicative competence. At the same time, they assess communication styles and communicative interactions between the child and others. Speech-language therapists are concerned with the communication skills of children in the context of social interactions with peers and family members in school and in various community settings. This concern is critical within the ecological congruence model, since lack of congruence can easily result from misunderstanding of communication styles or communicated messages. The regular kindergarten teacher who encounters a developmentally delayed child in her classroom for the first time finds that she must provide that child with additional or qualitatively different types of communicative cues. At the same time, she may need professional help in understanding the child's articulation errors in order to understand what the child is saying.

Another important area of expertise for many speech-language therapists is feeding. Speech-language therapists understand the oral cavity and the muscles and nerves of the face and jaws. Often they can apply this knowledge to difficult feeding situations, such as those brought about by a tracheostomy (Simon & McGowan, 1989) or oral hypersensitivity. Nurses, occupational therapists, physical therapists, and nutritionists may also have expertise in assessing feeding and providing feeding interventions.

The Role of the Pediatrician

Pediatricians, like nurses, are concerned primarily with the child's health status. Unlike nurses, pediatricians are often available only as consultants and are less likely to have contact with the child and family as part of a team. Their primary mission is to assist families in the promotion of optimal health, growth, and development of their infants and young children by providing health services. These services include assessment of the child's physiological state and general health, and the treatment of illness when present. Pediatricians can assess the need for drug therapy, both for remediation of illness and for maintaining health. They can provide information about both the beneficial and the adverse effects of drugs, and can educate other team members as to what danger signs to look for. They are also key to the as-

sessment and monitoring of physical growth, and in assessing the immunization status of the child. Pediatricians may also provide important information on how a physical condition or chronic illness might affect the child's ability to learn and develop.

The Role of the Physical Therapist

Physical therapists are concerned mainly with the assessment and development of gross motor function. They focus on the child's neuro-skeletal-muscular function, but may also assess the child's cardiopulmonary function and degree of general fitness. Physical therapists are important in assessing the congruence between the child and his or her physical environment and are able to design adaptive equipment for positioning and mobility that will help a child get maximum benefit from the stimuli present in the environment, thus increasing congruence. They are also well versed in the physical management of children with motor problems, and can be a resource for caregivers on how best to lift, move, or position a child. As suggested above, such information is often critical in improving the fit between child and caregiver.

The Role of the Occupational Therapist

Like the physical therapist the occupational therapist is concerned with sensory motor function. Occupational therapists, however, more often focus on fine motor, rather than gross motor, function. They also focus on the child's self-help abilities and adaptive and functional responses to the environment. Like speech therapists, many occupational therapists have particular expertise in feeding and feeding problems. This expertise grows from their orientation to expand and develop those functional abilities that are particularly dependent on the use of fine motor skills. Like physical therapists, occupational therapists assess the need for adaptive devices that facilitate motor function and increase the congruence between the child and the environment.

The Role of the Audiologist

More and more recognition is being given to the role of audiologists in serving infants and young children with handicaps. Audiologists provide and coordinate services to infants and children with auditory handicaps and screen infants and children to determine whether such handicaps exist. They focus on hearing handicaps, but also assess auditory perception in children whose auditory acuity may be within normal limits. Audiologists also have expertise in assessing the role of auditory function in the communicative process. They use a variety of techniques to assess audition, and can assess what types of amplification or assistive devices might aid children with hearing loss.

The Role of the Nutritionist

There is a growing recognition of the role of nutritionists in early intervention. Nutritionists are particularly important in assessing the nutritional needs of infants and young children with metabolic disorders, such as diabetes, phenlyketonuria, and galactosemia, and in structuring the special diets necessary for these children. They also have expertise in providing general nutritional information to parents and other professionals to help ensure that the infants and young children being served are receiving adequate nutrition and well-balanced meals. Nutritionists focus on ways to maximize the health and nutritional status of infants and preschool children through developmentally appropriate nutrition services within the

family and community environments. Together with professionals from other disciplines they may be concerned with food intake and feeding problems. They might concentrate more on ways to prepare the food for easier ingestion than on techniques to facilitate the use of the oral feeding mechanism, as speech therapists or occupational therapists might.

The Role of the Parents

Parents can and should be an integral part of the team that plans and implements services for them and their children. Outside of the child, parents are the greatest single source of information about the child's characteristics and level of functioning. Parents are important agents in the ecological system, and can be a major source of both congruence and incongruence. Unfortunately, it is often difficult to include parents as full team members because the parents may feel inferior to the professionals. To use parental expertise to its fullest, professionals must be mindful of the significant contribution parents can make to team planning, and must communicate with and treat parents in a way that makes them feel that they are important members of the team. Accomplishing this is sometimes difficult, not only because of parents' perceived inferiority, but also because it is not usually possible to confer with parents as often as it is with the professionals on the team.

While parents are a valuable source of input about their children and should be included in the team process whenever possible, it must be remembered that the purpose of early intervention is to meet the needs of parents and other family members, as well as the infants and preschool children being served. Thus, it is important to keep in mind that parents are both participants in team function and clients. At first glance this may seem to create a paradoxical situation. However, once parents are viewed as active participants in determining their own fate and that of their children, the apparent paradox is resolved.

Team Function and Case Management

For a team to function properly, it must have a leader. The leader can be permanent, or responsibility can shift and be related to case management. Each program plan and its implementation must have a case manager. This responsibility is assigned to the professional with the most significant role in provision of services or who has the best rapport with the family involved. Regardless of which leadership strategy is employed, it must facilitate team decision making.

Johnston and Magrab (1976) have summarized the essence of effective team function in the following statement:

> The problems of developmentally disabled children transcend the domain of any single profession. It is a challenge for all of us to develop creative and innovative modes for the many professionals involved to interact in an interdisciplinary way. . . . At a minimum each of us can become aware of the kinds of contributions each discipline has to offer and, at the optimum, become open to the interdependent relationships that can develop. (p. 12)

Johnston and Magrab's statement has added meaning when the basic concern is programming for increased ecological congruence.

A FORMAT FOR PLANNING

A planning format should be used to plan effectively for increasing ecological congruence. Figure 10.2 provides a planning format that allows team participants to summarize the program plan. This format is a guide, and users are urged to modify it to meet particular needs. The main features of the planning for-

mat are explained here and illustrate how various intervention strategies can be employed based upon this planning format.

Identifying Information Identifying information includes the family's name, child's name and date of birth, the specific ecological unit and/or activity for which the plan is being developed, the case manager, and the person primarily responsible for intervention in this particular ecological unit.

Source of Incongruence The source of incongruence should be specifically identified. For example, in the case of Ann and her father, discussed earlier, the source of incongruence could be described as a father's not accepting less-than-independent toileting ability by his daughter, who performs at her highest ability level.

Possible Necessary Conditions Possible conditions to account for the lack of congruence should be listed. With Ann and her father these could include the father's frustration over Ann's condition, Ann's incompetence in independent toileting behavior, the father's expectations of 5-year-old children, and the father's incompetence in helping Ann.

Objectives for the Child Specific objectives include the components suggested by Mager (1962) and discussed earlier in this chapter. In our example, no specific objectives would be indicated for Ann.

Strategies for Child Change Suggested strategies for meeting the objectives developed for the child are listed. The list might include specific instructional techniques, such as those discussed in the next chapter, or specific materials or curricular approaches. In our example, no strategies would be listed, since no changes are expected of Ann.

Objectives for System Change This category is analogous to the one listing objectives for the child, except that system objectives

Child's name _____ Date of birth _____ Case manager _____
Family's name _____ Ecological unit/activity _____ Primary interviewer _____

Source of incongruence	Necessary conditions	Objectives for child change	Strategies for child change	Objective for system change	Strategies for system change	Strategies for evaluation

Figure 10.2. Program planning sheet based on the ecological congruence model.

are listed. Thus, the objectives delineated for Mr. Ray on page 221 would be listed in this column.

Strategies for System Change   This category includes specific techniques and procedures that could bring about the desired changes in the environment. For Mr. Ray, these strategies might include individual counseling sessions to discuss his feelings, and his daily recording of his statements regarding Ann and her toileting behavior. It might also include Mrs. Ray preparing special dinners for him on any day that he assisted Ann with her toileting needs three times or more.

Evaluation   This category is used to describe the evaluation strategy to be employed. The strategy should include assessment of both child change and system change where appropriate, and should indicate whether an increase in ecological congruence took place. Some statement about the length of time necessary for the achievement of the specified objectives should also be made. A description of evaluation for our example might be that Mr. Ray was expected to meet his objectives within two months. Assessment might also include statements from the case manager or primary interventionist, as well as data collected by Mr. Ray regarding his own assistance of Ann with her toileting. Quite possibly, the strategy would also include Mrs. Ray collecting data on her husband's assistance of Ann and his positive and negative statements regarding her. The strategy would also include a baseline before intervention began so that the effectiveness of the intervention could be measured. Finally, it might be desirable to assess the quality of Ann's interaction with her father as his level of tolerance of her increased.

THE INDIVIDUALIZED FAMILY SERVICE PLAN

PL 99-457 calls for the development of an Individualized Family Service Plan (IFSP) for each infant and family served under the law. The planning format described above can form the centerpiece of an IFSP by focusing on the family ecology. The law requires an IFSP to contain the following: 1) a statement of the child's current levels of development; 2) a statement of the family's strengths and needs; 3) a statement of the major outcomes expected to be achieved for the child and the family; 4) the criteria, procedures, and timelines for determining progress; 5) the specific early intervention services necessary to meet the unique needs of the child and the family, including the method, frequency, and intensity of service; 6) the projected dates for the initiation of services and their expected duration; 7) the name of the case manager; and 8) procedures for transition from early intervention into the preschool program. An IFSP must be evaluated every year and must be reviewed at least every 6 months. Most of the information required by an IFSP can be incorporated onto the form illustrated in Figure 10.1. Other information, such as the plan for transition, statements of family strengths and needs, and specific program placements, can be included on a cover sheet designed to incorporate this information. A sample cover sheet is shown in Figure 10.3

It is interesting to note that some authors (i.e., Dunst, Trivette, & Deal, 1988) have already suggested that the IFSP is doomed to failure because of the nature of the relationship it sets up between professionals and parents, and because it emphasizes long-term rather than short-term outcomes. More perspective will be gained on this issue in Chapter 12.

Family name_____ Case manager_____

Date_____ Target child_____ DOB_____

Family members   **Date of birth**   **Relationship to target child**

Statement of family strengths and needs

Present program placement
                Target child   Other family members

Transition plan

Approvals

Name	Position	Date	Name	Position	Date
Name	Position	Date	Name	Position	Date
Name	Position	Date	Name	Position	Date
Name	Position	Date	Name	Position	Date

Figure 10.3. Individualized family service plan cover sheet.

SUMMARY

This chapter has dealt with some of the issues and techniques involved in individualized program planning. The need for an approach that plans for intervention designed for both child change and systems change is put forth. This approach, which has its origins in the ecological congruence model (Thurman, 1977), in many ways depends on existing techniques, like the construction of well-formulated program objectives. In essence, program planning should be designed with the entire ecology of the child in mind, and the purpose of the plan, therefore, should be focused on increasing the fit between the child and his or her environment. This approach requires the use of professionals from a variety of disciplines who operate as an interdisciplinary or preferably as a transdisciplinary team. The specific expertise of each discipline is also discussed. Finally the chapter provides a planning format that can be used for the development of individualized plans, including IFSPs.

11

Implementing Individualized Program Plans

1. How do major features of the learning environment affect the young child with special needs?
2. What are the potential negative side effects of punishment?
3. What is the role of antecedents in the implementation of individualized program plans?
4. How are the strategies discussed in this chapter compatible with both the developmental approach and the ecological congruence model discussed in earlier chapters?

THE PREVIOUS CHAPTER WAS devoted to a discussion of the program planning process and the way that process can be carried out in accordance with the ecological congruence model. This chapter addresses program implementation, and deals with strategies for both child change and system change, as well as factors relating to the physical management of infants and preschool children with handicaps. The last section of this chapter addresses ways changes in both children and environmental systems can be assessed.

Changes in a child result from his or her interaction with the environment. The way the child interacts with the environment is a function, in part, of the child's own charac-

teristics. Effective change strategies for the child depend on an understanding of the typical patterns of development of young children. The earlier chapters of this book provide this basic information. More important, however, is an understanding of the particular patterns of developmental characteristics of the child under consideration.

THE LEARNING ENVIRONMENT

If one accepts that developmental changes in children result from children's interaction with the environment, then it becomes important to examine features of the learning environment that may influence chil-

235

dren's development. By learning environment we mean any setting in which purposeful planned instructional intervention takes place. Such settings include classrooms, group homes, residential institutions, hospitals and natural homes. Virtually any setting can be a learning environment if purposeful instruction takes place there. This is not to suggest that learning and development do not take place without purposeful instruction. Certainly, they do. But it is important to establish learning environments for children with handicaps to ensure that these environments have the characteristics and resources necessary to maximize the child's development. In establishing an effective learning environment it is important to consider the physical structure, the affective structure, the materials used, and the human resources available. Each of these factors is considered below.

Physical Structure

The physical structure of an effective learning environment provides open access to the child. Tables and chairs are of the proper size and are arranged so that children can move about freely. Children with physical disabilities may require special equipment, such as walkers, wheelchairs, and standing tables, to take educational advantage of the environment. Other structural modifications for physically disabled children include wide doorways and entrance ramps.

In addition, children may require special equipment to ensure that they are properly handled and positioned. Utley, Holvoet, and Barnes (1977) and Campbell, Green, and (1989), and Utley, Holvoet, and Barnes (1977) provide some excellent suggestions on how to position children correctly and how to provide them with the necessary prosthetic and adaptive equipment. Campbell, Green, and Carlson provide the following suggestions for selecting and positioning equipment:

1. Make sure that the child's position is maximal for performing feeding or dressing skills. Sitting balance should be well developed (either independently or through equipment) to the point that the child is able to free both of his arms to use for the activity rather than for balance.

2. Make sure the child's position is such that [muscle] tone is normalized. If the child is very stiff or too hypotonic [flaccid], he will be unable to use his arms for function.

3. Know exactly what function you want the child to perform and exactly what motor action and skill are required. Select equipment to perform or to assist in performing those motor skills the child is unable to do on his own.

4. Equipment will not teach a child how to chew or hold a spoon, or take off his shirt. Equipment will only make it more possible for him to perform the motor skills. He still will have to be taught how to do the activity. (p. 307)

Classroom equipment must be appropriate to the task and, along with physical prostheses and braces, must be maintained in proper working order. Venn, Morganstren, and Dykes (1979) have suggested that "the primary role of the teacher [or other learning environment manager] regarding ambulation devices is daily observation of the student's use and care of his or her equipment" (p. 54). They go on to provide checklists to assess leg braces, leg prostheses, and wheelchairs. These checklists are useful aids to the learning environment manager and should be consulted in situations that require the use of these devices. In addition, physical and occupational therapists are valuable consultants in the proper use and maintenance of prosthetic and positioning devices, and the learning environment manager is urged to take advantage of their expertise. Finally, since special equipment often takes up large amounts of space, it may be necessary to serve fewer children in a given area, or to make other arrangements to ensure learning environments of the proper physical dimensions.

Space The physical structure of the learning environment must be such that children have adequate space to move from place to place. In addition, crowding must be avoided. Animal studies, such as that of Calhoun (1962), suggest that crowding adversely affects behavior. Results with human populations are less definitive and, as Moos (1976) suggests in summarizing the literature:

the age and individual characteristics of experimental subjects may affect the results of crowding studies. No research has compared the effects of density on individuals of various ages, yet children and adults may react to density differently. Similarly although the personal factors that mediate an individual's reaction to density have not been explored in depth, individuals undoubtedly differ in their reactions to density situations. . . . There is evidence that each individual has a "body-buffer-zone" or "personal space" surrounding him or her, and if this zone is invaded, feelings of stress appear. (pp. 160–161)

Smith, Neisworth, and Greer (1978) have also suggested that successful mainstreaming of children with and children without handicaps may require sufficient space so that "individuals and groups [can] keep their distance from each other while they are in the process of getting accustomed to each other" (p. 137).

Light Another factor affecting the structure of the physical environment is illumination. Smith, Neisworth, and Greer (1978) suggest that light levels should vary and should be appropriate for the activity being undertaken, "for example with brighter lighting at reading areas and softer lighting in areas used primarily for discussion" (p. 133). They believe that varying levels of light reduce the institutional look of a classroom.

Temperature Hickish (1955) studied factory workers to determine their comfort zone for indoor temperature. His standard suggests a comfort zone of 69–74° F during summer months. This is probably a reasonable comfort zone for most young children. High temperature, however, seems to be related to poor task performance and irritability. Pepler (1971) discovered that student performance in nonclimate-controlled rooms was more variable than student performance in climate-controlled rooms when temperatures were high both inside and outside. In another experiment, Baron and Lawton (1972) showed an increased tendency of subjects to imitate modeled aggressive responses. The room they used in their experiment was extremely hot, however (100° F). Given the current trend toward energy conservation, it is unlikely that higher temperatures present a problem in most learning environments. Unfortunately, the effects of relatively lower indoor temperatures are less well studied and the reader is urged to follow the advice of Smith, Neisworth, and Greer (1978), who suggest

"that to the extent that rooms [in the learning environment] are individually controlled, the teacher [parent, or caregiver] may want to experiment with somewhat lower temperatures; this should be done gradually, however, so that the children have the opportunity to modify their clothing habits." (p. 133)

It is also advisable to make sure that the children's internal temperature maintenance mechanisms are intact, since changes in external temperature may pose significant problems in their ability to maintain body temperature.

Noise A well-functioning learning environment may contain a certain amount of noise. Noise should be related to learning activities, however; extraneous noise from the environment can distract children. Since many young children, especially those with disabilities, are easily distracted, the degree of extraneous noise in the learning environment should be kept at a minimum. Research by Glass and Singer (1972) suggests that noise can have effects on human performance even after the noise has stopped.

Moos (1976) has concluded that "the full extent of the psychic cost of the adaptation to noise is unknown," but cautions nonetheless about "the risk of underestimating the harmful consequences of noise" (p. 190).

Affective Structure

Just as important as the physical structure of a learning environment is the affective structure. The proper affective structure sets the stage for the trust and nurturance necessary for learning and development to occur at the most rapid pace. The person who controls the learning environment generally determines the nature of the affective structure. In the case of the classroom, the teacher is the main determiner of affective structure. In the home, the same role falls to parents, although it is more often ascribed to mothers. In a residential facility, a charge aide or whoever is in control at a given point in time may determine the affective structure.

Smith et al. (1978) identified five continua that characterize the affective structure of a learning environment. While their major concern was in describing critical dimensions of teachers' behavioral styles, their conceptualization is applicable to any learning environment. The five dimensions that Smith and his colleagues identify are: 1) the positive-negative dimension, 2) the planned-haphazard dimension, 3) the flexible-rigid dimension, 4) the consistent-inconsistent dimension, and 5) the understanding-intolerant dimension. Each of these dimensions is discussed below.

Positive-Negative Dimension Some years ago a bumper sticker appeared that read "Courtesy is Contagious." The same might be said about being positive and, regrettably, about being negative. Learning environment managers' attitudes are soon detected and imitated by children. Positive affective structures lead to trust and comfort on the part of the children.

Lotman (1980) described what she labeled *contingency climates*. A contingency climate is the ratio of the number of positively reinforcing consequences a person receives to the number of negative or punishing consequences. Thus, if a positive consequence was experienced five times for every one time a negative experience was experienced, then the contingency climate would be a five to one positive climate. Lotman's research demonstrated that severely retarded children exhibited better performance in a four to one positive climate than they did in a one to one climate, and that their performance was even better in an eight to one positive climate. Positive attitudes in expectations have also been shown favorably to affect student outcome (cf. Rosenthal & Jacobsen, 1968, 1975). Using Bandura's (1971) arguments on modeling effects as their foundation, Smith et al. (1978) conclude that "it is critical . . . that teachers be positive and enthusiastic whenever possible and that a continuing pattern of negative attitudes and behavior will inevitably affect the children in many unfortunate ways, such as student passivity, withdrawal, and fear" (p. 85).

Planned-Haphazard Dimension A planned environment ensures consistency and provides children with a feeling of familiarity. When the environment is planned, children can more clearly see the purpose of activities and are more able to predict expected outcomes. Lewis and Goldberg (1969a, b) examined the importance for children of learning generalized expectancies in infancy and preschool years. They suggest how consistent responding from the environment leads to children's recognition of their own effect on the environment. More recently, Thurman (1978) studied the role of environmental contingencies and the development of expectancy in infants with handicaps. Simply stated, planned environments provide more consistent contingency structures than do haphazard environments. Hence, children develop a knowledge of their own effectiveness most readily in planned environments. This knowledge is important for both cognitive growth and recognition and awareness of self. Finally, as Smith et al. (1978) suggest, a planned learning environment promotes the participation of every child by giving each an opportunity to engage in appropriate learning activities.

Flexibility-Rigidity Dimension Flexibility and rigidity also play an important role in establishing the affective structure of the classroom. Flexibility increases fairness in the environment and creates a setting in which new ideas, curricula, and techniques are tried in an open and objective manner. In short, a flexible climate is more responsive to the individual needs of the students. The variability in the needs and abilities of young children with handicaps makes flexibility a prerequisite for establishing effective learning environments for these children.

Consistency-Inconsistency Dimension Closely related to the conditions necessary for a planned environment is consistency. Like a planned environment, a consistent environment helps children feel comfortable and allows them to know what to expect. This in turn leads to feelings of trust and security, and reduces the anxiety associated with learning situations. In a consistent environment, rules and standards are clearly stated, and children receive consistent consequences for their behavior based upon these standards. It is important to remain flexible, however, and flexibility should be used in setting up rules for the classroom. In addition, learning environment managers must be flexible enough to modify rules and standards when necessary. Consistency need not connote rigidity. The manager merely acts in accordance with established rules, retaining the ability to renegotiate them.

Understanding-Intolerance Dimension

Mutual tolerance and acceptance is a key factor in establishing a homeostatic balance and ecological congruence between children and their environments. Learning environment managers must understand and accept their students if they are to provide meaningful programs matched to the characteristics of each child. Knowledge of the student's needs will not be gained by the person who is intolerant and who casts upon the child a series of expectations.

Materials and Equipment

While they will not lead to an effective intervention program in and of themselves, materials and equipment are important in establishing meaningful learning environments. The materials chosen must meet the needs of the children being served. They must be appropriate to the children's developmental level. That is, they must stimulate involvement, but not be so difficult that they lead to rapid frustration. As was suggested in the discussion of cognitive development in Chapter 4, cognition is advanced when the environment is just different enough to stimulate a child's natural curiosity to interact. Materials should be chosen with this principle in mind.

Children with sensory handicaps require materials with appropriate stimulus features. Young children with visual impairments relate best to auditory and tactile stimulation. Materials for these children should be brightly colored and, when possible, have large, distinct features. This allows these children to make maximum use of their residual vision. Children with auditory impairments must rely more heavily on visual modes in order to learn. Materials for these children should also make use of any residual hearing.

Equipment can be important in providing access to the learning environment. Specialized wheelchairs and other physical prostheses should be used to provide the necessary learning experiences for children with physical handicaps. Of course, many children with sensory handicaps can benefit from hearing aids and eyeglasses. Learning environment managers should consult the appropriate professionals on their interdisciplinary team to make sure that they understand the use and maintenance of specialized equipment. Improper use of this equipment often can interfere with learning.

In choosing materials, the learning environment manager should also consider cost and durability. While there are many excellent materials on the market, materials can often be made that are of comparable quality. Homemade materials usually cost less than purchased ones, and have the added advantage of being designed for a particular child. Most areas of the country have instructional materials centers funded by governmental sources that lend out materials for classroom use. Teachers and other learning environment managers are urged to borrow materials before spending money only to find that a material is not useful for the particular purpose or the type of child the teacher had in mind. For suggestions on effective use of the materials budget, as well as on the selection, management, and adaptation of instructional materials for exceptional children, see Stowitschek, Gable, and Hendrickson (1980).

In a well-planned learning environment, the physical and affective structure, materials and equipment, and human resources are all taken into account.

Human Resources

While the manager is a primary human resource in any learning environment, other human resources can also be used in the learning environment. These resources include parents, volunteers, aides, and the children themselves.

Parents Using parents and other family members as change agents in learning environments is a well-established practice. Many programs for preschool children with handicaps rely almost entirely on parents as primary change agents for the children. Some of these programs are described in Chapter 13. These programs have demonstrated that parents can create meaningful learning environments for the children reasonably independently. Even when parents are not the primary change agents in a program, their skills and talents can be put to use in the classroom. Parents can help prepare and develop materials and implement instructional procedures. Just as important, however, is the information parents can provide about a child. Whether parents are the primary change agents, in programs such as that described by Shearer and Shearer (1976), or whether they serve as informants and aides, as in the program described by Bricker and Bricker (1976) (see Chapter 13), parents are powerful and important human resources who should be part of the learning environments serving their children. Chapter 12 provides a number of strategies to make parents more effective in their children's learning environments, and also discusses avenues for their involvement in early intervention programs.

Volunteers and Paraprofessionals Volunteers and paraprofessionals, such as teacher's aides, client care workers, and assistant teachers, can also be useful human resources. Like parents, they can help develop and prepare materials, as well as implement

instructional programs. The PEERS Project (Losinno, n.d., see Chapter 13), has been successful, in part, because of its effective use of volunteers. Use of volunteers has the additional advantage of being extremely inexpensive. If properly recruited, trained, and recognized, volunteers of all ages can be an important human resource in programs serving preschool children with handicaps and their families. It should be stressed that volunteers and paraprofessionals must be given the support and, most of all, the recognition they need and deserve if they are to be active participants with ongoing involvement in programs for young children with handicaps. Recently, Tingey and Stimell (1989) have described the use of volunteers in early intervention. The interested reader is referred there for more information.

Children One often overlooked human resource in learning environments is children. Program peers and older children who provide volunteer services can be important human resources for preschool children with handicaps. In the family setting, siblings can provide useful and constructive input into their brother's or sister's development. Hartup (1978) has discussed the importance of peers in the socialization process of young children with handicaps. He suggests that peers influence each other through mechanisms such as reinforcement, modeling, and tutoring. (See discussion in Chapter 6.) A number of authors have provided evidence that preschool peers can be effective models (e.g., Apolloni, Cooke, & Cooke, 1977; Guralnick, 1976; Peck, Cooke, & Apolloni, 1981; Strain, Kerr, & Ragland, 1981) and facilitators of social interaction (Devoney, Guralnick, & Rubin, 1974; Guralnick, 1981; Snyder, Apolloni, & Cooke, 1977; Strain, 1985; Strain, Hoyson, & Jamieson, 1985; Strain & Odom, 1986; Strain & Timm, 1974) for their peers with handicaps. The research of these authors clearly illustrates the important role that children without handicaps can play in the development of their peers with handicaps. It is difficult to ignore the exciting human resources that children can provide in any learning environment.

STRATEGIES FOR CHILD CHANGE

While the learning environment sets the stage for behavior change and provides the context for it, it is the development of specific strategies for modifying behavior that leads to effective behavior change. This is not to say that development will not occur without specific intervention. But the types of behavior change required to bring about ecological congruence require specific, well-thought-out behavior change strategies.

Just as a child's level of cognitive development or the lack of ecological congruence can be accounted for by some set of necessary and sufficient conditions, so, too, can a child's behavior. Thus, learning environment managers should identify as many as possible of the conditions that might account for a child's behavior or developmental state. By so doing, managers may often save endless hours, conserve resources, and eliminate stress for themselves and the children. Careful examination of conditions may reveal a simple, direct means of establishing congruence. The following story illustrates this point clearly.

A young boy residing in a state residential facility for retarded children was continually observed picking his nose—a behavior that created enough incongruence in the ecology that his program management team decided to change his behavior. After consultation, they decided verbally to reprimand the boy whenever he began picking his nose. They found this procedure effective as long as it

was used consistently. They found, however, that the boy would begin picking his nose as soon as they stopped reprimanding him. They decided to use a stronger procedure. This time they coupled their verbal reprimands with 30 seconds of restraint to the boy's arm. Again, the procedure was effective. Gradually, however, even though the procedure was still in use, the boy's nose picking behavior resumed. Several other interventions were planned and implemented with similar results. Just as the program team ran out of ideas and was ready to concede failure, the boy was scheduled for his annual physical examination. While looking up the boy's nose, the physician discovered the spring from a ball point pen mechanism lodged in the boy's nostril. The next day, the boy was brought to the infirmary and the spring was removed. After that he was rarely seen picking his nose. The obvious point is that the program management team, in their desire to increase congruence, overlooked an important condition accounting for the boy's behavior. Had they examined more conditions, they would have saved themselves a lot of effort and saved the boy a lot of discomfort and interference in his life. Before using any of the behavior change strategies discussed below, it is important to rule out other conditions that might account for or contribute to lack of ecological congruence and lack of expected behavior patterns or development levels in a child.

The Role of the Environment

All behavior is partially a function of environmental events. Some of these events follow behavior and are referred to as *consequences*. Others precede behavior and are referred to as *antecedents*. These consequences and antecedents can be modified and controlled to change an individual's behavior.

This section deals with the systematic changes that can be introduced in consequences and antecedents to bring about desired behavioral change in young children with handicaps.

Environmental Consequences In the discussion of Piaget's theory in Chapter 4, it was pointed out that by the end of the sensorimotor period of development children have learned that their behavior affects the environment. Children's understanding of means-ends relationships comes from their action on the environment and the recognition that their behavior has an effect. Simply, children's behavior provides the means to certain ends in the environment. Even children in the very earliest stages of the sensorimotor period modify their behavior in response to environmental consequences. For example, Sameroff (1968) demonstrated that 5-day-old infants changed their sucking responses depending upon which component of sucking was followed by the delivery of a nutrient solution. Thus, it can be seen that, virtually from the beginning of life, the consequences of our behavior affect the way we will behave in the future. For the most part, people emit behavior (i.e., exercise means) that lead to desired consequences (i.e., ends). Thus, the ebb and flow of behavior is a function of the interplay between children's acquired means (i.e., behavior patterns) and the ends (i.e., available consequences) in the environment.

The relationship between behavior and its consequence is referred to as a *contingency*, or as being characterized by a *contingent relationship*. A contingency can be thought of as an if-then situation. That is, if a child behaves in a particular manner, then that behavior leads to a particular end. Through identifying and understanding the contingent relationships between a child's behavior and the consequences of that behavior, effective strategies for behavior change can be developed.

Contingent consequences have three possible effects on a child's behavior: they may increase, decrease, or have no effect on the behavior that they follow. A consequence that increases behavior is referred to as a *reinforcing consequence*. A consequence that decreases behavior is referred to as a *punishing consequence*. A consequence that does not affect behavior is referred to as a *neutral consequence*. Reinforcing, punishing, and neutral consequences are defined in terms of their actual function on behavior, not on their perceived or ascribed function. Thus, the mother who yells at her child systematically for kicking the dog and claims to be punishing the child in this way is, in fact, not punishing the child at all unless the frequency with which the child kicks the dog declines over time. This mother could even be reinforcing the child by yelling at him if the yelling is linked to the child's continued kicking of the dog. The nature of a contingent consequence is not known unless the effects of that consequence on behavior can be demonstrated empirically. Later in this chapter we discuss data collection techniques that can be used to assess the effect of various contingent consequences on behavior.

Reinforcing Consequences There are two basic types of reinforcing consequences, *primary reinforcing consequences* and *secondary, or conditioned, reinforcing consequences*. Primary reinforcing consequences are effective because they provide a basic resource to the child's biological system. Primary reinforcing consequences include food, water, sleep, and sensory stimulation. Primary reinforcing consequences, then, increase behavior in a child without the child's need to learn that such consequences are reinforcing. Secondary, or conditioned reinforcing consequences, however, depend on learning. Neutral consequences may be presented simultaneously with primary reinforcing consequences. As a result, these neutral consequences begin to take on the reinforcing function of the primary reinforcing consequences. Many of the social consequences that are reinforcing to us are conditioned this way. For example, primary reinforcing consequences are used in training severely and profoundly retarded children or young retarded children. If the child makes a correct response to a discrimination problem, he or she is given a small edible treat or a sip of juice or soft drink. At the same time, the child is verbally praised with a statement such as, "That's good work," or "I like the way you showed me the circle." Over time, through being consistently paired with the food or liquid, the trainer's statements come to have reinforcing properties in and of themselves. When that happens, verbal praise has become a secondary or conditioned reinforcing consequence. A child's mother often becomes a source of reinforcement in a similar way. During infancy and early childhood, a child's mother is often the major source of primary reinforcing consequences. Because of this, the child's mother herself can become reinforcing to the child. Her mere presence or her attention to the child can act as a reinforcing consequence, and a powerful one at that. For this reason, a mother's attention may reinforce a child's undesired behavior, even though she has put forth a consequence she thinks of as punishing. This phenomenon explains the earlier suggestion that a mother's yelling at her child for kicking the dog may actually maintain or increase the child's kicking behavior, even though yelling is viewed as a negative consequence. In essence, the maternal attention the child receives as a result of the yelling has a stronger effect on the behavior than does the yelling itself. This phenomenon is more likely to occur when the mother provides attention to the child primarily when the child is behaving in an undesired manner. Parents, teachers, and other learning environment managers must always keep in mind the powerful effects their attention can have on the behavior of children.

Reinforcing consequences can be used to develop and maintain desired behavior in preschool children with handicaps. To do this, learning environment managers must follow three steps. First, they must identify in specific terms the behavior to be changed. Second, they must identify the consequences that are reinforcing to the child. Third, they must set up a consistent contingent relationship between the desired behavior and a consequence desired by the child. Steps one and two were discussed in the previous chapter. Recall that any well-stated instructional objective includes a precisely defined, observable behavior, and that strategies for identifying reinforcing consequences include observing the child and providing various consequences for the performance of simple tasks (e.g., hand clapping) to see which consequences result in the greatest increase in behavior.

Suppose an evaluation revealed a lack of congruence in the ecology because a 3-year-old child failed to make social contact with other children in her class and the other children did not establish contact with her. Two objectives to establish congruence might state:

Given a free play situation Sally, Belle, and Tanya will offer to share toys with Alice at least two times each for 5 consecutive days.

Given a free play situation, Alice will take a toy from Sally, Belle, or Tanya at least four times for 5 consecutive days.

Alice is the child who is not making social contact. From these two objectives, the following observable behaviors can be defined:

Sally, Belle, or Tanya offers a toy to Alice. Offering a toy is defined as approaching Alice closely enough that she could take the toy and extending the arm toward Alice while holding the toy in the hand of the extending arm.

Alice takes the toy from Sally, Belle, or Tanya. Taking the toy is defined as Alice extending her hand, placing it on the toy, and removing the toy from the hand of the other child.

Next, the learning environment manager chooses a consequence to make contingent upon the identified behaviors. For Alice, an appropriate consequence might be a tidbit of cereal paired with verbal praise and several strokes on her arm or back. For Sally, Belle, and Tanya, an appropriate consequence might be verbal praise alone. The contingencies, then, are verbally to praise Sally, Belle, or Tanya whenever they offer a toy to Alice, and to give Alice a tidbit of cereal along with physical and verbal praise if she takes the toy when offered. If over time Sally, Belle, and Tanya offer toys to Alice more frequently, then verbal praise is a reinforcing consequence. Likewise, if Alice takes the toy from the other girls more frequently, the consequences arranged for her behavior are also reinforcing.

Reinforcement sometimes can occur when a particular behavior results in the contingent removal of or escape from a previously presented stimulus. Suppose firm pressure is applied to a child's upper arm or shoulder when he wanders around the room. When he returns to his seat, the child is released. Thus, his behavior contingently results in the trainer letting go of the child. If this contingent consequence is effective, the child will return to his seat more quickly in the future. Ultimately, he may learn to avoid the firm grip altogether by not even leaving his seat unless told to do so. While such techniques can be successful in increasing desired behavior (cf. Lovaas, Schaeffer, & Simmons, 1965), it is usually more desirable to present children with positive consequences for their behavior. Thus, in the present example, the child would be given verbal praise for remaining in his seat, or the teacher would stand by him and stroke his arm as long as he remained seated.

Punishing Consequences As was noted above, contingent consequences can also lead to decreases in behavior. These consequences are said to be punishing consequences. Punishing consequences should be employed only when effective behavior change cannot be brought about using positively reinforcing consequence, or when a decrease or cessation of a particular behavior is necessary for the safety or welfare of the child or others in the setting. Use of punishing consequences in situations other than these is, in our opinion, to be avoided. Some authors have recently suggested that the demonstrated effectiveness of aversive procedures in and of itself does not justify their use (Guess, Helmstetter, Turnbull, & Knowlton, 1987). They suggest instead the implementation "of a systematic treatment plan to alter the conditions which maintain the problem behavior and to teach functional alternative positive behaviors to replace them" (p. 40). Inappropriate use of punishing consequences is at best an exercise of poor judgment and at worst a breach of basic human morality. Keep in mind, also, that punishment is almost always used to modify behavior viewed as deviant or intolerable, and that a primary reason for using punishment is that it is the traditional way in which our culture deals with problem behavior (La Vigna, 1987). Before implementing a punishment procedure, program teams should assess the appropriateness of placing the burden of change solely on the child. Kazdin (1975) has summed up the use of punishment aptly. He states:

> the best use of punishment in applied settings is an ancillary technique to accompany positive reinforcement. At best, punishment will only suppress undesirable responses but

not train desirable behaviors. Reinforcement is essential to develop appropriate behaviors which replace the suppressed behaviors. (p. 167)

Guess et al. (1987) and Kazdin have pointed out that punishment can lead to a number of undesirable side effects including emotional reactions, escape and avoidance, aggression, modeled punishment, and perpetuation of punishment. Each of these deserves some elucidation.

Punishing consequences often lead to emotional reactions on the part of both the child being punished and the person doing the punishing. These emotional reactions interfere with the ongoing activities of the setting and lessen the opportunity for the child to learn an appropriate pattern of behavior. Kazdin (1975) suggests that the person offering the punishment may, over time, come to "elicit similar emotional reactions even in the absence of punishment" (p. 161). These reactions may adversely affect the relationship between the child and the learning environment manager and may eventually interfere with the child's opportunity to learn.

After repeated punishment, children learn to avoid or escape from punishing situations. This action may reduce their opportunities to learn more adaptive patterns of behavior because they avoid situations in which punishment often occurs. At the same time, they may learn to avoid the person who issues the punishment. Such avoidance behavior can set the stage for significant levels of incongruency in the ecological system. It may, in fact, suppress behavior to the point that the child becomes "nonbehaving," that is, withdraws from interaction with the environment to avoid the possibility of punishment.

Punishment can lead to aggressive interaction between punished parties. Early work of Azrin and Holz (1966) demonstrated that laboratory animals who were frequently punished using electrical shock were very prone to attack each other during nonpunishment periods. Kazdin (1975) concludes that although "these phenomena have not been demonstrated with the wide range of punishing events used in applied settings . . . using punishment of any kind there is the possibility that the punished individual will aggress toward the punishing agent" (p. 161) and, thus, temporarily remove the punishing events.

Another potential drawback in the use of punishment is the model presented to the child by the punishing agent. The fact that children imitate adult models has been well documented in the literature (cf. Bandura, 1971). Thus, children are prone to imitate patterns of behavior associated with punishment. They may come to use punishment as their mode of interacting with other children. The tendency to imitate the punishing model increases the likelihood of aggressive behavior, since many punishing events could be classified as aggressive.

A final undesirable side effect of punishment suggested by Kazdin (1975) is its tendency to perpetuate itself. He suggests that successful punishment almost immediately brings about reduction of undesired behavior. Consequently, the punishing agent (e.g., the learning environment manager) is reinforced by the cessation of the child's undesired behavior. This reinforcement increases the likelihood that the person will use punishment in the future to manage or modify a child's behavior. The effectiveness of punishment in reducing undesirable behavior thus leads to the perpetuation of its use.

Punishing consequences can take many forms, some of which are milder and less dependent upon physical means. When punishment is necessary to bring about behavior change in young children, it is preferable to impose the mildest form of punishment that is effective, since this somewhat reduces the undesired side effects. Thus, if a 2-year-old will stop beating on the goldfish tank with a wooden mallet (an obviously dangerous behavior) upon sharply being told "NO!", then it is not necessary to slap his hand, send him to the corner for 5 minutes, or deprive him of lunch. In point of fact, physical punishment is almost never needed with young children with handicaps. Learning environment managers other than parents should never use physical punishment and should receive clearance from parents and program administrators before using any form of punishment other than the mildest kind. Parents should be instructed in ways of managing behavior without physical punishment. They, too, should rely on the mildest form of punishment that is effective and should be thoroughly familiarized with the negative side effects of punishment and the particular dangers of physical punishment.

Alternatives to physical punishment include techniques such as verbal reprimands, time out, and response cost. All of these techniques can be used successfully with preschool children with handicaps.

Verbal reprimands consist of giving a child verbal feedback about a particular behavior. These can take the form of a sharply spoken word, such as "NO!" or "STOP IT!" or they can be affect-laden statements, such as "I don't like it when you hit children." The latter approach has the advantage of letting the child know specifically what he or she is doing that is undesirable. It is based on the assumption that expressed displeasure on the part of an adult is sufficiently aversive to decrease the child's behavior. This may or may not be the case. Sharply spoken words typically are more aversive for the child, and are more likely to lead to decrease in behav-

ior. A third approach to verbal reprimands is to combine a sharp word with an explanation of what the undesired behavior is, for example, "STOP HITTING!" All three of these can be effective verbal reprimands. The advantages of each should be weighed by the learning environment manager before choosing the best one for the situation.

A technique referred to as *time out* is also effective in punishing a child. Time out refers to time out from positive reinforcement. If a child emits an undesired behavior, he or she is not given any positive reinforcement for some period of time. There is no reason for the time out period ever to exceed 5 minutes, especially if the child is isolated in a stimulus-free room or cubicle. This type of physical isolation represents the most extreme form of time out, and should be used only when milder forms of isolation prove ineffective. It is rarely necessary to use a time out room with preschool children with handicaps because their behavior can be managed with less drastic types of time out procedures. With young children, time out can be accomplished by adults in the learning environment halting their interaction for 30 to 60 seconds. This technique is effective because adults are the primary source of positive reinforcement in the learning environment and control children's access to it. In addition, while it may not seem like a long period of time for an adult, 60 seconds can represent an eternity for a young child. Another effective means for implementing time out with young children is the traditional practice of having a child stand or sit in the corner. In implementing this procedure, the learning environment manager should arrange an area of the room where the child can sit or stand face to the wall, reasonably isolated from the ongoing activities. The child should be required to spend no more than 2 or 3 minutes in the corner. Many managers find it effective to set a kitchen timer for 2 or 3 minutes when the child goes to the corner. This tells both the child and the manager when the time is up and prevents the manager from forgetting that a child is in time out. While most children will go to the time out corner upon command from the manager, some will not. These children should be guided firmly to the corner without fanfare. The manager may also find it necessary to monitor these children to prevent them from leaving the corner prematurely. Regardless of the type of time out used, children should understand the contingency and be told specifically why they are being sent to time out. This enables them to begin to distinguish appropriate behavior from inappropriate behavior, and to begin to internalize the control of their own behavior.

Control of undesirable behavior can also be accomplished by a procedure known as *response cost.* Response costs are fines. That is, a particular behavior results in the loss of some portion of a desired resource or activity. In the preschool classroom, response cost could consist of withholding lunch time dessert, a portion of free play, or the opportunity to engage in a favorite activity or to play with a particular toy. In essence, children pay the cost of emitting undesired behaviors by giving up something they desire. As with time out, it is important for children to understand the contingency and the exact reason for the response cost.

Although response cost can be effective, it also has certain drawbacks. First, it can set the stage for additional misbehavior by making children angry. Since punished children have already lost a desired activity or item, they may feel that nothing else can be lost by additional misbehavior. To prevent this from happening, managers should take away only a portion of a desired consequence. For example, 5 minutes of a 15 minute free play period rather than the entire period can be re-

moved. It is also more effective to make it the last 5 minutes rather than the first, so that the children pay their "fine" when it is felt most fully. In addition, children can be given the opportunity to earn the time or activity back through emitting desired behavior. Again, it is important for children to know specifically what must be done to regain the lost resources. One cannot merely say, "If you're good, you can gain your free play time back."

Another drawback to response cost is the time that typically passes between the undesired behavior and the payment of the cost. Contingent consequences are generally more effective if they are immediate. To get around this problem, response cost procedures are sometimes used in conjunction with token systems, in which children receive tokens for desired behavior and give up tokens for undesired behavior. Tokens are then used to gain access to desired events, items, or activities. Unfortunately, token systems can be quite cumbersome, and many young children have difficulty understanding the value of tokens and how they can be used. In spite of these limitations, response cost can be an effective means for decreasing undesired behavior in preschool children with handicaps.

Extinction Extinction, like punishment, provides a means for decreasing undesired behavior. However, it does not bring with it the undesired side effects associated with punishment. Extinction occurs when a previously reinforced response is no longer reinforced. Allen and colleagues (1964) offer an interesting example of extinction with a preschool child. In their study, a 4-year-old girl was socially withdrawn from her peers. Observation in the classroom revealed that her teacher attended to her whenever she was isolated from her peers. By ignoring the child when she was isolated and giving her attention when she played with other children, the teacher was able significantly to increase the child's social interaction. While extinction can be effective by itself, its effectiveness is usually increased when another, more desirable response is reinforced simultaneously. Allen and colleagues were able to reinforce an alternative behavior that was also incompatible with the undesired behavior. This procedure is sometimes referred to as *differential reinforcement of incompatible behavior,* or *DRI.* DRI is frequently used in conjunction with extinction or with various forms of punishment. Since extinction tends to decrease the rate of behavior more slowly than does punishment, it is good practice to combine extinction with a DRI procedure in order more rapidly to build behaviors that are desirable. Before using extinction, the learning environment manager should be sure that the reinforcer consequence that is maintaining the undesired behavior can be identified. In addition, the manager should be aware that an increase in undesired behavior may be noticed at the inception of extinction. For example, when extinction is used to decrease temper tantrums in young children, the length and intensity of the tantrums may increase for the first few days. The reason for this is that children try to acquire the reinforcing consequence that usually follows the tantrum. The lack of expected reinforcers may also lead to frustration and anger, which can be minimized by increasing the amount of reinforcement for desired behavior.

Another technique that can decrease undesired behavior is *differential reinforcement of other behavior,* or *DRO.* DRO can be used alone or in conjunction with various forms of punishment. In a DRO procedure, a child is reinforced for any behavior other than the undesired behavior. The procedure usually is set up so that a child is reinforced after some period of time, provided that the undesired behavior has not occurred. Suppose that a developmentally delayed preschool child had periodic episodes of self-stimulat-

ing behaviors during the day. The learning environment manager could set up a DRO procedure by providing the child reinforcement for time periods during which self-stimulation did not occur. The more often the reinforcement occurred the more effective the procedure would be. Thus, the manager might elect to start by reinforcing the child for very brief periods of time, say, 45 to 90 seconds, lengthening the time between reinforcements gradually. A kitchen timer can be set for various lengths of time, and reinforcement can be provided when the timer rings if the undesired behavior has not occurred. When it does occur, an undesired behavior can either be ignored (extinguished) or followed by a punishing consequence. In either case, the timer is reset so that the child is given a new opportunity for reinforcement. Several authors (e.g., Homer & Peterson, 1980; La Vigna & Donnellan, 1986) have indicated the strength of DRO procedures as an alternative to punishment.

Environmental Antecedents Antecedent events can be just as important as consequences in bringing about effective behavior change in young children. Antecedent events are particularly useful when a child is learning a behavior for the first time. They set the stage for behavior and provide models and cues for the child to follow. The effective use of antecedent events is necessary if young children with handicaps are to learn adaptive patterns of behavior.

Task Analysis and Instructional Objectives
The use of task analysis and instructional objectives as they relate to the program planning process was discussed in the previous chapter. These two techniques also play important roles in the actual instructional process. Recall that task analysis is the process by which relatively complex patterns of behavior are broken down into small, discrete steps. Each of these steps is the basis for en route and terminal instructional objec-

tives. In combination, these activities are the blueprint for instruction. More importantly, they are a way to identify the necessary antecedent events for effective instruction. Each behavioral step in a task is an antecedent to the step that follows it. For example, in the process of brushing one's teeth, opening the toothpaste is an antecedent event to putting the toothpaste on the toothbrush. Through task analysis, such events are identified and properly sequenced.

The givens, or the conditions, stated in a well-constructed instructional objective simply identify antecedents. For example, consider the following objective:

Given two red squares and a blue square and a verbal command, "Point to the one that is different," the child will point to the blue square four out of five times for 3 consecutive days.

The condition stated in this objective provides for several antecedent events before the child can emit the desired behavior. The trainer must provide three squares (two red and a blue) and a verbal command (point to the one that is different). Without these antecedent events—and, of course, without the child's attention to them—accomplishment of the objective stated above is impossible.

Setting Events Setting events are those antecedents of behavior that cue the child that a response is expected or necessary. In the example, the setup of the materials and the placement of the child at a table opposite the trainer are considered general setting events. Each of these events suggests to the child, "Now is the time to respond." The actual verbal command by the teacher ("Point to the one that is different") is the specific setting event that immediately precedes the child's response. Over time, these setting events lead to the development of a learning, or response set, on the part of the child. That is, repeated exposure to these antecedents lead to a readiness on the part of the child to

respond to cues provided. This is particularly true if the child is positively reinforced for responding.

Discriminative Stimuli Discriminative stimuli, or S^Ds, are defined by the functional relationship between an antecedent event and the child's behavior. A discriminative stimulus is an antecedent event in whose presence responding leads to positive reinforcement. In the example, the desired S^D is the blue square. Only as the child makes correct responses to the trainer's verbal command does the blue square become an S^D, however. The child's correct response is followed by a reinforcing consequence and the blue square acquires the properties of an S^D. However, a punishing consequence would follow the child's incorrect responding (i.e., if he or she pointed to a red square). This punishing consequence would be mild and would be designed to correct the child's incorrect response. Thus, the trainer might say, "No, that's not right" and point to the blue square and say, "This one is different." We would hope that from this action the child would learn that the red squares were incorrect antecedents, given the trainer's verbal command. Over time, in the same way the blue square becomes an S^D, the red squares become S-deltas (S^{Δ}s), or antecedents in whose presence responding does not result in positive reinforcement.

Consistent use of setting events and S^Ds is critical in establishing an effective learning environment, because it helps children learn when to respond. In addition, it lets children know which responses are expected in which learning situations. A number of instructional techniques designed to develop new behavior patterns rely heavily on the effective use of antecedent events. We do not suggest that antecedent events play a more important role than consequences; we do believe that antecedents must be considered in the instructional process. Instruction procedures that depend on antecedent events include modeling, cueing, chaining, shaping, and fading.

Modeling In modeling, a desired behavior is demonstrated by the trainer while the child watches. The intent is that the child will imitate the trainer and subsequently be reinforced. Some children, especially those with cognitive deficits, must actually be taught to imitate modeled responses (cf. Bricker & Dennison, 1978). Modeling is particularly useful in teaching social, self-help, and motor skills. Bricker and Dennison (1978) suggest that it be used in teaching prerequisites to verbal language. Apolloni, Cooke, and Cooke (1977) discuss techniques that can be used to establish a peer without a handicap as a model for a peer with a handicap in a preschool setting. The use of peer models is a rational for the integration of preschool children with and without handicaps (Bricker, 1978), but does not necessarily occur naturally (Snyder, Apolloni, & Cooke, 1977). It is important that both adult and child models be provided to preschool children with handicaps, and that the necessary techniques to bring about imitation of these models be implemented. Shaping procedures, discussed below, can be used to build imitative responses in preschool children with handicaps (cf. Baer, Peterson, & Sherman, 1967).

Cueing Like modeling, cueing uses antecedent events to bring about desired behavior change. Cueing consists of increasing the salience of an antecedent event. In the example in which the child was asked to point to the different color, a cue was provided by the trainer's pointing to the blue square while giving the verbal command. Other types of cues include physical prompts, instructions, and increasing the stimulus dimensions of an antecedent. In the case of a physical prompt, the trainer might actually hold the child's hands while performing a particular task, or might give the child physical guidance by touching or pointing to the child's hands. Instructions such as "Do this," or "Follow me," or "Pick the one that I point to" are also cues. Sometimes the physical properties of the antecedent event can be changed to provide a cue. In the example of the red and blue squares, the blue square could also have been bigger or lighter or darker in hue than the red squares, thus increasing the blue square's salience. Gordon and Haywood (1969) have shown that such stimulus enrichment (i.e., increase in salience) can increase the performance of children with mental retardation.

Chaining Chaining grows out of task analysis and depends upon each step in the task analysis being established as an S^D for the preceding step. Chaining may start with the first step of a behavioral sequence and proceed to the last (*forward chaining*), or it may begin with the last step of the sequence and proceed to the first (*backward chaining*). In backward chaining, the trainer completes the sequence except for the final step. Backward chaining is often the preferred procedure, because it allows the child to complete the entire sequence by performing the last step, which is followed by a positive reinforcer. When the child learns the last response, he or she is expected to perform the last two responses, then the last three, and so on until the entire chain has been learned. Some behavior sequences (e.g., toileting,) cannot be meaningfully taught using a backward chaining procedure. In these instances, the trainer employs forward chaining or graduated guidance. *Graduated guidance* consists of the trainer putting various degrees of pressure on the child's hands while performing a behavior sequence from beginning to end. Popovich (1981) provides the following description of graduated guidance. She also provides an excellent discussion of the way chaining procedures are implemented:

> During full graduated guidance, the instructor keeps her hands in full contact with the student's hands throughout the trial and praises the student continuously as long as the student is moving his hands in the desired direction. During partial graduated guidance, the instructor only guides the student's hands as necessary, while in shadowing the instructor does not physically touch the student's hands but keeps her hands within an inch of the student's hands as the student completes the trial. (p. 128)

Graduated guidance can be used effectively when the child has not learned all the specific behaviors necessary to complete the task being taught. Thus, as Popovich (1981) suggests, graduated guidance "is especially useful for students who do not understand simple verbal and gestural prompts and for students who need a great deal of physical prompting" (p. 133).

Shaping   Shaping is used to develop new behaviors in children. It depends upon positive reinforcement rewarding closer and closer approximations of a desired behavior. Kazdin (1975) contrasts chaining with shaping by suggesting that the former "is used to develop a sequence of behaviors based on responses that are already present in the individual's repertoire while shaping is used to develop new behaviors" (p. 40). Chaining and shaping are often used in concert, since a child may have mastered some but not all of the necessary behaviors for a particular behavior sequence. Shaping often uses models, cues, and prompts. These antecedents are used to encourage the performance of a particular behavior. If the child performs the behavior in even the grossest manner, reinforcement is given. However, future reinforcement is given only as the child's responses more and more closely approximate the response that is finally desired. Suppose, for example, a child is being

taught to ask for things rather than to point. Since asking is a new behavior, shaping is an appropriate behavior change technique. The first time a child is told, "Ask for it, say 'I want,'" the child may do nothing more than make an inarticulate sound. Since such a sound is the first approximation of the desired response, reinforcement follows. Further reinforcement is contingent upon the child's increasingly approximating the words, "I want." In this particular example, the reinforcing consequence could be the child being given what was asked for. In other situations, shaping reinforcers may be either primary or consist of social praise.

Fading   Up to this point, our discussion of environmental antecedents has focused on the importance of introducing antecedents that bring about desired responses in children. However, many of the antecedents used in the development of desired behavior outcomes are not readily available in many environmental settings. Thus, it is important that children's responses become more and more a function of internalized contingencies and the general recognition of the stimulus properties of various settings. Fading is often used to begin to meet this goal. Fading is a procedure by which the arranged antecedents for a child's behavior are gradually reduced or faded away. In our earlier example, the blue square might be illuminated in some manner at the same time the child was asked to point to the one that was different. As suggested earlier, this light is a cue, increasing the salience of the S^D being trained. As the child began to make more and more correct responses, the degree of illumination could be gradually reduced. Thus, the cue would gradually be faded, in this case literally. Fading can also be used to reduce the amount of physical guidance necessary for a child to perform a task. The earlier discussion of graduated guidance illustrates this idea quite well. The degree of actual guidance given to a child in completing the behavioral sequence being trained depends on the degree of independence the child expressed in carrying out the sequences. In other cases, when more than one antecedent is arranged, one may be faded out while the other is left intact. Imitation training, referred to earlier, is a good example of this. When children are being taught to imitate, it is important that they perform the same behavior as the model. In this training paradigm, the model usually performs a gross motor movement (e.g., placing the hands over the head), simultaneously saying, "Do this." Children may or may not imitate the model. If they do not, prompting is necessary. The trainer may have to take their hands and move them over their heads. Gradually, however, these physical prompts are faded out and children respond to the model and the verbal command alone. Children who are taught to respond in this way to several different gross motor behaviors often learn spontaneously to imitate the models' behavior. Essentially, children learn to emit the behavior that follows the command, "Do this." This procedure has been successful with severely and profoundly retarded young children, and can be used to train both gross motor responses and manual and verbal communicative responses.

Behavioral Formula Several authors (e.g., Bijou, Peterson, & Ault, 1968; Bijou, Peterson, Harris, Allen, & Johnston, 1969; Lindsley, 1964) have suggested formulas for demonstrating the relationship between environmental antecedents and consequences and behaviors specifically targeted for behavioral change. Program planning is a prerequisite to successful program implementation. The planning strategy inherent in the following behavioral formula is specific to the development of interventions designed to change a particular behavior in a given child. In addition, this formula gives an example of the relationship between antecedents, specific behavioral responses, and consequences. Table 11.1 shows a planning format, which is discussed below. This format originated in suggestions made by Lindsley (1964) and Bijou and colleagues (Bijou et al., 1968; Bijou et al., 1969). Readers should find this strategy useful in planning specific interventions.

This planning format is completed by asking a series of questions. Tables 11.2 and 11.3 are examples of the way the planning format is used. These samples are based on earlier examples used in this chapter. Table 11.2 is based on the example of the red and blue squares. Table 11.3 is based on the example of a child receiving verbal reprimands for hitting other children. Readers are urged to develop their own plans using other techniques discussed in this chapter. These specific intervention plans are a useful supplement to the more general planning strategy discussed in the previous chapter.

Table 11.1. Planning format for behavior change

Name of child: _____

Name of manager: _____

Specific objective: _____

Purpose: What is being done and why?

Setting: Where and when is the intervention taking place?

Antecedents: What events are to occur that may increase the likelihood of the desired behavior occurring?

Desired behavior: What specific behavior is desired to occur more often?

Consequence of desired behavior: What specific consequence will happen when the desired behavior occurs?

Undesired behavior: What specific behavior is desired to occur less often?

Consequence of undesired behavior: What specific consequence will happen when the undesired behavior occurs?

Table 11.2. Use of the planning format to teach the concept "different from"

Name of child: Billy R.

Name of manager: Sandy L.

Specific objective: Given two red squares and a blue square, Billy will point to the blue square 8 out of 10 times for 4 consecutive days when asked to point to the one that is different.

Purpose: To teach Billy the concept of different

Setting: The preschool class during individual instruction period

Antecedents: Two red squares and a blue square and the verbal request to "point to the one that is different"

Desired behavior: Billy points to the blue square

Consequence of desired behavior: Verbal praise and a small bit of orange juice

Undesired behavior: Billy points to a red square

Consequence of undesired behavior: Verbal feedback ("No Billy") and manager points to blue square and says "this one is different"

Table 11.3. Use of the planning format to decrease hitting behavior

Name of child: Patrice L.

Name of manager: Allen W.

Specific objective: Given Patrice in a classroom situation, she will not hit other children all day for 5 consecutive days.

Purpose: To get Patrice to stop hitting other children

Setting: Preschool classroom during the entire day

Antecedents: None

Desired behavior: Any appropriate behavior other than hitting

Consequence of desired behavior: Periodic verbal praise and attention for appropriate behavior

Undesired behavior: Hitting other children

Consequence of undesired behavior: Verbal feedback ("No hitting, Patrice")

Developmental Interaction Behavioral technology, as described above, with its emphasis on the process by which children may be taught skills or concepts, does not address the question of content, that is, the decision of what to teach or whether certain skills or concepts are appropriate for a given child at a given time. To decide what to teach at any given time, the planner must examine developmental consequences for nonhandicapped children and determine what skills are appropriate for each child. This information can be provided through a sound assessment program, as described in Chapters 8 and 9.

It is important to arrange the environment to motivate children to learn the skill or concept. An important aspect of motivation is readiness. We do not apply this concept to children with handicaps in the same way that Gesell and his associates (cf. Ilg & Ames, 1965) applied it to nonhandicapped children. However, the idea that children must be ready for a new learning in order for it to be meaningful is sound. For example, studies of children's spontaneous language acquisition have shown that children spontaneously imitate only those forms of adult grammar that they are about to incorporate into their own repertoires, ignoring other more complex forms (Bloom, 1973). It is particularly important, therefore, to be sure that whatever skill we are attempting to teach is developmentally appropriate. This will ensure that the children will aid, rather than resist, the process.

Another aspect of motivation comes from Piaget's theory of the construction of knowledge. Recall from Chapter 4 that Piaget (1952) considered cognitive development to be the result of a recurring state of disequilibrium. It is this state of disequilibrium, brought about when new information is at odds with previously held ideas, that is responsible for children adapting their thinking to take into account the new information and thus attaining a higher level of knowledge. The state of disequilibrium is necessary, therefore, for new learning to occur. Without this important process, learning is likely to be restricted to a superficial rote level. It is important in program implementation to so engineer the environment that disequilibrium occurs.

In order to accomplish this, a developmental interaction model (Biber, Shapiro, & Wickens, 1971; Bricker, Dennison, & Bricker, 1976) is suggested. This model combines the two ideas introduced above; that is, the need to base intervention on a sound developmental sequence, and the need to organize the learning environment so that optimal interaction may occur. Optimal interaction occurs when children are ready for the learning and when the interaction promotes a state of disequilibrium that fosters the adaptive process.

Shapiro and Biber (1972) have defined developmental interaction as follows:

Developmental refers to the emphasis on identifiable patterns of growth and modes of perceiving and responding which are characterized by increasing differentiation and progressive integration as a function of chronological age. Interaction refers, first, to the emphasis on the child's interaction with the environment—adults, other children, and the material world—and second, to the interaction between cognitive and affective spheres of development. The developmental interaction formulation stresses the nature of the environment as much as it does the patterns of the responding child. (pp. 59–60)

This model emphasizes experiences that allow children to try out new concepts, progress at their own pace, and engage in the kind of interaction that makes possible the assimilation of experience, the achievement of new integrations, and the resolution of conflict in both the cognitive and emotional realms (Shapiro & Biber, 1972).

In the Bank Street view, specific educational objectives for a particular child evolve from continuous analysis of the child's progress. Teachers must have a repertoire of teaching strategies from which to choose as individual situations dictate (Evans, 1975). The teacher is thus the most important variable in the child's learning environment. Other considerations for ensuring appropriate environmental interactions include a flexible arrangement of classroom equipment, a large variety of materials, an atmosphere of trust, learning activities that are focused around concrete personal experiences, and an interweaving of work and play in the classroom (Evans, 1975).

Bricker's (1978) concept of the developmental interaction process is compatible with the traditional Bank Street model. Unlike the Bank Street model, Bricker's model was conceived for use with children with handicaps. It stresses arranging the environment (curriculum) to ask more of the children each day in order to see change and growth. Behavior progresses from the simple to the complex in a specific developmental sequence. Targets are based on normal development and on functional competence within a setting. By placing children in a state of disequilibrium and then arranging the environment to promote meaningful interactions, the teacher ensures maximum growth.

In summary, the planning and implementation of individual educational programs for young children with handicaps must include considerations for both process and content. It must take account of both the child and the learning environment, and it must provide for meaningful experiences at the proper developmental level. To accomplish this, we have suggested a combination of behavioral technology and developmental interaction strategies designed to maximize the effects of intervention.

STRATEGIES FOR SYSTEMS CHANGE

The ecological congruence model discussed in the previous chapter is as concerned with changing systems as it is with changing the behavior of individuals. Although a technology for changing systems has not been developed to the same point as has the technology for individual behavior change, there are some strategies that can be employed in an attempt to change systems. These strategies often use contingent consequences in the same way that changing the behavior of a child does. Systems, after all, are controlled by people, and people respond to changes in the contingency structure of their environments. Some readers may be familiar with the book *Rules for Radicals* (Alinsky, 1971) that was popular in the early 1970s among people interested in effecting social and political change. Alinsky suggested that systems could be changed by identifying sacred or important elements in the system and then in some way interfering with the availability of these elements. For example, he maintained that O'Hare Airport is significant enough to the city of Chicago that one could bring about change in that city by effectively interfering with O'Hare's function. Alinsky's suggestion was to muster a cadre of people to occupy every stall of every bathroom at O'Hare until the city responded to whatever demands were being made. While Alinsky's strategy is a bit avant garde, and to our knowledge has never been successfully used, it does illustrate a principle by which system change can be brought about. Alinsky's strategy was essentially one of negative reinforcement: when the city of Chicago behaved in the manner Alinsky desired, he

would remove the aversive event (i.e., vacate the stalls at the airport). The point is that systems respond to contingent consequences just as individuals do, and these consequences can be used to bring about desired systems change. Remember that contingencies can be used in a more positive manner to help bring systems changes needed to establish ecological congruence.

Systems change can often be brought about by effective negotiation, leading to a compromise. Viewed from one perspective, a compromise is an agreed upon set of contingencies that are offered by each party. Presumably, the rewards gained through negotiation are stronger in maintaining desired outcomes than is the punishment rendered through giving up some desired consequences.

Suppose you were case manager for Ann, the young girl with cerebral palsy mentioned in the previous chapter. You may recall that Ann's father was intolerant of her inability to toilet herself independently, and that his intolerance coupled with Ann's lack of function created an incongruence in the family ecology. To increase Mr. Ray's tolerance of Ann, certain contingencies were implemented in the environment. For example, Ann's mother was to prepare special dinners for her husband on days when he assisted Ann with her toileting needs more than three times. Such contingencies might require negotiation to arrange. Mrs. Ray would need to be shown the benefits she would reap from preparing special dinners. In this situation, Mrs. Ray's cooperation would no doubt depend on how much importance she placed on having her husband assist with Ann's toileting needs.

Negotiation, while an important skill in bringing about systems change, is not always easily learned, nor is it always easy to accomplish. Successful negotiation depends on the following:

1. Understanding the nature of the system involved
2. Understanding the individuals in the system
3. Picturing clearly the desired outcome of the negotiation
4. Picturing clearly what consequences you are willing to offer for desired ends
5. Picturing clearly what consequences you are not willing to offer for desired ends
6. Being patient and tolerant of other people's view
7. Being committed enough to take the time and make the effort to complete the negotiation

Even if these guidelines are followed, negotiation may not always be successful. Any negotiator must be willing to accept failure and to find reward in the fact that he or she did whatever could be done. In developing congruent ecologies, it is necessary to have a commitment to negotiation and to be an advocate for both systems and individual change.

Although it can be useful in bringing about necessary changes in the physical and contingency structures of a social system, negotiation is often less successful in creating necessary attitude change. Attitude change depends on modifying internal feelings and contingencies that mediate a person's behavior. Sometimes a change in attitude can result from a negotiation—if the negotiated outcome demonstrates a point. For example, if a Down syndrome child's entrance into a regular kindergarten class could be successfully negotiated and implemented, the attitudes of the kindergarten teacher and other school personnel toward the acceptance of other children with developmental delays might become more favorable. Attitude change may also result from an examination of a person's internal state, an exercise that requires discussion and analysis over time. This is not to suggest that attitudes cannot also be changed by changing behavior, since the way we behave is a factor in determining the way we feel and the attitudes we express. The point is that attitude change usually requires relatively long-term interventions, which are carried out through systematic counseling and behavior change strategies. In Chapter 12 we discuss the use of these strategies as they apply to parents and other family members.

SUMMARY

This chapter has reviewed techniques and strategies for implementing individualized program plans. The affective and physical features of the learning environment are discussed and their importance to the intervention process are highlighted. The intervention techniques discussed stress the use of positive program and behavior management and focus on how environmental antecedents and consequences can be arranged to bring about effective learning and behavior change. A format is provided that can be used to structure specific interventions for an infant or young child. The importance of systems change is discussed from the ecological perspective, and some techniques for such change are put forth.

12

Family Needs and Services

1. How is a partnership with families different from more traditional models of intervention?
2. What are some of the emotions parents may go through in adapting to a young child with special needs?
3. What are some of the ways these emotions might be expressed?
4. What are the unique effects on mothers, fathers, and siblings of young children with special needs?
5. What are some avenues for parental involvement within an early intervention program?

THE PASSAGE OF PL 99-457 has forced early intervention professionals to take a new look at their relationship with parents and other family members. According to the law, family strengths and needs must be identified and an Individualized Family Service Plan (IFSP) must be developed by the professional in cooperation with the family. Some authors (e.g., Dunst, Trivette, & Deal, 1988) have suggested that parents should be responsible for developing strategies to meet their own needs, thus defining the role of the professional as one of helper and facilitator.

The role that is emerging for professionals is one of a partner working with families to achieve goals set by the family. This differs from more traditional early intervention models, which have posited the professional as the designer and implementer of programs. This emerging practice is one that approaches the family as the unit of concern and deals with the infant or young child within the context of that unit. As Dunst, Trivette, and Deal (1988) point out:

> this shift in role emphasis has occurred, in part, as a result of the recognition that the child is a member of a family system and that events both within and outside the family unit impinge upon the success of early intervention efforts. Indeed, it is now safe to say that early intervention programs that employ a broader-based, family systems approach will likely have positive influences on all family members, whereas traditional, child-focused inter-

Allen Sandler was co-author of this chapter and made a major contribution to it.

vention practices will produce meager results at best. (p. ix)

Developing a partnership with parents and other family members requires that professionals be knowledgeable concerning the emotions that family members experience in responding to an infant or young child with a disability. These emotions include anger, guilt, stress, grief, and shock. In addition, professionals must understand the means by which parents can become empowered to gain competence and control in their lives and the lives of their children. Finally, professionals must understand the various means by which parents can become directly involved in early intervention programs. These topics are discussed in this chapter and provide the reader with the knowledge necessary to begin to form an effective partnership with parents. Chapters 9, 10, and 11 may also be of interest.

FAMILY REACTIONS TO A CHILD WITH A HANDICAP

A family's reaction to a child's handicap begins at the point of diagnosis or confirmation of disability. Parents may experience anxiety over their child's development prior to the confirmation of the disability. Once the diagnosis is confirmed, however, the problem becomes real and parents must deal with it. For some parents, recognition and confirmation of a problem are made at birth, as, for example, in the cases of Down syndrome or spina bifida. In other cases, the disability will become manifested and confirmed only as the child fails to meet appropriate developmental milestones. In either instance the parents are faced with a reality to which they must respond and by some means adapt. This adaptation begins with a wide range of emo-

tions, some of which may never be fully resolved.

Early conceptualizations of parental reactions to children with handicaps tended to portray parents as uniformly neurotic—pathologically overcome by feelings of grief and guilt (Wolfensberger, 1967). More recent research has shown that such feelings are experienced along with a host of other emotional responses often experienced by essentially healthy individuals as they adjust to what Featherstone (1980) has termed "a difference in the family." Moreover, not all families experience grief and guilt.

Very few comparisons between parents of children with handicaps and parents of children without handicaps have been made. One of the few control group studies reported (Boles, 1959) failed to support the commonly held views that mothers of children with handicaps were more anxious, more socially withdrawn, more rejecting, more unrealistic in their attitudes, and more guilt ridden than mothers of children without handicaps. The bulk of work in this area has been theoretical, and based upon anecdotal reports and case studies. Familiarity with the available information in this area contributes substantially to one's ability to assist family members as they undergo what is often a continuing process of adjustment.

Blacher (1984) has hypothesized that parents may move through several stages of adjustment in adapting to the birth of an infant with a handicap. These stages are useful in providing a framework for the emotions experienced by parents in response to the confirmation of a handicap in an older child. It may be useful to keep these stages in mind while reading the following sections on parental emotions.

The first stage hypothesized by Blacher is that of shock and denial. Parents in this stage will often shop around in order to find a cure for their child. Generally, a cure does not exist, but often there are programs that can serve the needs of these parents and their children. Parents in this stage will often fail to "hear" what is being said to them about their child.

Blacher hypothesizes that the second stage of adjustment involves a period of emotional disorganization. It is during this stage that parents experience such emotions as anger, grief, and guilt. It is important for the early intervention professional to acknowledge these parental emotions and to support parents as they begin to cope with the reality of having a child with a disability. These emotions should not be judged, but rather should be viewed as natural reactions to a stressful and uncertain situation.

Finally, Blacher suggests that parents will come to accept the situation and continue to adapt to their child. It must be remembered that adaptation is a dynamic and ongoing process. It is not uncommon for parents who have accepted their situation to become advocates for their children as well as for children with handicaps generally. They may also be ready to participate in volunteer activities, such as fundraising, classroom assistance, or formation of support groups. Repeated clinical experience also suggests that parents will come to participate meaningfully in parent training activities only after they have been able to work through some of their emotions and begun to accept their child's disability.

It is important to remember that parents may move through the acceptance and adjustment process at very different rates. The emotions that parents experience may disappear and reappear; emotions that appear to have passed may reappear unexpectedly, or be triggered by medical or behavioral crises of the child. The good early intervention professional will be adept at recognizing paren-tal emotions and responding to them in an empathetic and supportive manner.

Grief

The period immediately after the identification of a child as disabled is usually the most difficult for parents. When an infant is identified as handicapped at birth, parents are dealt a blow at a time that, even under the best of circumstances, is one of great physical and psychological stress. The birth of any child requires dramatic adjustments in the roles and lifestyles of family members. The added stress of a newborn with a handicap may cause shock, bewilderment, confusion, anxiety, and despair. Wolfensberger and Menolascino (1970) have suggested that the critical issue is not so much the reality of the situation (i.e., the fact that the child has a disability), but the sudden shattering of expectations. They call this phenomenon "novelty shock."

Parents generally anticipate the birth of a child anxiously, with idealized expectations regarding the child-to-be. They often expect not merely a typical infant, but a perfect one. Grief is thought to result from the loss of this fantasized perfect child. Buscaglia (1975) describes the situation in this way:

> To go through a time of self-pity and mourning is to be expected. All parents have a dream of a perfect child, a new life which will to some extent reflect their own but go beyond them. They have dreams of their child being the football hero or the belle of the ball. . . . These may be unconscious feelings, but they are known to be very human dynamics in the psychology of birth. They believe that these dreams have been permanently shattered. They pity the child. They pity themselves. They have a right to go through a time of mourning as they would mourn the death of a loved one—for to some extent, the reality of a disabled child is the death of a loved dream of the perfect child they hoped for. (p. 101)

There are, however, important differences between mourning the birth of a child with a handicap and mourning a death (Featherstone, 1980). The implications of a child's disability are not nearly so clear-cut as those of a death. Confusion and lack of certainty about the future may create ambiguity. Parents do not know what the future holds, because professionals are often unable to make definitive judgments regarding a child's future development at so early an age. Contradictory feelings—of love and of sadness—may also be present. And, there are new caregiving demands:

> Instead of an aching hole—the empty bed, the now-useless baby clothes—parents face the insistent demands of a child who needs even more care than an ordinary infant would. They must shoulder the heavy responsibility of leading the child into life, and love him as though he embodied all their dreams. While death provides a moment's respite from ordinary demands, disability generates new tasks and necessities. (Featherstone, 1980, p. 234)

The manner in which parents are informed by the physician of their child's condition may exacerbate the difficult adjustment process. Parents look to the physician during this period for support and counsel. However, both the extent of the information conveyed by the physician and the way in which it is presented are often unsatisfactory. In several studies (e.g., Abramson, Abramson, & Sommers, 1977; Pueschel & Murphy, 1976) only about 50% of the parents reported satisfaction with the advice they received. Twenty-five percent of the parents surveyed by Pueschel and Murphy indicated that their physician was abrupt and unsympathetic. Two parents were informed of their child's condition by mail. Providing the parents with the opportunity to express their sorrow and receive support for the legitimacy of their grief may be especially important at this critical time. The physician's lack of support and sensitivity may cause anger and resentment.

The identification of a handicap some time after birth is also likely to cause sorrow and grief. At this time, however, parents may also experience a sense of relief. A significant period of time often elapses between the time a problem is first suspected by the parents and the time the presence of a disability is confirmed. During this period of uncertainty, parents may remain unconvinced by the reassurances of friends and family and feel powerless in the face of their fears. Sorrow may accompany the confirmation of the child's disability, but, in the words of one parent, "I also was free now to proceed to do something, to gain some control over the situation, instead of feeling like a helpless victim" (Kovacs, 1972, pp. 29–30).

Anger

Parents may be angry with God, fate, society, and professionals. They also may feel anger toward the child with the handicap. The birth of a child with a handicap may cause parents to question and sometimes rebel against basic assumptions about life's meaning. A satisfactory answer to the question "Why me?" may evade parents who were previously secure in viewing the world as an orderly place in which good deeds are rewarded and only wrongdoing punished. Parents may rebel in anger at the unfair burden meted out to them by God or fate. Featherstone (1980) describes one parent's reaction to another parent's observation that, "God never gives you more troubles than you can bear." The parent raised a clenched fist and responded, "I don't even believe in God, but sometimes I look up and tell Him that I hate Him" (p. 49). Parents may feel cheated by life, angry at life for having violated the rules (Featherstone, 1980).

Society's neglect of the problems of the handicapped may also cause anger in parents. Inadequate funding and reductions in funding by government may make needed services unavailable, although the implementation of PL 99-457 should help correct this situation.

Anger over threatened program cuts, however, may lead to action that positively affects parents' sense of competence and self-worth. In Featherstone's words, "Anger keeps us fighting . . . . We take a stand and raise ourselves to defend our own, like a mother bear with cubs" (1980, p. 49).

Medical and educational professionals are frequent targets of parents' anger. As we have already discussed, the manner in which a child's initial diagnosis is presented to parents may provoke anger. Parents may also experience considerable frustration as they seek accurate diagnosis of a child with a less readily identifiable problem. Too often a child's problem is minimized with statements such as, "He's just a little bit slow," or "He'll outgrow it," and valuable time is lost. Parents may become angry when they are not given adequate direction—when the diagnosis is a dead end without information about services available for the child and family.

Parents of autistic and severely emotionally disturbed children have been dealt the hardest blow by professionals, because they have often been blamed for their child's disability. One father of an autistic child responded to the National Society for Autistic Children's definition of autism with this letter:

Do you hear that out there Bruno Bettleheim? Are we getting through to you? We said: *No known factors in the psychological environment of a child have been shown to cause autism* . . . .

That means we didn't do it, Bruno . . . . It means that careful, objective, scientific people have carried out study after study . . . and have written paper after paper in journal after journal which show that we, the parents of autistic children, are just ordinary people. Not any crazier than others. Not "refrigerator parents" any more than others . . . . Not neurotic or psychopathic or sociopathic or any of those other words that have been made up.

It means, Dr. Bettleheim, that you, and all those others like you who have been laying this incredible guilt trip on us for over twenty years, you are wrong and ought to be ashamed of yourselves.

"Feral mothers" indeed! You are a feral mother, Bruno. Take that and live with it for awhile. It doesn't feel very good, does it?

And "parentectomy?" It is my considered professional opinion, after having carefully examined all of the facts, that nothing short of a Bruno-ectomy will improve conditions in this case. And a Freud-ectomy. And a psychiatrist-ectomy. And a jargon-ectomy. And a professional baloney-ectomy. (Warren, 1978, p. 195)

Finally, parents may feel anger toward their child. Feelings of resentment may build as extraordinary demands are made on parents' time, patience, physical endurance, and financial resources. Personal plans for the future may be thwarted, as parents look ahead to their child's continued dependence. Parents may be frustrated by their child's failure to progress at the pace they had anticipated; they may be angered by their child's apparent inability to learn. Behavior problems may cause anger, especially when they occur in public.

It may be difficult for parents to acknowledge anger toward their special child. In one of the few control group studies involving parents of children with handicaps, Cummings, Bayley, and Rie (1966) found that mothers of mentally retarded children experienced greater difficulty handling anger at their children than mothers of nonretarded children. As Featherstone puts it:

Because these children do not willfully choose to disobey or destroy, anger at them may appear as senseless as anger at fate itself. When disability magnifies a child's vulnerability, parents feel they owe him total devotion, unqualified and unremitting love. It takes courage to face rage and resentment . . . and the guilt these feelings bring. (p. 46)

Guilt

Redner (1980) found that college students' expectations about mothers of children with handicaps are consistent with Featherstone's thesis. Students expected mothers to be affected negatively by but be more devoted to a child with a handicap. The conflict between personal and social expectations and the reality of a child who inevitably brings parents frustration may cause guilt. Unable to accept feelings of rejection or hostility, parents may blame themselves for experiencing emotions unbefitting a good and loving parent, especially a parent of a child so in need of love and exceptional care. Parents are not prepared for the ambivalence that frequently characterizes the emotional interplay between a parent and a child with a handicap. The emotional maturity required to feel confident of one's love in the face of anger or resentment may be difficult to achieve.

Guilt may lead to overprotection of the child, as parents attempt to compensate for anger or rejection. Self-sacrifice and martyrdom may help parents feel atonement for the perceived sin of failing to love their child wholeheartedly. However, overprotection may occur in response to reality factors, such as immaturity of the child and uncertainty regarding his or her capabilities (Cummings, Bayley, & Rie, 1966). Overprotective behavior may also enhance a parent's feelings of satisfaction and self-worth, gained through meeting the dependency needs of the child (Ryckman & Henderson, 1965).

Guilt may also be related to a parent's feeling that something he or she did, or failed to do, caused a child's disability. This may be particularly true of parents of autistic or severely emotionally disturbed children, for, as we have seen, professionals have often attributed the problems of these children to parental inadequacy. Mothers of children identified at birth may feel guilt associated with some aspect of their pregnancy or the delivery: why didn't they refuse pain medication, or insist on a Cesarian—did they get enough rest, choose the right doctor, eat the right foods?

Parents may also feel guilt associated with their child's handicap simply because the child is theirs. Just as parents take pride in a healthy baby, they may feel guilt and shame because they have given birth to a child who is disabled, and thereby failed in the biological aspect of their role as parent.

Sorrow

Loss of self-esteem, loneliness, and what has been termed chronic sorrow (Olshansky, 1962, 1970) are among other possible reactions to a child with a handicap. Cummings, Bayley, and Rie (1966) found that mothers of mentally retarded children expressed higher levels of depressive affect and lower levels of self-esteem relative to their role as parent than did mothers of nonretarded children. Sorrow and feelings of inadequacy often continue beyond the adjustment period immediately following a child's initial diagnosis. The presence of a child with a handicap may provide parents with a continuing reminder that they have, in a sense, failed in their role as progenitors. Parents' self-esteem may also be affected negatively if they see a child's limited progress as evidence of their own lack of competence as parents. The opportunities for failure are as great for parents as they attempt to teach a child appropriate social behavior, language, or toileting skills, as they are for the child. The child's failure may reinforce an existing sense of failure in the parents. This may be especially true for fathers, who appear to view their role as guide and teacher as a fundamental aspect of their role as fathers (Boles, 1959).

Although it has been over 25 years since Olshansky (1962) first urged professionals to abandon "the simplistic and static concept of parental acceptance," theories that portray parents as progressing through various stages culminating in a final stage of acceptance continue to be popular. Olshansky instead offered the view that parents experience chronic sorrow associated with their child's lifelong state of dependency. The following passage, written by the father of a mentally retarded child, supports Olshansky's position:

> Parents of retarded people, the theorists tell us, learn to live with their children's handicaps. They go through stages of reaction, moving through shock, guilt, and rejection to the promised land of acceptance and adjustment.
>
> My own experience as the father of a retarded child did not fit this pattern. Instead, it convinced me that most people seriously misunderstand a parent's response to this situation . . . .
>
> Professionals could help parents more—and they would be more realistic—if they discarded their ideas about stages and progress. They could then begin to understand something about the deep, lasting changes that life with a retarded son or daughter brings to parents. And they could begin to see that the negative feelings . . . never disappear but stay on as a part of the parents' emotional life. (Searle, 1978, p. 27)

In addition to the occasion of a child's initial diagnosis, later situations may evoke sorrow in parents of disabled children. Although parents may accept their child, this state of acceptance may be very different from the "final harmony" suggested by stage theories. It is an acceptance that includes periods of pain and sadness — periodic sorrow within an overall context of acceptance (Featherstone, 1980; Wikler, Masow, & Hatfield, 1981). Some situations that might rekindle sorrow in parents of young children with handicaps include the following: 1) the child reaching the age when peers without handicaps begin to walk or talk, 2) a younger sibling overtaking the handicapped child's abilities, 3) the child beginning to attend a school program, and thus being publicly labeled as "different," and 4) parental management of a crisis (behavior problem, seizure disorder, other health problem) unique to the child (Wikler et al., 1981). Any situation that forces parents to confront their child's deviation from normal performance may cause sorrow.

Social Isolation

There are a number of possible explanations for the social isolation and loneliness sometimes experienced by parents. Some isolation results from embarrassment. Parents may hesitate to take their child out because of the child's appearance or behavior. The stigma associated with their child's disability may make parents themselves feel stigmatized and set apart from others. Parents may feel lonely because they are different, with problems and responsibilities unique to their role. Lack of understanding of these problems by others may intensify their feelings of aloneness. One parent described her rage in response to a stranger's suggestion that she let her 4-year-old daughter walk independently:

> I explained that she couldn't walk, that she was severely retarded. The stranger's face softened; her attitude was warm and understanding. "Oh," she said, "they are such wonderful children, and all they need is loving." Perhaps I had a premonition even then of how many years of assistance and training it would take before she would be able to walk, not to mention toilet herself, feed herself, and dress herself, which she still cannot do at age fifteen. One comes out of such interviews feeling very much alone,

burdened by the obligation to explain, educate, and reassure others because they know so little about our children and so very little about how to help. (Morton, 1978, pp. 145–146)

Parents may experience social isolation as a result of the physical requirements of parenting a child with a handicap. The time and energy needed to see friends, attend meetings, or enjoy an evening out with one's spouse may not be available to parents burdened with the extraordinary caregiving demands often required by a child with a handicap. Holt (1975) found that 30% of the 272 couples he surveyed never went out together, with the mother's only relief from care coming when the father took over. Many parents are either unwilling to leave their child with a sitter or unable to find a suitable sitter for their child. Gallagher, Cross, and Scharfman (1981) found changes in vacations, social activities, and recreation to be among the major sources of stress reported by parents of preschool children with handicaps.

Stress

All families experience stress; stress is a normal part of life. How a family responds to stress will be important in determining how it will respond and adjust to their young child with special needs. Each family and each family member is unique in its ability to respond to stress.

Wikler (1986) has suggested that Hill's ABCX model (Hill, 1949, 1958; McCubbin & Patterson, 1983) provides a useful framework for the analysis of family stress. Within the model, "A" represents the stressor event; "B," the resources of the family; and "C," the perception of the event by the family or the meaning attached to the event. "X" represents the degree of crisis experienced by the family or, put another way, how the family adapts. McCubbin and Patterson suggest that

bonadaptation occurs when there is "(a) the maintenance or strengthening of family integrity; (b) continued promotion of both member development and family unit development; and (c) the maintenance of family independence and its sense of control over environmental influences" (p. 20). Maladaptation, however, occurs when there is "(a) deterioration in family integrity; (b) a curtailment or deterioration in personal health and development of a member or the well-being of the family unit; or (c) a loss or decline in family independence and autonomy" (p. 20).

The Stressor Event "A" The stressor event in the present context is the birth or identification of an infant or young child with a special need. This may be a temporary special need (e.g., an infant in the neonatal intensive care unit with a resolving infection without complications), or it may be an ongoing special need (e.g., a child with Down syndrome). Of course, most children with special needs would be a source of ongoing stress to their families. Young children in general are a source of stress in many families. McCubbin and Patterson (1983) have also suggested that there can be what they call a "pile up" of stress when several sources of stress impinge upon the family at one time.

Family Resources "B" Family resources includes both physical and emotional resources. Physical resources include money, housing, health care, early intervention, clothing, and so forth. Emotional resources come primarily from a family's social support system. Social support has been repeatedly identified as an important mediator of stress (Cohen & Syme, 1985; Dunst, Trivette, & Deal, 1988; Pilisuk & Parks, 1983). The absence or relative lack of family resources may be defined as family needs. Assessment of the family's social support network and other resources is examined in Chapter 9.

Family Perception "C" How the family perceives the stressor event will depend on its social and religious values and its philosophy of life. The types of emotional reactions that a family experiences may also affect how the family perceives a stressful event. A man who is angry about the birth of a daughter with Down syndrome may perceive that event much differently from his spouse, who may feel guilty about the birth, or his older son, who may feel ashamed. The sum of these emotions may help determine the family's perception of the stressor event. McCubbin and Patterson (1983) have suggested that families who can redefine the stressor event and give it new meaning are often best able to cope.

What McCubbin and Patterson (1983) so eloquently point out is that the ABCX model must be seen as a dynamic model rather than a static one. This means that the stressors, resources, and perceptions of families are ever changing and in constant interaction with each other. The early intervention professional must be mindful of this dynamic quality of families.

Ongoing Sources of Stress Caregiving demands were the best predictor of stress in a survey of mothers of infants with handicaps (Beckman-Bell, 1981, Beckman, 1983). When added to the ordinary responsibilities of maintaining a household and attending to the needs of nonhandicapped siblings, the additional demands of caring for a child with a handicap can be overwhelming. Reality demands may be so excessive that parents experience "burn out" (Boggs, 1978; Schell, 1981). Physical exhaustion may result from long hours of caregiving without respite. Feeding, bathing, attending to special medical needs, carrying out home therapy programs, and providing other forms of therapeutic intervention all may contribute to a state of chronic fatigue. This aspect of parental stress

has often been overlooked by professionals, who have focused instead on parental psychopathology:

> What goes on in training programs in the name of education is sometimes shocking . . . . I cringe at the thought of some of the course syllabi I have reviewed. In many of these courses, very little attention is directed toward helping parents solve the day-to-day problems which almost invariably are encountered, yet weeks are devoted to the "psychological insight approach to parental guilt." Many such courses are a fraud and tend to insure further conflict and unsatisfactory relationships between parents and professionals. (Turnbull, 1978, p. 138)

Parents sometimes experience stress related to the need to provide stimulation and training to their child at home. This may be particularly true when a child is involved in a home-based program or in a program with a strong parent training emphasis. The pressure to provide training at home may prevent a mother from meeting her own needs for relaxation or time with friends and make it difficult for her to attend to other responsibilities around the home:

> I think you are always going to feel more pressure if your little one is handicapped, there's no way around it. When you get a little one who doesn't do anything until you're the catalyst . . . it almost becomes an obsession . . . because you feel like he'd be sitting there, and you know that either you're going to sew . . . or you could get him to learn his "K" sounds. (Winton & Turnbull, 1981, pp. 14–15)

Other reality sources of stress include financial responsibilities, management of behavior problems, and efforts to obtain appropriate educational services. Children with severe handicaps and children with physical disabilities are likely to require medical care that is not covered by ordinary medical insurance. Regular visits to the pediatrician, neurologist, or orthopedist, or specialized equipment, such as adaptive chairs, prone boards, or side-lyers, may be necessary. When financial resources are limited, the pressure to pay for needed services can be a significant source of stress (Beckman-Bell, 1981; Turnbull, 1978).

The presence of severe behavioral problems may be a source of considerable stress for parents. Special procedures are often necessary successfully to remediate problems such as self-injurious, stereotypical, or aggressive behavior, or tantrums. Parents may experience stress related to both the behavior problem itself and to the intervention approach recommended to remediate the problem (Beckman-Bell, 1981; Bray, Coleman, & Bracken, 1981).

Events related to educational services were the most common source of stress among parents of a heterogeneous group of children with handicaps participating in a survey reported by Bray, Coleman, and Bracken (1981). The impact of the child's initial diagnosis and the emotional impact of the child's disability on a specific family member were ranked as the next most common sources of stress. Parental concerns about educational services involved the suitability of placement; availability, relevance, or duration of services; and the child's adjustment to the educational program. In a related survey (Winton & Turnbull, 1981) parents of preschool children with handicaps indicated concern about the competence and sensitivity of their child's teacher. They were concerned not only because of the effect of the teacher's ability on their child's expected progress, but because the competence of their child's teacher affected their own ability to relax and obtain a break from the responsibilities involved in their child's care. Sixty-five percent of the mothers expressed the need for a break from the pressure of full-time educational responsibility for their child.

Effect on Marital Stability

Marital stability may be seriously threatened by the presence of a child with a handicap. Especially when a relationship is already problematic, the added stress related to rearing a child with a disability may lead to severe marital discord. Love (1973) reported three times as many divorces among parents of mentally retarded children as among parents of nonretarded children. Fatigue may cause irritability and lack of tolerance for frustration, which may in turn lead to arguments and outbursts of temper. Anger associated with the handicapped child's behavior may be misdirected at a spouse. Featherstone offers the following insight from her own experience as a parent:

> As Jay and I struggle to understand the anger we felt toward one another in the second year of Jody's life, it seems to us that our inability to focus our frustration on Jody himself might have contributed. When our dreams lay in fragments at our feet, when a crying baby interrupted every activity, fury and frustration were inevitable. But how could we blame Jody, who suffered, through no fault of his own, more than anyone else? Longing for solutions that no one could provide, we turned on one another. (1980, p. 98)

Another source of conflict may be disagreement over issues related to the handicap. Parents may disagree about the nature and extent of their child's disability and about implications for the future. This may be especially true in the case of children who are initially difficult to diagnose. Disagreements may concern the extent to which the needs of a child with a handicap should be permitted to interfere with normal family routines and the needs of other family members. Another possible source of conflict, especially important because of its potential impact on the child with the handicap, is parental disagreement over management of behavior problems. Parents may disagree over the extent to which the child should be held accountable for his or her own behavior and about the type of disciplinary approach, if any, to be used. Differences of opinion about other aspects of the child's training, especially as they affect the time and energy of other family members, may also cause conflict.

Boles (1959) found significantly higher levels of marital conflict reported by mothers of cerebral palsied children than by mothers of children without handicaps. He offered two possible explanations. First, differences in traditional maternal and paternal roles may enable mothers to achieve greater fulfillment through mothering, sheltering, and sacrificing for the child with the handicap, while fathers may find the helpless dependency of a child with a severe handicap frustrating and more of a liability. The difficulty each parent has in understanding the satisfactions or frustration of the other may contribute to marital conflict. Boles also hypothesized that maternal involvement with the child may be so great that the husband and other children become neglected. This may result in feelings of resentment by the husband and lead to tension and unresolved conflict in the marriage. Other authorities have suggested similar explanations for marital discord among families with a child with a handicap (Buscaglia, 1975; Berger & Fowlkes, 1980; Featherstone, 1980).

Borrowing the terminology and perspective of family therapy (Minuchin, 1974), we may state the problem in terms of a breakdown in the boundary that normally exists between the subsystem of husband and wife and the subsystem that includes their children. Maintaining the integrity of this boundary appears necessary for family stability. Problems may occur when the family system is unbalanced by an alliance between one parent and a child that isolates the other

parent. Parent training programs that include only the mother may contribute to boundary problems in a family by promoting increased levels of interaction between the mother and her child at the expense of transactions between husband and wife (Sandler, Coren, & Thurman, 1983).

Effect on Fathers

Fewer professionals have turned their attention to fathers, the "forgotten parents" (Crowley, Keane, & Needham, 1982). "Parent" support groups and "parent" training programs have rarely been set up to accommodate both mothers and fathers. Although mothers and their children are far more accessible targets of intervention, and mothers generally do assume the major share of caregiving responsibility for a child with a handicap, neglect of the needs of fathers can have an undesirable impact upon overall family adjustment and marital stability.

Cummings (1976) investigated the effect of a child with a handicap on the father. As might be expected, he found that fathers of mentally retarded children experienced significantly greater levels of psychological stress than fathers of nonretarded children. Fathers of retarded children scored higher on measures of depressive affect and preoccupation with their child and scored lower on a measure of self-esteem related to paternal competence. Fathers of mentally retarded children also demonstrated a relative lack of gratification from relationships with their wives, with other children in the family, and with their retarded child. Cummings suggests that the traditional paternal role of family provider limits a father's opportunities to act directly to help his retarded child, thereby providing evidence of his love and concern, and counterbalancing the feelings of grief, frustration, and anger he may experience.

Enacting other traditional paternal roles, such as physical playmate and socializing agent/model, may also be difficult for fathers, especially when the child with a handicap is a male (Gallagher, Cross, & Scharfman, 1981; Tallman, 1965).

Achieving greater satisfaction with their role in the family may be a critical need of fathers. Their difficulty defining an appropriate role is underscored by findings reported by Gallagher, Cross, and Scharfman (1981). Fathers judged both "average" and "successful" in their overall adjustment to a child with a handicap indicated that they felt they should be more actively involved in all six child care roles explored (teaching, nursing, child discipline, transporter, clothing selector, and recreation leader). Their wives agreed, and felt that the fathers should be more actively involved in 12 of 14 additional general family roles. Fathers appear to experience difficulty, however, in determining how to be involved with a child with a handicap. The following responses by fathers of deaf children express a common need to know more about how they might assist in promoting the growth of their children: "Knowing what to do is half the struggle;" "I need to know there is something I can do and to know what to do;" "Tell us what to do and we'll do it" (Liversidge & Grana, 1973, p. 175).

The traditional image of the strong, silent male may further interfere with adjustment to a child with a handicap. Mothers often complain that fathers do not talk about their feelings. Featherstone provides this example:

Elizabeth Black's experience is not atypical. She described taking Kimberly in for an evaluation because she worried about the little girl's slow development. Gary went with her. The news was shattering. But Gary went off to work, straight from the appointment, leaving her to cope alone with the crying baby and her feelings. "No support," she remarked concisely. He returned home at 10 p.m., after work and overtime.

"How are you?" Elizabeth asked.

"Oh, I'm fine."

"No, I mean how are you really?"

"Oh. Well, I guess I'm not feeling so great, after what they said this morning." She waited, but that was all. (1980, p. 124)

The inability or lack of willingness openly to express feelings may make it difficult for fathers to reduce the burden of stress they bear. Participation in a group with other fathers, however, may help some fathers open up (Liversidge & Grana, 1973). Unfortunately, support groups for fathers are not generally available, and when they are organized, participation is often limited. Interested fathers may simply lack the energy to attend an evening function. Successful groups for fathers have been described in the literature, however, and these descriptions are a valuable resource for professionals attempting to start a fathers' group (see Crowley, Keane, & Needham, 1982; Delaney, Meyer, & Ward, 1977; Erickson, 1974; Liversidge & Grana, 1973).

Fathers who do not feel comfortable participating in a sharing group may derive peer support through various activities centered on their children's school program. Group projects involving physical work, such as constructing a picnic table for the school yard, or putting up a new piece of playground equipment, may allow fathers to experience comradeship and also may enhance fathers' self-esteem. Other avenues for involvement that are consistent with traditional male roles include participation in organizational functions, such as serving as an officer of the parent group, becoming involved in fundraising, and joining in lobbying efforts of public officials.

Effect on Siblings

The effects of a child with a handicap on the family are not limited to the parents. Such emotions as sorrow, anger, and guilt may be experienced by both parents and siblings. Intertwined with these reactions, however, are others more uniquely experienced by siblings. These include identification with the handicapped sibling, embarrassment, and resentment.

Based upon her experience conducting a support group for siblings, Kaplan (1969) suggests that avoiding identification with a brother or sister with a handicap is the primary concern of siblings. Just as the community views the family as a social unit, so children identify themselves as family members, sharing and internalizing characteristics of their family. When a family's identity is heavily influenced by the presence of a child with a handicap, siblings' identity cannot escape a similar influence. Children may also identify with their sibling because of a physical resemblance (Featherstone, 1980). The process of identification may lead nonhandicapped brothers and sisters to question their own normalcy. They may fear that like their sibling they are in some way deficient.

Children often feel embarrassed and ashamed of a sibling with a handicap. Embarrassment caused by the stares of strangers may be so painful that a brother or sister may try to avoid accompanying a sibling with a handicap in public. Siblings who display obvious physical stigma or exhibit inappropriate social behavior, such as self-stimulation, are especially likely to cause embarrassment. The sister of an adult with a severe handicap related her feelings at age 11 in this way:

> I can remember being actually embarrassed by the ill-concealed stares our family re-
ceived . . . . I was certain that everyone was looking at my brother with his obvious handicap and their wondering what was wrong with the rest of us. As a result of the feelings aroused in me by these occurrences, I began to refuse to go out to dinner or shopping with my family and took precautions to avoid being seen on the street or in the yard with Robin.
>
> These avoidance procedures on my part were not taken without an accompanying sense of guilt. I knew that it was wrong for me to be ashamed of my brother. (Helsel, Helsel, Helsel, & Helsel, 1978, p. 110)

The significant amounts of time and money that may be spent on a disabled brother or sister may cause resentment among siblings. Children may feel deprived of the attention or resources they want and feel they need (Grossman, 1972). They may resent the embarrassment they face and the extra responsibilities they must shoulder. Holt (1975) found approximately 10% of the siblings in 201 families he surveyed to be extremely resentful of the attention given to a retarded brother or sister.

In the past, parents were often counseled that keeping a mentally retarded child at home would harm the siblings. Although, as we have seen, responses to a disabled sibling may be negative in certain respects, positive reactions are also commonly reported (Cleveland & Miller, 1977; Farber, 1963; Featherstone, 1980; Schreiber & Feely, 1975). These reactions include increased maturity, compassion, tolerance for individual differences, patience, and sense of responsibility; a greater appreciation for family bonds and for good health; and increased sensitivity to prejudice and other social welfare issues. Grossman (1972) found positive reactions such as these to be reported about as commonly by college age siblings as various negative reactions.

At particular risk for the development of adjustment problems, however, may be the oldest female sibling (Cleveland & Miller, 1977; Fowle, 1968; Gath, 1973, 1974). This risk may be related to the increased likelihood that she assumes parent-surrogate responsibilities in relation to a brother or sister with a handicap. Family supports, such as respite care, may help lessen this risk, allowing time for more normal peer relationships, dating, and the like. Many siblings benefit from participation in a group that provides information and a supportive atmosphere for the sharing of feelings. Sibling groups have been described by Kaplan (1969); Cansler, Martin, and Valand (1975); and Schreiber and Feely (1975).

In summarizing the literature, Simeonsson and McHale (1981) have identified various factors associated with positive and negative adjustments to siblings with handicaps. They conclude that positive sibling adjustment is more likely to take place when the family is small in size, when the handicapped sibling is a male, when siblings are of the same gender, when the sibling with the handicap is older, and when the handicap is severe and the impairment is undefined or ambiguous in nature (e.g., mental retardation). Conversely, they suggest that the following factors are related to negative adjustment of siblings: large family size, handicapped child being female, handicapped sibling of different gender, the handicapped sibling being younger, mild handicap in the sibling and impairment visible and clearly defined (e.g., blindness). It is important to consider the interaction of these factors when attempting to determine the adjustment of children to their brothers and sisters with handicaps.

A more recent analysis of the literature by Simeonsson and Bailey (1986) concludes that:

1) Regardless of the specific chronic and/or handicapping condition, siblings demonstrate similar personal and social reactions; 2) younger and closer age-spaced siblings seem to have more difficulty adjusting; and 3) the handicapping condition per se does not appear to determine whether the sibling reaction will be positive or negative. (p. 74)

What is clear is that siblings of children with handicaps can be affected in both positive and negative ways (Gallagher & Powell, 1989; Powell & Ogle, 1985), and that a number of interacting and often conflicting variables may account for their overall adjustment to having a sibling with a disability. This reality suggests that early intervention professionals should adopt an individualized approach to children with siblings with handicaps. Such an approach will help ensure that a variety of factors will be considered and that the needs of these children will be identified and meaningfully responded to.

THE FAMILY SYSTEMS APPROACH

Since the mid-1970s, early intervention professionals have recognized that families represent a system and that what affects one member of the family is likely to affect others in the family (Minuchin, 1974). Understanding that the family is a system is important, because it forces the early intervention professional to consider the implications of any given intervention for other members of the family. Rather than examine the effects of a child with a disability on individual family members, a systems approach would suggest that these effects are not isolated but in fact, interact with each other. Thus, the way in which a mother reacts to her child may influence, and in turn be influenced by, how the father reacts. Family-focused intervention, discussed in Chapters 9 and 13, is based on a family systems approach. This approach is reflected in public policy and has resulted in the provision in PL 99-457, calling for the development of Individualized Family Service

Plans (IFSPs) for infants, and the recognition that family training is an appropriate and re-imburseable service to families with pre-school children with disabilities.

Recent literature suggests that a family-focused approach should emphasize family strengths and should build a sense of compe-tence and power within the family system (Turnbull, Summers, & Brotherson, 1986; Dunst, Trivette, & Deal, 1988). To do this it is necessary to gather information about family structures, strengths, needs, and desires. Techniques for gathering such information are described in Chapter 9. An outcome of this approach will be families who feel com-fortably in control of their own lives. This ap-proach requires that a partnership be formed with families, and that the role of the profes-sional become one of facilitator and advo-cate. Case management should flow from this partnership and should actively involve family members. Maximum empowerment results when the management of the case is in the hands of the family.

Although we agree that empowerment is an important goal toward which service pro-viders should work, a word of caution is needed. Some families may choose not to be empowered, and are more comfortable if de-cision making remains with the professional. Each family must be responded to on an indi-vidual basis, and early intervention pro-viders, who are more and more committed to family empowerment, must realize that fam-ilies, like children, differ. In summary, fami-lies should be given control over their lives, but it should also be remembered that some families will be more willing and able to take that control. Other families may feel em-powered by making the decision to put con-trol into the hands of the professionals. In es-sence, good early intervention service deliv-ery depends on a philosophy that gives deci-sion-making power to families whenever possible. Professionals, of course, have the obligation to be responsive to the individual differences among families.

AVENUES FOR FAMILY INVOLVEMENT

Early intervention service providers can give families a variety of opportunities for in-volvement in different activities. The more types of opportunities for family involve-ment, the more likely it is that a large per-centage of parents will participate. Since only about 50% of parents with center-based programs will participate in home program-ming (Fredericks, Baldwin, & Grove, 1974), it is important to offer other avenues for par-ticipation. These activities may be directly re-lated to the child, as in the case of family training or program planning, or they may be focused on activities of broader benefit, such as volunteering or program advocacy. Keep in mind that the family-focused approach discussed above would suggest that parents should choose the number and types of ac-tivities in which to become involved. It is important to recognize that families, as well as early intervention programs, can benefit from this involvement.

Volunteer Activities

The importance of volunteer activities in maintaining early intervention services has recently been discussed by Tingey and Stim-ell (1989). What these authors fail to ac-knowledge is that family members can often engage in volunteer services and can gain a sense of worth and contribution by doing so. Volunteer activities can provide a major ave-nue for families to participate in early inter-vention programs and can help family mem-bers feel a sense of ownership of the pro-gram. These volunteer activities can take many forms and can be structured to meet both program needs and the needs of individual family volunteers. As with any mechanism for family involvement, volunteerism should be viewed as one of a number of options. "Required volunteerism" should be avoided. Family members should control their own participation and should determine the frequency and extent of their activity.

Family members can volunteer and bring needed services to an early intervention program in a number of ways. Each person must decide what types of volunteer activities make sense for him or her. Professional staff can be helpful in assisting family members in deciding whether to volunteer and if so, how. Ideally, these choices will be in the best interests of both the family member and the early intervention program. Options for volunteer participation by family members include acting as a classroom or therapy aide; helping to build equipment or renovate space; planning and implementing fundraising activities; serving on boards; assisting with clerical and office work; writing and mailing newsletters; participating in advocacy and lobbying activities; and managing support groups. Each of these options is discussed below.

Acting as a Classroom or Therapy Aide
Parents, or even teenage siblings, can often be effective as classroom or therapy aides. With proper planning and training it is often possible to use family volunteers to supplement classroom and therapy staff. For example, a teenage sibling may have to complete a school project in which he or she must teach a particular skill to a young child. This might be accomplished through participating in the early intervention program of a younger sibling. One mother may have special musical talents and can volunteer to develop and provide musical activities that enhance learning for the children in the early intervention program.

Another mother may be willing to assist in feeding children during mealtimes.

Whether a family member should volunteer in the classroom of its own child or sibling depends on the particular circumstances and should be discussed by professionals and family members together.

If family volunteers are to be effective ongoing classroom aides their involvement cannot be approached casually. Fredericks et al. (1974) suggest guidelines to help ensure a successful program. These include: 1) providing a brief initial training experience, including a description of the program, the volunteer's responsibilities, and a review of some basic teaching principles; 2) providing teaching tasks that are appropriate to a family member's teaching ability by initially having him or her teach in a single area only (e.g., self-help, fine motor); 3) providing regular feedback regarding performance through observation by professional staff; and 4) providing flexible scheduling so that the inevitable missed days will not be overly disruptive to classroom routine.

Building Equipment Special adaptive equipment is sometimes needed for young children with special needs. Such equipment can be costly. There may be parents, grandparents, or older siblings of children served by an early intervention program who have skills as carpenters, electricians, or metal workers who can build adaptive equipment. Often these individuals can build equipment to exact specifications, or can modify existing equipment to meet the needs of a particular child. Family volunteers may also assist with equipment maintenance, or help with space renovations or other construction projects. Family members may feel particularly pleased to build equipment or do renovation projects for an early intervention program and may see it as a tangible means to pay back the program for the services they have received.

Fundraising Family volunteers can take responsibility for fundraising activities. Such activities can include bake sales, Monte Carlo nights, raffles, cookbooks, bingo games, and car washes, to name just a few. Often a fundraising activity can be organized to support a particular need, such as money for classroom trips, new equipment, or educational materials, or to bring in a guest speaker. Although the amount of money generated by family volunteers through fundraising may not be substantial, such efforts are often significant because they make families feel as though they are contributing to their child's early intervention program. In addition, because fundraising activities can take so many forms, they require people with a variety of skills and abilities and, thus, open the possibility of including a large number of family volunteers.

Boards Most early intervention programs have advisory boards, or boards of directors. These boards provide another means for families to volunteer. As consumers and taxpayers, family members have a right to be involved in program policy issues. Family input concerning possible program changes makes it more likely that programs will meet child and family needs. With the best of intentions, professionals sometimes make program decisions that are overly influenced by administrative concerns and do not fully recognize the needs of families and children. Family members who serve on boards may be involved in hiring staff, reviewing budgets, setting spending priorities, and influencing important program changes (e.g., implementing a home-based program for children on the waiting list) (Sandler & Coren, 1981).

Clerical and Office Work Some family members who may not have the skills or inclination to volunteer in classrooms may be willing and able to provide clerical support. As with classroom volunteer activities, these services can be structured to meet the needs of both the individual volunteer and the early intervention program. For example, an early intervention center may be preparing a mass mailing for its annual giving campaign. The center may need extra clerical help to get the mailing out. At the same time there may be a mother who is thinking about going back into the work force who needs the opportunity to use her skills and regain her confidence. Through volunteering to help with this mailing this mother could benefit not only the center but also herself.

Newsletters Another volunteer activity that may be meaningful for family members is the publication of newsletters. A newsletter can provide a vehicle through which parents and staff can share ideas and information or announce upcoming events. A newsletter can also be used to welcome new staff or new families to the program. The publication of a newsletter requires individuals with organizational abilities, clerical abilities, writing skills, and artistic talent. Depending on how frequently it is published a newsletter can be a major undertaking, but it can serve to involve a number of family members in a meaningful and useful volunteer effort.

Advocacy and Lobbying Family members can often be effective advocates for their children and their children's programs. They can use their advocacy skills to lobby legislative and governmental officials for additional funds or needed legislation. Parental advocacy was important in bringing about PL 94-142 and PL 99-457. To be effective advocates family members must be knowledgeable about their child's educational needs, understand state and federal laws pertaining to early intervention and special education services, and be assertive. Early intervention programs can set up training programs to help family members develop advocacy skills. The process of empowering parents and giving them a feeling of confidence and competence can also facilitate their effectiveness as advocates.

It is important that family members, especially parents, gain advocacy skills when their children are young, so that they will be prepared to use those skills throughout their lifetime. As we move toward more family-focused models of service provision, advocacy by parents will be more and more directed at funding and policy issues at local, state, and federal levels. Successful family-focused intervention models should result in less need for parental advocacy with local program administrators, since these models lead to parental empowerment and place decision making about program services in the hands of families.

In times of dwindling public resources, it is especially important that parents be advocates in seeking services for their children. Lobbying efforts by parents are often helpful in preventing planned cuts in funding, or in seeking increases in funding to provide adequate programming. Parents of infants and preschool children with handicaps should be encouraged to advocate on behalf of expanded services for older children and adults with disabilities. They should be encouraged to view their parental role as encompassing advocacy on behalf of their child through the child's life span (Cartwright, 1981). It is only through such advocacy efforts combined with those of professionals that existing programs will be maintained and expanded services put into place.

FAMILY TRAINING

As we have seen, parents vary considerably in their response to a child with a handicap. Differences in the past experiences of parents, the status of the marital relationship, the se-

verity of a child's handicap, and other factors may influence not only the emotional adjustment of parents, but the degree to which they are able and willing to become actively involved in their child's educational program. As we turn to parent training methods, we pay special attention to the degree various approaches allow for differing levels of parent participation. We urge the reader to keep in mind that rigid adherence to any one professional role in working with parents is likely to lead to less than optimal results. Parents will often open up and express their feelings in the context of a parent training session. The professional must be willing to listen carefully as parents share their feelings, shifting easily from a parent training role to a supportive role more commonly associated with counseling. The approach used must depend upon the needs of a given parent at a particular time. Sensitivity and an open mind are required to discern what these needs may be.

Training programs for parents are generally provided within either a center-based or a home-based context. In either case, the following components are among those likely to be included:

1. Review of normal child development and developmentally sequenced instruction
2. Explanation of handicapping conditions and an overview of their treatment
3. Instruction in child management techniques
4. Instruction in teaching techniques, often including data collection
5. Observation of modeled teaching sequences involving child
6. Opportunity to practice teaching and receive feedback from professional staff (Welsh & Odum, 1981)

It is important that parents understand the basis for selecting skills to be taught to their child. Meaningful parent involvement in formulating goals and objectives requires familiarity with the concept of developmentally sequenced instruction. This may be facilitated by providing parents with a copy of a developmental checklist, and using it with them as a resource in choosing skills for their child. Parents often lack a clear understanding of the nature of their child's handicap and its implications for the future. A review of the causes and characteristics of the major handicapping conditions and their treatment may help parents to develop more realistic expectations and to understand better their role in promoting their child's growth.

Most research on parent training has involved training parents to remediate behavior problems in their children (Johnson & Katz, 1973; Kaiser & Fox, 1986; O'Dell, 1974). Parents often take their children's good behavior for granted and respond with negative attention to undesirable behavior. Thus, the child receives attention, albeit negative attention, following behavior that is disturbing to parents. This strengthens the disturbing behavior. Intervention involves teaching the parent to praise or otherwise reinforce appropriate behavior and to replace negative attention (e.g., scolding, repeated commands, reprimands, threats) with either systematic ignoring or an effective punishment procedure, such as time out. The effort required to teach the appropriate use of time out in the home should not be underestimated; repeated home visits are often required.

Among the most common behavior problems at home are noncompliance (refusal to follow commands) and tantrums. Procedures for reducing noncompliant behavior include reinforcing compliance; teaching the parent to provide clear commands and to limit the number of repetitions of an initial command; and either putting the child through the desired behavior without attention, or providing a warning ("If you don't

_____, you'll go in time out") and following through with time out if the warning is not heeded. Children have tantrums either to avoid something aversive (going to bed, taking a bath), or to obtain something they desire (a cookie, a chance to go outside). When a parent gives in to a child's demand, the acquiescence is negatively reinforced by the termination of the child's tantrum, and the parent will therefore be more likely to give in again in the future. The child's tantrum behavior is also reinforced when the parent gives in, because the child either gets something pleasant or avoids something unpleasant. Intervention involves teaching parents to avoid giving in to demands made during a tantrum and to otherwise ignore tantrum behavior.

Despite research support for the effectiveness of techniques such as these in treating behavior problems at home, prominent researchers in this area have questioned the generality of parent training results (Bernal, Klinnert, & Schultz, 1980; Wahler, 1980). Not all parents are likely to profit equally from training; Bernal, Klinnert, and Schultz suggest that a large proportion of parents with children who have conduct problems may fail to become effective change agents for their children.

A combination of small group and individual sessions is effective for providing instruction in techniques. General information may be conveyed through group sessions, which use professional time economically and enable parents to benefit from the encouragement and support of their peers. Individual sessions give parents an opportunity to observe as their child receives training and to work individually with their child and receive feedback from the parent trainer or other staff person. A variety of instructional methods may be used. Reading material, such as *Steps to Independence: A Skills Training Guide for Parents and Teachers of Children with*

Special Needs, Second Edition (Baker & Brightman, 1989) is helpful for presenting basic information (other parent training manuals are reviewed by Bernal and North, 1978). Videotaped sequences demonstrating various instructional techniques can be used, as can live modeling and role playing. Videotaping parents as they teach their child and reviewing the taped sequence afterwards is an effective way to provide feedback to parents.

Parent training programs often include instruction in data-keeping procedures (Bricker & Bricker, 1976; Fredericks, Baldwin, & Grove, 1974; Hayden & Haring, 1976; Shearer & Shearer, 1976). Although some parents' experience with data keeping is positive (see Figure 12.1), others find data keeping burdensome, and question its necessity for adequate instruction at home. Parents may feel under too much pressure to record data, and may even fabricate data in response to program pressure (Sandler & Coren, 1981). We agree with Lansing and Schopler (1978) that data keeping by parents may be unnecessary "for the development of a consistent and rational approach with the child" (p. 449). It is recommended that in-

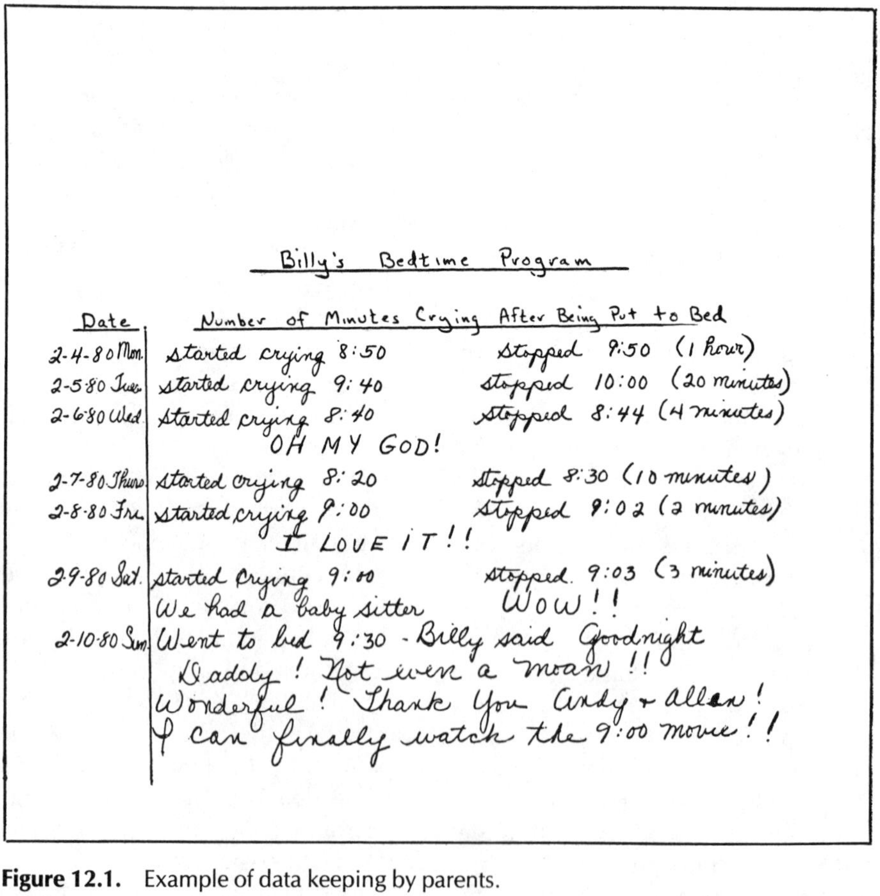

Billy's Bedtime Program

Date | Number of Minutes Crying After Being Put to Bed

2-4-80 Mon. started crying 8:50 stopped 9:50 (1 hour)
2-5-80 Tues. started crying 9:40 stopped 10:00 (20 minutes)
2-6-80 Wed. started crying 8:40 stopped 8:44 (4 minutes)
OH MY GOD!
2-7-80 Thurs. started crying 8:20 stopped 8:30 (10 minutes)
2-8-80 Fri. started crying 9:00 stopped 9:02 (2 minutes)
I LOVE IT!!
2-9-80 Sat. started crying 9:00 stopped 9:03 (3 minutes)
We had a baby sitter WOW!!
2-10-80 Sun. Went to bed 9:30 - Billy said Goodnight Daddy! Not even a moan!! Wonderful! Thank You Andy & Allan! I can finally watch the 9:00 movie!!

Figure 12.1. Example of data keeping by parents.

struction in data keeping be provided only to those parents who express an interest in this procedure. Here, as in other areas of work with parents, their diversity of interests must be respected.

Family training, while traditionally focused on parents, may also include siblings. Powell and Ogle (1985) have suggested that children can be trained to be teachers of their siblings with handicaps. They point out that such activity can increase sibling interaction and promote better relationships. However, they relate that such training may enhance status differences between siblings. They offer the following guidelines to those interested in training children to teach their siblings with handicaps:

> Clarify treatment expectations; do not force either child to participate; arrange the environment so that success is ensured; both children should be rewarded for participation in the teaching sessions; generally speaking, the sibling teacher should be chronologically older than the handicapped child. (pp. 129–130)

In implementing any family training program, trainers should be certain that participants are involved voluntarily. Trainers should make sure that training experiences are relevant and provide family members with information or skills that they desire and that are useable to them. They should present material so that it is easily understood and should provide opportunities for family members to ask questions and receive feedback. Finally, professionals should keep in mind that family members have other responsibilities and commitments. Too many demands from a family training program may cause additional stress, feelings of inadequacy on the part of participants, or withdrawal from the program. Thus, trainers should make sure that expectations are realistic and that a family member's needs are being met through his participation in the training program.

PROGRAM PLANNING

The provisions of PL 99-457 require that parents be given the opportunity to participate in program planning for their child. The law extends the provisions of PL 94-142 to children between 3 and 5 with handicaps. This means that educational agencies serving this population must develop individualized education programs (IEPs) for these children and that parents must be given the final say regarding what is included in the program. Thus, parents must have the opportunity to participate in program planning activities, and must sign off on any programs that are implemented on behalf of their child.

Additional provisions of PL 99-457 that apply to infants require the development of individualized family service plans (IFSPs). Without active parental participation in the program planning process, the development of IFSPs would be extremely difficult, if not impossible. As we suggested earlier, the needs and strengths of each family must be examined and plans then developed and implemented based on the data gathered.

It is the obligation of professionals continually to engage all parents and to provide them with ongoing information regarding their children. Professionals should do what they can to facilitate the involvement of parents in the program planning process.

For many parents with children in early intervention, the team planning meeting may be the first time they have ever sat down with a group of professionals to discuss their child. This situation may cause parents to feel intimidated and anxious. Professionals should not respond defensively to these parental feelings, but rather should attempt to establish a warm and accepting setting for parents. Efforts to talk with parents in nontechnical terms can help them feel part of the team process. In addition, it is often helpful to ask parents direct questions and actively to solicit their feedback on issues concerning their child and family. Building a partnership with families and aiding them in taking control of the decision-making process can facilitate their involvement on program planning teams, as well as encourage their participation in other activities.

Turnbull, Strickland, and Goldstein (1978) have suggested that the following strategies may be helpful in facilitating the active participation of parents at team planning meetings: 1) professionals on the team should model question asking as well as statements of diverse views during team meetings; 2) professionals should direct questions toward parents; 3) professionals should reinforce parental responses and suggestions; and 4) professionals should encourage parents to voice special concerns regarding their child or their child's programs. Of course, any concerns expressed by the parents should be given careful consideration by the team. Assigning one team member the role of parent advocate, with the responsibility for directing questions toward parents, reinforcing their contributions, and so on can be an effective strategy for facilitating active parental involvement during team meetings (Goldstein & Turnbull, 1982).

It should be pointed out that despite the best professional efforts, some families will not participate in the planning process. The demands of daily living or other stressful situations make it difficult for some families to participate in program planning or other types of program activities. These families should be supported with necessary services

and should not be judged as unmotivated, unconcerned, or uncaring.

SUPPORT GROUPS

Although the support provided to families by professionals can be important in helping them adjust to their situation and in providing them needed information about programs and development, it is often the support that families get from each other that is most helpful. A family experiencing a crisis or difficult period with a child may find useful support from another family who has had a similar experience. The establishment of family support groups can put families in contact with each other and can facilitate the development of informal family support networks. In many early intervention programs such family support activities are run by the families themselves and receive minimal input from the professional staff. Such family-run support groups can facilitate a family's feeling of control and lessen their dependence on professionals.

It can be particularly helpful if new families are teamed up with more experienced families. Parents, in particular, may achieve a sense of support through the process of resocialization that they undergo as they participate in a parent support group and come to identify with the concerns of other parents, adopting a shared perspective on their new role (Berger & Foster, 1976).

It can be helpful to establish support groups for specific family members. For example, fathers may want to discuss their own concerns with each other without their spouses being present. The same may be true for mothers. Siblings may also want time to discuss their feelings with each other. In some instances, it may even be helpful to develop support groups for grandparents. Again, it should be remembered that support groups should be focused on the agenda of the participants and should be facilitated, not dominated, by professional staff. Professional guidance and impetus are often necessary to establish a support group. However, the ongoing management of support groups should be handled by family members to as great an extent as is possible.

SUMMARY

Family members experience a variety of emotions in adapting to a young child with a handicap. To be effective, interventions must focus on the family and be responsive to a family's particular strengths and needs. To do this, early intervention professionals must empower families and create a partnership with them that helps ensure that each family feels a sense of competence and control. The family represents the major ecology for the infant or young child with special needs. To focus solely on the child while overlooking the family is to overlook a major factor in the provision of early intervention services.

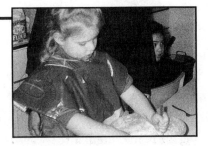

13

Intervention Models for Infants and Young Children with Special Needs

1. What are the major differences between Anastasiow's classification scheme and Beller's classification scheme?
2. What features are common to all early intervention programs for children with handicaps?
3. Do those programs that depend on parents seem to be mindful of the issues discussed in Chapter 12?
4. What features would you want to be sure to include in an early intervention program that you were planning?
5. Why do transitions require careful coordination of services?
6. What is the social validation approach to program evaluation?

SINCE ANCIENT TIMES HUMAN society has been committed to educating and protecting its children. In this way the mores and values of a culture are passed from generation to generation. It is through education that socialization and acculturation of individuals takes place; that is, individuals come to understand the rules and limits of the culture in which they live. While very early socialization usually takes place in families, there have always been young children whose families were unable to care for them. In such cases alternatives to natural families, such as orphanages and foster homes, have been provided. While the quality of these placements has varied greatly, they continue to exist because "the [perceived] role of adult society, be that parent or homes for children, has been considered to be one of protection . . . carrying out elementary socialization tasks related to biological needs of the infant" (Beller, 1979, p. 852) and young child.

In the last 75 to 100 years, society has witnessed significant shifts in the roles of women. More women are expressing their independence, working outside of the home, and pursuing more education. As a result, their traditional role in the basic socialization process has shifted. Because of the changes in the nuclear family brought about by the economic and moral necessities of women leaving the home, alternative socialization structures have developed that have major influences on infants and young children. These structures have taken the form of day care centers, kindergartens, and preschool education programs. All have grown out of society's historical commitment to provide socialization experiences to young children.

Early childhood programs had their beginnings in the theories of Freud and Montessori and later drew empirical support from authors such as Spitz (1945) and Goldfarb (1943). It was in the 1960s, however, that early childhood education blossomed. The forceful theoretical writings of Hunt (1961, 1964) and Bloom (1964) provided impetus for changes. The new social consciousness and the resulting government funding of preschool programs provided a major thrust for the development and maintenance of preschool programs. The establishment of Head Start in 1965 epitomized the trend that began in the 1960s.

Preschool programs were initially developed to reach populations deemed "culturally deprived" or, more precisely, those of lower socioeconomic status. The rationale for prototypic programs such as Head Start and Demonstration and Research Center for Early Education (DARCEE) (Klaus & Gray, 1968) was that the deleterious effects of poverty in the preschool years could be prevented and/or remediated by effective, intensive, preschool programming. This belief was important in shifting the emphasis of preschool and infant programs from one of custodially oriented caregiving to one of programming for developmental change.

Preschool education can minimize the effects of risk and lead to fewer manifestations of handicap in later years. This rationale was strong enough to lead to the establishment in 1968 of the Early Childhood Assistance Program of the Bureau of Education for the Handicapped (BEH). This program provided funds for the development of model preschool programs for children with handicaps. From this mandate the Handicapped Children's Early Education Program (HCEEP) was born and special education for preschool children began to flourish. HCEEP led to the development of a number of prototypic models for providing educational services to children from birth to 6 with handicaps. In addition, the program provided a means for disseminating critical aspects of these prototypic models to other sites. Throughout the early and mid-1970s, HCEEP was a major source of support for innovated program development for preschool children with handicaps; in 1979, 86% of the 24 originally funded programs were still operational (DeWeerd, 1980). In 1987, 79 model demonstration projects were funded through HCEEP; 30 outreach projects designed to disseminate their results by training and replication at other sites were also funded. HCEEP now operates as part of the Office of Special Education and Rehabilitation Services of the U. S. Department of Education.

Several Titles (e.g., I and II) of the Elementary and Secondary Education Act (ESEA) also included provision for funding preschool programs for children with handicaps. These funds, however, were distributed and monitored through state education agencies and generally did not have as great an impact as HCEEP. This is not to say that some innovative and worthwhile programs were not developed via ESEA provisions. Rather, because of the linking of these funds to state education agencies, visibility and dissemination of programs was generally not as great as of those funded through HCEEP.

Some early childhood programs for children with handicaps were funded in the 1970s through the Social Security Act and its Amendments. Initially this funding was provided via Title IV-A and later through Title XX. Many local programs were supported through these titles, which were distributed and monitored through state welfare programs. These funds were often critical in establishing and maintaining local social welfare programs and so led to the provision of educational programs for preschool children with handicaps within the broader context of social services provision to low income populations. Title IV-A and Title XX funds were also often important in providing ongoing program support after programs had completed their funding cycles through HCEEP, whose funds were strictly for model development, rather than long-term program maintenance. HCEEP now operates as part of the Office of Special Education and Rehabilitation Services (OSERS) of the U.S. Department of Education.

A new form of funding for preschool programs for children with handicaps appeared in the late 1970s. This funding stream was made possible through PL 94-142, the Education for All Handicapped Children Act, passed in 1975. This legislation and the appropriation that followed it made funding available to local districts to provide programs for preschool children with handicaps. PL 94-142 created a means by which local school districts receive $300 per child per year for every preschool child with handicaps served. They receive this $300 in addition to the regular funding they receive for children with handicaps. In December, 1983, with the passage of PL 98-199 (the Educa-

tion of the Handicapped Act Amendments of 1983), preschool incentive funds could be used to support programs for children with handicaps down to birth. In addition, these amendments made grants available to states to develop and implement comprehensive plans to provide early childhood education to all children with handicaps from birth to 5. More and more local school districts developed services for preschool children with handicaps as a result of these incentive grants. Generally, however, the preschool population has been underserved and poorly defined (Lessen & Rose, 1980). The provisions of PL 99-457 should be instrumental in bringing services to this population and in identifying parameters that define it.

As a result of the impetus provided by these various funding sources, many programs for preschool children with handicaps have been developed throughout the country. The remainder of this chapter is devoted to a discussion of the major models for preschool education of children with handicaps that have emerged as a result of these program development efforts over the last 2 decades. In addition, some major programs for infants and preschool children with handicaps are described.

MODELS OF EARLY INTERVENTION

Beller (1979) has described several models of preschool education. Although these models are discussed in terms of early intervention programs designed primarily to serve children from lower socioeconomic groups, they are generally applicable to young children with handicaps and young children who are considered at risk.

Beller provides a categorization based upon the service delivery strategy employed by various programs. Service delivery models are home based or center based, and parent oriented or child oriented. *Home-based* programs provide services in the homes of individual clients, whereas *center-based* programs provide services primarily in some central location, such as a church or school. *Parent-oriented* programs give parents skills to facilitate the development of their children more effectively. That is, these programs see parents as the major agents for intervention. Professional staff provide training and support to parents. *Child-oriented* programs, however, emphasize direct intervention with the child. In general, home-based programs tend to be parent-oriented, although this need not be the case. At least one child-oriented, home-based program has been described by Schaefer and Aaronson (1972), who relate how tutors were sent into the home to facilitate the cognitive development of infants from lower-income families.

Although many early intervention programs for infants and young children with handicaps can still be classified using Beller's system, a new approach is emerging. This approach is the ecological systems approach, which in part provided the basis for this book. In this approach the focus is neither child oriented nor parent oriented, but rather *family systems oriented*. Thus, the family system is seen as the target of intervention. Although specific interventions may still be planned and implemented for the child, the approach is a broader one that emphasizes the functioning of the family, the need for social support, the necessity for families to make their own decisions, and the roles of family members vis-à-vis each other as well as the community. These programs see the family ecology as the main focus for intervention, and interventions for a particular child are planned and implemented only within the context of the family ecology. Such programs may be either home based or center based and often combine these two approaches. The provision in PL 99-457 calling for the development of Individualized Family Service Plans is a step toward the recognition of the importance of family-focused approaches to early intervention. Family-focused approaches are among those at the cutting edge of early intervention service delivery. Other program characteristics also define best practice in early intervention. These characteristics are highlighted in the next section.

According to Beller (1979), home-based infant programs are as effective as center-based programs. The choice of service delivery model, then, may depend less on empirical verification than on practical constraints, such as geography, costs, and philosophical orientation toward parental involvement in infant and preschool programs. The Portage Project (Shearer & Shearer, 1976), for example, used a home-based approach because geography prevented transporting children to a central location. Home-based models often enjoy additional flexibility and have the advantage of providing intervention within the child's natural environment. However, home-based programs often put additional stress on parents, especially mothers, because they do not provide a means for them to have a respite from their children. In addition, parent-oriented programs, especially home-based ones, place a good deal of added responsibility for successful intervention on parents. While proper support can reduce the degree of parent failure, when parents do fail to intervene effectively they may feel guilty and inadequate. A number of programs have begun to incorporate both home-based and center-based activities, minimizing the weaknesses of both approaches while maximizing their strengths.

Like Beller (1979), Anastasiow (1978) has taken a broad categorical approach to the classification of preschool models. Anastasiow's conceptualization differs from Beller's in two significant aspects. First, it is clearly directed to programs that may include preschool children with handicaps and, second, and perhaps more importantly, it provides a basis for categorization based upon the theoretical and conceptual basis of programming rather than the service delivery structure. Anastasiow provides four basic preschool models, described below.

Behavioral Model

The behavioral model is based in large part on the work of Skinner and his followers (e.g., Bijou, 1966; Bijou & Baer, 1961). Thus, it suggests an intervention strategy based on the manipulation of environmental contingencies. Desired behavior is reinforced and undesired behavior is extinguished (ignored) or in some cases punished. This model views the child as a passive learner whose dignity depends upon overt manipulation of the environment by the teacher or interventionist. As Anastasiow (1978) points out, the model has its greatest usefulness with children exhibiting severe behavior problems or very significant delays in development.

Normal Developmental Model

The normal development model is based on a belief in the natural unfolding of development. The model is guided by maturational sequences such as those delineated by Gesell (1954). This model provided the impetus for maturational preschools, which provided the environments in which children could be nurtured sufficiently so that their development would unfold as a matter of course. In the normal developmental model, chil-

dren are seen as naturally active and engaging the environment. The teacher's role is to provide a nurturant environment full of learning opportunities. The teacher provides guidance and children learn and develop as a result of their maturational readiness to do so. Heavy emphasis is placed on group instruction and socialization.

Since this model is based upon a belief in the natural life cycle of development, it is, in a sense, antithetical to the early education of high-risk preschool children or preschool children with handicaps. These children, by definition, display developmental patterns noticeably different from the norm. Consequently a normal developmental model is not likely to be effective with them, unless the teacher is willing to individualize the instructional approach. In fact, Anastasiow (1978) believes "that the failure of the normal developmental model to provide for individual differences is what led parents of impaired children to set up their own schools and experiment with ways to facilitate impaired children's learning" (p. 102).

Cognitive Developmental Model

The cognitive developmental model gets its support from Piaget and in some respects parallels the normal developmental model. As was discussed in Chapter 4, Piaget's theory suggests a relatively fixed unfolding of cognitive structures as the child gets older. These structures unfold because the child actively seeks information from the environment. As in the normal developmental model, the teacher becomes a facilitator whose role it is to arrange the environment to ensure that the child has the experiences necessary for cognitive growth to take place. Where the normal developmental model is more concerned with socialization and conformity, the cognitive developmental model emphasizes cognitive growth. Knowledge of the social world is believed to come about through the development and application of existing cognitive structures. This model is applicable to children with delays in development to the extent that the teacher provides experiences novel enough to stimulate curiosity and application of existing cognitive structures to the environment. Only through further assimilative and accommodative processes does development occur.

Cognitive Learning Model

Anastasiow (1978) credits the Brickers (1974, 1976) with the development of what he has termed the cognitive learning model. Anastasiow chose this name "because the Brickers integrate the utilization of operant procedures for lesson strategies and remediation while drawing upon cognitive, psycholinguistic, and perceptual theories to diagnose the child's level of development and to plan intervention programs" (p. 105). With children with significant delays, it may first be necessary to teach exploratory strategies to facilitate further development. At the same time, such children can be taught specific cognitive skills using contingency management. These skills are the basis for the development of more complex cognitive abilities. Thus, in a sense children begin as passive learners, as in the behavioral model, but are transformed into an active mode both by structuring the necessary contingencies into the environment and by providing small instructional steps leading to more complex cognitive abilities. A strict Piagetian viewpoint would question whether such a strategy could be employed. Duckworth (1979), for example, might suggest that such instruction would not benefit the child who is not ready (cognitively) for it, or that such instruction would come too late, since the child had already begun to exhibit cognitive skills in the developmental sequence without any

formal instruction. Programs such as those of the Brickers (1974, 1976) and others (e.g., Robinson & Robinson, 1978) are accumulating data that attest to the success of this approach.

Best Practices in Early Intervention

Before describing some early intervention programs that represent a wide variety of approaches, it is useful to discuss briefly best practices in early intervention. McDonnell and Hardman (1988) have recently identified a series of best practices that appear to have empirical or ideological support in the field. They characterize services into the following best practice catagories: 1) integrated (i.e., handicapped and nonhandicapped children are served in the same settings), 2) comprehensive (i.e., a full array of services is offered), 3) normalized (i.e., instruction is stressed across a number of settings), 4) adaptable (i.e., the program employs flexible procedures), 5) peer and family referenced (i.e., curriculum is referenced to the child, family, and community), and 6) outcome based (i.e., there is an emphasis on development of skills for future usefulness). Table 13.1 includes a synthesis of best practice guidelines as suggested by McDonnell and Hardman. The programs described below all exemplify these best practices. In fact, some of these programs have been responsible for the establishment of the parameters of best practice. The reader is urged to refer to Table 13.1 while reading these program descriptions.

SOME ILLUSTRATIVE PROGRAMS

This section is devoted to descriptions of various infant and preschool programs for handicapped children. These programs are chosen

Table 13.1. A synthesis of "best practice" guidelines for early childhood services

Integrated

Supported placement in generic early childhood service sites

Systematic contact with nonhandicapped peers

Planned integration at all levels

Comprehensive

Comprehensive assessment, planning, programming, service coordination, and evaluation

Models theoretically and procedurally well defined

Transdisciplinary approach to the delivery of related services

Direct instruction of generalized responding

Normalized

Support for parenting role

Age-appropriate skills and instructional strategies

Concurrent training across skill areas

Distributed practice across settings

Establishment of self-initiated responding

Avoidance of artificial reinforcement and aversive control techniques

Adaptable

Flexible procedures within noncategorical models

Support of different family structures

Emphasis on function rather than form of response

Programming changes based on individual, formative evaluation

Peer and family referenced

Curriculum is referenced to individual child, family, peers, and community

Parents are full partners in educational planning and decision making

Systematic communication between family and service providers

Planned enhancement of child's skill development within daily family routine

Outcome based

Variety of outcome measures

Preparation for future integrated settings

Curricular emphasis on skills with present and future utility

Transition planning

From McDonnell, A., and Hardman, M. (1988). A synthesis of "best practice" guidelines for early childhood services. *Journal of the Division for Early Childhood, 12,* 328–341. Reprinted by permission.

for illustrative purposes and are meant to provide the reader with an overview, not an exhaustive look. The programs described include home-based and center-based programs that are either child oriented, parent oriented, or family oriented. They cut across various conceptual models and they serve a variety of children with handicaps. Each program will be described in terms of its conceptual/theoretical orientation, population, program goals, general program activities, assessment strategies, and relative strengths and weaknesses.

Center-Based Programs

The Infant, Toddler, and Pre-school Research and Intervention Programs The Infant, Toddler and Pre-school Research and Intervention Program (Bricker & Bricker, 1971, 1972, 1973, 1976) began as a model program based at George Peabody College in Nashville, Tennessee, in 1970. The program employed a cognitive learning model by incorporating developmental theories with operant technology. The program was originally designed to serve toddlers (18 to 36 months) and was later expanded to serve children from birth to age 5. The program spread "its service base across the preschool development range, across the economic continuum from poverty to affluence, and across a broad range of ethnic backgrounds" (Bricker & Bricker, 1976, p. 546). The program included both children with and children without identifiable delays in development (e.g., Down syndrome, autistic-like behavior, brain damage). Approximately 25% of the children served were "normal," 25% were "normal" but "at risk," and 50% were noticeably delayed in development.

Bricker and Bricker (1976) identified the following goals for the infant component of their programs:

1) the creation of individual programs to develop the child's competencies in the areas of gross motor skills, fine motor skills, sensorimotor,

self-help, and social skills; 2) the operationalization and empirical validation of such Piagetian concepts as causality, means-end, object permanence, imitation, and functional usage; 3) the development of a library of video tapes of infant behavior to be used for research, teaching, and parent training; and 4) the provision for each child to develop certain prerequisite forms of behavior necessary for adaptive functioning in the toddler unit. (p. 560).

Activities for each infant were very flexible and individualized to meet particular needs. Goals for the toddler unit included:

1) daily group or individual language training; 2) individually programmed gross and fine motor activities; 3) the opportunity to engage in self-directed activities; 4) a consistent environment established and maintained through the application of contingency management techniques; 5) opportunities to develop appropriate cognitive skills such as labeling, problem solving, and concept formation; and 6) adaptive skills necessary for entrance into the preschool unit. (p. 561)

The day's activities typically consisted of opening group time, individual and small group programming and skill building, free play, gym, snack, and closing activities.

The goals for the preschool unit represented in large measure an upward extension of the goals of the infant and toddler units. Like the earlier goals, they reflect a cognitive learning model. These goals included:

1) to develop pre-operational cognitive skills; 2) to develop further and refine more difficult self-help skills; 3) to develop increasingly independent behavior without teacher supervision or continuous reinforcement; 4) to correctly formulate three-word phrases; and 5) to develop certain prerequisite or useful early elementary education skills. (p. 562)

Daily activities were similar to those of the toddler unit, with more stress being placed on language and concept training as well as more independence on the part of the children.

Although this program was child oriented, heavy emphasis was placed on parental involvement. Parents were asked to participate in their child's classroom at least once a week. Project staff were expected to provide parent training and generally support parents through counseling and advocacy in acquiring additional services outside the project (e.g., medical services, welfare services).

Assessment strategies employed a number of informal classroom measurement systems. Through such systems, instruction and assessment become ongoing and interrelated processes. In addition, more standardized means of assessment, such as the Bayley Scales of Infant Development (Bayley, 1969) or the Cattell Infant Intelligence Scale (Cattell, 1960), were used.

The strengths of the Brickers' project include its application of services to both children with and children without handicaps, a practice whose rationale has been well documented from social-ethical, legal-legislative, and psychological-educational points of view (Bricker, 1978; Guralnick, 1978b). The ability to provide individualized programming with the cognitive learning model adds to its efficiency in serving both children with and children without handicaps by making it "most adaptable to environmental changes required to successfully integrate" (Anastasiow, 1978, p. 108) these children.

Another strength of the program was the level of support provided for parents. Parents not only received training designed to enhance their understanding of their children and their development, they also learned skills that help them facilitate their children's education and training at home. In addition, families received emotional support through counseling, referral, and advocacy services.

One obvious weakness was the program's rather loosely defined evaluation strategy. No evaluation design is reported by the Brickers that would substantiate the benefits of the program for both children with and children without handicaps. In essence, the standardized measure employed documented that the nonhandicapped children's development "was progressing as expected or better with no regression effects noted" (Bricker, 1978, p. 20), although no data indicate that the development of the education of the children without handicaps was in any way facilitated.

Another weakness of this model is its highly idealized nature. This program was affiliated with a university complex, where high levels of expertise and student participation created a situation that cannot be replicated in the real world service delivery system. While this high level of resources was undoubtedly beneficial for the children being served, it also reduced the replicability of the program in nonuniversity settings.

Finally, although the Brickers' program is theoretically adaptable to diverse populations of young children as suggested above, some data suggest that the children with handicaps and the children without handicaps in the program may not have been as well integrated as an initial perusal of the program would lead one to believe (cf. Porter et al., 1978; Ray, 1974a).

The Down Syndrome Program The Down Syndrome Program at the University of Washington's Experimental Education Unit has been described by Hayden and Dmitriev (1975) and Hayden and Haring (1976). According to Hayden and Dmitriev, the program sought to bring the Down syndrome child's development as close to normal as possible. Thus, "the children's progress [was measured] in relation to established developmental norms for *normal* children the same age, on precisely the same activities and learned tasks" (p. 194). This program then approximates what Anastasiow (1978) has termed a normal developmental model, although, like the Brickers (1976), Hayden

and Dmitriev report some dependence on task analysis and reinforcement contingencies to facilitate learning.

The program was designed to serve Down syndrome children exclusively, and included children from birth to 6. Children were subdivided into four age groupings resulting in an infant class (children 5 weeks–18 months); an early preschool class (18 months–3 years); an advanced preschool class (3–5 years); and a kindergarten class (4½–6 years). The infant class met once a week and provided 30 minutes of individualized training in early motor sensory development with the parent(s) and infant together. The other classes met 4 days a week, 2 hours a day.

All four classrooms in the program had the following common goals relating to children:

1. To increase the rate of sensory, vocal, and motor development of Down syndrome children to approximate more nearly the sequential development of normal children
2. To increase the subsequent rate of preacademic, academic, and social performance of these children, with the goal of including them in regular and special education programs in the public schools
3. To involve parents in full participation and full cooperation with the intervention team in the training of their children
4. To promote full cooperation of educators and child peers in accepting these children in school and community programs
5. To record continuous measurement data on the children's progress and to base all decisions and teaching activities on such data (Hayden & Dmitriev, 1975, p. 195)

Activities for the infant program were highly individualized and involved parents. Training goals were developed individually for infants based on the Denver Development Screening Test (Frankenburg & Dodds, 1969) and on the norms provided by Gesell and Amatruda (1969). Specific training activities were then developed based on the goals for each infant.

In the early preschool class, activities were designed to enhance fine and gross motor skills, self-help skills, individual concept learning, and social interaction. Children were given exercises to aid development of standing and walking. In addition, manipulative and creative materials, such as crayons, dolls, and puzzles, were made available. Concept development was facilitated through one-on-one instruction and all children were trained in toileting and hand washing when ready. Daily activities also included an opening routine, snack time (used for developing eating and communication skills), story time, music, and a departure routine. Activities in the advanced preschool class were similar to those in the early preschool class, but were designed to deal with more complex developmental skills.

In the kindergarten class, activities continued to stress self-help and motor development, but an emphasis on cognitive development was added. Children were exposed to calendars, seasons, and holidays. They were also given instruction in academic subjects, including sight words, basic number concepts, letter recognition, simple printing (e.g., their names), and phonics. Parents were involved in all phases of the program throughout their children's involvement.

Besides individualized continuous data systems, the program used standardized tests of development. These included the Denver Developmental Screening Test and Gesell norms for infants, and the Peabody Picture Vocabulary Test (PPVT) (Dunn, 1959) for preschool and kindergarten children. The PPVT was administered once a year and used because it "enables children with low verbal skills to demonstrate their receptive and associative capabilities without penalizing them for their verbal deficits" (Hayden & Haring, 1976, p. 595).

The greatest strength of this program was the commitment of the staff to approximate normal development in Down syndrome children. Many children in this program made significant developmental progress that probably would not have occurred without the program orientation toward normal development. The success of the Down Syndrome Program has done a great deal toward modifying the expectations of both parents and professionals as to the developmental potentials of Down syndrome children. This success has been so far-reaching that the program has been replicated in Australia (De-Weerd, 1980).

Another strength of the program was its overriding concern with parental involvement. Parents were critical members of the program's team. They were viewed as "powerful educators [who require] training, encouragement, and acknowledgement of [their] contribution to their child's development" (Hayden & Haring, 1976, p. 589).

The Milwaukee Project   One of the best known preschool projects for high-risk children is described by Heber and Garber (1975). Beller (1979) and Garber (1988) characterize this program as being equally oriented to the child and the parent. The program was based on the prediction that certain children will exhibit characteristics associated with cultural-familial mental retardation if significant changes are not made in their life situations during their first 6 years. *Cultural-familial retardation* is most often associated with children from lower socioeconomic families who show no biological or organic basis for mental retardation and who come from families in which one or more members is classified as mentally retarded. People with cultural familial retardation typically fall within the mild to moderate range of retardation, exhibiting IQ scores between 50 and 75.

Because of their belief that cultural-familial retardation results largely from environmental factors, Heber and Garber (1975) set up selection criteria based on family characteristics for the infants to be included in their program. Infants were selected from low SES black families in which the mother's measured IQ scores on the Wechsler Adult Intelligence Scale (Wechsler, 1955) was 75 or less. Families selected were assigned to either an experimental or a control group.

The program that was implemented was a "family intervention program which was designed to modify adverse factors in the environments of the experimental infants. The objective was to provide the kind of learning opportunities that facilitate the acquisition of cognitive skills" (Heber & Garber, 1975, p. 406). To meet this goal, two parallel intervention programs were developed. One sought to provide mothers with better vocational, homemaking, and child-rearing skills. The other, directed at infants, was designed to facilitate the development of cognitive, language, and social abilities. The program was designed to start in infancy and continue until the children entered first grade. While general goals were the same for each child, programs were individualized "to maximize the effects of the educational experiences for each child" (Heber & Garber, 1975, p. 408). During infancy, babies were assigned to one primary caregiver during program hours. This practice ensured a secure environment for each infant and provided for one-on-one programming.

During the preschool years the program stressed a combination of small group learning and individual, child-directed activities. Most activities were geared toward cognitive and language development. Language was taught through the use of the Peabody Language Development Kit and "each child participated in informal reading, science, music,

and art activities" (Heber & Garber, 1975, p. 413). Each child was assessed every two weeks using the goals in the curriculum sequence.

Both experimental and control children were assessed periodically in physical development, language development, and measured intelligence. In addition, the mother-child interaction of each family was assessed through observation. Physical development was assessed by periodic medical examinations. These assessments showed no overall differences in height, weight, or abnormal birth conditions between the experimental and control groups.

The Gesell Developmental Schedule revealed the first significant differences in language development at 18 months. These differences in favor of the experimental groups were manifested from that point on. Analysis of language samples also revealed differences between experimental and control children in amount of conversation and lexical growth. Articulation was better in the experimental group, as was grammatical comprehension. All children were given the Illinois Test of Psycholinguistic Abilities (ITPA) (Kirk, McCarthy, & Kirk, 1968) at 54 months of age. The control group was found to be 18 months behind the experimental group in psycholinguistic development.

Periodic measurement of intelligence using standardized tests, such as the Cattell (Cattell, 1960), Stanford-Binet (Terman & Merrill, 1973), and the Wechsler Preschool and Primary Scale of Intelligence (Wechsler, 1967) yielded differences in IQ of 20 to 30 points between 24 and 66 months of age. "Thus, the performance [of these children] on standardized tests of measured intelligence indicates a remarkable intellectual development on the part of Experimental subjects who have been exposed to the infant stimulation program" (Heber & Garber, 1975, p. 429). This statement assumes, of course, that IQ tests are valid measures of intellectual development and not just measures of learning outcomes.

The Milwaukee Project has a strong conceptual base, recognizing the need for family-based intervention. The project drew its strength from improving the performance and competence of both children and their parents. Although the theory of such an approach can hardly be disputed, at least one critic, Page (1975), has questioned the validity of Heber's results. Page suggests that there were significant sampling errors resulting in nonequivalence of the experimental and control groups. He further contends that measurements may have biased due to the specific skills measured by the IQ tests employed. He further points out the lack of clarity in describing the intervention program and the curriculum employed. Heber, however, has since indicated where this information is available (Heber & Garber, 1975). To our knowledge, the Milwaukee Project has not been replicated. Perhaps through replication the effectiveness of this conceptually sound model can be confirmed.

The Ypsilanti High Scope Program   The Ypsilanti High Scope Program began in the early 1960s. It was initiated by Weikart and his associates as the Ypsilanti Perry Preschool Project, and was designed "as a long-term effort to assist educationally disadvantaged Negro children in developing the concepts and abilities necessary for academic success in the public schools" (Weikart, Rogers, Adcock, and McClelland, 1971, p. 1). The program used a cognitive developmental model based on Piaget's theory. Several excellent accounts of Piagetian-based curricula have been formulated (e.g., Kamii, 1972; Weikart, 1974; Weikart, Rogers, Adcock, & McClelland, 1971) and the interested reader is referred to these sources for more detailed information.

Long-term follow-up of the population served in the original Perry Preschool Project indicates that the effects of this early intervention were evident as long as 15 years later (Berrueta-Clement, Schweinhart, Barnett, Epstein, & Weikart, 1984; Schweinhart & Weikart, 1981). These follow-up studies have helped to demonstrate both the cost-effectiveness of early intervention programs and their effectiveness in bringing about positive long-term behavioral outcomes.

Ispa and Matz (1978) describe how children with handicaps have been integrated into a preschool program employing the High Scope curriculum. Classrooms were set up with 2 teachers and 15 children, 10 of whom did not have handicaps and 5 of whom did. The children with handicaps had a variety of difficulties, including heart defects, hemiplegia, spinal curvature, language delay, Down syndrome, and partial hearing loss. Daily activities allowed children to plan and execute their own activities. During planning time each child planned activities to do during work time. In the work time that followed, children carried out their plan "with the support and assistance of adults and peers [they] actively pursue[d] the ideas, activities, and projects they [had] planned for at planning time" (Ispa & Matz, 1978, p. 169). Work time was followed by snack and small group activity. Children were also given an outdoor activity designed to include large motor activities when possible. The last activity of the day was circle time, which typically included songs and musical games. Because the Cognitively Oriented Curriculum is universalistic, Ispa and Matz (1978) believe it can be adapted with equal success to both children with and children without handicaps. They state that:

> because each child works at activities that are developmentally appropriate, he or she has the opportunity to grow and experience success

without infringing on the needs of other children for a faster (or slower) pace or for an activity that is more personally interesting. (p. 171)

To assess the effects of integrating preschool children with and preschool children without handicaps, Ispa and Matz (1978) developed an observation scheme for assessing naturally occurring interactions. Each child was observed for a total of 48 minutes, divided into four 12 minute observations. Observations were carried out during work time only "and only when at least two handicapped children were present" (Ispa & Matz, 1978, p. 175). Analysis of the data collected by these procedures indicated that the children with handicaps less frequently conversed with peers, verbally expressed pride to peers, and gave and showed materials to peers. In addition Ispa and Matz (1978) report that the observed and expected number of times children interacted with disabled and nondisabled children were similar. Thus, they conclude that the children were socially integrated. These results, while somewhat different from those of Devoney, Guralnick, and Rubin (1974), Guralnick (1976), Porter and colleagues (1978), and Ray (1974a) may be accounted for by differences in the populations studied and by the ratio of children with handicaps to children without handicaps. Finally, it is also possible that the dependent variables accounted for these differences. As Guralnick (1980) suggested, all of these factors may be important in determining the degree of social integration between preschool children with and preschool children without handicaps in the same classroom.

Ispa and Matz report the use of the McCarthy Scales of Children's Abilities (McCarthy, 1970) as a means of assessing developmental progress in children. Children were pretested and posttested with this scale. All children made equivalent gains in all areas except for motor areas. Ispa and Matz (1978) account for this result by the physical disabilities of some children, which may have made it "unreasonable to expect progress analogous to that of nonhandicapped children [in the motor area]" (p. 187).

Ispa and Matz (1978) presented an effective model of educating preschool children with relatively mild handicaps. That social integration seems to have occurred is of particular interest and supports the effectiveness of child-directed programs for both preschool children with and preschool children without handicaps.

If parents were involved either in classroom programming or in counseling or training sessions, Ispa and Matz fail to mention it in their report. Weikart, Rogers, Adcock, and McClelland (1971) point to the importance of home visits in the implementation of the High Scope Model. It is reasonable to conclude that Ispa and Matz chose to stress the effects of classroom activities on social integration rather than to deal with parent components. The role of parents in the program (assuming there was a role) may have contributed in part to the program's apparent success and should have been mentioned.

Home-Based Programs

The Portage Project The Portage Project began in 1969 as a model program under HCEEP (Shearer & Shearer, 1976). More recently, the project has operated as a PL 91-230 Title IV-C project in cooperation with a regional education agency in rural Wisconsin. Because of the relative geographic isolation of the population being served, the Portage Project is home based. In addition, the project employs a behavioral model, and uses parents as teachers of their own children. This latter practice is characteristic of most home-based programs for preschool children with handicaps. The project serves any child up to age 6 who lives within the project's catchment area.

Besides the pragmatic necessity for a home-based project in a rural area such as that served by the Portage Project, the project staff has come to believe "that there are inherent *educational* advantages in utilizing the home-based precision teaching model" (Shearer & Shearer, 1976, p. 336). Shearer and Shearer (1976) list these educational advantages:

1. Learning occurs in the natural environment.
2. There is constant access to the full range of child's behavior as it naturally occurs.
3. There is more likelihood of maintenance and generalization.
4. All members of the family can participate in the teaching process and support the child's learning.
5. Training parents will presumably provide them with skills with which to deal more effectively with new behaviors as they arise in the child's repertoire.
6. Individualization is enhanced because the teacher is able to work on a one-on-one basis with the parent, who in turn works on a one-on-one basis with the child.

All in all, the home-based approach is believed to improve the ability of children to gain competencies in language, cognitive, self-help, motor, and socialization skills.

Activities vary from child to child in the program and are prescribed on an individualized basis. Each home teacher spends about an hour and a half a week with each child assigned to him or her. Instruction during the remainder of the week is the responsibility of the parent. Prescriptions are modified according to each child's individual weekly progress. Three new behavior targets are identified each week, and it be-

comes the parent's responsibility to provide instruction on these behaviors between the weekly visits of the home teacher. The home teacher collects data both before and after instruction to monitor each child's progress. The home teacher, in addition, helps parents sharpen their teaching skills. Model techniques are presented by the home teacher and parents are given an opportunity to try them out and receive feedback each week. All project staff act as home teachers, even though they come from varied professional disciplines (e.g., special education, speech, psychology). Some home teachers are paraprofessionals.

Ongoing assessment of children is accomplished through the individualized data charts referred to above. In addition, the Alpren-Boll Developmental Profile (Alpren & Boll, 1972) is administered to all children for screening and curriculum planning. The Portage Guide to Early Education (Bluma, Shearer, Frohman, & Hillard, 1976) was developed by project staff to aid in curriculum planning and to assess ongoing progress of the children. This assessment procedure is based on a series of developmental checklists that cover the age range from birth to 6. The Portage Guide has been widely accepted and suggested for older children who are severely or profoundly delayed (cf. VanEtten, Arkell, & VanEtten, 1980) and for young children with handicaps.

Both the Stanford-Binet and Cattell Infant Test have been used to assess the progress made by children in the Portage Project Program. These measures were employed on a pre-post test basis and showed that "the average child in the Project gained 15 months in an 8 month period" (Shearer & Shearer, 1976, p. 348). Project children also showed significantly greater gains on these measures and on the Alpren-Boll Developmental Profile and the Gesell when compared with a group of control children who were drawn randomly from preschool classes serving culturally and economically disadvantaged children. Shearer and Shearer (1976) believe that the use of these standardized, norm-referenced measures should be phased out of the program since "the staff believes that the only purpose for testing should be to program curriculum more effectively for children" (p. 338). They stress instead "informal assessment, which includes observing and recording how a child accomplishes a task, or why he fails to accomplish it, as well as behavioral checklists" (p. 338).

The success of the Portage Model can be seen in its wide dissemination and replication. DeWeerd (1980) reports that a program modelled after the Portage Project has been implemented in Japan. Another strength of the Portage Project can be seen in the development and dissemination of the Portage Guide to Early Education (Bluma et al., 1976), the assessment aspect of which was discussed above. The guide also includes a set of curriculum cards that correspond to the assessment checklist and incorporate almost 600 objectives in the area of infant stimulation, self-help, language socialization, and cognitive skills. While the manual gives overall instructions on the use of the guide, each card provides a specific "how to do it" statement related to each curriculum goal.

The Portage Project places significant responsibility on parents by casting them in the role of teacher. High expectations are held for parents, and the amount of support provided by project staff is relatively low. The support that is provided tends to be centered on the development of teaching and data collection skills. Parent support in the emotional and affective domain is seen as coming from other service agencies suggested by project staff. It is difficult to determine whether the lack of socialization with other children hinders the development of children served by the project. Although the Shearers present data suggesting advances in socialization, these data may actually refer to adaptive interaction with other children. The home-based approach of the Portage Project seems to overlook the significant contribution of peers to the development of children with handicaps.

Project EDGE   The project for Expanding Developmental Growth through Education (EDGE) has been described by Rynders and Horrobin (1975) as a program designed to facilitate the development of Down syndrome children through home instruction in infancy. After a period of home instruction, children enter the EDGE preschool at 30 months of age. Like several of the projects already described, Project EDGE received its initial funding through HCEEP. It was based at the University of Minnesota's Research, Development, and Demonstration Center in Education of Handicapped Children.

Several important principles undergirded Project EDGE and provided the basis for the program's activities. According to Rynders and Horrobin (1975):

1. Each activity should engage mother and child in affectionate, focused, sensorimotor interaction

2. Each activity should engage mother and child in sensorimotor activity, and should require, at the same time, that the mother talk with her child about the activities

3. Mothers should be taught to use a hierarchy of teaching strategies

4. Children should be systematically exposed to the fact that three-dimensional objects, photographs of the objects, and their printed labels have related meaning

5. Mothers should be encouraged to involve nonhandicapped siblings during the time they work with their Down syn-

drome child so as to minimize the risk of sibling jealousy

6. Sufficient structure should guide the mother's activities so that the execution of curricular principles can be guaranteed but, at the same time, does not stifle her unique maternal style

7. Every lesson should be paired in all possible lesson combinations in order to capitalize on the reinforcement value of relative novelty

These principles recognize the important role of the mother in the education and development of Down syndrome infants. In addition, they indicate a cognitive learning model, and stress the development of language and cognitive skills in particular.

Mothers of children enrolled in the infant program were expected to engage in specified training activities for one hour daily. Individual daily lessons were based on the EDGE curriculum, and each mother is provided with 20 sets of simple materials that could be used in carrying out the daily lessons. "The lessons provide enough structure to help the mother to be goal-directed by allowing considerable freedom for her to use materials to suit her style preferences" (Rynders & Horrobin, 1975, p. 178). The mother continued these daily lessons until the child reached 30 months of age, at which time the child entered the EDGE preschool, which continued to emphasize the development of communication skills. Even after the child enters the preschool program, the mother was expected to continue to provide daily stimulation by working with the child for 30 minutes daily. Thus, the EDGE approach combined a home-based approach for infants with a center-based approach for preschool children.

While mothers were seen as the hub of the program, Project EDGE staff recognized the need to augment maternal tutoring with other services. This recognition led to the implementation of certain ancillary services that lessened mothers' burden in providing education and training to their children while recognizing their importance. In addition to the preschool program mentioned above for the older children in the project, several other services were provided to support the efforts of the mothers with infants. These included an itinerant teacher, provision of respite care, and a mobile education unit. The itinerant teacher conducted lessons in the home and provided counseling and instructional support for parents (Rynders & Horrobin, 1975). Through their activity, the itinerant teachers provided mothers with a certain amount of free time and at the same time sharpened mothers' skills through modeling and feedback.

Respite care services provided parents an opportunity to get away from their children for short periods of time. Such care must be provided in safe, home-like settings if it is to be most effective (cf. Ray, 1974b).

A mobile unit was used as a classroom on wheels and was taken to various locations. The unit was a base for instruction in a classroom-like environment. Mothers were initially included in the instructional activities, but were gradually faded out. Instruction was carried out by two undergraduate students who "were selected because of their ability to relate to young children effectively, for their careful driving habits, excellent language skills, and willingness to help create and then carefully implement lesson plans" (Rynders & Horrobin, 1975, p. 187). Three hours of instruction were provided weekly to eight children through the mobile unit. Rynders and Horrobin (1975) conclude that a mobile unit is an effective and relatively inexpensive means for providing educational services to Down syndrome infants. They suggest that mobile units may be particularly useful in rural areas, although theirs was used in a primarily metropolitan setting. Finally, they point out that the "mobile program was used to *augment* a mother's teaching, not to supplant it" (p. 189).

Project EDGE used a strong evaluation design by assigning 20 children to the intervention group and 20 children to a control group. It is unclear from the description provided by Rynders and Horrobin what level of intervention, if any, the control children received. According to preliminary data, experimental children were showing positive performance differences "in concept formation, expressive language, on-task behavior, and IQ score as compared with their non-enrolled (control) counterparts" (Rynders & Horrobin, 1975, p. 184). Rynders and Horrobin do not report the means by which these data were collected, nor do they mention the specific assessment instruments employed. In a later presentation of their data Rynders, Spiker, and Horrobin (1978) state:

> we would point out that the 17 children in our early education treatment programs have shown, on the average, gains in IQ score (on the Stanford-Binet). Nevertheless, in the group of 18 Down's syndrome children not receiving our experimental treatment, fully 45 percent scored at or above the educable level. (Most of these children received differing forms of early intervention.) (p. 446)

Clearly, a strength of the EDGE program was the recognition by its staff that although mothers can provide an important link in education of Down syndrome infants, they must receive additional services to augment their efforts at home. An examination of Project EDGE will demonstrate that service delivery to families with Down syndrome infants and young children is challenging and complex, and that multiphasic modes must be employed to carry out this task well.

Perhaps a weakness of the project is its university base, for although the university provides a multitude of resources, its context is not easily replicable in the world beyond its campus. In general, Project EDGE represents an innovative and well-thought-out approach to preschool education of children with handicaps and has positive implications for providing educational services to other groups of infants and young children with developmental disabilities.

Parents as Effective Early Education Resources (PEERS)   Like several projects already described, the PEERS project (Losinno, n.d.) received funding through HCEEP after its inception as a volunteer program. More recently, it has been funded through PL 89-313 and the County Office of Mental Health and Mental Retardation in Philadelphia, Pennsylvania. PEERS is currently run by a community service agency in northeast Philadelphia and maintains a basic philosophy "that any child who is developmentally delayed must be involved in a consistent training program as soon as a delay in any developmental area is identified" (Losinno, n.d., p. 4). The basis of the PEERS program lies in the beliefs that, given proper information and training, parents can best serve as the child's teacher during the early years, and that parents and volunteers are effective primary intervention agents. The idea that early intervention can alleviate developmental delay is critical. Thus, the PEERS program employs a home-based, parent-oriented model of service delivery and adheres to what Anastasiow (1978) would classify as a cognitive developmental model.

The PEERS project has operated on a zero reject model of acceptance and has served between 20 and 40 families a year. These families all have children between the ages of 3 weeks and 3 years who are manifesting developmental delays in one or more areas. Many of these children also attend other training programs. The basic goals of the program are to provide stimulation and create an optimum learning environment for the child in home, and to provide intensive training for the child's parents and family. Project staff believe that attainment of these goals will minimize the degree of handicap exhibited by a child upon reaching preschool or kindergarten age.

The program activities are divided into three areas—parent training, home visits, and individualized child evaluations and prescriptive programming. Parent training is accomplished through seminars and lectures, for which parents come together as a group on Saturday mornings. These Saturday sessions are arranged to coincide with the individualized prescriptive/evaluative program sessions held for the children. About 80% of the families enrolled in the program attend these Saturday sessions on a typical Saturday and about 60% of the time both parents attend. These sessions are both a means for formal instruction and a social and emotional support group for the parents. The course of instruction for parents is designed to last two years and covers "basic concepts in child development; a review of methods and means of assessment; a discussion of community resources; and guidelines in dealing with sibling problems, parent/child problems, child problems, future planning, toy selection, child management, and other related topics" (Losinno, n.d., pp. 8–9).

Home visits are conducted by a project teacher once a month. The home visit focuses on parent concerns, and the teacher provides parents with input concerning prescriptions and procedures for implementing them. New lesson plans are explained to parents and are left for their use in training sessions. Parents are urged to set aside 30 minutes for training every day, and are encouraged to keep a log of their child's activities and progress. These anecdotal records are seen as important sources of data for assessing both parent and child progress.

Children also come in on Saturdays for evaluation and individualized prescriptive programming. These sessions last 3 hours and are conducted by community volunteers and project staff. Children are worked with individually and in small groups. These Saturday sessions provide the children with an opportunity to become socialized to other children, and give project staff an opportunity formally to assess children's progress. In addition, parents are excused from their training session periodically and given an opportunity to work with their children with all project staff available for feedback and information. This opportunity occurs approximately once every 6 weeks. Saturday morning sessions are also used by staff to assess and update individual prescriptions for children about once every 3 months.

Formal evaluation of each child is done every 6 months. Children are evaluated with standardized tests, such as the Bayley Scales of Infant Development (Bayley, 1969), the Vineland Scale of Social Maturity (Doll, 1964), and the Bzoch-League Receptive-Expressive Emergent Language Scales (Bzoch & League, 1971). In addition, children's progress on self-help skills, fine motor skills, gross motor skills, cognitive concepts, social skills, and expressive and receptive language skills is assessed using an internal evaluation device known as the PEERS instrument, which Losinno reports correlates in the range of .83 to .96 with the standardized measures used.

Sower (1978) compiled an extensive report on the effectiveness of the PEERS project. The method of compensated and noncompensated post ages developed by Irwin and Wong (1974) was used as the main means of evaluating gains in children's development. A multivariate analysis of pre- and post-scores of the Bayley, Vineland, Bzoch-League, and the seven domains on the PEERS instrument revealed an overall significant effect for both compensated and noncompensated scores. This analysis included 17 subjects. Sower (1978) concludes that:

> these multivariate analyses suggest that the total impact of the PEERS program on the 17 subjects as evaluated by the seven sub-tests is indeed considerable. Note that even the analysis that employs the compensated post ages [scores] is significant. This analysis is more rigorous from their conventional post analysis because it subtracts from the actual increase the mathematical projection of the increase that could have been predicted by maturational factors alone. (p. 21)

Even using compensated scores, it is difficult to interpret the true effect of the PEERS project, since many of the children were also served by other programs.

One strength of the PEERS project is the support that parents of the project provide each other. The regularly scheduled Saturday morning meetings greatly facilitate the development of this support. These types of group meetings are unique and do not usually occur in parent-oriented programs, which are typically oriented to the individual family. In essence, the PEERS project provides a means by which parents become resources to their own children and to each other. The PEERS project staff realizes that parents need not only training, but psychological and emotional support in dealing with their children.

A relative weakness of the project is the infrequency with which parents were visited by home teachers. While this deficiency was offset to some degree by the weekly Saturday meetings, which provided access to staff, these meetings were typically of a general nature and were designed to give group input to the parents. Another weakness was the relatively long time span (3 months) between changes in prescription. A child who spends a full 2 years in the program receives only eight different prescriptions during his tenure in the program.

The UCLA Infant Studies Program   According to a description of the UCLA Infant Studies Program provided by Bromwich and Parmelee (1979), "the educational intervention program . . . was oriented primarily to support and enhance the quality of interaction between parent and infant in light of considerable research evidence regarding the powerful influence of parent-infant interaction on the development of the infant" (p. 389). The program served high-risk, preterm infants between the ages of 10 months and 2 years. To be eligible for the program, infants had to be less than 37 weeks in gestational age and weigh less than 2,500 grams at birth. In addition, they had to be evaluated as being at risk using the cumulative risk measures described by Parmelee, Sigman, Kopp, and Haber (1975, 1976) and Sigman and Parmelee (1979). The families of these infants spanned the spectrum of ethnic and socioeconomic groups. The program employed a home-based, parent-centered approach that followed cognitive developmental models.

The overall goal of the program was to enhance the parents' enjoyment of and sensitivity and responsiveness to their infants and thus to increase their motivation and ability to provide opportunities and experiences that would further the infant's development (Bromwich & Parmelee, 1979). The staff was concerned with infant development in the social-affective, cognitive-motivational, and language areas. To reach its goal with parents and infants, the staff developed an individualized plan for each family. In general, goals focused on making parents responsive to cues given by the infant; giving parents ways of motivating infant responses; giving parents observational skills enabling them to assess the infant's competence and then select appropriate ma-

terials and play activities; increasing parents' awareness of prelinguistic skills and
the necessity for reciprocal communication;
and providing parents with skills to motivate infant language.

The activities of the intervention program
centered on home visits. During the several
home visits, staff were primarily concerned
with establishing rapport with the family and
completing a baseline assessment on the infant. After the first three sessions, an intervention plan for the family was developed.
Every 4 months staff prepared case summa-
ries that included:

(a) an assessment of the infant, parenting behavior, parent-infant interaction, and home
environment of the infant; (b) a discussion of
changes in any of the areas that were assessed;
and (c) an evaluation of the concept and process of intervention with subsequent revisions
of the intervention plan as indicated by the
evaluation." (Bromwich & Parmelee, 1979, p.
392)

Bromwich and Parmelee point out that the
staff followed a number of guidelines that
they believe were central to their approach:

1. parent remains in control
2. dealing with parent's priorities and concerns
3. avoiding the "authority-laymen" gap
4. respecting parent's goals for infant
5. respecting individual styles of parent-infant
   interaction
6. parent participation in planning
7. building on strengths of parents
8. reinforcement is not enough
9. parent as observer of infant's play
10. giving parents an "out"
11. experimenting can be fun for parent (pp.
    394–396).

Two instruments were developed by project staff to assess the effectiveness of the intervention program in modifying parent-infant interaction. The first of these was the
Parent Behavior Progression (PBP), designed
to assess parenting behavior at six levels.
These levels ranged from assessing a parent's

basic enjoyment of his or her infant to assessing the parent's ability independently to gen-
erate developmentally appropriate and interesting experiences for the infant. Project
staff also developed the Play Interaction
Measure (PIM). Unlike the PBP, the PIM was
designed for use in the laboratory rather than
the home. The PIM is divided into three sections, which measure play-related behaviors, social-affective behaviors, and language
behaviors. In addition, children were assessed using the Gesell and the Bayley measures.

The program employed a control group
that did not participate in the intervention
program. It is interesting to note that Bromwich and Parmelee found no significant differences between the 1-year or 2-year Gesell
or Bayley scores for the intervention and the
nonintervention groups. They conclude that
"it is clear that the intervention did not alter
this trend" (Bromwich & Parmelee, 1979, p.
400).

Staff assessed the intervention program as
being successful for families in the intervention group. Fourteen families were rated as
mixed successes and five were considered
unsuccessful. From these cases, the 11 most
successful were compared with the 10 least
successful on percentage gain on the PBP and
the PIM. The total gain on all levels of the
PBP was 46% for the successful group, as
compared with an average gain of only 10%
for the unsuccessful group. On the PIM, the
average gain for the successful group was
34% as compared with 23% for the unsuccessful group. These results may be con-
founded by the fact that the staff may have
known PBP and PIM scores, and that that
knowledge affected which families were
viewed as successful and which families
were not.

While the philosophical tenets of this program appear sound, the data that Bromwich
and Parmelee (1979) present raise some

questions as to the actual effectiveness of the intervention program. Since the authors do not specify precisely what procedures were employed in their intervention program, it is difficult to assess why the evaluation data do not show a higher degree of successes. The authors suggest that the effects of the program may appear in the long term rather than the short term. In addition, they report that the control group actually received certain medical and social services through the time of the program. These services may have been as effective in facilitating development as those offered through the intervention program. In summary, the strength of this program lies in its theoretical and philosophical underpinnings, which were drawn from a substantial literature on the relationship between mothers and their infants and how these relationships can foster optimal infant development.

Family-Focused Programs

The Liaison Infant Family Team (LIFT) The Liaison Infant Family Team (LIFT) (Thurman, Cornwell, & Korteland, 1989) is a family-focused intervention program designed to serve families with infants in neonatal intensive care. The program, which began as a HCEEP demonstration project, serves about 30 families a year. Housed in a community hospital in suburban Philadelphia, LIFT treats a variety of premature and otherwise ill or compromised infants. Families served by LIFT represent a cross section of socioeconomic backgrounds. According to Thurman, Cornwell, and Korteland, LIFT is based on the following principles:

1. Interventions should be designed to increase goodness of fit and ecological congruence within the family.
2. The needs and desires of the family should drive the type and extent of service responses.
3. Families should develop independence

from service providers and should be empowered to have their own needs met.
4. Families are dynamic, complex, and ever changing systems.

The LIFT model focuses on the fit between the infant and other family members while at the same time stressing the facilitation of the infant's development. The model is predicated on the belief that families whose infants receive neonatal intensive care should also receive intensive support and services. Services to families begin within 24 hours of their infant's admission to the hospital and continue as long as the family feels it needs the services provided by LIFT. An individual program plan is developed, implemented, and monitored for each family. Families are visited in the hospital and in their homes. LIFT also facilitates the fit between the family and the community by aiding in the transition of the infant from hospital to home and by helping to arrange needed community services.

The team consists of four professionals, each of whom has a distinct role within the model. The infant coordinator has primary responsibility for activities directed at facilitating the development of the infant. These activities include enhancing parent-child interaction, providing developmental assessment, providing infant stimulation, developing specific interventions, assisting parents in carrying out interventions, and providing technical assistance to early intervention programs in which the infants are placed.

The family coordinator has primary responsibility for the dynamics of the family. Specifically, the family coordinator seeks to aid the family with the stress associated with neonatal intensive care and its aftermath. The family coordinator assesses the family stress levels and social support mechanisms and provides services based on the results of these assessments. The overall goal of the family coordinator is to develop and maintain levels of family function that reduce stress, increase support, and begin to lay the groundwork for the development of a good fit between the infant and the family, as well as among other family members.

The liaison coordinator's role focuses on linking families with community resources as needed. Again the emphasis is on developing support mechanisms; however, these mechanisms are extra-family mechanisms rather than intra-family mechanisms, which are facilitated by the family coordinator. The liaison coordinator seeks to link families and the appropriate service agencies that are needed to provide support.

The role of the team coordinator is primarily that of team manager. The role stresses the development of team function and focuses on the coordination of team activities. Another aspect of this role is the facilitation of cooperation with the staff of the neonatal intensive care unit.

Although these roles appear somewhat separate and distinct, in fact they overlap with each other. Thus, there is a certain amount of role release between team members. This role release is characteristic of teams operating in a transdisciplinary mode; however, since this team is not disciplinarily based, it is somewhat inappropriate to apply this term to its function. The term, however, is helpful in characterizing the level of team function associated with LIFT.

LIFT staff meet on a weekly basis to discuss families and infants. During the rest of the week they are in regular contact with families and are engaged in ongoing assessment, intervention, and support activities. The LIFT model takes a highly individualized approach to service delivery and develops individualized plans that incorporate the intra- and extra-family support needs and the developmental needs of the infant. Each family

plays a major role in identifying these needs. The service plan is unified through the construct of goodness of fit and is developed to increase the adaptive fit between family members and the infant, as well as between the family and community service agencies that may be needed to support the family after the infant's discharge from the hospital. Families and infants are assessed using a variety of formal and informal techniques. Thus, the LIFT model employs an individualized approach both in assessment of families and infants and in the type of interventions it employs.

Because of the highly individualized approach that LIFT employs, program evaluation has depended primarily on a case study format. Case studies on families are developed and then analyzed to determine how goals were established, interventions developed, and outcomes attained. In addition, case studies are examined to assess to what degree the guiding principles in the model were evident. The LIFT model has been effective in demonstrating the importance and usefulness of a family-focused approach to early intervention that begins during the hospitalization of an infant in neonatal intensive care.

Helping Agencies Promote Parent Empowerment Through Networking (HAPPEN) Another program that emphasizes a family-focused approach and stresses the empowerment of families is project HAPPEN (Helping Agencies Promote Parent Empowerment Through Networking). Initially funded as an HCEEP model demonstration project (Cornwell & Snyder, in press), Project HAPPEN focused on the empowerment of families with special needs children from birth to age 8. It served 20 to 25 families annually. Priority was given to minority families or families with underserved children living in four rural counties in western North Carolina. The project mediated linkages between families and service providers and between families and informal support networks. Families that required networking of services among different agencies were targeted.

Project HAPPEN provided families with advocacy training, physical and emotional support, and communication training designed to enhance a parent's ability to ensure that the child's needs would be met. Families were aided in identifying their own needs, locating community resources to meet those needs, exploring options for action, and choosing those options that were best for them. Parents also evaluated their own actions and developed support networks within their own communities. The amount of support given to parents in carrying out these activities depended on the needs and abilities of individual parents. Parents were given no more support than was necessary to accomplish their goals and were given more and more independence in carrying out activities as the project progressed.

Results of the project suggest that the empowerment process used promotes a family's sense of competence in identifying and meeting its needs. Children in the project were assessed quarterly using a variety of tools. The particular assessment tools employed depended on the age and functional level of the child; they included the Bayley Scales of Infant Development, the Learning Accomplishment Profile, and the Stanford-Binet Intelligence Scale. Parents also administered a developmental checklist to their children every 6 months.

TRANSITION TO PUBLIC SCHOOL

A major concern of early intervention professionals is the transition of children from preschool programs to public school. Bron-fenbrenner (1977) has pointed out that transitions in early life affect not only the lives of children, but also those of their parents. Early intervention programs often provide a level of support to parents that is not typically available in the public schools. Research also suggests that parents may receive more support from early intervention professionals than from the public schools during the actual transition process (Hamblin-Wilson & Thurman, in press). Because of the stressful nature of this transition for parents, special efforts must be made to accommodate parental needs. Hanline (1988) has recently reported that parents have major concerns related to lack of information about school district services, anxiety about working with an unfamiliar agency, and uncertainty as to whether their child will receive appropriate services. Thus, it is important to include parents in the transition process (Egelston, Maddox, & Tazioli, 1985) and for service providers to coordinate activities for parents and the sending and receiving programs (Bricker, 1986).

Diamond, Spiegel-McGill, and Hanrahan (1988) have recently suggested an ecological developmental approach to the transition process. Their model recognizes the differences between the ecological structure of the preschool program and the ecological structure of the public school classroom. They assert that smooth transition depends on parental involvement and on the development of effective interrelationships between systems. They propose a 15-step approach to operationalize the transition process. Their approach suggests that planning for the transition should begin in September of one school year and end in October of the next. Table 13.2 illustrates the steps that Diamond et al. suggest for planning and implementing the transition process.

Gallagher, Maddox, and Edgar (1984) have provided materials to implement a

Table 13.2. Steps in planning and implementing the transition process

Preliminary transition plans (September and October)
1. The IEP
2. Identification of preschool liaison with school district
3. Parent education

Initiating contacts with the school district (November through February)
4. Referral to the school district's multidisciplinary team
5. Parent conference to discuss child's level of functioning and parents' expectations for school placement
6. Informal contact with the school
7. Assessment reports provided to school and parents

Developing placement options (February through June)
8. Planning meeting with multidisciplinary team chairperson
9. Visits to proposed school programs
10. Continued parent education focusing on due process rights
11. Multidisciplinary team meeting to recommend an appropriate placement and develop the Phase 1 IEP

Continuing the transition planning process (June through August)
12. Visit by public school teacher to the preschool
13. Visit by the child to the public school
14. School records sent to the public school and parents by the preschool program

Follow-up (October)
15. Follow-up contact with the public school

From Diamond, K.E., Spiegel-McGill, P., & Hanrahan, P. (1988). Planning for school transition: An ecological developmental approach. *Journal of the Division for Early Childhood, 12,* 245–252. Reprinted by permission.

multi-step interagency transition program and Hanline and Knowlton (1988) have suggested a similar series of steps for smoothing the transition from infant intervention to preschool programs in the public schools.

EVALUATION OF EARLY INTERVENTION PROGRAMS

The need for professional and financial accountability demands the development of effective models of program evaluation. If the mandates of PL 99-457 are to be met it is necessary to develop cost-effective programs that bring about the desired outcomes for children and families. Weatherford (1986) has suggested at least three reasons for evaluating early intervention programs. First, he suggests, is the need to acquire knowledge about the learning and development of this population. Essentially, Weatherford is suggesting that we can learn more about the learning processes of infants and young children with disabilities by evaluating the effects of various specific interventions on specific learning or developmental outcomes in children. Dunst (1986) has made a similar point by suggesting that evaluation strategies should begin to focus on which dimensions of early intervention are related to different outcomes. He asserts that we should no longer focus on the question of whether early intervention works, but rather on how it works.

A second reason identified by Weatherford for program evaluation is moral obligation. He states that, "it is incumbent upon us to provide the most effective programs possible for these children" (Weatherford, 1986, p. 2). One problem that arises from this statement is the definition of effectiveness. The outcome variables of one program may be very different from those of another program, and yet both may be equally effective. Consider, for example, the respective outcomes associated with project HAPPEN and project EDGE. Although each program may have been equally effective in bringing about specific outcomes, the basic differences in the two programs makes it difficult to compare them. In fact, it may be that the outcomes associated with project HAPPEN should not be expected in a program such as project EDGE, nor should those associated with project EDGE be expected of project HAPPEN. The notion of moral obligation, while important, must be tempered by evaluating program effectiveness based on the purposes and outcomes defined by a given program. To do otherwise would be analogous to asking a medical researcher to assess the effectiveness of a cancer treatment for treating diabetes.

The third reason Weatherford puts forth for program evaluation is accountability, the "need to account for or justify the value of given activities or programs" (Weatherford, 1986, p. 3). Such accountability can be measured by cost effectiveness and cost-benefit models. These models compare a program's costs with its outcomes. Barnett and Escobar (1989) asserts that cost-benefit analysis is concerned with "the state of the world with a program, [as compared with] the state of the world without the program" (p. 60). "Cost-effectiveness analysis seeks to estimate the economic value of all the resources used by a program [and] is correctly applied when two or more programs, with the same goals, are analyzed and compared" (p. 61). Cost-benefit analysis is often more difficult to perform, because it requires that monetary value be associated with outcomes and benefits that are often difficult to measure in monetary terms (e.g., an improved relationship between a father and a child). Cost effectiveness, however, assigns value to the resources used to bring about a particular outcome (e.g., an improved relationship between a father and a child), but does not place a monetary value on that outcome. Cost effectiveness is concerned with determining the relative cost of producing an outcome, whereas cost-benefit analysis is concerned with the overall benefits of a particular out-

come. For a more complete discussion of these approaches the reader is referred to Barnett (1986).

Another means of assessing accountability is social validation. Social validation refers to the desirability, or value, placed on a particular program or program outcome by society (Wolf, 1978). Head Start, for example, has a high degree of social value in our society and, thus, has been socially validated. The degree of social validation is usually determined by soliciting the opinions of users of a program (Kazdin, 1977). Parents, for example, might be asked to express their level of satisfaction with the type of behavior change brought about in their child, or their satisfaction with the procedures used to bring about the change. The overall philosophy, purpose, and methods of the program are all targets for social validation. Social validation is an important technique for program evaluation because it defines the social importance and social relevancy of a particular program. Social validation measures are also necessary to help ensure that the program is accountable to its users. The construct of ecological congruence and goodness of fit discussed in earlier chapters help ensure that programs are socially valid, since the establishment of fit in the system depends on what is desirable to individuals in the system. Employing a family-focused approach to services such as those discussed above can also help ensure the social validity of a program.

The design of a program evaluation should take into account several factors. According to Smith (1986), these factors include the purpose of the evaluation (e.g., to assess the quality of what has been achieved, to obtain accreditation); the primary audiences for the evaluation (e.g., program staff, legislators, program funding agencies); and the aspects to the program that are of concern (e.g., program goals, family outcomes, management procedures). Smith also suggests that program evaluation strategies are influenced by the types of questions being asked. These questions may center on such issues as need, quality of service, efficiency, and impact. What is important to realize is that the exact type of program evaluation design and methods to be employed must address the factors and questions identified as relevant by those conducting the evaluation. Data on independent and dependent variables must be collected in such a way as to ensure that the necessary answers will be obtained. Program staff often require additional expertise from consultants in setting up and maintaining effective program evaluation strategies. These consultants are available through colleges and universities, as well as through local, state, and federal agencies. For a more thorough discussion of program evaluation, the reader is referred to Smith (1986) and Shadish (1986).

EFFECTIVENESS OF EARLY INTERVENTION

The effectiveness of early intervention remains an issue of interest to service providers, legislatures, parents, and funding agencies. Although much remains to be learned about early intervention, several studies have reported on its positive impact (see Casto & Mastropieri, 1986). These reports typically examine the effects of a particular program technique or methodology on the outcome of specified behavior or developmental targets in children or families. Even as resources become tighter, early intervention programs must continue to provide data on their effectiveness so that the long-term effectiveness of early intervention can be measured. While several studies have demonstrated that early intervention can be effective in increasing the likelihood of placement in integrated settings (e.g., Hayden, Morris, & Bailey, 1977; McNulty, Smith, & Soper, 1983), little research has been done that compares the long-term developmental and behavioral outcomes of children who have had early intervention with those who have not. One notable exception is the work of Berruerta-Clement and colleagues (1984), which established long-term positive effects of an early intervention program. Their study examined the effectiveness of the Perry Preschool Project, which served low-income children with high environmental risk, rather than children with identified handicaps. There is some question as to whether the same results would obtain with a population of children with handicaps.

Another issue related to assessing the effectiveness of early intervention is the ethical issue of denying service to some children in order to establish a control group. Such a practice is probably illegal under PL 99-457 and certainly raises serious ethical questions. As an alternative, researchers must conduct studies that randomly assign children and families to different intervention programs and then collect data to determine which programs are most effective both in the short term and the long term.

SUMMARY

This chapter has discussed major program approaches to the provision of early intervention services, many of which had their origins in model demonstration projects. These program approaches can be categorized using classification systems that stress program focus and conceptual base. The chapter enumerates the features of early intervention programs that have been identified as best practice. A number of programs are described that provide center-based or home-based services and that are child oriented, parent oriented, or family focused in approach. Issues concerning the transition of children and families from early intervention programs to public schools are highlighted.

Finally, the critical issues of program evaluation and effectiveness were discussed. In addition, specific approaches to program accountability are described, such as cost-benefit analysis and social validation.

References

Abbeduto, L., & Rosenberg, S. (1987). Linguistic communication and mental retardation. In S. Rosenberg (Ed.), *Advances in applied psycholinguistics: Vol. 1. Disorders of first language development*. Cambridge: Cambridge University Press.

Abel, E.L., Randall, C.L., & Riley, E.P. (1983). Alcohol consumption and prenatal development. In B. Tabakoff, P.B. Sutker, & C.L. Randall (Eds.), *Medical and social aspects of alcohol abuse*. New York: Plenum.

Abidin, R.R. (1983). *Parent-stress index*. Charlottesville, VA: Pediatric Psychology Press.

Abramson, P., Gravink, M., Abramson, L., & Sommers, D. (1977). Early diagnosis and intervention of retardation: A survey of parental reactions concerning the quality of services rendered. *Mental Retardation, 15*, 28–31.

Abroms, K.I., & Bennett, J.W. (1980). Current genetic and demographic findings in Down's syndrome: How are they presented in college textbooks on exceptionality? *Mental Retardation, 18*, 101–107.

Achenbach, T.M., & Edelbrook, C.S. (1981). Behavioral problems and competencies reported by parents of normal and disturbed children aged 4 through 16. *Monographs of the Society for Research in Child Development, 46*, Serial Nos. 1 & 188.

Adelson, E., & Fraiberg, S. (1975). Gross motor development in infants blind from birth. In B.Z. Friedlander, G.M. Sterrit, & G.E. Kirk (Eds.), *Exceptional infant: Assessment intervention* (Vol. 3). New York: Brunner/Mazel.

Adler, S. (1983). *The non-verbal child* (3rd ed.). Springfield, IL: Charles C Thomas.

Ainsworth, M.D., Blehar, M.C., Waters, E., & Walls, S. (1978). *Patterns of attachment: A psychological study of the strange situation*. Hillsdale, NJ: Lawrence Erlbaum Associates.

Ainsworth, M.D., & Wittig, B. A. (1969). Attachment and exploratory behavior of one-year-olds in a strange situation. In B.M. Foss (Ed.), *Determinants of infant behavior*. London: Methuen.

Alinsky, S.D. (1971). *Rules for radicals*. New York: Random House.

Allen, K.E., et al. (1964). Effects of social reinforcement on isolate behavior of a nursery school child. *Child Development, 35*, 511–518.

Alpren, G., & Boll, T. (1972). *The developmental profile*. Indianapolis, IN: Psychological Development Publishers.

American Academy of Pediatrics. (1988). AIDS Task Force Pediatric guidelines infection control of HIV (AIDS virus) in hospitals, medical offices, schools, and other settings. *Pediatrics, 82,* 801–807.

American Academy of Pediatrics Task Force on Pediatric AIDS. (1988). Perinatal human immunodeficiency virus infection. *Pediatrics, 82*, 941–944.

Anastasi, A. (1958). Heredity, environment and the question of "how"? *Psychological Review, 65*, 197–208.

Anastasi, A. (1976). *Psychological testing* (4th ed.). New York: Macmillan.

Anastasiow, N.J. (1978). Strategies for models for early childhood intervention of handicapped and nonhandicapped children. In M.J. Guralnick (Ed.), *Early intervention and the integration of handicapped and nonhandicapped children*. Baltimore: University Park Press.

Anastasiow, N.J. (1981). Socioemotional development: The state of the art. *New Directions for Exceptional Children, 5*, 1–12.

Anastasiow, N.J. (1986). *Development and disability: A psychobiological analysis for special educators.* Baltimore: Paul H. Brookes Publishing Co.

Anatov, A.N. (1947). Children born during the siege of Leningrad in 1942. *Journal of Pediatrics, 30,* 250.

Anisfeld, M. (1984). *Language development from birth to three.* Hillsdale, NJ: Lawrence Erlbaum Associates.

Apgar, V. (1953). A proposal for a new method of evaluation of the newborn infant. *Anesthesia and Analgesia, 32,* 260–267.

Apgar, V. (1965). Drugs in pregnancy. *American Journal of Nursing, 65*(3), 104–105.

Apgar, V., Holaday, D.A., James, L.S., Berrien, C., & Weisbrot, I.H. (1958). Evaluation of newborn infants—second report. *Journal of the American Medical Association, 168,* 1958–1988.

Apgar, V., & James, L.S. (1962). Further observations on the newborn scoring system. *American Journal of the Diseases of Children, 104,* 419–428.

Apolloni, T., Cooke, S.A., & Cooke, T.P. (1977). Establishing a normal peer as a behavioral model for delayed toddlers. *Perceptual and Motor Skills, 44,* 231–241.

Armstrong v. Kline, 476 F. Supp. 583 (E.D. Pennsylvania 1979).

Aslin, R.N., Pisoni, D.B., & Jusczyk, P.W. (1983). Auditory development and speech perception in infancy. In P.H. Mussen (Ed.), *Handbook of child psychology: Vol. 2. Infancy and developmental psychology* (4th ed.). New York: John Wiley & Sons.

Atkinson, R.C., & Shiffrin, R.M. (1968). Human memory: A proposed system and its control processes. In K.W. Spence & J.T. Spence (Eds.), *The psychology of learning and motivation: Advances in research and theory* (Vol. 2). New York: Academic Press.

Austin, J. (1962). *How to do things with words.* London: Oxford University Press.

Avery, C.D. (1971). A psychologist looks at the issue of public versus residential school placement for the blind. In R.L. Jones (Ed.), *Problems and issues in the education of exceptional children.* Boston: Houghton Mifflin.

Ayres, J. (1972). *Sensory integration and learning disorders.* Los Angeles: Western Psychological Services.

Ayres, J. (1986). *Southern California Sensory Integration Tests, manual revised.* Los Angeles: Western Psychological Services.

Azrin, N.H., & Holtz, W.C. (1966). Punishment.

In W.K. Honig (Ed.), *Operant behavior: Areas of research and application.* New York: Appleton-Century-Crofts.

Baer, D.M., Peterson, R.F., & Sherman, J.A. (1967). The development of imitation by reinforcing behavioral similarity to a model. *Journal of Experimental Analysis of Behavior, 10,* 405–409.

Bagnato, S.J., & Neisworth, J.T. (1987). *Perceptions of developmental status: A system for planning early intervention.* University Park: Pennsylvania State University.

Bailey, D.B., Clifford, R.M., & Harms, T. (1982). Comparison of preschool environments for handicapped and nonhandicapped children. *Topics in Early Childhood Special Education, 2*(1), 9–20.

Bailey, D.B., Palsha, S., & Huntington, G.S. (1988). *Preservice preparation of special educators to work with handicapped infants and their families: Current status and training needs.* Chapel Hill: University of North Carolina, Carolina Institute on Infant Personnel Preparation, Frank Porter Graham Center.

Bailey, D.B., & Simeonsson, R.J. (1988). *Family assessment in early intervention.* Columbus, OH: Charles E. Merrill.

Bailey, D.B., & Wolery, M. (1989). *Assessing infants and preschoolers with handicaps.* Columbus, OH: Charles E. Merrill.

Baker, B.L., & Brightman, A.J. (1989). *A skills training guide for parents and teachers of children with special needs* (2nd ed.). Baltimore: Paul H. Brookes Publishing Co.

Baldwin, A. (1968). *Theories of child development.* New York: John Wiley & Sons.

Bandura, A. (1971). Psychotherapy based on modeling principles. In A. Bergin & S.L. Garfield (Eds.), *Handbook of psychotherapy and behavior change: An empirical analysis.* New York: John Wiley & Sons.

Bandura, A., & Menlove, F.L. (1968). Factors determining vicarious extinction of avoidance behavior through symbolic modeling. *Journal of Personality and Social Psychology, 8,* 99–108.

Banks, M.S., & Ginsburg, A.P. (1987). Early visual preferences: A review and a new theoretical treatment. In H.W. Reese (Ed.), *Advances in child development and behavior.* New York: Academic Press.

Banks, M.S., & Salapatek, P. (1983). Infant visual perception. In P.H. Mussen (Ed.), *Handbook of child psychology: Vol. 2. Infancy and developmental psychobiology* (4th ed.). New York: John Wiley & Sons.

Barker, R.G. (1955). *One boy's day.* New York: Harper & Row.

Barker, R.G. (1968). *Ecological psychology.* Palo Alto: Stanford University Press.

Barker, R.G., & Wright, H.F. (1955). *Midwest and its children.* New York: Harper & Row.

Barnes, A.C. (1968). *Intra-uterine development.* Philadelphia: Lea & Febiger.

Barnett, W. S. (1986). Methodological issues in economic evaluation of early intervention programs. *Early Childhood Research Quarterly, 1,* 249–268.

Barnett, W.S., & Escobar, C.M. (1989). Understanding program costs. In C. Tingey (Ed.), *Implementing early intervention* (pp. 49–62). Baltimore: Paul H. Brookes Publishing Co.

Baron, R.A., & Lawton, S.F. (1972). Environmental influences on aggression: The facilitation of modeling effects by high temperatures. *Psychonomic Science, 26,* 80–82.

Bartel, N.R., & Guskin, S.L. (1980). A handicap as a social phenomenon. In W.M. Cruickshank (Ed.), *Psychology of exceptional children and youth* (4th ed.). Englewood Cliffs, NJ: Prentice-Hall.

Bates, E. (1975). Peer relations and the acquisition of language. In M. Lewis & L. Rosenblum (Ed.), *Friendship and peer relations.* New York: John Wiley & Sons.

Bates, E. (1976a). *Language and context.* New York: Academic Press.

Bates, E. (1976b). Pragmatics and sociolinguistics in child language. In D. Morehead & A. Morehead (Eds.), *Normal and deficient child language.* Baltimore: University Park Press.

Bates, E., Bretherton, I., Beeghly-Smith, M., & McNew, S. (1982). Social bases of language development: A reassessment. In H.W. Reese & L.P. Lipsitt (Eds.), *Advances in child development* (Vol. 16). New York: Academic Press.

Batshaw, M.L., & Perret, Y.M. (1986). *Children with handicaps: A medical primer* (2nd ed.). Baltimore: Paul H. Brookes Publishing Co.

Batuev, A.S. (1987). *Higher integrative systems of the brain* (J.H. Appleby, Trans.). New York: Gordon and Breach.

Bayley, N. (1935). The development of motor abilities during the first three years. *Monographs of the Society for Research in Child Development, 1.*

Bayley, N. (1969). *Bayley Scales of Infant Development* (rev.). New York: Psychological Corporation.

Bayley, N. (1970). The development of mental disabilities. In P.H. Mussen (Ed.), *Carmichael's manual of child psychology* (Vol. 1). New York: John Wiley & Sons.

Beckman, P.J. (1983). Influences of selected child characteristics on stress in families of handicapped infants. *American Journal of Mental Deficiency, 88,* 150–156.

Beckman-Bell, P. (1981). Child-related stress in families of handicapped children. *Topics in Early Childhood Special Education, 1,* 45–53.

Beckwith, L. (1979). Prediction of emotional and social behavior. In J.D. Osofsky (Ed.), *The handbook of infant development.* New York: John Wiley & Sons.

Beez, W.V. (1968). Influence of biased psychological reports on teacher behavior and pupil performance. *Proceedings of the Seventy-Fifth American Psychological Association Annual Convention,* Washington, DC.

Beller, E.K. (1979). Early intervention programs. In J.D. Osofsky (Ed.), *Handbook of infancy research.* New York: John Wiley & Sons.

Belsky, J., Rovine, M., & Taylor, D. (1984). The Pennsylvania infant and family development project, III: The origins of individual differences in infant-mother attachment: Maternal and infant contributions. *Child Development, 55,* 718–728.

Benoit, E.P. (1959). Toward a new definition of mental retardation. *American Journal of Mental Deficiency, 63,* 559–565.

Berdine, W.H., & Cegelka, P.T. (1980). *Teaching the trainable retarded.* Columbus, OH: Charles E. Merrill.

Berger, M., & Foster, M. (1976). Families with retarded children: A multivariate approach to issues and strategies. *Multivariate Experimental Clinical Research, 1,* 1–21.

Berger, M., & Fowlkes, M.A. (1980). Family intervention project: A family network model for serving young handicapped children. *Young Children, 35,* 22–32.

Bernal, M.E., Jr. (1977). Introduction: Perspectives on nondiscriminatory assessment. In T. Oakland (Ed.), *Psychological and educational assessment of minority children.* New York: Brunner/Mazel.

Bernal, M.E., Klinnert, M.D., & Schultz, L.A. (1980). Outcome evaluation of behavioral parent training and client centered parent counseling for children with conduct problems. *Journal of Applied Behavior Analysis, 13,* 677–691.

Bernal, M.E., & North, J.A. (1978). A survey of parent training manuals. *Journal of Applied Behavior Analysis, 11,* 533–544.

Berrueta-Clement, J.R., Schweinhart, L.J., Barnett, W.S., Epstein, A.S., & Weikart, D.P. (1984). *Changed lives: The effects of the Perry Preschool Program on youths through age 19.* Ypsilanti, MI: High/Scope Press.

Bettelheim, B. (1950). *Love is not enough: The treatment of emotionally disturbed children.* Glencoe, IL: The Free Press.

Biber, B.E., Shapiro, E., & Wickens, D. (1971). *Promoting cognitive growth: A developmental interaction point of view.* Washington, DC: National Association for the Education of Young Children.

Bijou, S.W. (1966). A functional analysis of retarded development. In N.R. Ellis (Ed.), *International review of research in mental retardation* (Vol. 1). New York: Academic Press.

Bijou, S.W., & Baer, D.M. (1961). *Child development: A systematic and empirical theory* (Vol. 1). New York: Appleton-Century-Crofts.

Bijou, S.W., Peterson, R.F., & Ault, M.H. (1968). A method to integrate descriptive and experimental field studies at the level of data and empirical concepts. *Journal of Applied Behavior Analysis, 1,* 175–191.

Bijou, S.W., Peterson, R.F., Harris, F.R., Allen, K.E., & Johnston, M.S. (1969). Methodology for experimental studies of young children in natural settings. *Psychological Record, 19,* 177–210.

Bingol, N., Fuchs, M., Diaz, V., Stone, R.K., & Gromisch, D.S. (1987). Teratogenicity of cocaine in humans. *Journal of Pediatrics, 110,* 93–96.

Bixler, R.H. (1980). Nature versus nurture: The timeless anachronism. *Merrill-Palmer Quarterly, 26,* 153–159.

Blacher, J. (1984). Sequential stages of parental adjustment to the birth of a child with handicaps: Fact or artifact? *Mental Retardation, 22,* 55–63.

Bloom, B.S. (1964). *Stability and change in human characteristics.* New York: John Wiley & Sons.

Bloom, L. (1970a). *Language development: Form and function in emerging grammars.* Cambridge, MA: MIT Press.

Bloom, L. (1970b). Child language, adult model. Review of P. Menyuk, Sentences children use. *Comtemporary Psychology, 15,* 182–184.

Bloom, L. (1973). *One word at a time: The use of single-word utterances before syntax.* The Hague, Netherlands: Mouton.

Bloom, L., & Lahey, P. (1978). *Language development and language disorders.* New York: John Wiley & Sons.

Bloom, L., Lightbrown, P., & Hood, L. (1975). Structure and variation in child language. *Monographs of the Society for Research in Child Development, 40* (Serial No. 160).

Bluma, S.M., Shearer, M.S., Frohman, A.H., & Hillard, J.M. (1976). *Portage guide to early education.* Portage, WI: Cooperative Educational Service Agency 12.

Bobath, B., & Bobath, K. (1975). *Motor development in the different types of cerebral palsy.* London: Heinemann.

Boehm, A.E. (1971). *Boehm Test of Basic Concepts.* New York: Psychological Corporation.

Bogdan, R. (1980). What does it mean when a person says, "I am not retarded"? *Education and Training of the Mentally Retarded, 15,* 74–79.

Boggs, E.M. (1978). Who is putting whose head in the sand or in the clouds as the case may be? In A.P. Turnbull & H.R. Turnbull, III (Eds.), *Parents speak out: Growing with a handicapped child.* Columbus, OH: Charles E. Merrill.

Boles, G. (1959). Personality factors in mothers of cerebral palsied children. *Genetic Psychology Monographs, 59,* 195–218.

Borke, H. (1971). Interpersonal perception of young children: Egocentrism or empathy. *Developmental Psychology, 5,* 263–269.

Bourne, L.E., Jr., Dominowski, R.L., & Loftus, E.F. (1979). *Cognitive processes.* Englewood Cliffs, NJ: Prentice-Hall.

Bower, E., Bersamin, K., Fine, A., & Carlson, J. (1974). *Learning to play, playing to learn.* New York: Human Sciences Press.

Bowerman, M. (1973). *Early syntactic development: A cross-linguistic study with special reference to Finnish.* London: Cambridge University Press.

Bowlby, J. (1969). *Attachment.* New York: Basic Books.

Brackbill, Y. (1979). Obstetrical medication and infant behavior. In J.O. Osofsky (Ed.), *Handbook of infant development.* New York: John Wiley & Sons.

Brandt, R.M. (1972). *Studying behavior in natural settings.* New York: Holt, Rinehart & Winston.

Bray, N.M., Coleman, J.M., & Bracken, M.B. (1981). Critical events in parenting handicapped children. *Journal of the Division for Early Childhood, 3,* 26–33.

Brazelton, T.B. (1969). *Infants and mothers: Difference in development.* New York: Delacorte Press.

Brazelton, T.B. (1973). *Neonatal behavioral assessment scale*. Philadelphia: J.B. Lippincott.

Brazelton, T.B. (1984). *Brazelton Neonatal Behavioral Assessment Scale* (2nd ed.). Philadelphia: Spastic International Medical Publications, J.B. Lippincott.

Brazelton, T.B., Koslowski, B., & Main, M. (1974). The origins of reciprocity: The early mother-infant interaction. In M. Lewis & L.A. Rosenblum (Eds.), *The effect of the infant on its caregiver*. New York: John Wiley & Sons.

Bricker, D.D. (1978). A rationale for the integration of handicapped and nonhandicapped preschool children. In M.J. Guralnick (Ed.), *Early intervention and the integration of handicapped and nonhandicapped children*. Baltimore: University Park Press.

Bricker, D.D. (1986). *Early education of at-risk and handicapped infants, toddlers, and preschool children*. Glenview, IL: Scott, Foresman.

Bricker, D.D. (1988). Commentary: The future of early childhood/special education. *Journal of the Division for Early Childhood, 12,* 276–278.

Bricker, D.D., & Bricker, W.A. (1971). Toddler research and intervention project report: Year I. *IMRID Behavior Science Monograph* (No. 20). Nashville, TN: Institute on Mental Retardation and Intellectual Development, George Peabody College.

Bricker, D.D., & Bricker, W.A. (1972). Toddler research and intervention project report: Year II. *IMRID Behavior Science Monograph* (No. 21). Nashville, TN: Institute on Mental Retardation and Intellectual Development, George Peabody College.

Bricker, D.D., & Bricker, W.A. (1973). Infant, toddler and preschool research and intervention project report: Year III. *IMRID Behavior Science Monograph* (No. 23). Nashville, TN: Institute on Mental Retardation and Intellectual Development, George Peabody College.

Bricker, D.D., & Dennison, L. (1978). Training prerequisites to verbal behavior. In M.E. Snell (Ed.), *Systematic instruction of the moderately and severely handicapped*. Columbus, OH: Charles E. Merrill.

Bricker, D.D., Dennison, L., & Bricker, W.A. (1976). A language intervention program for developmentally young children. *University of Miami, MCCD Monograph* (Series No. 1).

Bricker, D.D., & Slentz, K. (1989). Personnel preparation: Handicapped infants. In M.C. Wang, H.J. Walberg, & M.C. Reynolds (Eds.), *The handbook of special education research and practice* (Vols. 1–3). Oxford: Pergamon Press.

Bricker, W.A., & Bricker, D.D. (1974). An early language training strategy. In R.L. Schiefelbusch & L.L. Lloyd (Eds.), *Language perspectives: Acquisition, retardation, and intervention*. Baltimore: University Park Press.

Bricker, W.A., & Bricker, D.D. (1976). The infant, toddler, and preschool research and intervention project. In T.D. Tjossem (Ed.), *Intervention strategies with high risk infants and young children*. Baltimore: University Park Press.

Brierley, J.K. (1987). *Give me a child until he is seven: Brain studies in early childhood education*. New York: Falmer Press.

Brigance, A.H. (1978). *Brigance Diagnostic Inventory of Early Development*. Worchester, MA: Curriculum Associates.

Bromwich, R.H. (1978). Working with parents and infants. (Appendices A and B, Parent Behavior Progression). Austin, TX: PRO-ED.

Bromwich, R.M., Fust, S., Khokha, E., & Walden, M. (1981). *Play Assessment Checklist for Infants Manual*. Unpublished manuscript, California State University, Northridge.

Bromwich, R.M., & Parmelee, A.H. (1979). An intervention program for pre-term infants. In T.M. Field (Ed.), *Infants born at risk: Behavior and development*. New York: Spectrum Publications.

Bronfenbrenner, U. (1977). Toward an experimental ecology of human development. *American Psychologist, 32,* 513–531.

Brooten, D. (1983). Issues for research on alternative patterns of care for low birthweight infants. *Images: The Journal of Nursing Scholarship, 15,* 80–83.

Brown, A.L., Campione, J.C., Bray, N.W., & Wilcox, B.L. (1973). Keeping track of changing variables: Effects of rehearsal training and rehearsal prevention in normal and retarded adolescents. *Journal of Experimental Psychology, 101,* 123–131.

Brown, D., Simmons, V., & Methuin, J. (1979). *The Oregon project for visually impaired and blind preschool children*. Medford, OR: Jackson County Education Service District.

Brown, R. (1973). *A first language: The early stages*. Cambridge, MA: Harvard University Press.

Brown, R., & Bellugi, U. (1964). The processes in the child's acquisition of syntax. *Harvard Educational Review, 34,* 133–151.

Brown, R., Cazden, C., & Bellugi, U. (1969). The child's grammar from one to three. In J.P. Hill (Ed.), *Minnesota Symposia on Child Psychology* (Vol. 2). Minneapolis: University of Minnesota Press.

Brown, R., & Fraser, C. (1963). The acquisition syntax. In C.N. Cofer & B. Musgrave (Eds.), *Verbal behavior and verbal learning: Problems and process*. New York: McGraw-Hill.

Brown, S.L., D'Eugenio, D.D., Drews, J.E., Haskin, B.S., Lynch, E.W., Moersch, M.S., & Rogers, S.J. (1981). *Preschool developmental profile*. Ann Arbor: University of Michigan Press.

Bruner, J.S. (1972). Nature and uses of immaturity. *American Psychologist, 27,* 687–708.

Bruner, J.S. (1975). The ontogenesis of speech acts. *Journal of Child Language, 2,* 1–19.

Bruner, J.S., Jolly, A., & Sylva, K. (Eds.). (1976). *Play: Its role in development and evolution*. New York: Basic Books.

Bryen, D. (1982). *Inquiries into child language*. Boston: Allyn & Bacon.

Buncic, J.R. (1980). Disorders of vision. In S. Gabel & M. Erickson (Eds.), *Child development and developmental disabilities*. Boston: Little, Brown.

Buscaglia, L. (1975). *The disabled and their parents: A counseling challenge*. Thorofare, NJ: Charles B. Slack.

Buss, A.H., & Plomin, R. (1975). *A temperamental theory of personality development*. New York: John Wiley & Sons.

Butler, N.R., & Alberman, E.D. (Eds.). (1969). *Perinatal problems: The second report of the 1958 British Perinatal Morality Study*. Edinburg, Scotland: Livingston.

Butterfield, E.C., Wambold, C., & Belmont, J.M. (1973). On the theory and practice of improving short-term memory. *American Journal of Mental Deficiency, 77,* 654–669.

Bzoch, K., & League, R. (1971). *Receptive-Expressive Emergent Language Scales*. Baltimore: University Park Press.

Caldwell, B.M., & Bradley, R.H. (1978). *Home Observation and Measurement of the Environment Inventory*. Little Rock: University of Arkansas, Center for Child Development and Education.

Calhoun, J.B. (1962). Population density of social pathology. *Scientific American 206,* 139–148.

Cameron, J.R. (1977). Parental treatment, children's temperament, and the risk of childhood behavioral problems: Relationships between parental characteristics and changes in children's temperament over time. *American Journal of Orthopsychiatry, 47,* 568–576.

Cameron, J.R. (1978). Parental treatment, children's temperament, and the risk of childhood behavioral problems. *American Journal of Orthopsychiatry, 48,* 140–147.

Campbell, P.H., Green, K.M., & Carlson, L.M. (1977). Approximating the norm through environmental and child-centered prosthetics and adaptive equipment. In E. Sontag (Ed.), *Educational programming for the severely and profoundly handicapped*. Washington, DC: Council for Exceptional Children, Division on Mental Retardation.

Cansler, D.P., Martin, G.H., & Valand, M.C. (1975). *Working with families*. Winston-Salem, NC: Kaplan Press.

Capobianco, R.J., & Cole, D.A. (1960). Social behavior of mentally retarded children. *American Journal of Mental Deficiency, 64,* 638–651.

Carey, W.B. (1970). A simplified method of measuring infant temperament. *Journal of Pediatrics, 77,* 188–194.

Carey, W.B., & McDevitt, S.C. (1978). Stability and change in individual temperament diagnoses from infancy to early childhood. *Journal of the American Academy of Child Psychiatry, 17,* 331–337.

Carlson, N.R. (1986). *Physiology of behavior* (3rd ed.). Boston: Allyn & Bacon.

Carter, C.H. (Ed.). (1975). *Medical aspects of mental retardation* (2nd ed.). Springfield, IL: Charles C Thomas.

Carter, S. (1975). Assessing prognosis for a child's first febrile seizure. *National Spokesman, 5,* 5–11.

Cartwright, C.A. (1981). Effective programs for parents of young handicapped children. *Topics in Early Childhood Special Education, 1,* 1–9.

Cassarett, L.J., & Doull, J. (Eds.). (1975). *Toxicology, the basic science of poisons*. New York: Macmillan.

Cassidy, J. (1986, December). *The exploratory behavior of securely and insecurely attached infants*. Paper presented at the Second Annual Training Institute, National Center for Clinical Infant Programs, Washington, DC.

Casto, G., & Mastropieri, M.A. (1986). The efficacy of early intervention programs: A meta-analysis. *Exceptional Children, 52,* 417–424.

Cattell, P. (1960). *The measurement of intelligence of infants and young children*. New York: Psychological Corporation.

Chasnoff, I.J., Burns, W.J., Schnoll, S.H., & Burns, K.A. (1985). Cocaine use in pregnancy. *New England Journal of Medicine, 313,* 666–669.

Children's Defense Fund. (1974). *Children out of school in America*. Washington, DC: Author.

Chomsky, N. (1959). Review of *Verbal behavior* by B.F. Skinner. *Language, 35,* 26–58.

Chomsky, N. (1965). *Aspects of the theory of syntax*. Cambridge, MA: The MIT Press.

Cicchetti, D.E. (1984). The emergence of developmental psychopathology. *Child Development, 55,* 1–7.

Cicchetti, D.E., & Schneider-Rosen, K. (1984). Theoretical and empirical considerations in the investigation of the relationship between affect and cognition. In C. Izard, J. Kagan, & R. Zajonc (Eds.), *Emotions, cognitions and behavior.* New York: Cambridge University Press.

Cleveland, D.W., & Miller, N. (1977). Attitudes and life commitments of older siblings of mentally retarded adults: An exploratory study. *Mental Retardation, 15,* 38–41.

Cohen, G., & Martin, M. (1975). Hemisphere differences in an auditory stroop test. *Perception and Psychophysics, 17,* 79–83.

Cohen, L.B. (1981). Examination of habituation as a measure of aberrant infant development. In S. Friedman & M. Sigman (Eds.), *Preterm birth and psychological development.* New York: Academic Press.

Cohen, S., & Syme, S.L. (Eds.). (1985). *Social support and health.* Orlando, FL: Academic Press.

Cole, M., & Bruner, J. (1971). Cultural differences and influences about psychological processes. *American Psychologist, 26,* 867–876.

Cooper, L.Z., & Krugman, S. (1966). Diagnosis and management: Congenital rubella. *Pediatrics, 37,* 335.

Copeland, M.E., & Kimmel, J.R. (1989). *Evaluation and management of infants and young children with developmental disabilities.* Baltimore: Paul H. Brookes Publishing Co.

Cornwell, J.C., & Snyder, K.D. (in press). Community networking in partnership with families. *Rural Special Education Quarterly.*

Cratty, B.J. (1986). *Perceptual and motor development in infants and children* (3rd ed.). Englewood Cliffs, NJ: Prentice-Hall.

Crowley, M., Keane, K., & C. Needham (1982, February). Fathers: The forgotten parents. *American Annals of the Deaf,* pp. 38–40.

Cummings, S.T. (1976). The impact of the child's deficiency on the father: A study of fathers of mentally retarded and chronically ill children. *American Journal of Orthopsychiatry, 46,* 246–255.

Cummings, S.T., Bayley, H., & Rie, H. (1966). Effects of the child's deficiency on the mother: A study of mothers of mentally retarded, chronically ill, and neurotic children. *American Journal of Orthopsychiatry, 36,* 595–608.

Dale, P.S. (1976). *Language development: Structure and function.* New York: Holt, Rinehart & Winston.

Dansky, J.L. (1980). Cognitive consequences of sociodramatic play and exploration training for economically disadvantaged preschoolers. *Journal of Child Psychology and Psychiatry and Allied Disciplines, 21,* 47–58.

Davis, C.J. (1980). *Perkins-Binet Tests of Intelligence for the Blind.* Watertown, MA: Perkins School for the Blind.

Davis, H.P., & Squire, L.R. (1984). Protein synthesis and memory: A review. *Psychological Bulletin, 96*(3), 518–559.

Dawson, G. (1983). Lateralization of brain function in autism. *Journal of Autism and Developmental Disorders, 13,* 369–386.

Delaney, S.W., Meyer, D.J., & Ward, M.J. (1977). *Fathers and infants class: A model for facilitating attachment between fathers and their infants.* Seattle: University of Washington Experimental Education Unit, Child Development and Mental Retardation Center.

Dennis, W., & Najarian, P. (1957). Infant development under environmental handicap. *Psychological Monographs, 71* (No. 7).

Department of Health, Education, and Welfare. (1978). *Mainstreaming children with handicaps* (Series No. OHDS 78-311110). Washington, DC: Office of Human Development Services.

Devoney, C., Guralnick, M.J., & Rubin, H. (1974). Integrating handicapped and nonhandicapped preschool children: Effects on social play. *Childhood Education, 50,* 360–364.

DeWeerd, J. (1980). Handicapped children's early education program: A retrospective. In S. Friedman (Ed.), *Handicapped children's early education program.* Washington, DC: Bureau for the Education of the Handicapped.

Dexter, L.A. (1964). On the politics and sociology of stupidity in our society. In H.S. Becker (Ed.), *The other side: Perspectives on deviance.* New York: Free Press.

Diamond, K.E., Spiegel-McGill, P., & Hanrahan, P. (1988). Planning for school transition: An ecological developmental approach. *Journal of the Division for Early Childhood, 12,* 245–252.

Doke, L., & Risley, T.R. (1972). The organization of daycare environments: Required versus optional activities. *Journal of Applied Behavior Analysis, 5,* 405–420.

Doll, E.A. (1964). *The Vineland Scale of Social Maturity.* Circle Pines, MN: American Guidance Service.

Drage, J.S. et al. (1966). Five-minute Apgar scores and 4-year psychological performance. *Developmental Medicine and Child Neurology, 8,* 141.

Drillen, C.M. (1964). *The growth and development of*

the prematurely born infant. Baltimore: Williams & Wilkins.

Duckworth, E. (1979). Either we're too early and they can't learn it or we're too late and they know it already: The dilemma of "applying Piaget." *Harvard Educational Review, 49,* 297–312.

Dunn, L.M. (1959). *Peabody Picture Vocabulary Test.* Circle Pines, MN: American Guidance Service.

Dunn, L.M. (1968). Special education for the mildly retarded—Is much of it justifiable? *Exceptional Children, 35,* 5–22.

Dunst, C.J. (1981). *Infant learning: A cognitive-linguistic intervention strategy.* Hingham, MA: Teaching Resources.

Dunst, C.J. (1986). Overview of the efficacy of early intervention programs. In L. Bickman & D.L. Weatherford (Eds.). *Evaluating early intervention programs for severely handicapped children and their families.* Austin, TX: PRO-ED.

Dunst, C.J., Cooper, C.S., Weeldreyer, J.C., Snyder, K.D., & Chase, J.H. (1988). Family Needs Scale. In C.J. Dunst, C. Trivette, & A. Deal (Eds.), *Enabling and empowering families: Principles and guidelines.* Cambridge, MA: Brookline Books.

Dunst, C.J., Jenkins, V., & Trivette, C.M. (1984). Family Support Scale: Reliability and validity. *Journal of Individual, Family and Community Wellness, 1,* 45–52.

Dunst, C.J., & Trivette, C.M. (1985). Measures of social support, parent stress, well-being and coping and other family level behavior. *Monograph of the Technical Assistance Development System* (No. 1). Chapel Hill: University of North Carolina.

Dunst, C.J., Trivette, C.M., & Deal, A.G. (1988). *Enabling and empowering families: Principles and guidelines for practice.* Cambridge, MA: Brookline Books.

Dunst, C.J., Trivette, C.M., & Jenkins, V. (1988). Family Support Scale. In C.J. Dunst, C.M. Trivette, & A. Deal (Eds.), *Enabling and empowering families: Principles and guidelines for practice.* Cambridge, MA: Brookline Books.

Edmonds, M. (1976). New directions in theories of language acquisition. *Harvard Educational Review, 46,* 29–40.

Egelston, C., Maddox, M., & Tazioli, P. (1985). *Interagency transition for young handicapped children: Problems and solutions.* Unpublished manuscript, University of Washington, Seattle.

Epstein, J.L. (1986). Friendship selection: Development. E.C. Mueller & C. Cooper (Eds.), *Process and out-

come in peer relationships.* New York: Academic Press.

Erickson, E.H. (1963). *Childhood and society* (2nd ed.). New York: Norton.

Erickson, M., Sroufe, L.A., & Egeland, B. (1985). The relationship between quality of attachment and behavior problems in preschool in a high-risk sample. In I. Bretherton & E. Waters (Eds.), Growing points of attachment theory and research. *Monographs of the Society for Research in Child Development, 50*(1–2, Serial No. 209), 147–166.

Erickson, M.P. (1974, November–December). Talking with fathers of young children with Down's syndrome. *Children Today,* pp. 22–25.

Erlenmeyer-Kimling, L. (1968). Studies on the offspring of two schizophrenic parents. In D. Rosenthal & S. Kety (Eds.), *The transmission of schizophrenia.* Elmsford, NY: Pergamon Press.

Escalona, S.K., & Corman, H.H. (1969). *Albert Einstein Scales of Sensorimotor Development.* New York: Albert Einstein College of Medicine, Department of Psychiatry.

Evans, E.D. (1975). *Contemporary influences in early childhood education* (2nd ed.). New York: Holt, Rinehart & Winston.

Farber, B. (1963). Interaction with retarded siblings and life goals of children. *Marriage and Family Living, 25,* 96–98.

Farber, B. (1968). *Mental retardation: Its social context and consequences.* Boston: Houghton Mifflin.

Featherstone, H. (1980). *A difference in the family.* New York: Basic Books.

Fein, D., Skoff, B., & Mirsky, A.F. (1981). Clinical correlates of brainstem dysfunction in autistic children. *Journal of Autism and Developmental Disorders, 11,* 303–316.

Feitelson, D., & Ross, G.S. (1973). The neglected factor—play. *Human Development, 16,* 202–223.

Ferguson, C. (1977). Baby talk as a simplified register. In C. Snow & C. Ferguson (Eds.), *Talking to children.* Cambridge: Cambridge University Press.

Fewell, R.R. (1986a). The measurement of family functioning. In L. Bickman & D.L. Weatherford (Eds.), *Evaluating early intervention programs for severely handicapped children and their families.* Austin, TX: PRO-ED.

Fewell, R.R. (1986b). *The Play Assessment Scale (experimental edition).* Seattle: University of Washington, Experimental Education Unit.

Fewell, R.R., & Kaminski, R. (1988). Play skills development and instruction for young children with handicaps. In S.L. Odom & M.B. Karnes (Eds.), *Early intervention for infants and children with handicaps* (pp. 145–158). Baltimore: Paul H. Brookes Publishing Co.

Fillmore, C. (1968). The case for case. In E. Bach & R.T. Harms (Eds.), *Universals in linguistic theory.* New York: Holt, Rinehart & Winston.

Finnie, N.R. (1975). *Handling the young cerebral palsied child at home* (2nd ed.). New York: E.P. Dutton.

Fiorentino, M. (1972). *Normal and abnormal development: The influence of primitive reflexes on motor development.* Springfield, IL: Charles C Thomas.

Fitzhardinge, P.M., & Ramsey, M. (1973). The improving outlook for the small prematurely born infant. *Developmental Medicine and Child Neurology, 16,* 709–728.

Flavell, J. (1977). *Cognitive development.* Englewood Cliffs, NJ: Prentice-Hall.

Folio, M., & Fewell, R. (1983). *Peabody Developmental Motor Scales.* Hingham, MA: Teaching Resources.

Folkman, S., & Lazarus, R.S. (1980). An analysis of coping in a middle-aged community sample. *Journal of Health and Social Behavior, 21,* 219–239.

Folkman, S., & Lazarus, R.S. (1985). If it changes it must be a process: Study of emotion and coping during three stages of a college examination. *Journal of Personality and Social Psychology, 48,* 150–170.

Folkman, S., Lazarus, R.S., Dunkel-Shetter, C., DeLorgis, A., & Gruen, R.J. (1986). The dynamics of a stressful encounter: Cognitive appraisal, coping and encounter outcomes. *Journal of Personality and Social Psychology, 50,* 992–1003.

Fowle, C.M. (1968). The effect of the severely mentally retarded child on his family. *American Journal of Mental Deficiency, 73,* 468–473.

Fowler, S.A. (1982). Transition from preschool to kindergarten for children with special needs. In K.E. Allen & E.M. Goetz (Eds.), *Early childhood education: Special problems, special solutions.* Rockville, MD: Aspen Publishers.

Fox, N. (1978). *Infant "at risk": The consequences of low birth weight on the physical and mental health of the child.* Princeton, NJ: Institute for the Study of Exceptional Children, Educational Testing Service.

Fraiberg, S. (1971). Intervention in infancy: A program for blind infants. *Journal of the American Academy of Child Psychiatry, 10,* 381–405.

Fraiberg, S. (1975). Intervention in infancy: A program for blind infants. In B.Z. Friedlander, G.M. Sterritt, & G.E. Kirk (Eds.), *Exceptional infant: Assessment and intervention* (Vol. 3). New York: Brunner/Mazel.

Fraiberg, S., & Adelson, E. (1973). Self representation in language and play: Observations of blind children. *Psychoanalytical Quarterly, 42,* 539.

Fraiberg, S., Smith, M., & Adelson, E. (1969). An educational program for blind infants. *Journal of Special Education, 3*(2), 121–139.

Frankenburg, W., & Dodds, J. (1969). *Denver Developmental Screening Test.* Denver, CO: University of Denver.

Frankenburg, W.K., Dodds, J., & Fandal, A.W. (1982). *Denver Developmental Screening Test—Revised.* Denver, CO: Denver Developmental Materials.

Fredericks, H.D., Baldwin, V.L., & Grove, D. (1974). A home-based parent training model. In J. Griggs (Ed.), *Training parents to teach: Four models.* Chapel Hill, NC: Technical Assistance Development System (EC 071447).

Friedrich, W.N., Greenberg, M.T., & Crnic, K.A. (1983). A short-form of the questionnaire on resources and stress. *American Journal of Mental Deficiency, 88,* 41–48.

Freud, S. (1915). *Instincts and their vicissitudes.* London: Hogarth Press.

Freud, S. (1926). *Inhibitions, symptoms, and anxiety.* London: Hogarth Press.

Fullard, W., McDevitt, S.C., & Carey, W.B. (1984). Assessing temperament in one- to three-year old children. *Journal of Pediatric Psychology, 9,* 205–217.

Furey, E.M. (1982). The effects of alcohol on the fetus. *Exceptional Children, 49,* 30–34.

Gallagher, G., Maddox, M., & Edgar, E. (1984). *The Early Childhood Interagency Transition Model.* Bellevue, WA: Edmark.

Gallagher, J.J., Cross, A., & Scharfman, W. (1981). Parental adaptation to a young handicapped child: The father's role. *Journal of the Division for Early Childhood, 3,* 3–14.

Gallagher, J.M., & Reid, D.K. (1981). *The learning theory of Piaget and Inhelder.* Monterey, CA: Brooks/Cole.

Gallagher, P.A., & Powell, T.H. (1989). Brothers and sisters: Meeting special needs. *Topics in Early Childhood Special Education, 8*(4), 24–37.

Garber, H. (1988). *The Milwaukee Project: Preventing mental retardation in children at risk.* Washington, DC: American Association on Mental Retardation.

Garnica, O. (1977). Some prosodic and paralinguistic features of speech to young children. In C. Snow & C. Ferguson (Eds.), *Talking to children*. Cambridge: Cambridge University Press.

Garvey, C. (1986). Peer relations and the growth of communication. In E.C. Meuller & C. Cooper (Eds.), *Process and outcome in peer relationships*. New York: Academic Press.

Gath, A. (1973). The school-age siblings of mongol children. *British Journal of Psychiatry, 123,* 161–167.

Gath, A. (1974). Sibling reactions to mental handicap: A comparison of the brothers and sisters of mongol children. *Journal of Child Psychology and Psychiatry, 15,* 187–198.

Gath, A. (1977). The impact of an abnormal child upon the parents. *British Journal of Psychiatry, 130,* 405–410.

Gazzaniga, M.S., & Blakemore, C. (Eds.). (1975). *Handbook of psychobiology*. New York: Academic Press.

Gazzaniga, M.S., & LeDoux, J.E. (1978). *The integrated mind*. New York: Plenum.

Gearheart, B.R. (1972). *Education of the exceptional child: History, present practices, and trends*. Scranton, PA: International Textbook Co.

Gersten, M., Coster, W., Schneider-Rosen, K., Carlson, V., & Cicchetti, D. (1987). The socioemotional bases of communicative functioning: Quality of attachment, language development and early maltreatment. In M. Lamb, A.L. Brown, & B. Rozoff (Eds.), *Advances in developmental psychology* (pp. 306–322). Hillsdale, NJ: Lawrence Erlbaum Associates.

Gesell, A. (1949). *Gesell developmental schedules*. New York: Psychological Corporation.

Gesell, A. (1954). The ontogenesis of infant behavior. In L. Carmichael (Ed.), *Manual of child psychology* (2nd ed.). New York: Wiley.

Gesell, A., & Amatruda, C. (1969). *Developmental diagnosis*. New York: Harper & Row.

Gianascol, A.J. (1973). Psychodynamic approaches to childhood schizophrenia: A review. In S.A. Szurek & I.N. Berlin (Eds.), *Clinical studies in childhood psychosis: 25 years in collaborative treatment and research*. New York: Brunner/Mazel.

Ginsberg, H., & Opper, S. (1979). *Piaget's theory of intellectual development* (2nd ed.). Englewood Cliffs, NJ: Prentice-Hall.

Glass, D.S., & Singer, J.E. (1972). *Urban stress: Experiments on noise and social stressors*. New York: Academic Press.

Gleason, J. (1973). Code switching in children's language. In T. Moore (Ed.), *Cognitive develop-ment and the acquisition of language*. New York: Academic Press.

Glover, M.E., Preminger, J.L., & Sanford, A.L. (1978). *The early learning accomplishment profile*. Winston-Salem, NC: Kaplan.

Gold, M.W. (1976). Task analysis of a complex assembly task by the retarded child. *Exceptional Children, 43,* 78–84.

Golden, M., & Birns, B. (1976). Social class and infant intelligence. In M. Lewis (Ed.), *Origins of intelligence*. New York: Plenum.

Goldfarb, W. (1943). The effects of early institutional care on adolescent personality. *Journal of Experimental Education, 12,* 106–129.

Goldstein, J., & Turnbull, A.P. (1982). Strategies to increase parent participation in IEP conferences. *Exceptional Children, 48,* 360–361.

Goodman, K. (1986). *What's whole in whole language?* Portsmouth, NH: Heinemann.

Goodwin, W., & Driscoll, L. (1980). *Measurement and evaluation in early childhood education*. San Francisco: Jossey-Bass.

Gopnik, A., & Meltzoff, A. (1987). Early semantic developments and their relationship to object permanence, means-ends understanding, and categorization. In K.E. Nelson & A. Van Kleek (Eds.), *Children's language, Vol. 6* (pp. 191–213). Hillsdale, NJ: Lawrence Erlbaum Associates.

Gordon, J.E., & Haywood, H.C. (1969). Input deficit in cultural-familial retardates: Effects of stimulus enrichment. *American Journal of Mental Deficiency, 73,* 604–610.

Gottlieb, G. (1965). Prenatal auditory sensitivity in chickens and ducks. *Science, 147,* 1596–1598.

Gottlieb, G. (1983). The psychobiological approach to developmental issues. In P.H. Mussen (Ed.), *Handbook of child psychology: Vol. 2. Infancy and developmental psychobiology* (4th ed., pp. 1–27). New York: John Wiley & Sons.

Gottlieb, J., & Leyser, Y. (1981). Friendship between mentally retarded and nonretarded children. In S. Asher & J. Gottman (Eds.), *The development of children's friendships*. Cambridge, England: Cambridge University Press.

Grady, M.P. (1984). *Teaching and brain research*. New York: Longman.

Graham, M.D. (1967). *Multiply-impaired blind children: A national problem*. New York: American Foundation for the Blind.

Green, H.B. (1974). Infants of alcoholic mothers. *American Journal of Obstetrics and Gynecology, 118,* 713–716.

Gregg, N.M. (1941). Congenital cataract following German measles in the mother. *Transactions of the Opthalmological Society of Australia, 3,* 35.

Grossman, F.K. (1972). *Brothers and sisters of retarded children: An exploratory study.* Syracuse, NY: Syracuse University Press.

Grossman, H.J. (Ed.). (1973). *Manual on terminology and classification in mental retardation.* Washington, DC: American Association on Mental Deficiency.

Grossman, H.J. (1983). *Classification in mental retardation.* Washington, DC: American Association on Mental Deficiency.

Gruenwald, P. (1965). Some aspects of fetal distress. In M. Dawkins & W.G. MacGregor (Eds.), *Gestational age, size, and maturity.* London: Spastics Society.

Guess, D., Helmstetter, E., Turnbull, H.R., & Knowlton, S. (1987). *Use of aversive procedures with persons who are disabled: An historical review and critical analysis.* Seattle: The Association for Persons with Severe Handicaps.

Guralnick, M.J. (1976). The value of integrating handicapped and nonhandicapped preschool children. *American Journal of Orthopsychiatry, 42,* 236–245.

Guralnick, M.J. (Ed.). (1978a). *Early intervention and the integration of handicapped and nonhandicapped children.* Baltimore: University Park Press.

Guralnick, M.J. (1978b). Integrated preschools as education and therapeutic environments: Concept, design and analysis. In M.J. Guralnick (Ed.), *Early intervention and the integration of handicapped and nonhandicapped children.* Baltimore: University Park Press.

Guralnick, M.J. (1980). Social interactions among preschool children. *Exceptional Children, 46,* 248–253.

Guralnick, M.J. (1981). Peer influences on the development of communicative competence. In P.S. Strain (Ed.), *The utilization of classroom peers as behavior change agents.* New York: Plenum.

Guthrie, R.D. et al. (1977). The newborn. In D.W. Smith (Ed.), *Introduction to clinical pediatrics.* Philadelphia: W.B. Saunders.

Haith, M.M. (1980). *Rules that babies look by.* Hillsdale, NJ: Lawrence Erlbaum Associates.

Hallahan, D.P., & Kauffman, J.M. (1982). *Exceptional children: Introduction to special education* (2nd ed.). Englewood Cliffs, NJ: Prentice-Hall.

Hamblin-Wilson, C., & Thurman, S.K. (in press). Transition from early intervention to kindergarten: Parental satisfaction and involvement. *Journal of Early Intervention.*

Hanline, M.F. (1988). Making the transition to preschool: Identification of parent needs. *Journal of the Division for Early Childhood, 12,* 98–107.

Hanline, M.F., & Knowlton, A. (1988). A collaborative model for providing support to parents during their child's transition from infant intervention to preschool special education public school programs. *Journal of the Division for Early Childhood, 12,* 116–125.

Hannafin, M.J. (1986). Special education assessment. In D.L. Wodrich & J.E. Joy (Eds.), *Multidisciplinary assessment of children with learning disabilities and mental retardation* (pp. 77–108). Baltimore: Paul H. Brookes Publishing Co.

Hans, S.L., Marcus, J., Jeremy, R.J., & Auerbach, J.G. (1984). Neurobehavioral development of children exposed in utero to opioid drugs. In J. Yanai (Ed.), *Neurobehavioral teratology.* Amsterdam: Elsevier.

Hansen, H. (1978). Decline of Down's syndrome after abortion reform in New York State. *American Journal of Mental Deficiency, 83,* 183–185.

Harbin, G. (1977). Educational assessment. In L. Cross & K. Goin (Eds.), *Identify handicapped children: A guide to casefinding, screening, diagnosis, assessment, and evaluation.* New York: Walker & Co.

Harms, T., & Clifford, R.M. (1980). *Early Childhood Environment Rating Scale.* New York: Teacher's College Press.

Harms, T., & Clifford, R.M. (1983). Assessing preschool environments with the Early Childhood Environment Rating Scales. *Studies in Educational Evaluation, 8,* 261–269.

Harms, T., & Clifford, R.M. (in press). *The Family Day Care Rating Scale.* New York: Teacher's College Press.

Harms, T., Cryer, D., & Clifford, R.M. (in press). *Infant/Toddler Environment Rating Scale.* New York: Teacher's College Press.

Harris, S.R., Swanson, M.W., Andrews, M.S., Sells, C.J., Robinson, N.M., Bennett, F.C., & Chandler, L. (1984). Predictive validity of the "Movement Assessment of Infants." *Journal of Developmental and Behavioral Pediatrics, 5,* 336–342.

Hart, V. (1979). Crippling conditions. In M.S. Lilly (Ed.), *Children with exceptional needs.* New York: Holt, Rinehart & Winston.

Hartup, W.W. (1978). Peer interaction and the

processes of socialization. In M.J. Guralnick (Ed.), *Early intervention and the integration of handicapped and nonhandicapped children*. Baltimore: University Park Press.

Hartup, W.W. (1983). Peer relations. In P.H. Mussen & E.M. Hetherington (Eds.), *Carmichael's manual of child psychology* (Vol. 4, 4th ed.). New York: John Wiley & Sons.

Hayden, A., & Beck, G.R. (1982). The epidemiology of high-risk and handicapped infants. In C.T. Ramey & P.L. Trohanis (Eds.), *Finding and educating high-risk and handicapped infants*. Baltimore: University Park Press.

Hayden, A.H., & Dmitriev, V. (1975). The multidisciplinary preschool program for Down's syndrome children at the University of Washington Model Preschool Center. In B.Z. Friedlander, G.M. Sterritt, & G.E. Kirk (Eds.), *Exceptional infant: Assessment and intervention* (Vol. 3). New York: Brunner/Mazel.

Hayden, A.H., & Haring, N.G. (1976). Early intervention for high risk infants and young children: Programs for Down's syndrome children. In T.D. Tjossem (Ed.), *Intervention strategies for high risk infants and young children*. Baltimore: University Park Press.

Hayden, A.H., Morris, K., & Bailey, D. (1977). *Final report: Effectiveness of early intervention for handicapped children*. Washington, DC: Bureau of Education for the Handicapped.

Hayes, D. (1986). Audiological assessment. In D.L. Wodrich & J.E. Joy (Eds.), *Multidisciplinary assessment of children with learning disabilities and mental retardation* (pp. 109–131). Baltimore: Paul H. Brookes Publishing Co.

Hebb, D.O. (1949). *The organization of behavior*. New York: Wiley & Sons.

Heber, R. (1959). A manual on terminology and classification in mental retardation. *Monograph Supplement, American Journal of Mental Deficiency, 64*.

Heber, R.F. (1961). A manual on terminology and classification in mental retardation (rev. ed.). *American Journal of Mental Deficiency Monograph* (Suppl. 64).

Heber, R., & Garber, H. (1975). The Milwaukee Project: A study of the use of family intervention to prevent cultural-familial mental retardation. In G.M. Sterritt & G.E. Kirk (Eds.), *Exceptional infant: Assessment and intervention* (Vol. 3). New York: Brunner/Mazel.

Hedrick, D.L., Prather, E.M., & Tobin, A.R. (1975). *Sequenced inventory of communication development*. Seattle: University of Washington Press.

Held, R., & Hein, A. (1963). Movement-produced stimulation in the development of visually guided behavior. *Journal of Comparative and Physiological Psychology, 56*, 872–876.

Hellman, L.M., & Pritchard, J.A. (1971). *Williams obstetrics* (14th ed.). New York: Appleton-Century-Crofts.

Helsel, E., Helsel, B., Helsel, B., & Helsel, M. (1978). The Helsels' story of Robin. In A.P. Turnbull & H.R. Turnbull, III (Eds.), *Growing with a handicapped child*. Columbus, OH: Charles E. Merrill.

Heward, W.L., & Orlansky, M.D. (1980). *Exceptional children*. Columbus, OH: Charles E. Merrill.

Hickish, D. (1955). Thermal sensations of workers in light industry in Southern England. *Journal of Hygiene, 53*, 112–123.

Hill, R. (1949). *Families under stress*. New York: Harper & Row.

Hill, R. (1958). Generic features of families under stress. *Social Casework, 49*, 139–150.

Hill, R.M., Craig, J.P., Chaney, M.V., Tennyson, L.M., & McCulley, L.B. (1977). Utilization of over-the-counter drugs during pregnancy. *Clinical Obstetrics and Gynecology, 20*, 381–394.

Hirshhorn, K. (1973). Chromosomal abnormalities I: Autosomal defects. In V.A. McKusick & R. Claiborne (Eds.), *Medical genetics*. New York: Hospital Practice Publishing.

Hobbs, N. (Ed.). (1975). *Issues in the classification of children*. San Francisco: Jossey-Bass.

Holden, R.H. (1972). Predictions of mental retardation in infancy. *Mental Retardation, 10*, 28–30.

Holroyd, J. (1974). The questionnaire on resources and stress: An instrument to measure family responses to a handicapped family member. *Journal of Community Psychology, 2*, 92–94.

Holt, K.S. (1975). Home care of severely retarded children. In J.J. Dempsey (Ed.), *Community services for retarded children*. Baltimore: University Park Press.

Homer, A.L., & Peterson, L. (1980). Differential reinforcement of other behavior: A preferred response elimination procedure. *Behavior Therapy, 11*, 449–471.

Howes, C. (1980). Peer Play Scale as an index of complexity of peer interaction. *Developmental Psychology, 16*(4), 371–372.

Hresko, W., Reid, K., & Hammill, D. (1984). *The Test of Early Reading Ability*. Austin, TX: PRO-ED.

Huggett, F.E. (1986). *Teachers.* London: Weidenfeld & Nicholson.

Hulme, I., & Lunzer, E.A. (1966). Play, language and reasoning in subnormal children. *Journal of Child Psychology and Psychiatry, 7,* 107.

Hunt, J. McV. (1961). *Intelligence and experience.* New York: Ronald Press.

Hunt, J. McV. (1964). The psychological basis for using preschool as an antidote for cultural deprivation. *Merrill-Palmer Quarterly, 10,* 209–248.

Hunt, J. V. (1976). Environmental risk in fetal and neonatal life. In M. Lewis (Ed.), *Origins of intelligence.* New York: Plenum.

Hunt, J.V., Tooley, W.H., & Harvin, D. (1982). Learning disabilities in children of birth weight under 1501 grams. *Seminar in Perinatology, 6,* 294–304.

Hutt, M.L., & Gibby, R.G. (1976). *The mentally retarded child: Development, education and treatment* (3rd ed.). Boston: Allyn & Bacon.

Hynd, G.W., & Willis, W.G. (1987). *Pediatric neuropsychology.* New York: Grune & Stratton.

Ilg, F.L., & Ames, L.B. (1965). *School readiness.* New York: Harper & Row.

Ingram, D. (1976). Current issues in child phonology. In D. Morehead & A. Morehead (Eds.), *Normal and deficient child language.* Baltimore: University Park Press.

Inhelder, B. (1968). *The diagnosis of reasoning in the mentally retarded.* New York: Day.

Ireland, W.W. (1900). *The mental affections of children: Idiocy, imbecility, and insanity.* Philadelphia: Balkiston.

Irwin, D.M., & Bushnell, M. (1980). *Observational strategies for child study.* New York: Holt, Rinehart & Winston.

Irwin, J.V., & Wong, S.P. (1974). Compensation for maturity in long range intervention studies. *Acta Symbolica, 5,* 47–66.

Ispa, J., & Matz, R.D. (1978). Integrating handicapped preschool children within a cognitively oriented program. In M.J. Guralnick (Ed.), *Early intervention and the integration of handicapped and nonhandicapped children.* Baltimore: University Park Press.

Jacobson, J.L., Tianen, R.L., Willie, D.E., & Aytch, D.M. (1986). Infant-mother attachment and early peer relations: The assessment of behavior in an interactive context. In E.C. Mueller & C. Cooper (Eds.), *Process and outcome in peer relationships.* New York: Academic Press.

Jakobson, R. (1968). *Child language, aphasia and phonological universals.* The Hague: Mouton.

Jervis, G. A. (1952). Medical aspects of mental deficiency. *American Journal of Mental Deficiency, 57,* 175–188.

John, E.R. (1976). A model of consciousness. In G.E. Schwartz & D. Shapiro (Eds.), *Consciousness and self-regulation: Advances in research* (Vol. 1). New York: Plenum.

Johnson, C.A., & Katz, R.C. (1973). Using parents as change agents for their children: A review. *Journal of Child Psychiatry and Psychology, 14,* 181–200.

Johnson, D.J., & Myklebust, H.R. (1967). *Learning disabilities: Educational principles and practices.* New York: Grune & Stratton.

Johnson, H.C. (1980). *Human behavior and the social environment: A new perspective. Behavior, psychopathology and the brain* (Vol. 1). New York: Curriculum Concepts.

Johnson, S.W., & Morasky, R.L. (1980). *Learning disabilities* (2nd ed.). Boston: Allyn & Bacon.

Johnson-Martin, N.M., Jens, K.G., & Attermeier, S.A. (1986). *The Carolina curriculum for handicapped infants and infants at risk.* Baltimore: Paul H. Brookes Publishing Co.

Johnston, J.R., & Schery, T.K. (1976). The use of grammatical morphemes by children with communication disorders. In D.M. Morehead & A.E. Morehead (Eds.), *Normal and deficient child language.* Baltimore: University Park Press.

Johnston, R.B., & Magrab, P.R. (1976). *Developmental disorders: Assessment, treatment, education.* Baltimore: University Park Press.

Jones, K.L. (1988). *Smith's recognizable patterns of human malformation* (4th ed.). Philadelphia: W.B. Saunders.

Jones, K.L., & Smith, D.W. (1974). Recognition of fetal alcohol syndrome in early infancy. *Lancet, 2,* 999–1001.

Jones, K.L., Smith, D.W., Ulleland, C.N., & Stressguth, A.P. (1973). Patterns of malformation in offspring of chronic alcoholic mothers. *Lancet, 1,* 1267–1271.

Kagan, J., Rosman, B.L., Day, D., & Phillips, W. (1964). Information processing in the child. *Psychological Monographs, 78* (1, Whole No. 578).

Kaiser, A.P., & Fox, J.J. (1986). Behavioral parent training research: Contributions to an ecological analysis of families of handicapped children. In J.J. Gallagher & P.M. Vietze (Eds.), *Families of handicapped persons: Research, programs, and policy issues* (pp. 219–235). Baltimore: Paul H. Brookes Publishing Co.

Kamii, C. (1972). An application of Piaget's theory to the conceptualization of preschool curriculum. In R.K. Parker (Ed.), *The preschool in action*. Boston: Allyn & Bacon.

Kanner, L. (1943). Autistic disturbances of affective contact. *Nervous Child, 2,* 217–250.

Kaplan, E., & Kaplan, G. (1971). The prelinguistic child. In J. Elist (Ed.), *Human development and cognitive processes*. New York: Holt, Rinehart & Winston.

Kaplan, F. (1969). Siblings of the retarded. In S.B. Sarason & J. Doris (Eds.), *Psychological problems in mental deficiency*. New York: Harper & Row.

Kaufman, A.S., & Kaufman, N.L. (1983). *Kaufman Assessment Battery for Children*. Circle Pines, MN: American Guidance Service.

Kazdin, A.E. (1975). *Behavior modification in applied settings*. Homewood, IL: Dorsey Press.

Kazdin, A.E. (1977). Assessing the clinical or applied importance of behavior change through social validation. *Behavior Modification, 1,* 427–451.

Kearsley, R.B. (1979). Iatrogenic retardation: A syndrome of learned incompetence. In R.B. Kearsley & I.E. Sigel (Eds.), *Infants at risk: Assessment of cognitive functioning*. Hillsdale, NJ: Lawrence Erlbaum Associates.

Keogh, B., & Becker, L.D. (1973). Early detection of learning problems: Questions, cautions, and guidelines. *Exceptional Children, 40,* 5–11.

Keogh, B., & Kopp, C. (1978). From assessment to intervention-an elusive bridge. In F. Minifie & L. Lloyd (Eds.), *Communication and cognitive abilities—early behavioral assessment*. Baltimore: University Park Press.

Kieth, T.Z. (1985). Questioning the K-ABC: What does it measure? *School Psychology Review, 14,* 9–20.

Kirk, S.A., & Gallagher, J.J. (1983). *Educating exceptional children* (4th ed.). Boston: Houghton Mifflin.

Kirk, S.A., McCarthy, J.J., & Kirk, W.D. (1968). *Examiner's manual: Illinois Test of Psycholinguistic Abilities* (rev. ed.). Urbana: University of Illinois Press.

Kitchen, W.H., Ford, G.W., Rickards, A.L., Lissenden, J.V., & Ryan, M.M. (1987). Children of birth weight < 1000 grams: Changing outcome between ages 2 and 5 years. *Pediatrics, 110,* 283–288.

Klapp, S.T., Marshburn, E.A., & Lester, P.T. (1983). Short-term memory does not involve the "working memory" of information processing: The demise of a common assumption. *Journal of Experimental Psychology, 112,* 240–264.

Klaus, R.A., & Gray, S.W. (1968). The early training project for disadvantaged children: A report after five years. *Monograph for the Society for Research in Child Development, 33*(Serial No. 120).

Knoblock, H., & Passamanick, B. (Eds.). (1974). *Gesell and Amatruda's developmental diagnosis* (3rd ed.). New York: Harper & Row.

Knoblock, H., Stevens, F., & Malone, A. (1980). *The Revised Gesell Developmental Schedules*. New York: Harper & Row.

Kodera, T.L., & Garwood, S.G. (1979). The acquisition of cognitive competence. In S.G. Garwood (Ed.), *Educating young handicapped children: A developmental approach*. Rockville, MD: Aspen Publishers.

Koelle, W.H., & Convey, J.J. (1982). The prediction of the achievement of deaf adolescents from self concept and locus of control measures. *American Annals of the Deaf, 127,* 769–778.

Kopp, C.B. (1983). Risk factors in development. In M.M. Haith & J. J. Campos (Eds.), *Infancy and development psychobiology,* P.H. Mussen (Ed.), *Handbook of child psychology* (4th ed., Vol. 2). New York: John Wiley & Sons.

Kovacs, D. (1972, April/May). The lonely search for help. *Exceptional Parent*.

Lachar, D. (1982). *Personality Inventory for Children (PIC): Revised format manual supplement*. Los Angeles: Western Psychological Services.

Lambert, N., Windmiller, M., Tharinger, D., & Cole, L. (1981). *AAMD Adaptive Behavior Scale, School Edition*. Washington, DC: American Association on Mental Deficiency.

Lansing, M.D., & Schopler, E. (1978). Individualized education: A public school model. In M. Rutter & E. Schopler (Eds.), *Autism: A reappraisal of concepts and treatments*. New York: Plenum.

Laosa, L. (1977). Nonbiased assessment of children's abilities: Historical antecedents and current issues. In T. Oakland (Ed.), *Psychological and educational assessment of minority children*. New York: Brunner/Mazel.

LaVigna, G.W. (1987). Non-aversive strategies for managing behavior problems. In D.J. Cohen & A.M. Donnellan (Eds.), *Handbook of autism and pervasive developmental disorder*. New York: John Wiley & Sons.

LaVigna, G.W., & Donnellan, A. (1986). *Alternatives to punishment: Solving behavior problems with non-aversive strategies*. New York: Irvington Publishers.

Lee, L.C. (1973, May). *Social encounters of infants: The beginning of popularity*. Paper presented at the biennial meeting of the International Society for the Study of Behavior Development, Ann Arbor, MI.

Leonard, L. (1987). Is specific language impairment a useful construct? In S. Rosenberg (Ed.), *Advances in applied psycholinguistics: Vol. 1. Disorders of first language development.* Cambridge, MA: Cambridge University Press.

Lerner, J., Mardell-Czudnowski, C., & Goldenberg, D. (1981). *Special education for the early childhood years.* Englewood Cliffs, NJ: Prentice-Hall.

Lessen, E.I., & Rose, T.L. (1980). State definitions of preschool handicapped populations. *Exceptional Children, 46,* 467–469.

Levenstein, P. (1972). But does it work in homes away from home? *Theory Into Practice, 11,* 157–162.

Levy, J. (1974). Psychobiological implications of bilateral asymmetry. In S.J. Dimond & J.G. Beaumont (Eds.), *Hemisphere function in the human brain.* New York: Halsted Press.

Levy, J., Trevarthen, C., & Sperry, R.W. (1972). Perception of bilateral chimeric figures following hemispheric deconnexion. *Brain, 95,* 61–78.

Lewis, M. (1976a). Infant intelligence tests: Their use and misuse. *Human Development, 16,* 108.

Lewis, M., & Brooks, J. (1978). Self-knowledge and emotional development. In M. Lewis & L.A. Rosenblum (Eds.), *The development of affect.* New York: Plenum.

Lewis, M., & Goldberg, S. (1969a). The acquisition and violation of an expectancy: An experimental paradigm. *Journal of Experimental Child Psychology, 7,* 70–80.

Lewis, M., & Goldberg, S. (1969b). Perceptual-cognitive development in infancy: A generalized expectancy model as a function of the mother-child interactions. *Merrill-Palmer Quarterly, 15,* 81–100.

Li, A.K.F. (1981). Play and the mentally retarded child. *Mental Retardation, 19*(3), 121–126.

Lilienfeld, A.M., & Pasamanick, B. (1956). The association of maternal age and fetal factors with the development of mental deficiency II. *American Journal of Mental Deficiency, 60,* 557–569.

Lindsay, P.H., & Norman, D.A. (1977). *Human information processing* (2nd ed.). New York: Academic Press.

Lindsley, O.R. (1964). Direct measurement and prosthesis of retarded behavior. *Journal of Education, 147,* 62–81.

Ling, D. (1984). *Early intervention for hearing impaired children: Total communication options.* New York: College-Hill Press.

Liversidge, E.B., & Grana, G.M. (1973, March). Hearing impaired child in the family: Parent's perspective. *The Volta Review, 75,* 128–133

Lorenz, K. (1957). Companionship in birdlife. In C.H. Schiller (Ed.), *Instinctive behavior.* New York: International Universities Press.

Lorenz, K. (1972). Psychology and phylogeny. In R. Martin (Ed. and Trans.), *Studies in animal and human behavior.* Cambridge, MA: Harvard University Press.

Losinno, A.K. (Ed.). (no date). *The P.E.E.R.S. program: An overview.* Philadelphia: Special People in the Northeast.

Lotman, H.A. (1980). *Effects of three contingency reinforcement climates on increasing on-task behavior in a classroom for trainable retarded.* Unpublished doctoral dissertation, Temple University, Philadelphia.

Lovaas, O.I., & Bucher, B.D. (1974). *Perspectives in behavior modification with deviant children.* Englewood Cliffs, NJ: Prentice-Hall.

Lovaas, O.I., Schaeffer, B., & Simmons, J.Q. (1965). Building social behavior in autistic children by use of electric shock. *Journal of Experimental Research in Personality, 1,* 99–109.

Love, H. (1973). *The mentally retarded child and his family.* Springfield, IL: Charles C Thomas.

Luria, A.R. (1963). Psychological studies of mental deficiency in the Soviet Union. In N.R. Ellis (Ed.), *Handbook of mental deficiency.* New York: McGraw-Hill.

MacMillan, D.L., Meyers, C.E., & Yoshida, R.K. (1978). Regular class teachers' perceptions of transition programs for EMR students and their impact on the students. *Psychology in the Schools, 15*(1), 99–103.

Mahler, M.S., Bergman, A., & Pine, F. (1975). *The psychological birth of the human infant.* New York: Basic Books.

Mahoney, G., Powell, A., & Finger, I. (1986). The Maternal Behavior Rating Scale. *Topics in Early Childhood Special Education, 6*(2), 44–56.

Main, M. (1983). Exploration, play, and cognitive functioning related to infant-mother attachment. *Infant Behavior and Development, 6,* 167–174.

Main, M., & Solomon, J. (1986). Discovery of an insecure disorganized/disoriented attachment pattern: Procedures, findings, and implications for the classification of behavior. In T.B. Brazelton & M. Yogman (Eds.), *Affective develop-*

ment in infancy (pp. 95–124). Norwood, NJ: Ablex.

Maratosos, M. (1973). Nonegocentric communication abilities in preschool children. *Child Development, 44,* 697–700.

Marcus, L.M., & Baker, A. (1986). Assessment of autistic children. In R.J. Simeonsson (Ed.), *Psychological and developmental assessment of special children.* Boston: Allyn & Bacon.

Mardell-Czudnowski, C., & Goldenberg, D. (1984). Revision and restandardization of a preschool screening test: DIAL becomes DIAL-R. *Journal of the Division of Early Childhood, 4,* 95–109.

McCall, R. (1971). New directions in psychological assessment of infants. *Proceedings of the Royal Society of Medicine, 64,* 465–467.

McCall, R.B., Hogarty, P.S., & Hurlburt, N. (1972). Transitions in infant sensorimotor development and the prediction of childhood I.Q. *American Psychologist, 27,* 728–748.

McCarthy, D. (1970). *Manual for the McCarthy Scales of Children's Abilities.* New York: Psychological Corporation.

McCarthy, D. (1972). *McCarthy Scales of Children's Abilities.* New York: Psychological Corporation.

McCollum, J., & Stayton, V. (1985). Infant/parent interaction: Studies and intervention guidelines based on the SIAI model. *Journal of the Division for Early Childhood, 9,* 125–135.

McCormick, L. (1987). Comparison of the effects of a microcomputer activity and toy play on social and communication behaviors of young children. *Journal of the Division for Early Childhood, 11,* 195–205.

McCubbin, H.I., McCubbin, M.A., Nevin, R.S., & Cauble, E. (1979). *Coping-Health Inventory for Parents.* St. Paul: University of Minnesota Family Social Science.

McCubbin, H.I., & Patterson, J.M. (1983). The family stress process: The double ABCX model of adjustment and adaptation. In H.I. McCubbin, M.B. Sussman, & J.M. Patterson (Eds.), *Social stress and the family: Advances and developments in family stress theory and research.* New York: Haworth Press.

McDonnell, A., & Hardman, M. (1988). A synthesis of "best practice" guidelines for early childhood services. *Journal of the Division for Early Childhood, 12,* 328–341.

McFie, J., & Robertson, J. (1973). Psychological test results of children with thalidomide deformities. *Developmental Medicine and Neurology, 15,* 719–727.

McNellis, K.L. (1987). In search of the attentional deficit. In S.J. Ceci (Ed.), *Handbook of cognitive, social and neuropsychological aspects of learning disabilities* (Vol. II). Hillsdale, NJ: Lawrence Erlbaum Associates.

McNulty, B., Smith, D.B., & Soper, E.W. (1983). *Effectiveness of early special education for handicapped children.* Denver: Colorado Department of Education.

Meadow, K.P. (1983). An instrument for assessment of social-emotional adjustment in hearing impaired preschoolers. *American Annals of the Deaf, 128,* 826–884.

Mellin, G.W., & Katzenstein, M. (1962). The saga of thalidomide. *New England Journal of Medicine, 267,* 1184–1193, 1238–1264.

Menyuk, P. (1964). Comparison of grammar of children with functionally deviant and normal speech. *Journal of Speech and Hearing Research, 7,* 109–121.

Menyuk, P., & Looney, P. (1972). A problem of language disorder: Length versus structure. *Journal of Speech and Hearing Research, 15,* 264–279.

Mercer, J.R. (1973). *Labeling the mentally retarded: Clinical and social systems perspectives on mental retardation.* Berkeley: University of California Press.

Miller, L.J. (1982). *Miller Assessment for Preschoolers.* Littleton, CO: Foundation for Knowledge in Development.

Miller, W., & Erwin, S. (1964). The development of grammar in child language. In U. Bellugi & R. Brown (Eds.), The acquisition of language. *Monographs of the Society for Research in Child Development, 29* (Serial No. 92).

Minuchin, S. (1974). *Families and family therapy.* Cambridge, MA: Harvard University Press.

Moerk, E.L. (1975). Verbal interactions between children and their mothers during preschool years. *Developmental Psychology, 11,* 788–794.

Mogford, K. (1977). The play of handicapped children. In B. Tizard & D. Harvey (Eds.), *Biology of play.* Philadelphia: J.B. Lippincott.

Monsell, S. (1984). Components of working memory underlying verbal skills: A "distributed capacities" view. In H. Bouma & D. Bouwhuis (Eds.), *International Symposium on Attention and Performance, X.* Hillsdale, NJ: Lawrence Erlbaum Associates.

Montagu, A. (1971). *The elephant man: A study in human dignity.* New York: Ballatine Books.

Moore, G.T. (1982). *Early Childhood Physical Environment Scales.* Milwaukee: Center for Architecture and Urban Planning Research.

Moore, J., & Fine, M.J. (1978). Regular and special class teachers' perception of normal and exceptional children and their attitudes towards mainstreaming. *Psychology in the Schools, 15,* 253–259.

Moores, D.F. (1982). *Educating the deaf: Psychology, principles and practices* (2nd ed.). Boston: Houghton Mifflin.

Moores, D., Weiss, K.L., & Goodwin, M.W. (1976). *Early education programs for hearing-impaired children* (Research Report No. 104). Minneapolis: University of Minnesota Research and Development Center in Education of Handicapped Children.

Moos, R.H. (1974). *Family Environmental Scale.* Palo Alto, CA: Consulting Psychologists Press.

Moos, R.H. (1976). *The human context: Environmental determinants of behavior.* New York: John Wiley & Sons.

Morehead, D., & Ingram, D. (1973). The development of base syntax in normal and linguistically deviant children. *Journal of Speech and Hearing Research, 16,* 330–352.

Morton, K. (1978). Identifying the enemy—A parent's complaint. In A.P. Turnbull & H.R. Turnbull (Eds.), *Parents speak out: Growing with a handicapped child.* Columbus, OH: Charles E. Merrill.

Msall, M.E., & Ichord, R. (1986). Developmental pediatric assessment. In D.L. Wodrich & J.E. Joy (Eds.), *Multidisciplinary assessment of children with learning disabilities and mental retardation* (pp. 195–226). Baltimore: Paul H. Brookes.

Mueller, E., & Lucas, T. (1975). A developmental analysis of peer interactions among toddlers. In M. Lewis & L. Rosenblum (Eds.), *Friendship and peer relations.* New York: John Wiley & Sons.

Mueller, E.C., & Cohen, D. (1986). Peer therapies and the little latency: A clinical perspective. In E.C. Mueller & C. Cooper (Eds.), *Process and outcome in peer relationships.* New York: Academic Press.

Mundy, P., Sigman, M., Sherman, T., & Ungerer, J. (1984, April). *Representational ability, nonverbal communication skills and early language development in autistic children.* Paper presented at the Fourth International Conference on Infant Studies, New York.

Musatti, T. (1986). Early peer relations: View of Piaget and Vygotsky. In E.C. Mueller & C. Cooper (Eds.), *Process and outcomes in peer relationships.* New York: Academic Press.

National Advisory Committee on the Handicapped. (1976). *The unfinished revolution: Education for the handicapped.* Washington, DC: U.S. Office of Education.

National Society for the Prevention of Blindness. (1966). *N.S.P.B. fact book: Estimated statistics on blindness and visual problems.* New York: Author.

Neisser, U. (1976). *Cognition and reality: Principles and implications of cognitive psychology.* San Francisco: W.H. Freeman.

Neisworth, J.T., & Bagnato, S.J. (1988). Assessment in early childhood special education: A typology of dependent measures. In S.L. Odom & M.B. Karnes (Eds.), *Early intervention for infants and children with handicaps: An empirical base* (pp. 23–49). Baltimore: Paul H. Brookes Publishing Co.

Nelson, K.E. (1987). Some observations from the perspective of the rare event cognitive comparison theory of language acquisition. In K.E. Nelson & A. Van Kleek (Eds.), *Children's language,* (Vol. 6, pp. 289–331). Hillsdale, NJ: Lawrence Erlbaum Associates.

Nelson, K.E., & Van Kleek, A. (1987). *Children's language* (Vol. 6). Hillsdale, NJ: Lawrence Erlbaum Associates.

Newborg, J., Stock, J.R., Wnek, L., Guidubaldi, J., & Svinicki, J. (1984). *Battelle Developmental Inventory.* Allen, TX: Teaching Resource.

Newcomer, B.L., & Morrison, T.L. (1974). Play therapy with institutionalized mentally retarded children. *American Journal of Mental Deficiency, 78,* 727–733.

Newland, T.E. (1971). *Manual: Blind Learning Aptitude Test.* Champaign: University of Illinois Press.

Nihara, K., Foster, R., Shellhaas, M., & Leland, H. (1969). *AAMD Adaptive Behavior Scale* Washington, DC: American Association on Mental Deficiency.

Nihara, K., Foster, R., Shellhaas, M., & Leland, H. (1974). *AAMD Adaptive Behavior Scale* (rev. ed.). Washington, DC: American Association on Mental Deficiency.

Norman-Murch, T., & Bashir, A. (1986). Speech-language assessment. In D.L. Wodrich & J.E. Joy (Eds.), *Multidisciplinary assessment of children with learning disabilities and mental retardation* (pp. 133–160). Baltimore: Paul H. Brookes Publishing Co.

O'Brien, J.S. (1971). How we detect mental retardation before birth. *Medical Times, 99,* 103–108.

O'Dell, S. (1974). Training parents in behavior

modification: A review. *Psychological Bulletin, 81,* 418–433.

Odom, S.L., Deklyen, M., & Jenkins, J.R. (1984). Integrating handicapped and nonhandicapped preschoolers: Developmental impact on the nonhandicapped children. *Exceptional Children, 51,* 41–49.

Odom, S.L., & McEvoy, M.A. (1988). Integration of young children with handicaps and normally developing children. In S.L. Odom & M.B. Karnes (Eds.), *Early intervention for infants and children with handicaps: An empirical base* (pp. 241–267). Baltimore: Paul H. Brookes Publishing Co.

Odom, S.L., & Warren, S.F. (1988). Early childhood special education in the year 2000. *Journal of the Division for Early Childhood, 12,* 263–273.

Olley, J.G. (1986). The TEACH curriculum for teaching social behavior to children with autism. In E. Schopler & G.B. Mesibov (Eds.), *Social behavior in autism* (pp. 351–374). New York: Plenum.

Olshansky, S. (1962, April). Chronic sorrow: A response to having a mentally defective child. *Social Casework,* 190–193.

Olshansky, S. (1970). Chronic sorrow: A response to having a mentally defective child. In R. Noland (Ed.), *Counseling parents of the mentally retarded.* Springfield, IL: Charles C Thomas.

Olson, D.R., Portner, J., & Lavee, Y. (1985). *Family Adaptation and Cohesion Evaluation Scale III.* St. Paul: University of Minnesota, Family Social Science.

Olson, S.L., Bates, J.E., & Bayles, K. (1984). Mother-infant interaction between affect and cognition in maltreated infants: Quality of attachment and the development of visual self-recognition. *Child Development, 55,* 648–658.

Ornitz, E.M., & Ritvo, E.R. (1977). The syndrome of autism: A critical review. In S. Chess & A. Thomas (Eds.), *Annual progress in psychiatry and child development.* New York: Brunner/Mazel.

Oro, A.S., & Dixon, S.D. (1987). Perinatal cocaine and methamphetamine exposure: Maternal and neonatal correlates. *Journal of Pediatrics, 111,* 571–578.

Ottenbacher, K., & Short, M.A. (1985). Sensory integrative dysfunction in children: A review of theory and treatment. In M.L. Wolraich (Ed.), *Advances in developmental and behavioral pediatrics* (Vol. 6, pp. 287–329). Greenwich, CT: JAI Press.

Page, E.B. (1975). Miracle in Milwaukee: Raising the I.Q. In B.Z. Friedlander, G.M. Sterritt, & G.E. Kirk (Eds.), *Exceptional infant: Assessment and intervention* (Vol. 3). New York: Brunner/Mazel.

Palmer, D.J. (1979). Regular classroom teachers' attributions and instructional prescriptions for handicapped and nonhandicapped pupils. *Journal of Special Education, 13,* 325–337.

Palmer, D.J. (1980). The effect of educable mental retardation descriptive information on regular classroom teachers' attributions and instructional descriptions. *Mental Retardation, 18,* 171–175.

Parmelee, A.H., Kopp, C.B., & Sigman, M. (1976). Selection of developmental assessment techniques for infants at risk. *Merrill-Palmer Quarterly, 22,* 177–199.

Parmelee, A.H., & Sigman, M.D. (1983). Perinatal brain development and behavior. In P.H. Mussen (Ed.), *Handbook of child psychology: Vol. 2. Infancy and development psychobiology* (4th ed.). New York: John Wiley & Sons.

Parmelee, A.H., Sigman, M., Kopp, C.B., & Haber, A. (1975). The concept of a cumulative risk score for infants. In N.R. Ellis (Ed.), *Aberrant development in infancy: Human and animal studies.* Hillsdale, NJ: Lawrence Erlbaum Associates.

Parmelee, A.H., Sigman, M., Kopp, C.B., & Haber, A. (1976). Diagnosis of the infant at risk for mental, motor, or sensory handicap. In T.D. Tjossem (Ed.), *Intervention strategies for high risk infants and young children.* Baltimore: University Park Press.

Parten, M.B. (1932). Social participation among preschool children. *Journal of Abnormal and Social Psychology, 27,* 243–269.

Patton, J.R., Payne, J.S., & Bierne-Smith, M. (1986). *Mental retardation* (2nd ed.). Columbus, OH: Charles E. Merrill.

Pavlov, I.P. (1927). *Conditioned reflexes.* London: Oxford University Press.

Peck, C.A., Apolloni, T., Cooke, T.P., & Raver, S. (1978). Teaching retarded preschoolers to imitate the free-play behavior of non-retarded classmates: Trained and generalized effects. *Journal of Special Education, 12,* 195–207.

Peck, C.A., Cooke, T.P., & Apolloni, T. (1981). Utilization of peer limitation in therapeutic and instructional contexts. In P.S. Strain (Ed.), *The utilization of classroom peers as behavior change agents.* New York: Plenum.

Penrose, L.S. (1949). *The biology of mental defect.* New York: Grune & Stratton.

Pepler, R. (1971). Variations in students' test performances and in classroom temperatures in climate controlled and non-climate controlled schools. *ASHRAE Transactions, 77* (Pt. 2), 35–42.

Persson-Blennow, I., & McNeil, T.F. (1982). Factor analysis of temperament characteristics in children at six months, one year and two years of age. *British Journal of Educational Psychology, 21,* 37–46.

Peterson, N.L. (1987). *Early intervention for handicapped and at-risk children: An introduction to early childhood-special education.* Denver: Love Publishing Co.

Pflaum, S.W. (1986). *The development of language and literacy in young children.* Columbus, OH: Charles E. Merrill.

Phillips, J. (1973). Syntax and vocabulary of mother's speech to young children: Age and sex comparisons. *Child Development, 44,* 812–185.

Piaget, J. (1932). *Child's conception of physical causality.* New York: Harcourt Brace.

Piaget, J. (1952). *The origins of intelligence in children* (2nd ed.). New York: International Universities Press.

Piaget, J. (1954). *The construction of reality in the child.* New York: Basic Books.

Piaget, J. (1962). *Play, dreams, and imitation in childhood* (C. Gattegno & F.M. Hodgson, Trans.). New York: Norton.

Piaget, J. (1977). *Science of education and the psychology of the child.* New York: Penguin.

Piaget, J., & Inhelder, B. (1969). *The psychology of the child.* New York: Basic Books.

Picone, T.A., Allen, L.H., Olen, D.N., & Ferris, M.E. (1982). Pregnancy outcome in North American women II: Effects of diet, cigarette smoking, stress, and weight gain on placentos, and on neonatal physical and behavioral characteristics. *American Journal of Clinical Nutrition, 36,* 1214–1224.

Pilisuk, M., & Parks, S.H. (1983). Social support and family stress. In H.I. McCubbin, M.B. Sussman, & J.M. Patterson (Eds.), *Social stress and the family: Advances and developments in family stress theory and research.* New York: Haworth Press.

Pinker, S. (1984). *Language learnability and language development.* Cambridge, MA: Harvard University Press.

Popovich, D. (1981). *Effective educational and behavioral programming for severely and profoundly handicapped students: A manual for teachers and aides.* Baltimore: Paul H. Brookes Publishing Co.

Porges, S.W. (1983). Heart rate patterns in neonates. In T. Fields & A. Sostek (Eds.), *Infants born at risk: Physiological, perceptual, and cognitive processes.* New York: Grune & Stratton.

Porter, R.H., Ramsey, B., Tremblay, A., Iaccobo, M., & Crawley, S. (1978). Social interactions in heterogeneous groups of retarded and normally developing children: An observational study. In G.P. Sackett (Ed.), *Theory and applications in mental retardation* (Vol. 1). Baltimore: University Park Press.

Powell, T.H., & Ogle, P.A. (1985). *Brothers and sisters—A special part of exceptional families.* Baltimore: Paul H. Brookes Publishing Co.

Prechtl, H.F. (1981). The study of neural development as perspective of neural problems. In K.J. Connolly & H.F. Prechtl (Eds.), *Maturation and development: Biological and psychological perspectives.* Philadelphia: J.B. Lippincott.

Pueschel, S.M., & Murphy, A. (1976). Assessment of counseling practices at the birth of a child with Down's syndrome. *American Journal of Mental Deficiency, 81,* 325–330.

Pye, C., Ingram, D., & List, H. (1987). A comparison of initial consonant acquisition in English and Quiche. In K.E. Nelson & A. Van Kleek (Eds.), *Children's language* (Vol. 6, pp. 175–190). Hillsdale, NJ: Lawrence Erlbaum Associates.

Quay, H.C., & Peterson, D.R. (1967). *Manual for the Behavior Problem Checklist.* Champaign, IL: Children's Research Center.

Raju, T.N.K. (1986). An epidemiologic study of very and very very low birth weight infants. *Clinics in Perinatology, 13,* 233–250.

Rawlings, G., Reynolds, E.O.R., Stewart, A., & Strange, L.B. (1971). Changing prognosis for infants of very low birth weight. *Lancet, 1,* 516–519.

Ray, J.S. (1974a). *Behavior of developmentally delayed and non-delayed toddler-age children: An ethological study.* Unpublished doctoral dissertation, George Peabody College, Nashville, TN.

Ray, J. (1974b). The family training center: An experiment in normalization. *Mental Retardation, 12*(1), 12–13.

Redner, R. (1980). Others' perceptions of mothers of handicapped children. *American Journal of Mental Deficiency, 85,* 176–183.

Reid, K., Hresko, W., & Hammill, D. (1985). *The Test of Early Language Development.* Austin, TX: PRO-ED.

Reynell, J. (1979). *Reynell-Zinkin Scales: Developmental scales for young visually handicapped children.* Windsor, England: NFER.

Rhodes, L.K., & Dudley-Marling, C. (1988). *Readers and writers with a difference: A wholistic approach to teaching learning disabled and remedial students.* London: Heinemann.

Ringler, N. (1975). *Mothers' language to their young children and to adults over time.* Unpublished doctoral dissertation, Case Western Reserve University, Cleveland, OH.

Robinson, C.C., & Robinson, J.H. (1978). Sensorimotor functions and cognitive development. In M.E. Snell (Ed.), *Systematic instruction of the moderately and severely handicapped.* Columbus, OH: Charles E. Merrill.

Robinson, L.E., & DeRosa, S.M. (1980). *Parent Needs Inventory.* Austin, TX: Parent Consultants.

Robinson, N.M., & Robinson, H.B. (1976). *The mentally retarded child* (2nd ed.). New York: McGraw-Hill.

Rogers, S.J. (1988). Cognitive characteristics of handicapped children's play: A review. *Journal of the Division for Early Childhood, 12,* 161–168.

Rogers, S.J., D'Eugenio, D.B., Brown, S.L., Donavan, C.M., & Lynch, E.W. (1981). *Early Intervention Developmental Profile.* Ann Arbor: University of Michigan Press.

Rogers, S.J., Herbison, J.M., Lewis, H.C., Pantone, J., & Reis, K. (1986). An approach for enhancing the symbolic, communicative, and interpersonal functioning of young children with autism and severe emotional handicaps. *Journal of the Division for Early Childhood, 10,* 135–148.

Rogers, S.J., & Puchalski, C.B. (1984). Development of symbolic play in visually impaired infants. *Topics in Early Childhood Special Education, 3,* 57–64.

Rose, S.A. (1981). Lags in the cognitive competence of prematurely born infants. In S. Friedman & M. Sigman (Eds.), *Preterm birth and psychological development.* New York: Academic Press.

Rosen, C.E. (1974). The effects of socio-dramatic play on problem-solving behaviors among culturally disadvantaged preschool children. *Child Development, 45,* 920–927.

Rosenberg, S.A., & Robinson, C.C. (1985). Enhancement of mothers' interactional skills in an infant educational program. *Education and Training of the Mentally Retarded, 20,* 163–169.

Rosenberg, S.A., & Robinson, C.C. (1986). Measures of parent-infant interaction: An overview. *Topics in Early Childhood Special Education, 6* (2), 32–43.

Rosenberg, S.A., & Robinson, C.C. (1988). Interactions of parents with their young handicapped children. In S.L. Odom & M.B. Karnes (Eds.), *Early intervention for infants and children with handicaps: An empirical base* (pp. 159–177). Baltimore: Paul H. Brookes Publishing Co.

Rosenthal, R., & Jacobsen, L. (1968). *Pygmalion in the classroom: Teacher expectation and pupil's intellectual development.* New York: Holt, Rinehart & Winston.

Rosenthal, R., & Jacobsen, L. (1975). What teacher behavior mediates. *Psychology in the Schools, 12,* 454–461.

Ross, B.M. (1976). Preferences for nonrepresentational drawings by Navajo and other children. *Journal of Cross-Cultural Psychology, 7*(2), 145–156.

Rossetti, L.M. (1986). *High risk infants: Identification, assessment, and intervention.* San Diego: College-Hill Press.

Rubin, K.H., Maioni, T.L., & Hornung, M. (1976). Free play behavior in middle- and lower-class preschoolers: Parten and Piaget revisited. *Child Development, 47,* 414–419.

Rubin, K.H., & Pepler, D.J. (1980). The relationship of child's play to social-cognitive growth and development. In H.C. Foot, A.J. Chapman, & J.R. Smith (Eds.), *Friendship and social relations in children.* New York: John Wiley & Sons.

Rubin, Z. (1980). Children's friendships. In J. Bruner, M. Cole, & B. Lloyd (Eds.), *The developing child.* Glasgow: Collins.

Ruggles, T.R. (1982). Some considerations in the use of teacher implemented observation procedures. In K.E. Allen & E.H. Goetz (Eds.), *Early childhood education: Special problems, special solutions* (pp. 77–104). Rockville, MD: Aspen Systems.

Rutter, M. (1975). *Helping troubled children.* New York: Plenum.

Rutter, M. (1984). Issues and prospects in developmental neuropsychiatry. In M. Rutter (Ed.), *Developmental neuropsychiatry.* New York: Guilford Press.

Rutter, M. (1985). Infantile autism and other pervasive developmental disorders. In M. Rutter & L. Hersov (Eds.), *Child and adolescent psychiatry: Modern approaches* (2nd ed.). Oxford, England: Blackwell.

Rutter, M. (1986). Infantile autism: Assessment, differential diagnosis and treatment. In D. Shaffer, A. Erhardt, & L. Greenhill (Eds.), *A clinical guide to child psychiatry.* New York: Free Press.

Ryckman, D.B., & Henderson, R.A. (1965). The meaning of a retarded child for his parents: A focus for counselors. *Mental Retardation, 3,* 4–7.

Rynders, J.E., & Horrobin, J.M. (1975). Project EDGE: The University of Minnesota's communication stimulation program for Down's syndrome infants. In B.Z. Friedlander, G.M. Sterritt, & G.E. Kirk (Eds.), *Exceptional infant: Assessment and intervention* (Vol. 3). New York: Brunner/Mazel.

Rynders, J.E., Spiker, D., & Horrobin, J.M. (1978). Underestimating the educability of Down's syndrome children: Examination of methodological problems in recent literature. *American Journal of Mental Deficiency, 82,* 440–448.

Sachs, J. (1977). Adaptive significance of linguistic input to prelinguistic infants. In C. Snow & C. Ferguson (Eds.), *Talking to children.* Cambridge, England: Cambridge University Press.

Safford, P.L. (1978). *Teaching young children with special needs.* St. Louis: C.V. Mosby.

Saltz, E., Dixon, D., & Johnson, J. (1977). Training disadvantaged preschoolers on various fantasy activities: Effects on cognitive functioning and impulse control. *Child Development, 48,* 367–380.

Sameroff, A.J. (1968). The component of sucking in the human newborn. *Journal of Experimental Child Psychology, 6,* 607–623.

Sameroff, A.J. (1979). Etiology of cognitive competence. In R.B. Kersley & I.E. Sigel (Eds.), *Infants at risk: Assessment of cognitive functioning.* Hillsdale, NJ: Lawrence Erlbaum Associates.

Sameroff, A.J., & Chandler, M.J. (1975). Reproductive risk and the continuum of caretaking casualty. In F.D. Horowitz, M. Hetherington, S. Scarr-Salapatek, & G. Sigel (Eds.), *Review of child development research* (Vol. 4). Chicago: University of Chicago Press.

Sameroff, A.J., & Zax, M. (1978). In search of schizophrenia: Young offspring of schizophrenic women. In L.C. Wynne, R. Cromwell, & S. Matthysse (Eds.), *Nature of schizophrenia: New findings and future strategies.* New York: John Wiley & Sons.

Samuels, S. (1981). *Disturbed exceptional children: An integrated approach.* New York: Human Sciences Press.

Sandler, A., & Coren, A. (1981). Integrated instruction at home and school: Parents' perspective. *Education and Training of the Mentally Retarded, 16,* 183–188.

Sandler, A., Coren, A., & Thurman, S.K. (1983). A training program for parents of handicapped preschool children: Effects upon mother, father, and child. *Exceptional Children, 49,* 355–358.

Sanford, A. (1974). *Learning Accomplishment Profile.* Winston-Salem, NC: Kaplan.

Sanford, A.R., & Zelman, J.G. (1981). *Learning Accomplishment Profile* (rev. ed.). Winston-Salem, NC: Kaplan.

Sarason, S.B., & Doris, J. (1979). *Educational handicap, public policy and social history.* New York: Free Press.

Schaefer, E.S., & Aaronson, M. (1972). Infant education research project: Implementation and implications of the home tutoring program. In R.K. Parker (Ed.), *The preschool in action.* Boston: Allyn & Bacon.

Schaefer, E.S., & Moerch, M.S. (1981). *Developmental programming for infants and young children.* Ann Arbor: University of Michigan Press.

Schell, G.C. (1981). The young handicapped child: A family perspective. *Topics in Early Childhood Special Education, 1,* 21–27.

Schlesinger, I. (1971). Production of utterances and language acquisition. In D. Slobin (Ed.), *The ontogenesis of grammar.* New York: Academic Press.

Schneider-Rosen, K., Braunwald, K., Carlson, V., & Cicchetti, D. (1985). Current perspectives in attachment theory: Illustration from the study of maltreated infants. In I. Bretherton & E. Waters (Eds.), Growing points of attachment theory and research. *Monographs of the Society for Research in Child Development, 50*(1–2, Serial No. 209), 194–210.

Schneider-Rosen, K., & Cicchetti, D.E. (1984). The relationship between affect and cognition in maltreated infants: Quality of attachment and the development of visual self-recognition. *Child Development, 55,* 648–658.

Schopler, E. (1978). Changing parental involvement in behavior treatment. In M. Rutter & E. Schopler (Eds.), *Autism: A reappraisal of concepts and treatments.* New York: Plenum.

Schopler, E., & Mesibov, G.B. (1986). Introduction to social behavior in autism. In E. Schopler & G.B. Mesibov (Eds.), *Social behavior in autism.* New York: Plenum.

Schreiber, M., & Feely, M. (1975). Siblings of the retarded: A guided group experience. In J.J. Dempsey (Ed.), *Community services for retarded children.* Baltimore: University Park Press.

Schwartz, E. (1974). Characteristics of speech and language development in the child with myelomeningocele and hydrocephalus. *Journal of Speech and Hearing Disorders, 39,* 465–468.

Schweinhart, L.J., & Weikart, D.P. (1981). Effects

of the Perry Preschool Program on youths through age 15. *Journal of the Division for Early Childhood, 4,* 29–39.

Scott, R.A. (1969). *The making of blind men.* New York: Russell Sage Foundation.

Searle, J. (1969). *Speech acts: An essay in the philosophy of language.* London: Cambridge University Press.

Searle, S.J. (1978, April). Stages of parental reaction. *Exceptional Parent,* pp. 27–29.

Self, P.A., & Horowitz, D. (1979). The behavioral assessment of the neonate: An overview. In J.D. Osofsky (Ed.), *Handbook of infant development.* New York: John Wiley & Sons.

Sell, E.J. (1986). Outcome of very very low birth weight infants. *Clinics in Perinatology, 13,* 451–460.

Shadish, W.R., Jr. (1986). Sources of evaluation practice: Needs, purposes, questions and technology. In L. Bickman & D.L. Weatherford (Eds.), *Evaluating early intervention programs for severely handicapped children and their families.* Austin, TX: PRO-ED.

Shapiro, E., & Biber, B. (1972). The education of young children: A developmental-interaction approach. *Teachers College Record, 74,* 55–79.

Share, J., Koch, R., Webb, A., & Graliker, B. (1964). The longitudinal development of infants and young children with Down's syndrome. *American Journal of Mental Deficiency, 68,* 689–692.

Shatz, M. (1987). Bootstrapping operations in child language. In K.E. Nelson & A. Van Kleek (Eds.), *Childrens' language* (Vol. 6, pp. 1–22). Hillsdale, NJ: Lawrence Erlbaum Associates.

Shatz, M., & Gelman, R. (1973). The development of communication skills: Modifications in the speech of young children as function of listener. *Monographs of the Society for Research in Child Development, 38*(Serial No. 152).

Shearer, D.E., & Shearer, M.S. (1976). The Portage Project: A model for early childhood intervention. In T.D. Tjossem (Ed.), *Intervention strategies for high risk infants and young children.* Baltimore: University Park Press.

Sheridan, M.D. (1968). *The developmental progress of infants and young children.* London: Her Majesty's Stationary Office.

Sheridan, M.D. (1975). The importance of spontaneous play in the functional learning of handicapped children. *Child Care, Health and Development, 1*(3), 118–122.

Short-DeGraff, M.A. (1986). Occupational therapy assessment. In D.L. Wodrich & J.E. Joy (Eds.),

Multidisciplinary assessment of children with learning disabilities and mental retardation (pp. 161–193). Baltimore: Paul H. Brookes Publishing Co.

Shugar, G.W., & Bokus, B. (1986). Children's discourse and children's activity in the peer situation. In E.C. Mueller & C. Cooper (Eds.), *Process and outcomes in peer relations* (pp. 196–228). New York: Academic Press.

Sigel, I.E. (1979). On becoming a thinker. A psychoeducational model. *Educational Psychologist, 14,* 70–78.

Sigman, M., & Parmelee, A.H. (1979). Longitudinal evaluation of the pre-term infant. In T.M. Field (Ed.), *Infants born at risk: Behavior and development.* New York: Spectrum Publications.

Simeonsson, R.J. (1986). *Psychological and developmental assessment of special children.* Boston: Allyn & Bacon.

Simeonsson, R.J., & Bailey, D.B. (1986). Siblings of handicapped children. In J.J. Gallagher & P.M. Vietze (Eds.), *Families of handicapped persons: Research, programs, and policy issues* (pp. 67–77). Baltimore: Paul H. Brookes Publishing Co.

Simeonsson, R.J., Huntington, G.S., Short, R.J., & Ware, W.B. (1982). The Carolina record of individual behavior: Characteristics of handicapped infants and children. *Topics in Early Childhood Special Education, 2*(2), 43–55.

Simeonsson, R.J., & McHale, S.M. (1981). Review: Research on handicapped children: Sibling relationships. *Child Care, Health and Development, 7,* 153–171.

Simmons, J.L. (1969). *Deviants.* Berkeley, CA: Glendessary Press.

Simon, B.M., & McGowan, J.S. (1989). Tracheostomy in young children: Implications for assessment and treatment of communication and feeding disorders. *Infants and Young Children, 1* (3), 1–9.

Sinclair, H. (1969). Developmental psycholinguistics. In D. Elkind & J. Flavell (Eds.), *Studies in cognitive development.* New York: Oxford University Press.

Sinclair, H. (1970). The transition from sensory motor behavior to symbolic activity. *Interchange, 1,* 119–126.

Sinclair, H. (1973). Language acquisition and cognitive development. In T. Moore (Ed.), *Cognitive development and the acquisition of language.* New York: Academic Press.

Siqueland, E.R. (1981). Studies of visual recognition memory in preterm infants: Differences in development as a function of perinatal morbidity factors. In S. Friedman & M. Sigman (Eds.), *Preterm birth and psychological development* (pp. 271–288). New York: Academic Press.

Skeels, H.M., & Dye, H.B. (1939). A study of the effects of differential stimulation on mentally retarded children. *Proceedings and Addresses of the American Association on Mental Deficiency, 44,* 114–136.

Skinner, B.F. (1957). *Verbal behavior.* New York: Appleton-Century-Crofts.

Smilansky, S. (1968). *The effects of sociodramatic play on disadvantaged preschool children.* New York: John Wiley & Sons.

Smith, D.D., & Snell, M.E. (1978). Classroom management and instructional planning. In M.E. Snell (Ed.), *Systematic instruction of the moderately and severely handicapped.* Columbus, OH: Charles E. Merrill.

Smith, D.W., & Wilson, A.A. (1973). *The child with Down's syndrome (mongolism).* Philadelphia: W.B. Saunders.

Smith, N.L. (1986). Evaluation alternatives for early intervention programs. In L. Bickman & D.L. Weatherford (Eds.), *Evaluating early intervention programs for severely handicapped children and their families.* Austin, TX: PRO-ED.

Smith, R.M., Neisworth, J.T., & Greer, J.G. (1978). *Evaluating educational environments.* Columbus, OH: Charles E. Merrill.

Snow, C. (1972). Mothers' speech to children learning language. *Child Development, 43,* 549–565.

Snow, C.E. (1983). Literacy and language: Relationships during the preschool years, *Harvard Educational Review, 53,* 165–189.

Snow, C.E., Perlmann, R., & Nathan, D. (1987). Why routines are different: Toward a multiple-factors model of the relation between input and language acquisition. In K.E. Nelson & A. Van Kleek (Eds.), *Children's language* (Vol. 6, pp. 65–98). Hillsdale, NJ: Lawrence Erlbaum Associates.

Snyder, L. (1975). *Pragmatics in language deficient children: Prelinguistic and early verbal performatives and presuppositions.* Unpublished doctoral dissertation, University of Colorado, Boulder.

Snyder, L., Apolloni, T., & Cooke, T.P. (1977). Integrated settings at the early childhood level: The role of nonretarded peers. *Exceptional Children, 43,* 262–266.

Solnit, A.J., & Provence, S. (1979). Vulnerability and risk in early childhood. In J.D. Osofsky (Ed.), *Handbook of infant development.* New York: John Wiley & Sons.

Sower, R. (Ed.). (1978). *Parents teaching children: P.E.E.R.S Model.* Philadelphia: Special People in the Northeast.

Sparling, J.W. (1980). The transdisciplinary approach with the developmentally delayed child. *Physical and Occupational Therapy in Pediatrics, 1* (2), 3–15.

Sparrow, S.S., Balla, D.A., & Cicchetti, D.V. (1984). *The Vineland Adaptive Behavior Scales.* Circle Pines, MN: American Guidance Service.

Sperry, R.W. (1974). Lateral specialization in surgically separate hemispheres. In F.O. Schmitt (Ed.), *The neurosciences, third study program.* Cambridge, MA: MIT Press.

Spitz, R.A. (1945). Hospitalism: An inquiry into the genesis of psychiatric conditions in early childhood. *The Psycho-Analytic Study of the Child, 1,* 53–74.

Springer, S., & Deutsch, G. (1985). *Left brain, right brain* (rev. ed.). San Francisco: W.H. Freeman.

Sproule, A. (1988). *The world at play.* London: MacDonald.

Squire, L.R. (1987). *Memory and brain.* New York: Oxford University Press.

Sroufe, L.A. (1979). Socioemotional development. In J.D. Osofsky (Ed.), *The handbook of infant development.* New York: John Wiley & Sons.

Sroufe, L.A. (1983). Infant-caregiver attachment and patterns of adaptation in preschool: The roots of maladaptation and competence. In M. Perlmutter (Ed.), *The Minnesota Symposia on Child Psychology* (Vol. 16). Hillsdale, NJ: Lawrence Erlbaum Associates.

Sroufe, L.A. (1985). Attachment classification from the perspective of infant-caregiver relationships and infant temperament. *Child Development, 56,* 1–14.

Sroufe, L.A., & Fleeson, J. (1986). Attachment and the construction of relationships. In W. Hartup & Z. Rubins (Eds.), *The nature and development of relationships.* Hillsdale, NJ: Lawrence Erlbaum Associates.

Stambak, M., & Verba, M. (1986). Organization of social play among toddlers: An ecological approach. In E.C. Mueller & C. Cooper (Eds.), *Process and outcome in peer relationships.* New York: Academic Press.

Stein, Z., Susser, M., Saenger, G., & Marolla, F. (1972). Nutrition and mental performance: Prenatal exposure to the Dutch famine of 1944–1945 seems not related to mental performance at age 19. *Science, 178,* 708–713.

Stephens, T.E., & Lattimore, J. (1983). Prescriptive checklist for positioning multihandicapped residential clients: A clinical report. *Physical Therapy, 63,* 1113–1115.

Stewart, R.B., Cluff, L.E., & Philip, R. (1977). *Drug monitoring: A requirement for responsible drug use.* Baltimore: Williams & Wilkins.

Stowitschek, J.J., Gable, R.A., & Hendrickson, J.M. (1980). *Instructional materials for exceptional children: Selection, management, and adaptation.* Rockville, MD: Aspen Publishers, Inc.

Strain, P.S. (1985). Programmatic research on peer-mediated interventions. In B.H. Schneider, K.H. Rubin, & J.E. Ledingham (Eds.), *Children's peer relations: Issues in assessment and intervention.* New York: Springer-Verlag.

Strain, P.S., Hoyson, M., & Jamieson, B. (1985). Normally developing preschoolers as intervention agents for autistic-like children: Effects on class deportment and social interaction. *Journal of the Division for Early Childhood, 9,* 105–115.

Strain, P.S., Kerr, M.M., & Ragland, E.V. (1981). The use of peer social initiations in the treatment of social withdrawal. In P.S. Strain (Ed.), *The utilization of classroom peers as behavior change agents.* New York: Plenum.

Strain, P.S., & Odom, S.L. (1986). Peer social initiations: Effective intervention for social skills development. *Exceptional Children, 52,* 543–552.

Strain, P.S., & Timm, M.S. (1974). An experimental analysis of social interaction between a behaviorally disordered preschool child and her classroom peers. *Journal of Applied Behavior Analysis, 7,* 583–590.

Strauss, A., & Lehtinen, L. (1947). *Psychopathology and education of the brain injured child.* New York: Grune & Stratton.

Strauss, A., & Warner, H. (1942). Disorders of conceptual thinking in the brain injured child. *Journal of Nervous and Mental Disease, 96,* 153–172.

Stuckless, E., & Birch, J. (1966). The influence of early manual communication on the linguistic development of deaf children. *American Annals of the Deaf, 111,* 425–460, 499–504.

Suess, J.F., Cotten, P.D., & Sison, G.F.P., Jr. (1983). The American Association on Mental Deficiency Adaptive Behavior Scale: Allowing credit for alternative means of communication. *American Annals of the Deaf, 128,* 390–393.

Suomi, S.J., & Harlow, H.F. (1975). The role and reason of peer relationships in rhesus monkeys. In M. Lewis & L.A. Rosenblum (Eds.), *Friendships and peer relations.* New York: John Wiley & Sons.

Suran, B.G., & Rizzo, J.V. (1979). *Special children:*

An integrative approach. Glenview, IL: Scott, Foresman.

Sylva, K. (1977). Play and learning. In B. Tizard & D. Harvey (Eds.), *Biology of play.* Philadelphia: J.B. Lippincott.

Tallman, I. (1965, February). Spousal role differentiation and the socialization of severely retarded children. *Journal of Marriage and the Family,* pp. 37–42.

Taylor, R.C. (1984). *Assessment of exceptional students.* Englewood Cliffs, NJ: Prentice-Hall.

Temple, C., Nathan, R., Burris, N., & Temple, F. (1988). *The beginnings of writing* (2nd ed.). Boston: Allyn & Bacon.

Terman, L.M., & Merrill, M.A. (1973). *The Stanford-Binet Intelligence Scale* (3rd rev.). Boston: Houghton Mifflin.

Terrell, B.Y., Schwartz, R.G., Prelock, P.A., & Messick, C.K. (1984). Symbolic play in normal and language impaired children. *Journal of Speech and Hearing Research, 27,* 424–429.

Thomas, A., Chess, S., & Birch, H. (1968). *Temperament and behavior disorders in children.* New York: New York University Press.

Thomas, A. et al. (1963). *Behavioral individuality in early childhood.* New York: New York University Press.

Thurman, S.K. (1977). The congruence of behavioral ecologies: A model for special education programming. *Journal of Special Education, 11,* 329–333.

Thurman, S.K. (1978). *A review of contingency in infants: Avenues for the handicapped infant.* Princeton, NJ: Institute for the Study of Exceptional Children, Educational Testing Service.

Thurman, S.K., Cornwell, J.R., & Korteland, C. (1989). The Liaison Infant Family Team (LIFT) Project: An example of case study evaluation. *Infants and Young Children, 2*(2), 74–82.

Thurman, S.K., & Lewis, M. (1979). Children's responses to differences: Some possible implications for mainstreaming. *Exceptional Children, 45,* 468–470.

Thurman, S.K., & Widerstrom, A. (1979). *A methodological synthesis for the study of social behavior.* Unpublished manuscript, Temple University, Philadelphia.

Thurstone, L., & Thurstone, T. (1954). *Science Research Associates primary mental abilities* (rev. ed.). Chicago: Science Research Associates.

Tingey, C., & Stimell, F. (1989). Increasing services through interagency agreements, volunteers, and donations. In C. Tingey (Ed.), *Implementing early intervention* (pp. 63–78). Baltimore: Paul H. Brookes Publishing Co.

Tizard, J. (1964). *Community services for the mentally handicapped.* Oxford, England: Oxford University Press.

Tizard, B., & Harvey, D. (Eds.). (1977). *Biology of play.* Philadelphia: J.B. Lippincott.

Tredgold, A.F. (1908). *Mental deficiency.* London: Bailliera, Tindall, and Fox.

Trembath, J. (1978). *The Milani-Comparetti Motor Development Screening Test.* Omaha: University of Nebraska Medical Center, Meyers Children's Rehabilitation Institute.

Trivette, C.M., & Dunst, C.J. (1988). Inventory of social support. In C.J. Dunst, C.M. Trivette, & A.G. Deal (Eds.), *Enabling and empowering families: Principles and guidelines for practice.* Cambridge, MA: Brookline Press.

Trivette, C.M., Dunst, C.J., & Deal, A.M. (1988). Family strength's profile. In C.J. Dunst, C.M. Trivette, & A.M. Deal (Eds.), *Enabling and empowering families: Principles and guidelines for practice.* Cambridge, MA: Brookline Press.

Tronick, E., Ricks, M., & Cohn, J. (1982). Maternal and infant affective exchange: Patterns of adaptation. In T. Fields & A. Fogel (Eds.), *Emotion and interaction: Normal and high risk infants.* Hillsdale, NJ: Lawrence Erlbaum Associates.

Turnbull, A.P. (1978). Moving from being a professional to being a parent: A startling experience. In A.P. Turnbull & H.R. Turnbull, III (Eds.), *Parents speak out: Growing with a handicapped child.* Columbus, OH: Charles E. Merrill.

Turnbull, A.P., Strickland, B., & Goldstein, S. (1978). Training professionals and parents in developing the IEP. *Education and Training of the Mentally Retarded, 13,* 414–423.

Turnbull, A.P., Summers, J.A., & Brotherson, M.J. (1986). Family life cycle: Theoretical and empirical implications and future directions for families with mentally retarded members. In J.J. Gallagher & P.M. Vietze (Eds.), *Families of handicapped persons: Research, programs, and policy issues* (pp. 45–65). Baltimore: Paul H. Brookes Publishing Co.

Turnbull, A.P., & Turnbull, H.R. (1982). Parent involvement in the education of handicapped children: A critique. *Mental Retardation, 20,* 115–122.

Udwin, O., & Yule, W. (1982). Validation data on Lowe and Costello's Symbolic Play Test. *Child Care, Health and Development, 8,* 361–366.

Umbreit, J., & Ostrow, L.D. (1980). The fetal alcohol syndrome. *Mental Retardation, 18,* 109–111.

Utley, B.L., Holvoet, J.F., & Barnes, K. (1977). Handling, positioning, and feeding the phys-

ically handicapped. In E. Sontag (Ed.), *Educational programming for the severely and profoundly handicapped.* Reston, VA: Council for Exceptional Children.

Uzgiris, I.C., & Hunt, J. McV. (1975). *Assessment in infancy: Ordinal scales of psychological development.* Urbana: University of Illinois Press.

VanEtten, G., Arkell, C., & VanEtten, C. (1980). *The severely and profoundly handicapped: Programs, methods and materials.* St. Louis: C.V. Mosby.

Venn, J., Morganstern, L., & Dykes, M.K. (1979). Checklists for evaluating the fit and function of ortheses, prostheses, and wheelchairs in the classroom. *Teaching Exceptional Children, 11,* 51–56.

Vernon, McK., & Kohn, S. (1970). Effects of manual communication on deaf children's education achievement, linguistic competence, oral skills, and psychological development. *American Annals of the Deaf, 115,* 527–536.

Vorhees, C.V., & Mollnow, E. (1987). Behavioral teratogenesis: Long-term influences on behavior from early exposure to environmental agents. In J.D. Osofsky (Ed.), *Handbook of infant development* (2nd ed.). New York: John Wiley & Sons.

Vygotsky, L.S. (1962). *Thought and language.* Cambridge, MA: The MIT Press.

Wahler, R.G. (1980). The insular mother: Her problems in parent-child treatment. *Journal of Applied Behavior Analysis, 13,* 207–219.

Warren, F. (1978). A society that is going to kill your children. In A.P. Turnbull & H.R. Turnbull, III (Eds.), *Parents speak out: Growing with a handicapped child.* Columbus, OH: Charles E. Merrill.

Weatherford, D.L. (1986). The challenge of evaluating early intervention programs for severely handicapped children and their families. In L. Bickman & D.L. Weatherford (Eds.), *Evaluating early intervention programs for severely handicapped children and their families.* Austin, TX: PRO-ED.

Wechsler, D. (1955). *Wechsler Adult Intelligence Scale.* New York: Psychological Corporation.

Wechsler, D. (1967). *The Preschool and Primary Scale of Intelligence.* New York: Psychological Corporation.

Wechsler, D. (1974). *Wechsler Intelligence Scale for Children–Revised.* New York: Psychological Corporation.

Wehman, D. (1977). *Helping the mentally retarded acquire play skills.* Springfield, IL: Charles C Thomas.

Weikart, D.P. (1974). Curriculum for early childhood special education. *Focus on Exceptional Children, 6*(1), 1–8.

Weikart, D.P., Rogers, L., Adcock, C., & McClelland, D. (1971). *The cognitively oriented curriculum: A framework for preschool teachers.* Washington, DC: National Association for the Education of Young Children.

Weiner, E.A., & Weiner, B.J. (1974). Differentiation of retarded and normal children through toy-play analysis. *Multivariate Behavioral Research, 9*(2), 245–252.

Weiss, G., & Hechtman, L.T. (1986). *Hyperactive children grown up: Empirical findings and theoretical considerations.* New York: Guilford Press.

Welsh, M.M., & Odum, C.S.H. (1981). Parent involvement in the education of the handicapped child: A review of the literature. *Journal of the Division for Early Childhood, 3,* 15–25.

Wender, P.H. (1987). *The hyperactive child, adolescent, and adult: Attention deficit disorder through the lifespan.* New York: Oxford University Press.

Werner, E.E., Honzik, M.P., & Smith, R.S. (1968). Prediction of intelligence and achievement at 10 years from 20-month pediatric and psychological examinations. *Child Development, 39,* 1063–1075.

Westby, C.E. (1980). Assessment of cognitive and language abilities through play. *Language, Speech and Hearing Services in Schools, 9,* 154–168.

Wexler, K., & Culicover, P.W. (1980). *Formal principles of language acquisition.* Cambridge, MA: MIT Press.

White, B. (1975). *The first three years of life.* Englewood Cliffs, NJ: Prentice-Hall.

White, O.R., Edgar, E., Haring, N., Affleck, J., Hayden, A., & Bendersky, M. (1981). *Unit from performance assessment system.* Columbus, OH: Charles E. Merrill.

Whittaker, C. (1980). A note on developmental trends in the symbolic play of hospitalized profoundly retarded children. *Journal of Child Psychology and Psychiatry, 20,* 253–261.

Wickstrom, R.L. (1983). *Fundamental motor patterns.* Philadelphia: Lea & Febiger.

Widerstrom, A.H. (1979). *A case study of early language disorder: A developmental-experiential approach to intervention.* Unpublished manuscript, Philadelphia, PA.

Widerstrom, A.H. (1982a). Mother's language and infant sensorimotor development: Is there a relationship? *Language Learning, 32,* 1.

Widerstrom, A.H. (1982b). Mainstreaming handicapped preschoolers: Should we or shouldn't we? *Childhood Education, 58*(3), 172–178.

Widerstrom, A.H. (1983). How important is play for handicapped children? *Childhood Education, 59*(1), 39–49.

Widerstrom, A.H. (1987a). Review of Test of Early Language Development. In D.J. Kayser & R.C. Sweetland (Eds.), *Test critiques* (Vol. V). Kansas City, MO: Test Corporation of America.

Widerstrom, A.H. (1987b). Review of Test of Early Reading Ability. In D.J. Kayser & R.C. Sweetland (Eds.), *Test critiques* (Vol. V). Kansas City, MO: Test Corporation of America.

Widerstrom, A.H., & Goodwin, L.D. (1987). Effects on the family of early intervention programs. *Journal of the Division for Early Childhood, 11*(2), 143–153.

Wikler, L. McD. (1986). Family stress theory and research on families of children with mental retardation. In J.J. Gallagher & P.M. Vietze (Eds.), *Families of handicapped persons: Research, programs, and policy issues* (pp. 167–195). Baltimore: Paul H. Brookes Publishing Co.

Wikler, L., Masow, M., & Hatfield, D. (1981). Chronic sorrow revisited: Parent vs. professional depiction of the adjustment of parents of mentally retarded children. *American Journal of Orthopsychiatry, 51,* 63–70.

Wilhelm, C., Johnson, M., & Eisert, D. (1986). Assessment of motor impaired children. In R.J. Simeonsson (Ed.), *Psychological and developmental assessment of special children.* Boston: Allyn & Bacon.

Wilkinson, P.F. (1980). *In celebration of play: An integrated approach to play and child development.* London: Croom Helm.

Willis, A., & Ricciuti, H. (1975). *A good beginning for babies: Guidelines for group care.* Washington, DC: National Association for the Education of Young Children.

Willis, W.G., & Widerstrom, A.H. (1986). Structure and function in prenatal and postnatal neurological development. In J.E. Obrzut & G. Hynes (Ed.), *Child neuropsychology.* Orlando, FL: Academic Press.

Willoughby-Herb, S.J., & Neisworth, J.T. (1983). *HICOMP preschool curriculum.* San Antonio, TX: Psychological Corporation.

Wilson, J.G. (1973). *Environment and birth defects.* New York: Academic Press.

Wilson, J.G. (1974). Teratologic causation in man and its evaluation in non-human primates. In B.V. Beidel (Ed.), *Proceedings of the Fourth International Conferences.* Dordrecht, Netherlands: Excerpta Medica.

Wing, L., Gould, J., Yeates, S.R., & Brierley, L.M. (1977). Symbolic play in severely mentally retarded and in autistic children. *Journal of Child Psychology and Psychiatry, 18,* 167–178.

Winick, M. (1970). Fetal malnutrition and growth process. *Hospital Practice, 5*(5), 33–41.

Winick, M., & Rosso, P. (1973). Effects of malnutrition on brain development. *Biology of Brain Dysfunction, 1,* 301–317.

Winton, P.J., & Bailey, D.B. (1988). The family focused interview: A collaborative mechanism for family assessment and goal-setting. *Journal of the Division for Early Childhood, 12,* 195–207.

Winton, P.J., & Turnbull, A.P. (1981). Parent involvement as viewed by parents of preschool handicapped children. *Topics in Early Childhood Special Education, 1,* 11–19.

Witt, J.C., & Cavell, T.A. (1986). Psychological assessment. In D.L. Wodrich & J.E. Joy (Eds.), *Multidisciplinary assessment of children with learning disabilities and mental retardation* (pp. 31–75). Baltimore: Paul H. Brookes Publishing Co.

Wodrich, D.L. (1986). The terminology and purposes of assessment. In D.L. Wodrich & J.E. Joy (Eds.), *Multidisciplinary assessment of children with learning disabilities and mental retardation* (pp. 1–29). Baltimore: Paul H. Brookes Publishing Co.

Wolf, M.M. (1978). Social validity: The case for subjective measurement or how applied behavior analysis is finding its heart. *Journal of Applied Behavior Analysis, 11,* 203–214.

Wolfensberger, W. (1967). Counseling the parents of the retarded. In A.A. Baumeister (Ed.), *Mental retardation: Appraisal, education and rehabilitation.* Chicago, IL: Aldine.

Wolfensberger, W. (1975). *The origin and nature of our institutional models.* Syracuse, NY: Human Policy Press.

Wolfensberger, W., & Menolascino, F.J. (1970). A theoretical framework for the management of parents of the mentally retarded. In F. J. Menolascino (Ed.), *Psychiatric approaches to mental retardation.* New York: Basic Books.

Woodcock, L.P. (1941). *Life and ways of the two-year-old.* New York: E.P. Dutton.

Wooten, M., & Mesibov, G.B. (1986). Social skills training for elementary school autistic children with normal peers. In E. Schopler & G.B. Mesibov (Eds.), *Social behavior in autism.* New York: Plenum.

Wright, H.F. (1960). Observational child study. In P.H. Mussen (Ed.), *Handbook of research methods in child development.* New York: John Wiley & Sons.

Wyne, M.D., & O'Connor, P.D. (1979). *Exceptional children: A developmental view.* Lexington, MA: D.C. Heath.

Zaichkowsky, L.D., Zaichkowsky, L.B., & Martinek, T.J. (1980). *Growth and development: The child and physical activity.* St. Louis: C.V. Mosby.

Zeaman, D., & House, B.J. (1963). The role of attention in retardate discrimination learning. In N.R. Ellis (Ed.), *Handbook of mental deficiency.* New York: McGraw-Hill.

Zeaman, D., & House, B.J. (1979). A review of attention theory. In N.R. Ellis (Ed.), *Handbook on mental deficiency: Psychological theory and research* (2nd ed.). Hillsdale, NJ: Lawrence Erlbaum Associates.

Zelazo, P.R. (1979). Reactivity to perceptual-cognitive events: Application for infant assessment. In R.B. Kearsley & I.E. Sigel (Eds.), *Infants at risk: Assessment of cognitive functioning.* Hillsdale, NJ: Lawrence Erlbaum Associates.

Zelazo, P.R. (1982). An information processing approach to infant cognitive assessment. In M. Lewis & L.T. Taft (Eds.), *Developmental disabilities: Theory, assessment, and intervention* (pp. 229–255). New York: Spectrum.

Zeskind, P.S. (1983). Production and spectral analysis of neonatal crying and its relation to other behavioral systems in the infant at risk. In T. Field & A. Sostek (Eds.), *Infants born at risk: Physiological, perceptual and cognitive processes.* New York: Grune & Stratton.

Index